Early Modern Capitalism

Early Modern Capitalism takes stock of recent research on the development of economic growth, and the development of capital and labour markets, during the centuries that preceded the Industrial Revolution. This book discusses important issues such as the nature of the late medieval crisis that has always been pictured as the 'start' of European capitalism; it examines the quantitative dimensions of economic growth, as well as more specific topics such as the consumption of energy in early modern Europe. Issues such as proto-industry, proletarianization, and labour mobility are also addressed.

The book emphasizes the diversity in the economic experience of early modern Europe and suggests how this diversity might serve as the foundation of a new conception of economic and social change, replacing the traditional dichotomies of pre-industrial versus industrial or pre-modern versus modern/post-modern.

Maarten Prak is Professor of Social and Economic History at the University of Utrecht. He has published widely on topics of early modern social history in international books and journals.

Routledge Explorations in Economic History

Early Modern Capitalism

Economic and social change in Europe,
1400–1800

Edited by Maarten Prak

London and New York

First published 2001
by Routledge
11 New Fetter Lane, London EC4P 4EE

Simultaneously published in the USA and Canada
by Routledge
29 West 35th Street, New York, NY 10001

Reprinted 2002

Routledge is an imprint of the Taylor & Francis Group

Typeset in Garamond by Steven Gardiner Ltd, Cambridge
Printed and bound in Great Britain by
TJI Digital, Padstow, Cornwall

British Library Cataloguing in Publication Data
A catalogue record for this book is available from the British Library

Library of Congress Cataloging in Publication Data
Early modern capitalism: economic and social change in Europe, 1400–1800
/ edited by Maarten Prak.
     p.   cm.
Includes bibliographical references and index.
1. Europe – Economic conditions. 2. Europe – Social conditions.
3. Capitalism – History. I. Economic and social change in Europe,
1400–1800. II. Prak, Maarten Roy, 1955–
HC240.E233.2000
338.94′009—dc21   00-35308

ISBN 0–415–21714–8

Contents

Figures

Tables

Contributors

Ian Blanchard is Professor of Medieval Economic History at the University of Edinburgh, and Recurrent Professor at the Central European University, Budapest.

Stephan Epstein is Reader in Economic History at the London School of Economics.

Edwin Horlings is a post-doctoral researcher at the History Department of the University of Amsterdam.

Ad Knotter is Director of the Sociaal-Historisch Centrum and Professor at the University of Maastricht.

Jan Lucassen is Director of Research at the International Institute of Social History in Amsterdam, and Professor of Social History at the Free University, also in Amsterdam.

Paolo Malanima is Professor of Economic History and Economics at the University of Catanzaro.

Maarten Prak is Professor of Social and Economic History of the University of Utrecht, and teaches at University College Utrecht.

Jürgen Schlumbohm is Professor at the Max-Planck-Institut für Geschichte in Göttingen.

Jan de Vries is Professor of Economic History at the University of California, Berkeley.

Jan Luiten van Zanden is Professor of Social and Economic History at the University of Utrecht.

Acknowledgements

As with so many collective volumes, this book started out as a set of conference papers. In 1991 the first *Journées Braudeliennes* were organized in Mexico City, initiated by Carlos Aguirre Rojas. The idea was to reflect on and further develop the intellectual legacy of Fernand Braudel. When it was my turn to organize the third Braudel Days in the Netherlands, it seemed appropriate to select the rise of capitalism in the early modern era, a subject central to both the history of the Netherlands and the work of Braudel, as the topic for discussion.

Given the initial focus on his work, many of the conference papers took Braudel as their point of departure. The conference discussions were particularly enlightened on this point by the remarks of Madame Paule Braudel, whose interest in our work is acknowledged here with special gratitude. When it came to making a book out of the conference papers, however, it was decided to broaden the scope to a more general discussion of economic and social change during the late Middle Ages and early modern era. Fernand Braudel's inspiration will nonetheless be visible throughout the book and even if not all of his conclusions are supported by every individual contributor, many of the chapters testify quite explicitly to Braudel's enduring influence and inspiration.

The conference took place at the Netherlands Institute for Advanced Study in Social Sciences and the Humanities (NIAS) in Wassenaar on 23 and 24 May 1997. It was co-organized by Immanuel Wallerstein and Maurice Aymard, whose help was vital in bringing together a distinguished group of scholars. The conference received financial aid as well as marvellous hospitality from NIAS; its director, H. L. Wesseling was instrumental in both areas. The staff at NIAS made our conference a most pleasant occasion. The Dutch Scientific Organization NWO also provided a grant that helped to make the meeting possible.

In addition to the contributors to this volume, papers were presented to the conference by Marjolein 't Hart, Lex Heerma van Voss, Clé Lesger, David Levine, Carlos Aguirre Rojas, and Milja van Tielhof. For various reasons they have not been included in this volume. Maurice Aymard, Karel Davids, Paul Klep, and Immanuel Wallerstein gave us the benefit of their wise comments. In preparing the papers for publication, I was helped by Michael Joseph. Thanks are due to all of them.

Maarten Prak
Utrecht, January 2000

1 Early modern capitalism

An introduction

Maarten Prak

Eric Hobsbawm once stated the issue in the clearest of terms. 'Nobody', Hobsbawm declared in *Marxism Today* in 1962, 'has seriously maintained that capitalism prevailed before the 16th century or that feudalism prevailed after the 18th' (Sweezy *et al.* 1978: 162). This statement maintains in effect that, during the early modern period, Europe was transformed from one type of society into another. The nature of this transition, as well as its precise outlines, have continued to fascinate historians and social scientists alike: this book seeks to add some new elements to our understanding of this crucial issue in the history of Europe, and indeed the world.[1]

Like all conceptual tools, the word 'capitalism' works on two levels simultaneously. It obviously refers to certain aspects of the realm of human experience, more specifically of the economic and social order of modern society. At the same time, 'capitalism' is self-referential, to the extent that the word can hardly be used innocently, in a purely descriptive sense. Whoever speaks or writes about 'capitalism' must immediately confront issues of definition and interpretation (Sombart 1930; Dobb 1946: chapter 1; Braudel 1982–84 Volume 2: 232–49; Hilger 1982). This book consequently includes both empirical and reflective contributions.

The use of the word 'capitalism' is not necessarily the prerogative of radical historians. It is a fact, nonetheless, that the history of the debate about the rise of capitalism in Europe reflects the ups and downs of the left-wing intellectual heritage in the West since World War II. Immediately after that war, communism as a political system, and therefore Marxism as an intellectual framework, struck many as offering a significant alternative to the prevailing doctrines of the time. However, the disclosures in 1956 by the Soviet authorities of Stalinist brutalities, as well as the subsequent economic prosperity and international successes of the Western countries during the later 1950s and the 1960s, did little to help the cause of Marxist historiography (Kaye 1984). It was only with the disenchantment of the Vietnam War and the subsequent economic recession that Marxism again became a force to reckon with, in the universities as well as on the streets. In the mid-1970s, in the span of only a few years, a number of seminal works on the rise of capitalism appeared, almost all of which contained extensive references to the work of Karl Marx. In 1974 Immanuel Wallerstein published the first volume of his *Modern World-System*; in 1976 Robert Brenner published his first essay in *Past and Present* about the agrarian roots of European capitalism; and in 1977 Peter Kriedte, Hans Medick, and Jürgen Schlumbohm proposed a fully developed theory of proto-industrialization. In the meantime the main contributions to the Dobb–Sweezy controversy were published in a single volume (1976), and shortly afterward (1979) Fernand Braudel produced his three-volume *Civilization and Capitalism 15th–18th Century*. Although Braudel was not obviously a Marxist, he had come under its influence and accepted several of its leading ideas; he was happy to quote Marx at key points in his work (Aguirre Rojas 1992).

Even if they drew inspiration from similar intellectual sources, these authors were not necessarily trying to explain the same things. At least three different sub-plots to the bigger story of capitalism during the early modern era can be distinguished, each with its own time-frame and explanatory models. The first sub-plot is concerned with the circumstances that helped to launch capitalism upon the world. These are most often located in the fourteenth and fifteenth centuries, in the so-called 'feudal crisis'. According to the proponents of this argument, the outbreak of plague in the middle of the fourteenth century that was to kill off a quarter or more of Europe's population was the most vivid expression of a fundamental crisis of the feudal economy and the social relations underpinning it. This issue is further discussed in S. R. Epstein's contribution to this volume.

The second sub-plot concerns the rise of capitalism proper. This story basically covers the early modern period. The debate here is about the nature of the new socio-economic system, and the extent to which the traditional elements in society had given way to the newly established capitalist relationships. Most of the essays in this book address this issue. As will be elaborated later in this Introduction, the debate in the 1970s alternated between the three main sectors of the economy: trade, agriculture and industry. Depending on their points of view, authors have dubbed the three centuries between the Great Discoveries in the New World and the Far East and the Industrial Revolution as a period in which capitalism became firmly established, as a time of transition, or as one characterized by a special type of capitalism, dominated by the merchants.

The idea of a specific 'merchant capitalism', or commercial capitalism, goes back to Marx, who may have taken his cue in turn from Adam Smith. In Book III of *The Wealth of Nations* (1776), Smith ascribed to towns, and merchants in particular, a crucial role in the transformation of the European economy. Marx, of course, was fully aware of the implications of the Industrial Revolution, and he was convinced that a fundamental distinction should be made between industrial capital, entrenched in the production process, and commercial or circulating capital. Significantly, Marx remarked that '[i]n the first phase of capitalist society trade overruled industry; in modern society it is the other way around' (Marx 1971, vol. 3: 335–49, quote on 342). But Marx never developed a theory of merchant capitalism, and the concept has remained open to the criticism that it was not a proper 'mode of production' precisely because merchant capitalism was characterized by a separation of commercial capital and presumably non-capitalist production.[2]

The third sub-plot in the debate over the origins of capitalism concerns the transition from pre-industrial to industrial society. As will be argued below, some authors see this as a development *within* the broader framework of capitalism. Others maintain that the Industrial Revolution was a fundamental discontinuity and inaugurated a truly new era in the history of Western society. If this is so, and one accepts that industrial society is capitalist (or socialist, in one of its later incarnations), by implication pre-industrial society must have been something other than capitalist. The debates about the Industrial Revolution that focus of course on the decades around 1800 thus have indirect but nonetheless significant consequences for the analysis of the preceding centuries. This topic is further discussed in Edwin Horlings' contribution to this volume.

The end of feudalism and the origins of capitalism

Maurice Dobb's *Studies in the Development of Capitalism*, published in 1946, was the first major post-war statement on the origins of capitalism (see also Kaye 1984: chapter 2). In many ways his proposals have defined the debate ever since, including some of the confusion that it has engendered. Dobb made a distinction between the demise of feudalism and the rise of capitalism. He claimed that trade, 'an alien body within the pores of feudal society', may have been an important contributing factor to the creation of capitalism, but that it was in itself not a 'sufficient' pre-condition for the establishment of a capitalist economy (Dobb 1963: 37–9). To understand why feudalism declined it was, Dobb claimed, of paramount importance to investigate the 'forces internal to [the] feudal economy' (*ibid.*: 42). Although relatively little was known about this, Dobb speculated that the feudal crisis was a combination of two factors. On the one hand, the manorial economy was incapable of long-term improvement. On the other, the pressures on the peasants to increase their output were rising because the number of lords was increasing, and their armed conflicts (e.g. the Crusades) were requiring ever greater sums of money. Although this pressure was initially absorbed by a rising population and the exploitation of newly cultivated lands, at the same time peasants were escaping from the countryside and seeking their fortunes in the towns. Rising levels of mortality around 1300, i.e. well before the great outbreak of plague in the middle of the fourteenth century, suggest that a breaking point had already been reached (*ibid.*: 42–50).

The crisis of feudalism did not directly lead to capitalism, however. According to Dobb bourgeois capital was accumulated in international trade, thanks to the political privileges and monopoly strategies of the early merchants, for whom the playing field had been levelled by the unravelling of feudalism. In the sixteenth century, merchant capital in England started to penetrate the sphere of petty production, in the seventeenth century the first industrial capitalists were rising from the ranks of petty producers. Capitalism had arrived (*ibid.*: 18, 70, 88, 109, 126, 134).

This interpretation was challenged by Paul Sweezy, like Dobb a Marxist economist, and not trained as an historian.[3] Sweezy maintained that Dobb's analysis of the feudal crisis was seriously flawed. Logically, it was unclear how a mode of production that had existed for ages, could transform itself without substantial inputs from outside. Sweezy also accused Dobb of misinterpreting Marx's own words. This, it seems, was a somewhat ambiguous argument, because in different places in Marx's writings one finds him emphasizing different elements in the process. In the third volume of *Capital*, for example, Marx stated unequivocally that '[i]n the early stages of capitalism commerce dominates industry' (Marx 1971 Volume 3: 342). He then went on to explain how the Great Discoveries and the development of commercial capital were (*ibid.*: 345)

> key moments . . . in the transition from a feudal system of production to a capitalist. The sudden expansion of the world market, the multiplication of goods in circulation, the competition among European nations to acquire the Asian products and American treasures for themselves, the colonial system, all made crucial contributions to cracking the feudal limitations on production.

In the *Grundrisse* there is a similar emphasis on the role of money and merchant capital, but at the same time an insistence that this in itself was not enough. For if mere wealth could create capitalism, then Ancient Greece and Rome should have travelled this road earlier (Marx 1964: 109). What was needed to transform monetary wealth into capital was its application to the exploitation of free labour. Hence, capitalism could only develop where a pool of free labour was available. Such a labour market was first created, Marx claimed, in the English countryside 'when the great English landowners dismissed their retainers, who had consumed a share of the surplus produce of their land; when their farmers drove out the small cottagers, etc.' (*ibid.*: 110–11).

If Marx proved to be an unreliable ally, Sweezy had another arrow to his bow. Historically, Sweezy said, it could easily be demonstrated that towns and their trade, in other words a cause 'external to the system', were crucial in the dissolution of the feudal economy. It was the towns that whetted the appetite for new luxuries among the propertied classes, which in turn forced them to increase the extraction of ever greater revenues from the peasants. At the same time, the towns were setting new standards of productivity and providing an alternative source of income for the oppressed peasants. This exposed the frailty of the feudal economy and created the crisis. Sweezy also pointed out another puzzling aspect of Dobb's interpretation, which had left a yawning historical gap between the dissolution of the feudal economy in the fourteenth century and the establishment of capitalism around 1600. Somehow it seemed unlikely that the feudal economy, having succumbed to its own internal contradictions, was succeeded by . . . nothing. Sweezy's own focus on towns and trade could resolve this problem too.

The Dobb–Sweezy controversy went through a second round of exchanges and was joined by other contributors, before petering out in the mid-1950s. Apart from the unfavourable general political climate, it also suffered from a lack of fresh input of historical data; quotations from Marx will only take one so far (cf. Hilton in Sweezy *et al.* 1978: 11, 153–8). The issues it raised, however, did not go away. In the 1970s the two sides re-emerged, albeit in slightly different forms.

Trade and the emergence of a world-economy

Superficially, the first volume of Immanuel Wallerstein's *Modern World-System* looked like a confirmation of the Sweezy position. Critics have been quick to point out the common features between Sweezy and Wallerstein.[4] The similarities are, nonetheless, limited. For one, Wallerstein, although politically an avowed socialist, was far less intellectually dependent on Marx than Sweezy was.[5] Moreover, Wallerstein's vision was truly global, where Sweezy remained transfixed by the European experience (Ragin and Chirot 1984). As a sociologist specializing in the plight of the young African nations, Wallerstein was less interested in explaining the rise of capitalism as a European phenomenon than in demonstrating the connection between the West's dominance and the poverty of the Third World.

Wallerstein's starting point is a simple statement: 'In the late fifteenth and early sixteenth century, there came into existence what we may call a European world-economy' (Wallerstein 1974: 15). This world-economy differed from earlier phases of economic expansion, because the space of the world-economy did not coincide with any single political unit. Whereas former world-economies had been transformed into empires, this new world-economy was held together by economic ties. The older world-economies had suffered from the tributary demands imposed by the political superstructure. Not so under the new system: 'What capitalism does is offer an alternative and more lucrative source of surplus appropriation' (*ibid.*: 16). By implication, the 'modern world-system' equalled capitalism (also Wallerstein 1979: chapter 1).

Given these definitions, several questions impose themselves. What preceded this new order? What circumstances caused the transition to capitalism? What was the shape of the new world-economy? Wallerstein describes the feudal economy as a series of 'relatively small, relatively self-sufficient economic nodules', strung together by a long-distance trade in luxury commodities. During the fourteenth century, however, the feudal economy was thrown into turmoil as a consequence of conjunctural factors (the available technology had exhausted its potential), of diminishing returns to feudal exploitation, and finally, a climatological turn for the worse, which caused agricultural productivity to decline (Wallerstein 1974: 18, 20, 36–7; quote on 36). To overcome the crisis, the propertied classes started to look for ways to make up for the loss in income. They found it in the 'capitalist world-economy' (*ibid.*, 37).

The establishment of this new order entailed three crucial developments. First and foremost, it required the expansion of what was originally a *European* world-economy into something truly global. Although this expansion did not necessarily imply that all of the globe was from the very start included into the new capitalist system, significant areas outside Europe in fact were. Second, it led to a divison of this world-economy into different zones, or regions, according to a specific hierarchy of exploitation. The core, semi-periphery and periphery, roughly coinciding with north-western Europe, southern Europe and the non-European worlds respectively, were also characterized by different systems of labour control (Wallerstein 1979: chapter 2; also 1974: 86–118). A third characteristic of the world-economy was the development of strong state-structures in the core area. As distinct from the economically crippling empires of yore, however, these new states acted to support the new capitalist dynamic.

Although there were some further developments, the basic structure of the capitalist world-economy was in place by the mid-seventeenth century. Thereafter, the system became enmeshed in a series of leadership contests. Initially the Dutch Republic captured the coveted role. It was a sweet, but brief interlude (Wallerstein 1980: chapter 2; also Aymard 1982), before France and Britain entered a long and exhausting struggle for economic and hence political hegemony. Britain, helped by its Industrial Revolution, eventually won out, as confirmed by the French Revolution and its military aftermath (Wallerstein 1989).

For Wallerstein (1979: 15; also 1974: 92), the early modern period is definitely *not* a specific era in the history of capitalism. He has rejected the idea that the centuries between 1500 and 1800 were a transitional stage, principally because declaring any period in time 'transitional' is an expression of muddled thinking. He also rejects the idea of 'merchant capitalism', because it suggests an opposition between merchant and industrial entrepreneur, whereas he (Wallerstein 1991: 204) maintains that it is precisely characteristic of the capitalist that he is both. Although in passing he refers to an 'era of agricultural capitalism' (Wallerstein 1979: 17), this looks more like a slip of the pen than a serious proposal. Capitalism, Wallerstein (1979: 6) maintains, is a market economy and the division of labour within the world-economy implies exchange throughout the system. Note, however, that capitalism is not necessarily a system of free labour. On the contrary, in the periphery a whole range of non-economic pressures is applied to a labour force, at times reduced not merely to poverty but rather to outright slavery. By implication, the capitalist system is not simply a market economy, where the 'invisible hand' does its beneficial work unopposed. In all parts of the system institutions have a role to play, either to maintain the leadership of the core states, or to organize the transfer of surplus from the direct producers to their lords and from the periphery to the core.

Wallerstein's claims have not gone unchallenged. The idea that the non-European world contributed decisively to Europe's economic development has been seriously criticized, and is no longer accepted by economic historians, if it ever was.[6] Nonetheless, perhaps more than any other sociological concept, the 'world-economy' has entered the mainstream of academic discourse. Its success rests no doubt on the coherence of Wallerstein's analysis. But it has been helped by the creation of several strategic institutional positions, notably the Fernand Braudel Center at the State University of New York at Binghamton, the publication of the scholarly journal *Review.* 'For the Study of Economies, Historical Systems, and Civilizations' (Arrighi 1998: 114), and perhaps most important, the alliance with the French historical school of *Annales* ('Économies, Sociétés, Civilizations') at the time of Fernand Braudel's leadership. For Wallerstein, the French provided access to much-needed data, as well as the blessing of the most renowned historical school for his specific brand of historical sociology. For *Annales*, and Braudel personally, Wallerstein opened the door to American social science and the English-speaking world more generally (Ragin and Chirot 1984: 287).[7] Nonetheless, there are substantial differences between the two authors, even though their analyses of capitalism share certain traits as well.

Like Wallerstein, Braudel saw capitalism as in many ways the opposite of what the classical economists wanted us to believe it was (cf. Wallerstein 1991: 207–17). Their capitalism was Braudel's market economy.[8] In Braudel's analysis of the economy, the market occupies some sort of middle ground.[9] He describes the market as a fairly open, routinized set of exchanges, where the laws of supply and demand introduce adjustments but basically everyone involved understands the name of the game and surprises are therefore unlikely. It is the natural habitat of trade over middle distances, of production for export markets where, once the connection has been made, a regular flow of commodities will be sold against more or less fixed prices. However, beyond the market there are two further realms of exchange, that Braudel labels 'daily life' or 'material civilization', and 'capitalism' respectively. At the lowest level of the early modern European economies, the market had not fully evolved. Even if villagers did more than simply barter their goods, the fortunes of the local bakers, blacksmiths and cobblers could hardly be said to be propelled by Adam Smith's invisible hand (Persson 1988: 50–4). On the contrary, exchanges were determined by tradition, moral standards about a 'just price', and similar non-economic considerations, as much as by market forces (Thompson 1991: chs. 4 and 5).

While on the ground-floor level of the economy (a metaphor Braudel reverts to on several occasions) it may have been too overcrowded for the market to impose itself, at the top of the building the air became too thin to support the regular flows of supply and demand necessary to trigger the price mechanism. Instead, this was the natural habitat of the really big wholesale merchants. They were few in numbers but their wealth, trade networks and political influence took them a very long way indeed. These were not self-made men because capitalism, according to Braudel, was a game only those who already made their fortunes elsewhere could afford. The capitalist was simply a very rich man (in a fascinating chapter Braudel demonstrates that this was the original meaning of the word) in the process of becoming richer still.

Capitalists who fit this description are, according to Braudel – and who would want to dispute this? – a feature of any economy. Their presence does not make an economy capitalist, however. Braudel's work seems ambiguous, at times excruciatingly so, about when precisely the European economy became 'capitalist' and what exactly defined it as such. He speaks freely about 'merchant capitalism' as a characteristic feature of the early modern age. When discussing the 'sphere of circulation', he says he does 'not hesitate to call [it] capitalist' (Braudel 1982–4 Volume 2: 248). But a little later he claims that capitalism in the countryside required no less than a connection to export markets, a form of 'rational' management, fixed capital investments, and last but not least, the employment of a wage-earning proletariat (*ibid.*: 251). Capitalism, Braudel tells us, made inroads into the industrial sector, but remained ultimately an intruder, not quite 'at home' there in the way it felt at home in wholesale trade. In a discussion of Braudel's work, Alberto Tenenti pointed out that, likewise, Braudel seemed to want to have it both ways simultaneously when discussing the Industrial Revolution. On the one hand he claimed that it was a fundamental rupture, on the other hand he denied that it changed the character of 'capitalism' (Braudel 1985: 143).

The root cause of this confusion (Braudel himself seemed baffled by Tenenti's remarks), and also the point where Wallerstein and Braudel part ways, is in their overall assessment of the economy. Wallerstein claims that, ultimately, the economy is unitary, and therefore it is either capitalist, or feudal, or something else still. Braudel sees the economy as layered and therefore, almost by definition, as capable of being many things at the same time. Thus he raises the question of why the wholesale trade that he did not hesitate to call capitalist 'should have lived as if in a bell-jar, cut off from the rest; why was it not able to expand and conquer the whole of society?' (Braudel 1982–4 Volume 2: 248).

It fits his metaphor that Braudel should picture capitalism almost exclusively an urban phenomenon. Here too his interpretation diverges from Wallerstein (e.g. 1980, chapter 2), who emphasized backward and forward linkages throughout the economy, as well as the importance of national governments in propping up the economic power of core states (see Skocpol 1977). The third volume of Braudel's *Civilization and Capitalism*, devoted entirely to early modern capitalism, discusses towns only. 'A world-economy', Braudel claimed, 'always has an urban centre of gravity, a city, as the logistic heart of its activity. [. . .] At varying and respectful distances around the centre will be found other towns, sometimes playing the role of associate or accomplice, but more usually resigned to their second-class role' (Braudel 1982–4 Volume 3: 27; cf. de Vries, 1984: 159–61). Such a picture could not be further removed from the analysis proposed by the American historian Robert Brenner.

The agrarian roots of European capitalism

In 1974 Brenner launched a head-on attack on what the author considered to be the misguided assumptions of the historical profession concerning the origins of capitalism in Europe. In a paper first presented at the annual convention of the American Historical Association in December 1974, Brenner sought to expose the fallacies of the two predominant explanations for this momentous change and replace them with a class-based analysis.

The first of Brenner's scape-goats were the so-called neo-Malthusians, who had become firmly established during the 1960s in the French *Annales* school, and whose foremost representative was Emmanuel Le Roy Ladurie.[10] In their massive studies of French rural regions during the late middle ages and early modern period, the *Annales* historians had established a powerful vision of the rural economy as at heart 'immobile', in the celebrated phrase of Le Roy Ladurie (1977). A permanent tension between population growth and food resources created long cycles of upswings and downturns. This 'secular trend' was driven by the inability, over the long run, of the rural economy to expand its output sufficiently to feed a growing population. As a consequence, the economy would collapse at regular intervals under the strain of rising food prices, which caused scarcity and ultimately starvation in the countryside. Depressed prices and a depopulation of marginal areas marked the beginning of a new cycle, which would ultimately lead to another crisis. Brenner, however, objected that this model failed to explain how similar demographic trends could have had widely different outcomes in eastern and western Europe. Even in the west, the agrarian economies of England and France developed along very different tracks after the fourteenth century, despite parallel trends during the preceding centuries (Brenner 1976: 37, 39, 61).

The commercial explanation for the rise of capitalism, on the other hand, took economic change too much for granted. The starting point of Brenner's analysis here was in fact very close to Dobb's position (Harvey 1984: 62): the expansion of international commerce could only have had the far-reaching impact claimed by the 'commercialists' if some sort of market economy was already in place. In other words, Brenner (1977: 31) claimed, the explanation for the rise of capitalism provided by the likes of Wallerstein already assumed the existence of a market economy and was thus merely going round in circles (also Meiksins Wood 1996: 212). To break out of that circle, one had to understand the changes in the sphere of production as a consequence of the feudal crisis (Kaye 1984: 173–5; Holton 1986: 79–91; Mooers 1991: 5–43). These changes, in turn, were the outcome of class struggles, Brenner maintained.

In the east, peasant communities were too weak to resist the onslaught of the lords, who were therefore able to impose a new serfdom on territories where initially the peasants had enjoyed greater freedom than anywhere else in Europe. In France, the landowning class was internally divided, and the crown hoped to gain the upper hand in this struggle by supporting (and subsequently taxing) the peasantry. Thus French peasants were able to become quasi-proprietors of the soil they cultivated, which ensured the continuation of the small family plot as the basic unit of French farming. In England the lords dominated the crown and enjoyed full ownership of the greatest share of the cultivated land. Peasant claims were successfully resisted and the landowners created tenant farms on their own terms. The relatively large, efficient farms broke down the self-imposed constraints of the feudal economy. The specific relationship between landlord and tenant-farmer in England was such that both parties would profit from farm investments and improvement of the land.

In the debate that followed the publication of Brenner's article in 1976 he was criticized for numerous sins: misrepresenting his opponents' points of view, lack of familiarity with the relevant data, over-simplifying what is in fact a very complex issue, and so on. Several of his critics pointed out that, while having a sharp eye for the shortcomings of his opponents, Brenner himself still shared one fundamental belief with them: he thought that only large-sized farms, worked by tenant-farmers, were able to apply modern attitudes and introduce efficient techniques, thus creating 'self-sustaining growth' (Brenner 1982: 17). Patricia Croot and David Parker, Emmanuel le Roy Ladurie, and J. P. Cooper all argued that he under-estimated the peasants (in Aston and Philpin 1985: 81, 105, 144–8). In ground-breaking studies of productivity in English and French agriculture, Robert Allen and Philip Hoffman have both confirmed that there is no relationship whatsoever between the size of farms and agricultural productivity (Allen 1992: 149, 208; Hoffman 1996: 146; also Overton 1996: 205). Allen's research on the English Midlands demonstrated that the large, enclosed, commercially operated farm only became general during the eighteenth century, as a consequence of a landlords' agricultural revolution. This revolution was, Allen argued, preceded by a yeomen's revolution of the sixteenth and seventeenth centuries that introduced the main innovations and productivity gains that were usually ascribed to the English landlords (Allen 1992: 21; also Allen 1991). The yeomen's revolution was stimulated by government policies that sought to minimize the social destabilization resulting from early enclosures (Allen 1992: 71–2). These policies are reminiscent of the policies Brenner considered typical of French absolutism. Allen also claimed that security of tenure played a crucial role in the yeoman's willingness to improve his farm (*ibid.*: 208). Again, this seems reminiscent of the situation Brenner describes as typically French, and responsible for the backwardness of the agricultural sector there.

Wrongly so, according to Hoffman, because in fact there were huge differences within France, precisely with regard to levels of productivity. Hoffman argued that it makes little sense anyway to discuss 'national' patterns of development in an era when the economy was susceptible to wide regional variations (Hoffman 1996: 136). More specifically, Hoffman was struck by the strong rise of productivity in the Parisian basin. There, productivity attained levels equal to those of English agriculture. Hoffman therefore concluded that 'the bulk of the evidence points to urbanization being the cause of agricultural productivity gains, not a result' (*ibid.*: 171).[11]

This ties in with a remarkable selectiveness in the geography of the Brenner debate. As Brenner's discussion of Europe's agricultural regimes limited itself mainly to England, France and east-central Europe, it conspicuously left out the zones traditionally associated with the rise of capitalism: northern Italy, Flanders, and the Dutch Republic. Even if one does not go along with the argument that towns and economic development are basically interchangeable (compare Holton 1986: chapter 4), this is nonetheless remarkable, because these areas have been known not merely for their commercial success but also as regions of agricultural progress. A recent survey by van Zanden confirms this strong correlation between urbanization and agricultural productivity, at least at a national level of comparison (van Zanden 1998; also Overton, Campbell 1991: 41; Grantham 1997; de Vries, 1974). Stephan Epstein (1991 and 1993), in his critique of the Brenner interpretation, has insisted that towns were not uniformly beneficial. They could exploit their institutional dominance over the countryside in ways not dissimilar to Brenner's 'system of lordly surplus extraction by means of extra-economic compulsion' (Epstein 1991: 14). But his analysis too avoids the over-simplified opposition of a rural, agrarian capitalism versus an urban, merchant-dominated capitalism.

Proto-industry and the transition to industrialization

After Wallerstein had made a claim for trade as the 'prime mover' in the transition to capitalism, and Brenner had made the case for agriculture, it was left to three German scholars to fly the colours of industry. The concept of proto-industry received its name and first formulation from Franklin Mendels in an article published in 1972. While Mendels had studied an area of Flanders, his paper discussed rural industry in more general terms: its organization, the demographic characteristics of the workforce, and the transition to modern industry. Much of what Mendels had to say was already familiar to experts. In 1960 for instance, the Swiss folklorist and social historian Rudolf Braun had published a study of rural industry in the hills and mountain valleys to the north and east of Zürich, which fitted the proto-industry model remarkably well (Braun 1960; also Pfister 1992).

What Mendels offered was a new perspective on these rural industries. Instead of presenting them as part of the pre-industrial world, Mendels argued that in fact they were the first phase of the industrialization process itself. The Industrial Revolution was only phase two, which built upon the fundamental changes that had preceded it. Mendels thereby achieved two things. First, he extended the concept of industrialization way back into the early modern period. Second, he put the seemingly modest business of rural industry on a pedestal, showing it off as one of the most important agents of change in the transition from the feudal world of the middle ages to the capitalist world of the modern age.

These implications might have been easily overlooked by the readers of Mendels' modest article. They were not lost, however, on Peter Kriedte, Hans Medick, and Jürgen Schlumbohm, who would provide the classical formulation of the theory of proto-industry in a few years' time. Their book *Industrialization before Industrialization*, first published in Germany in 1977, has been the touchstone for every subsequent discussion of rural industries in early modern Europe. The book contains six essays by the three authors, and two others by Franklin Mendels and Herbert Kisch respectively. Whereas Mendels and Kisch contributed regional studies of the development of rural industry, Kriedte, Medick and Schlumbohm provided a tightly argued digest of an impressive array of literature. Moreover, the three authors' collaboration had been so close as to suggest the point of view of a single individual. This impression was reinforced when on several occasions the three together reviewed new additions to the ever-growing literature on proto-industry (Kriedte, Medick and Schlumbohm 1993 and 1998).

In the very first sentence of the book (1981: 1), proto-industry is defined as 'gewerbliche Warenproduktion auf dem Land für den Massenabsatz auf inter-regionalen und internationalen Märkten in den Formationsperiode des Kapitalismus' ('industrial commodity production in the countryside for large inter-regional and international markets . . . during the formation period of capitalism'). Other authors would later add refinements, but this is what most historians would understand proto-industrial theory to be about. The definition contains several elements that merit closer inspection. Most important, perhaps, is the indeterminate character of 'rural industry'. Quite a few authors have assumed that the theory covers any industry in the countryside, as long as its products are destined for export (see for example several contributions in Ogilvie and Cerman 1996). This, however, is misleading. Although Kriedte, Medick and Schlumbohm never discuss the issue explictly in their book, they do state that some industries, notably iron founding and mining, were located in the countryside for no other reason than that, given the state of transport technology, it was impractical to move their raw materials (1977: 12). They also emphasized that proto-industry used unsophisticated technology and was labour-intensive (Pfister 1996: 137). Their book discusses at some length the transfer of former urban industries to the countryside (Kriedte, Medick and Schlumbohm 1981: 7, 21–2). Proto-industry proper, one is led to conclude from a spate of detailed case-studies, mainly concerns textile production.

Traditionally of course, textiles produced for export markets came predominantly from urban areas. But labour supply in the towns was too inelastic to allow urban textiles to expand rapidly. At the same time, urban guilds imposed restrictions on the development of the industry. These two circumstances, according to Kriedte, Medick and Schlumbohm, tempted urban entrepreneurs to try their luck in the countryside, where the seasonal work-cycle left the great majority of the population significantly under-employed. This was particularly true in areas of poor soil quality.

This had several important consequences. It provided new opportunities for poverty-stricken populations, who became entangled in an international web spun by merchant capital. This 'symbiosis' of cottage labour and merchant capital was what made proto-industry stand out as a special 'mode of production' (*ibid.*: 9–11). The spinners and weavers in proto-industry were not completely proletarianized from the outset because they retained some sort of independence. Under the *Kaufsystem* at least, they remained in command of their own tools and labour. At the same time, even a small strip of land allowed them to grow a substantial part of the food they needed to feed themselves and their families. Paradoxically, this connection with agriculture also allowed the proto-industrial workers to be paid below the subsistence wage.

A second consequence was that the whole demographic system of early modern Europe was upset by the new relations of production in the rural industries. As Hajnal had demonstrated, Europe's demographic system was dominated by a restrictive marriage pattern, including late age at marriage and high numbers of permanent celibates (Hajnal 1965). This system was in turn dominated by a strategy of capital inheritance: only when the farm or the workshop was due to be handed over to the next generation could a new household be established. Proto-industry, however, was a system regulated by wage-labour. Proto-industrial workers had no reason to wait for a farm or workshop that would never be theirs anyway. They could marry early. Moreover, families would produce children to help out at the spinningwheel or the loom. Children were 'the capital of the poor' (Kriedte, Medick and Schlumbohm 1981: 55). As a consequence, and paradoxically because they seemed least able to afford it, proto-industrial families were more numerous than those of other social groups. Thus, it was argued, proto-industry was a major factor contributing to the growth of the European population during the early modern era.

Third, proto-industry contributed significantly to the proletarianization of the European labour force and thus to the rise of capitalism. At first, merchants were satisfied with selling raw materials to rural spinners and weavers, and buying back the yarn and cloth they had produced. But as the industries expanded, they looked for tighter control. The so-called *Kaufsystem* gave way to *Verlag*, where the merchant would remain owner of the product through all the stages of production. Later again, some entrepreneurs began to centralize their workforce in manufactures, or proto-factories. Obviously, the workers were simultaneously travelling down the road from independent producer to wage labourer.

All of this underscored the role of proto-industry as one of the midwives of capitalism. The three authors differed about the specific place of proto-industry in this process of transformation, with Kriedte and Medick arguing that proto-industry was a specific mode of production, albeit a transitory one, and Schlumbohm of the opinion that it was simply a combination of feudal and capitalist elements, typical of a transitional stage between two modes of production (1981: 10). However this dispute seems more a question of definition than of substance and it has been largely ignored in the subsequent debate.

As Jürgen Schlumbohm's contribution to the present book makes clear, the debate about proto-industry has not only been intense and fruitful, it has also put in doubt some of the main tenets of the whole theory. In particular, the demographic component has had to contend with a broad range of results that were impressive more for their variation than for the support they provided for the original ideas about the connection between proto-industry and population growth. Historians are also less sure about the central role of proto-industry in the rise of capitalism. As Ulrich Pfister (1998: 46) recently stated:

> The dominant macro-formation of the early modern period was . . . the formation of a European world-economy. Merchant capitalism, in the shape of commercial empires, provided the over-arching organizational principles. Regional proto-industries were obviously no more than a sub-category of this macro-formation.

These developments notwithstanding, the theory of proto-industrialization has proved to be one of the most fruitful concepts in recent historical understanding. General history textbooks have come to use it as a matter of course. Major new books and articles are still published every year (see the surveys in Kriedte, Medick and Schlumbohm 1993 and 1998; Ogilvie and Cerman 1996; Ebeling and Mager 1997). And the theory's potential has still not been exhausted.

One area of possible development seems to be the geography of proto-industry. Proto-industry, it has been claimed, had an important impact on the formation and development of regions in early modern Europe. The rise of proto-industry entailed a shift in location of industrial production from town to countryside. Whereas during the middle ages towns had been at the forefront of industrial development, they subsequently lost their competitive edge because they lacked the flexibility to supply the developing European world-economy. For this the guilds were to blame, in part at least, but so too perhaps were the demographic mechanisms of early modern society. On top of all that, labour was much more expensive in towns than in the countryside (Kriedte 1982: 27–9). Therefore, merchant capital relocated export industries, with textiles of course the most important by far, to rural areas. However, it has been pointed out repeatedly that this does not mean the towns became insignificant to proto-industry. On the contrary, as Mendels himself emphasized, they remained an 'essential element' in the system's proper functioning, as centres of distribution and of co-ordination, as the place where capital was provided, and where the final (and often most valuable) stages of the production process were executed (Mendels 1981: 28; Kriedte 1982: 33; Hohenberg and Lees 1985: 125–34). Proto-industrialization thus helped to reinforce town–country relations (Pfister 1998: 29) in the small regions, consisting of a single town and its direct hinterland, that had been a hallmark of the European landscape already in the middle ages (Prak 1994: 31–5).

At the same time as it was reinforcing town–country connections *within* regions, proto-industry seems to have created a certain amount of specialization *between* regions, that is to say a spatial division of labour inside Europe. The pattern here is still far from clear, especially as proto-industry developed throughout western and central Europe simultaneously. But as Mendels suggested, one might expect a division of labour to arise between areas of good soil quality, where farmers would devote their energies more exclusively to the production of food, and those of poor soils, where proto-industry was taking root (Mendels 1981: 28–9). A recent survey of proto-industrial regions has, moreover, concluded that these were generally located in the 'core areas of old European urbanization' (Ebeling and Mager 1997: 41; see also Ogilvie and Cerman 1996). This seems to reinforce the point made in the previous section about the potential for growth in the most urbanized parts of Europe.

Economic growth and beyond

Since the 1970s the debate has shifted away from the high ground of general theory towards more mundane methodological considerations.[12] Many economic historians have become dissatisfied with Grand Theory and what they see as generally impressionist analyses. Instead, attempts have been made to apply the more rigorous methods of contemporary economics to the past.[13] The problems of quantitative testing for the pre-statistical era are of course nothing short of formidable. Nonetheless, estimates have been produced, notably by N. F. R. Crafts (1985), of England's gross domestic product (GDP) in the eighteenth century.

The application of methods and models drawn from modern economics to the early modern economy has had two major consequences. First, it has tended further to blur the distinction between pre-industrial and industrial economies. As we saw earlier, Wallerstein and Braudel, Brenner, and Kriedte, Medick and Schlumbohm, for various reasons all questioned the idea of a fundamental rupture in the decades around 1800. Crafts (1985) added another shattering blow to the idea of the Industrial Revolution as a watershed in history because in his tables it was all but invisible.

The second implication of the New Economic History was that 'capitalism' as a key-word was gradually replaced by 'economic growth'. This shift took the ideological sting out of a debate that had been dominated, as was argued above, mostly by Marxist historians. Analytically, the emphasis shifted from the economic (and social) *system*, to its *performance*. Of course it had always been understood that the rise of capitalism had been the driving force behind economic growth in the West.[14] But as the 1980s had once more demonstrated that capitalism was perfectly capable of economic self-destruction, the connection between capitalism and growth became less and less self-evident.

Methodologically, the replacement of 'capitalism' by 'economic growth' has had obvious advantages, most clearly the introduction of quantitative yardsticks to underpin arguments about the amount of change, or indeed lack of it. However, such firm indicators bring along their own problems. Not only are reliable figures hard to come by, as the discussion in van Zanden's contribution to this volume underscores, but results also tend to be biased by the unit of measurement. Sidney Pollard (1988), in his critique of *national* growth figures as an indicator of the amount of change during the Industrial Revolution, has pointed out that national figures tend to level out important variations between smaller units, such as regions (also Hudson 1989; Pollard 1994). That is even more true of arguments that deal with Europe as a whole.

This is precisely the point of Stephan Epstein's contribution in this book, a contribution that takes chronological precedence because it deals with the 'crisis of feudalism' of the fourteenth century. Epstein sets out to demonstrate that in many respects the traditional picture of the middle ages does an injustice to the complexities of the feudal economy. That picture is imbalanced because it over-emphasizes the peasant elements (food production, self-sufficiency, isolation from the market), and underestimates the impact of the market in the feudal economy. Long-term population growth in fact testifies to the potential for growth in the pre-industrial economy. This long-term growth was the result, Epstein argues, not of new technology but of the diffusion of techniques already available. The main problem of the feudal economy was the under-employment of critical resources, such as technology and labour. Their optimal use was impeded primarily by high transaction costs, in other words by market imperfections.

The 'feudal crisis' of the fourteenth century was an expression of these problems. It triggered a process of 'creative destruction' (in Schumpeter's words), both in the economic and in the political realm. Institutional integration and the clearing away of institutional obstacles to trade helped free the economy of its 'feudal' shackles. Widening and deepening of the market at the same time set in motion a process of regional specialization, which allowed some areas in Europe, mainly those with high levels of urbanization and low levels of institutional impediments, to embark upon a course of dynamic development.

From a slightly different angle Paolo Malanima's contribution on energy consumption reaches similar conclusions. Malanima discusses two transitions, both entailing the rise of new energy systems. In the thirteenth century the ancient Mediterranean energy system was replaced by a medieval system of energy production, characterized by the extensive use of draught animals, and the widespread use of water and wind-power to propel machines and vessels. This medieval energy system was in turn replaced at the end of the *ancien régime* by the industrial system, based on a large-scale exploitation of fossil fuels.

These stages, however, tell only half the story. Long before the Industrial Revolution the 'medieval' energy system experienced major changes. Indeed, fossil fuels were already used on a substantial scale during the early modern period, mainly as a replacement for ever-scarcer firewood. Their impact on overall energy consumption remained superficial, however. Significant progress, on the other hand, was made in the exploitation of natural energy resources during the later seventeenth and the eighteenth centuries. Most of these innovations occurred in agriculture. Population pressure, mainly in Europe's central regions where occupation densities were highest, challenged farmers to adopt new techniques. This extension of Europe's energy basis, especially in the central region, helped establish a foundation for the post-Industrial Revolution growth spurt.

These optimistic pictures of the early modern economy's growth potential are in marked contrast with Jan Luiten van Zanden's assessments of actual growth rates. It should be emphasized once again that any figure claiming to represent the economy of the pre-statistical age is open to discussion. Nonetheless, the picture painted in van Zanden's contribution is consistent and based on a broad set of data. These firmly establish that per capita economic growth, the ultimate test of an economy's performance, was extremely slow in early modern Europe. The agrarian sector in particular was holding back the economy. In trade and industry growth figures were more positive, but their impact is not large enough to relieve the gloom.

In some areas the picture is brighter, however. Especially in the regions where trade was concentrated, first in northern and central Italy, later in the Low Countries and southern England, the agrarian economy developed vigorously alongside (and as a consequence of) urban trade and industry. However, even there the economy seemed to be held back, as first the Italian Renaissance towns and later those of the Low Countries ran out of steam.

Edwin Horlings also emphasizes the very substantial differences between growth before the Industrial Revolution and afterwards. Horlings claims that a set of inter-locking mechanisms was responsible for this situation. The pre-industrial economy was poorly integrated. Due to physical obstacles, such as difficult transport, transaction costs were high. As a consequence of low-quality market access, regional variations in prices were significant and unpredictable. Investors were therefore cautious and found it hard to see how, in the absence of well-established property rights and integrated markets, they would be able to reap the benefits of investments in new technologies and other projects. Collective arrangements, such as guilds, further limited the options for innovation, as did institutional rigidities. High levels of income inequality made it difficult to find a mass market for any product other than food.

To be sure, these difficulties were not insurmountable. Population growth, particularly in densely populated areas, could give rise to a further division of labour, specialized production and a decrease in transaction costs. Hence towns, and more specifically regions with a high level of urbanization, became privileged nodes of economic development in pre-industrial Europe. But constraints of transport technology and other market imperfections ensured that these beneficial effects remained limited to a small area, and failed to transform the wider hinterland. Hence the constraints remained in place and would eventually overwhelm every region of strong economic growth, as the fates of Venice, Antwerp and finally Amsterdam testify.

Only the Industrial Revolution managed to break down the barriers and create a new economic order, where the interlocking modes of operation no longer exercised self-restraint, but instead initiated a process of self-sustained growth. The revolutionary breakthrough was, however, not so much a result of previous improvements but rather came from an exogenous shock, provided by the Napoleonic Wars. These created a new round of 'creative destruction', not unlike that of the feudal crisis four centuries earlier.

Capitalism, as Marx contended, is ultimately to be defined not by economic performance, but by its specific relations of production, i.e. the modes of operation and interactions of capital and labour. These are addressed by four further chapters in this book. Again the picture is far from consistent: Ian Blanchard and Jan Lucassen tend to emphasize major changes while Jürgen Schlumbohm and Ad Knotter suggest greater continuity.

Blanchard demonstrates convincingly that European money markets went through a series of stages. In the late middle ages interest rates in western and central Europe started to come down from ten per cent or more to about five per cent around 1500, while at the same time converging on the levels established in England and in the Lower Rhine regions (the Low Countries and German areas as far up-river as Trier). Population growth in the late fifteenth and sixteenth centuries was pressing rates in an upward direction, but the pressure was relieved by the exploitation of silver caches in central Europe. As a consequence, the base rate remained around five per cent. Central European silver, however, helped consolidate the re-location of Europe's money markets from Italy to Germany and the Lower Rhine area.

Then in the middle of the sixteenth century Europe's monetary system was once more relocated, as American silver came to dominate the money markets. The American silver boom made 'monetary', rather than 'real' profits a very attractive option to those with money on their hands. In England and along the Lower Rhine, however, enhanced savings created a secular decline in base rates and offered small businessmen, such as farmers, real opportunities to finance innovations with borrowed capital. Rising incomes in turn produced savings. During the first half of the seventeenth century money poured into the agrarian sector; after *c.* 1640 a reverse in the terms of trade saw capital moving out of agriculture and into commerce and industry. By the end of the century, Blachard assures us, 'the English and the Dutch capital markets were awash with money'. In the eighteenth century this capital increasingly sought new outlets abroad. Whereas initially the rest of Europe had helped finance prosperity in the areas bordering on the North Sea, this trend was now reversed.

If capital markets were going through a series of changes that one can hardly avoid calling 'progress', this was far less evident with labour, Jürgen Schlumbohm points out. Proletarianization was not exactly a one-way process. Proto-industry could in fact lead to re-agrarianization and de-proletarianization, as happened in the Osnabrück (Germany) region studied by Schlumbohm. What may look like proletrianization turns out on closer inspection to be merely a stage in an individual's life-cycle; people were often temporary proletarians.

The aim of Ad Knotter's contribution is to demolish completely the picture of a unilinear development from independent peasants and artisans to wage-labourers. The Golden Age of labour is a myth, Knotter claims, as is the suggestion that there was a family wage-economy stage between the feudal and the industrial economy. In fact, patterns of labour recruitment were always shaped by a variety of circumstances. More specifically, Knotter argues, during the early modern period when agriculture loomed so large in the economy, these circumstances were to an important extent determined by the ecology of the rural region.

Lucassen nonetheless does see a massive development of proletarian labour. This is not necessarily at odds with Schlumbohm and Knotter, because individual proletarians may have moved in and out of wage-labour jobs. The number of such jobs, Lucassen argues, increased under the impact of international trade and the Military Revolution, which both led to a quite specific type of labour recruitment. But again a broad range of circumstances imposed themselves as constraints or enabling factors, forcing states, elites and large companies to resort to forced (unfree) labour at various times in different parts of Europe. In fact, a completely free labour market for international migrants was established only in the Dutch Republic. The early modern period, Lucassen seeks to demonstrate, was a very specific phase in the development of labour markets precisely because of this variety of trajectories, which are in marked contrast to earlier and later stages, when the trend was much more one of convergence.

So what, after the debates of the 1970s and indeed the new approaches that have since been adopted and developed among economic historians, is there to say about the rise of capitalism during the early modern period? First, let us return once more to *capitalism*. Earlier contributors to the debate may have been strong on theoretical consistency, but tended to privilege just one particular aspect of what was, by common consent, a broad and complex transition. Braudel and other supporters of the trade-as-prime-mover approach underscored the pivotal role of towns in the development of markets, trade, and therefore capital accumulation. But in the sixteenth century, less than ten per cent of Europeans lived in a town. Brenner was therefore correct, on grounds of numbers if nothing else, to call attention to changes in rural society. Since he published his essays on agrarian capitalism, however, new evidence has been produced to demonstrate that increased productivity in agriculture was less the result of a capitalist approach to farming than a function of the proximity of urban markets. This town–country relationship also seems significant in the development of proto-industry in early modern Europe. Taken together, the debates of the 1970s and 80s seem to make a strong case for a regional approach to social and economic developments in early modern Europe (cf. de Vries 1999: 140).

The chapters in this book strongly reinforce that case. Epstein's contribution on the 'crisis of feudalism', Malanima's on energy consumption, van Zanden's on economic growth, Blanchard's analysis of the development of capital markets, and Lucassen's comparison of European labour markets all demonstrate that: patterns of development differed widely across Europe. This variation, however, was far from random. Time and again certain regions stand out, and all tend to be located close together around the North Sea. This was an area where several smaller regions, notably south-east England, northern France, the western Low Countries, and more generally the

Rhine valley, all displayed remarkable economic potential. But it was also an area that was integrated far better economically than politically. The Dutch and German regions in particular were characterized by strong urbanization and a low level of bureaucratization (compare Tilly 1990; 't Hart 1993). This clearly raises questions about the relation between economic and institutional development.

And what about *early modern* capitalism? Few historians, in this volume or anywhere else for that matter, would like to argue that the European economy in 1800 was still 'feudal'. At the same time, it would be equally difficult to say that it had been transformed completely into a capitalist economy by that time. So 'transitional', or an equivalent term that expresses the incompleteness of the transformation but acknowledges the fact that it was under way, seems appropriate after all. Indeed, several essays in this book provide strong evidence of the precariousness of such master processes as economic growth, or proletarianization. As Knotter's paper demonstrates, the available evidence can no longer support the popular image of a family economy broken down by the onslaught of capitalism. Both before and during early capitalism income strategies were flexible in ways that make it hard to describe workers as either 'self-employed' or 'proletarian'. Schlumbohm provides evidence of a counter-movement of proto-industrial workers who were able to establish themselves as independent petty producers; similarly, van Zanden concludes that substantial improvements in GDP during the early modern era were possible only in limited areas and proved to be short-lived as well. England stands out as the only exception to this pattern.

Nonetheless, and this is a point that Jan de Vries makes very strongly in the final chapter of this book, the early modern economy was indeed dynamic in all its different sectors, i.e. in trade and industry but also in agriculture. This dynamic may have been frail and easily extinguished, no doubt, but it never disappeared altogether. In some privileged regions, in general those with high levels of urbanization, a confluence of dynamic elements was capable of generating a broader dynamic, perhaps even something like self-sustained growth. Seen from this perspective, 'transitional' takes on a very specific meaning. Instead of an economy that moves from one stage (pre-industrial) to another (industrial), de Vries challenges us to start thinking in terms of simultaneity, of various trajectories of development existing side by side. If one accepts his invitation, the 'transition' is no longer a question of change from one economic system to another, but of a changing balance between fast-track regions and those travelling along more traditional routes at slower speeds.

This is not the time for another Grand Theory of the rise of capitalism. The history of the debate on the origins of capitalism suggests that the arrival of such a theory might ultimately depend on the survival of Marxism as an intellectual project. But if that new Grand Theory is eventually to appear, it will have to take into account two important results of the work presented here. First, we need a clearer understanding of the regional dynamics of early modern Europe. This in turn requires a better conceptualization of the developments within regions, as well as a far better understanding of the regional division of labour in Europe. Second, any new Grand Theory should reckon with the fact that over at least three centuries capitalism was struggling to emerge from a largely non-capitalist world. Acknowledging this fact demands a better conceptualization of the relationships between capitalist and non-capitalist economies that co-existed even within the relatively small spaces of individual European countries. As an intellectual enterprise, this might be of some historical importance. At the same time it could, perhaps, contribute to a better understanding of our present predicament.

Notes

1 Thanks are due to Stephan Epstein and Jan Luiten van Zanden for their comments on an earlier draft of this introduction. However, I accept full responsibility for any remaining shortcomings.

2 Recently van Zanden (1993: chapter 1) in his book on Dutch capitalism has provided what to my knowledge is the first attempt at an economic interpretation of merchant capitalism. See the ensuing debate in van Zanden *et al.* (1997: 189–270), with contributions by Ad Knotter, Catharina Lis and Hugo Soly, Immanuel Wallerstein, and van Zanden himself.

3 Rodney Hilton in Sweezy *et al.* (1976: 11–12). Sweezy's 'A Critique' and Dobb's 'A Reply' were both published in the Marxist quarterly *Science and Society* in the Spring of 1950. These and other contributions to the debate have been collected in Sweezy *et al.* (1976). See also Holton (1985).

4 Notably Brenner (1977: 33, 38–41, 53–4, 91). This criticism was justified to the extent that Wallerstein (1979: 9) himself has explicitly endorsed Sweezy's views.

5 The intellectual background of Wallerstein's work is described in Chirot and Hall (1982). The quantum leap in scholarship and hence availability of data also allowed Wallerstein an intellectual freedom far greater than Dobb or Sweezy enjoyed, as can be glimpsed from the bibliography in Wallerstein (1974: 359–86), consisting almost exclusively of post-1950 works.

6 O'Brien (1982) has provided the most systematic criticism of this aspect of Wallerstein's theory. But it was already rejected by de Vries (1976: 141–6).

7 Given Braudel's present fame, it is easy to overlook the fact that the first English translation of the *Méditerannée* was published only in 1972.

8 Most of the following paragraphs come from *The Wheels of Commerce*, Volume 2 of Braudel's huge work on the early modern economy, *Civilization and Capitalism, 15th–18th Century*, 1982–84, first published in French in 1979. For a more succinct statement of his position compare Braudel (1976).

9 Note that Wallerstein sees capitalism as a market economy.

10 This summary follows the argument as developed in Brenner's 'Agrarian Class Structure', and the later restatement of his case, in 'The Agrarian Roots of European Capitalism', *Past and Present* 79 (1982: 16–113), both reprinted in Aston and Philpin (1985).

11 This, incidentally, was already noted by Adam Smith (1986: 515) when he wrote: 'It is thus that through the greater part of Europe the commerce and manufactures of cities, instead of being the effect, have been the cause and occasion of the improvement and cultivation of the country'.

12 DuPlessis (1997) is a helpful survey of developments in agriculture and industry, but does not pretend to offer an over-arching explanatory framework for these transitions.

13 The specific technique is known as national accounts, and is applied in this volume by Jan Luiten van Zanden.

14 Thus, Brenner (1977: 32–3) explains: 'What therefore accounts for capitalist economic development is that the class (property/surplus extraction) structure of the *economy as a whole* determines that the reproduction carried out by its component 'units' is dependent upon their ability to increase their production (accumulate) and thereby develop their forces of production, in order to increase the productivity of labour and so cheapen their

commodities. In contrast, pre-capitalist economies, even those in which trade is widespread, can develop only within definite limits, because the class structure of the economy as a whole determines that their component units . . . neither can nor must systematically increase the forces of production, the productivity of labour, in order to reproduce themselves.'

Part I
Economic growth

2 The late medieval crisis as an 'integration crisis'

S. R. Epstein

During the 1950s and 1960s a distinguished generation of Marxist and neo-Malthusian scholars led by M. M. Postan (1973), Wilhelm Abel (1935), Ernest Labrousse (1933), Fernand Braudel (1982–84, Volume 2), Emmanuel Le Roy Ladurie (1966), Maurice Dobb (1946), and Rodney Hilton (1975; also Bois 1984) established the view – later to be enshrined as the so-called 'Brenner debate' (Aston and Philpin 1985) – that pre-modern, 'traditional' societies did not undergo significant long-run intensive per capita economic growth for lack of technological innovation. This view is now increasingly being challenged, and from two directions. First, earlier claims that pre-industrial agrarian technology was incapable of keeping food output in step with rising population are now viewed as too pessimistic, in the light of a growing body of archaeological and archival research that shows that the available agricultural techniques could produce much higher yields than was formerly believed. Second, historians are taking more cognisance of developments in rural by-employment and 'proto-industry', and of improvements in market organization and trade that earlier generations had largely ignored.

Perhaps the most significant aspect of the current revisionism is the suggestion that most pre-modern societies were operating significantly below their technological and productive potential. This proposition implies that pre-modern technology did not pose the fundamental economic constraint that earlier scholars assumed, and it offers a simple solution to an unanswered problem with 'stagnationist' models, which is to explain why the pre-modern European population growth maintained a long-term upward trend even though agrarian technology underwent little change. The answer is that food production was able to expand in line with population growth because there existed considerable technological and organizational slack. Nevertheless, towards 1300 only a handful of European regions – including parts of Essex and Kent, of Flanders and northern France, of the southern Rhineland, and of Lombardy, Tuscany and possibly Valencia – were coming within sight of the technological frontier of pre-modern agriculture, while in most other European regions agricultural systems were still unaffected by the most significant medieval innovations. The history of European agriculture between 1300 and 1800 is thus a story of the slow and frequently reversible diffusion of best practice from the more advanced to the more backward areas of the continent, rather than a tale of structural immobility and rustic *longue durée* as evoked so movingly by Fernand Braudel.

Technological innovation and organizational change were spurred by the gains from specialization, which occurred as opportunities to market improved; however, a complex array of institutional barriers to trade and frequent phases of commercial disintegration due to warfare made specialization fitful and subject to frequent setbacks. As a result, towards 1800 many parts of Europe had still not caught up with productive techniques that had been applied elsewhere since the late middle ages; the mechanization of agriculture and the introduction of chemical fertilizers replaced a bundle of ancient and medieval technology that had still to unfold its full productive capacity.[1]

The fact that pre-industrial societies could under some circumstances undergo intensive growth, which most postwar historians denied, raises the question why relatively few regions took such a path. Whereas both schools were happy to tar all pre-industrial economies with the same brush of stagnation (with England and Holland as generally unexplained exceptions to the rule), the argument we have just outlined takes regional economic diversity as a central element to be explained. It also suggests new answers to the old debate on the late medieval 'crisis' and the transition from feudalism to capitalism, which will be the topic of this chapter. The chapter begins by discussing current models of the 'feudal' economy that appeal to exogenous sources of change, and proposes an alternative model of endogenous development in which long-run intensive growth is one of several alternative outcomes. It then addresses the nature and causes of the demographic slowdown that occurred in many parts of western Europe from the late thirteenth century. Was it a systemic crisis, as neo-Malthusians and neo-Marxists claim, or was it a series of short-term difficulties or bottlenecks that could have been overcome had the catastrophe of the Black Death not struck? In other words, are claims about a 'general crisis' in the fourteenth century an instance of *post hoc* argumentation based on the social, economic and political upheaval following the Black Death? The chapter concludes with a model of the crisis that emphasizes general patterns of development but also sketches an answer to the question why long-run intensive growth in early modern Europe was so rhapsodic across time and space.

1 The 'traditional' feudal economy

Notwithstanding significant ideological and theoretical differences, post-war historians agreed that the period between the 1280s and the 1340s marked a watershed for the European economy. Most called it a general economic crisis. The arguments are well known and need to be sketched out only very briefly. The feudal economy, pictured as a one-good Ricardian economy devoted to the subsistence production of grain with no significant agricultural or manufacturing alternatives (Desai 1991), was unable to produce enough food to meet rising demand because of its primitive technology and low rates of investment (Hilton 1965; Postan 1967). Technological inefficiency was the effect of the prevailing set of property rights and incentive structures. Feudal lords obtained their income through military and legal ('extra-economic') coercion and therefore had little incentive to produce for, and compete in, the market; conversely, the lack of competitive markets gave them few incentives to innovate. The peasantry's preference for self-sufficiency to 'dependence' on the market – that is, their native risk aversion – was also compounded by the absence of true, 'capitalist' markets. Primitive technology meant that output could only be increased by bringing new land into cultivation, which was in any case subject to rapidly diminishing returns. The consequences of declining land productivity were intensified by the constantly rising costs of feudal warfare. Because the total size of the economic pie was not increasing, lords could only meet their escalating military costs by capturing a larger share of the social surplus. The contraction of the peasants' share cut into their capital investments and the availability of seed, thus exacerbating the decline in agricultural output. Famines increased, pushing the peasantry and the poor urban wage-earners to their physiological limits. Undernourishment increased rates of mortality and prepared the ground for the Black Death. The feudal system could no longer reproduce its economic base, and the Black Death brought the crisis of an entire society to a head.

The model faces problems on several important counts. The first concerns the regulation of medieval demography. The Ricardian–Malthusian conclusion that by 1300 the population was rapidly outstripping available resources arose from three distinct claims: first, that the marginal productivity of land was in long-run decline; second, that lower levels of food consumption, and particularly the greater incidence of harvest crises from the 1280s onwards, increased levels of background and crisis mortality and caused population to decline; and third, that medieval societies were incapable of applying preventive checks to nuptiality and natality that could mitigate the pressure on resources. None of these statements withstands closer scrutiny.

The only statistical evidence that long-term grain yields were in decline before the Black Death comes from a famous study by Postan and Titow of the Winchester lands between the mid thirteenth and mid fourteenth century. Contrary to their claims, however, modern analysis has shown that the Winchester yields display no statistically significant trend; grain yields were in fact stagnant in the century before the Black Death (Postan and Titow 1958–9; Desai 1991).[2] On the other hand, recent findings for other parts of England and Continental Europe suggest that in some regions average yields were still rising before the Black Death (Reinicke 1989; Mate 1988; Campbell 1995: 555; Cortonesi 1995). Evidence of demographic hardship before the Black Death is equally ambiguous, with places showing demographic stagnation or contraction appearing side by side with areas of continued growth in England (B. F. Harvey 1991; Smith 1991); in Iberia, where Catalonia and Castile were relatively underpopulated, Aragon and Navarre less so (Dufourcq, Gaultier Dalché 1976: 122–3; Bisson 1986: 163; Zulaica Palacios 1994; Berthe 1984); in Italy, where Tuscan and southern Italian stagnation or decline contrasted with continued growth in Lombardy (Pinto 1995: 46–54; Chiappa Mauri 1997; Epstein 1992: chapter 2); and in France (Dubois 1988: 242–63; Sivéry 1976: 607; Baratier 1961). The main indirect evidence for patterns of food production (yields) and consumption (population) is therefore far from clear-cut, since indirect intimations of economic problems within some regions and communities are matched by evidence of economic expansion elsewhere. While it would be wrong to extrapolate general trends

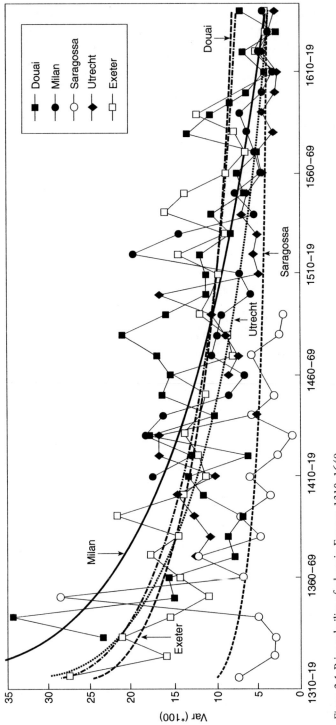

Figure 2.1 Price volatility of wheat in Europe, 1310–1649

from either finding, the evidence does not support claims of a general European crisis in the decades preceding the Black Death.

There are similar problems with the argument that background and crisis mortality increased from the late thirteenth century. Direct evidence of mortality is thin on the ground and difficult to interpret. Nearly all of it is based on estimates culled from tax records, most of which are of urban origin. Besides the problems in interpreting sporadic fiscal estimates that are often poorly understood, the sources seldom make it clear what caused a community's population to contract. The common assumption that net demographic losses were caused by mortality crises rather than other factors does not have strong statistical support. The most detailed study of pre-Black Death demography in a significantly sized region, Navarre, indicates that migrations caused by pestilence, warfare and other unknown factors caused extreme short- and medium-term changes in both rural and urban population. Evidence for thirteenth and early fourteenth-century Provence, while applying more to town than country, suggests similar levels of volatility (Berthe 1984; Baratier 1961). Although peasant mobility may have been more constrained in regions where serfdom was still a significant institution, those areas also included large numbers of economically marginal and potentially mobile individuals who could respond to local economic difficulties by migrating.

Because of the difficulties involved with accurate demographic estimations, Ricardian–Malthusian pessimists have searched for evidence of increased hardship elsewhere. They have focused in particular on the apparent increase in the volatility of grain prices on urban markets (rural prices being generally unknown), which they take as evidence of worsening harvests and of the increased liability of the urban poor to death by hunger. Both inferences are open to question. Price volatility is strictly speaking a function of the efficiency of urban supply structures rather than of the volatility of the neighbouring harvest. The two will only coincide if output is subject to identical shocks across a town's entire supply region, so the town is unable to compensate for declining output in one part of the supply area by importing food from elsewhere (if compensatory flows do arise, prices on the urban market will increase only by the difference in transport costs between the two locations). Thus the claim that the volatility of wheat prices accurately measures the volatility of harvest output assumes either that harvests were identical across very large regions or that the costs of transporting grain impeded commercial arbitrage between deficient and surplus areas. However, since the ecological determinants of output were in practice very localized and grain was actively traded within and across regions, we must conclude that any rise in price volatility from the 1280s onwards reflected increasing constraints on distribution rather than production.

Long-run developments in price volatility in European towns support this conclusion (figure 2.1). First, the fact that volatility remained very high for many decades after the Black Death, despite the sharp demographic contraction, proves that it was not caused by excess population driven onto marginal and increasingly unproductive land. The continued instability of grain prices during the weakly populated fifteenth century or later shows that the causes of volatility were largely social and institutional. Second, volatility in the longer run declined sharply even as population growth resumed.[3] The trend was common to regions with very different levels of agricultural productivity, so it seems unlikely that agricultural improvements can explain much of the gain; more plausibly, the decline in volatility was largely due to improvements in the efficiency of trade. Conversely, any significant increase in the volatility of urban grain prices is more likely to have been caused by difficulties in food supply than by fluctuations in output (Fogel 1992; Nielssen 1997; Epstein 1999).[4]

There were, of course, occasions when climatic disorders affected such a large region that it became nearly impossible to compensate for local hardship by importing food from neighbouring areas. The worst example of a natural calamity of this kind resulted in the north European Great Famine of 1315–17, often considered the archetypal 'Malthusian crisis' because it was associated in many places by sharply rising mortality.[5] But even though famine and mortality often coincided chronologically, modern epidemiological research does not confirm the neo-Malthusian postulate of a causal link between famine and mortality or even between malnutrition and disease: individuals seldom die of hunger and low levels of food intake do not automatically raise morbidity levels. According to epidemiologists and students of contemporary famines, the main cause of short-term mortality during a severe food shortage is the social and economic disruption to food allocation and sanitation, and to inefficient systems of distribution and welfare. The effects of famine will therefore differ by class, gender and time; the relation between population and food supply displays multiple equilibria.[6]

It seems reasonable to assume that pre-modern famines and crisis mortality were, like contemporary instances, the effect mainly of inefficient distribution systems and of underdeveloped systems of social welfare and support, which were unable to respond to short-term entitlement failures and move food supplies swiftly at times of need, and which exacerbated the problem by concentrating the best food supplies in the towns that attracted vast numbers of temporary immigrants. Mortality rose not strictly speaking because of nutritional failure, but because migrants spread diseases and put existing supply and sanitary systems under intolerable stress.[7]

As our critique of the late medieval 'Malthusian crisis' has suggested, there are grounds for questioning neo-Malthusian assumptions more generally. The model of the feudal economy sketched previously made three crucial claims: in demographic terms, that the population periodically overshot its resource base (or output 'ceiling') and had to be kept in check by rising mortality; in technological terms, that output could not keep up with rising population; and in structural terms, that the economy was nearly wholly employed producing grain for human consumption.

The belief that medieval peasants were unable to adapt their reproductive strategy to changing economic circumstances rests on the claim that they ignored basic contraceptive and abortifacient techniques and did not calibrate nuptiality to economic opportunity.[8] However, both medical texts and church moralists attest to the fact that contraceptives and abortifacients were well known during the high and late middle ages (Biller 1980; Riddle 1991). The frequently observed positive correlation between peasant wealth and family size also suggests that both active and passive methods of birth control (including infanticide, exposure, differential nutrition, and regulation of the age of first marriage) were being used, particularly by the poorer sections of the population, to restrict household size.[9] Migration was also an effective means for those not legally bound to the land of adapting to changing environmental constraints and opportunities. By the thirteenth century at the latest, therefore, European populations disposed of a portfolio of social and medical controls over fertility and nuptiality that could maintain them in homeostatic equilibrium with resources. Given the doubts cast on what neo-Malthusian historians have taken as evidence of overpopulation (declining grain yields, rising price volatility, and slowing demographic growth), we may reasonably conclude that medieval populations acted rationally – that is, preventively – to opportunities for, and constraints upon, family formation.

The second string to the neo-Malthusian bow, technological pessimism, was based on early estimates of pre-modern agricultural productivity that relied on crude measures of yield per unit of seed, which showed considerable stability over time. What these estimates did not do was to measure changes in output per unit of land and labour, and in the return to investment. Neo-Malthusian pessimists also took the lack of major crop and machine innovations between the fourteenth and the eighteenth centuries as evidence that productivity was stagnant. However, recent more sophisticated measurements of output and capital efficiency have substantially raised earlier estimates, and have gone on to suggest that the lack of major technical change before 1750 was not a significant constraint upon output at the prevailing levels of population. Substantial productivity gains supporting a larger population could still be made in eighteenth-century Europe by using available factors of production more efficiently and by introducing low-cost innovations (better drainage, new crop rotations, enclosure, etc.) based on practical technical knowledge that was available from the thirteenth century or before.

By the 1320s Norfolk and Kentish peasants had achieved levels of land productivity that were reached again only in the eighteenth century (Campbell and Overton 1993; Campbell 1995: 555). In thirteenth-century Tuscany, average agricultural productivity may have increased about 0.25 per cent per annum thanks to investments in drainage, reorganization of plots, the planting of higher value crops, and improvements in transport and distribution, that required no major technical change; these gains were associated with a rough doubling of the total population and a tripling of the proportion of urban residents in the region. Tuscany only achieved similar levels of population density and urbanization after 1800. Alain Derville (1987), Eric Thoen (1997), Christian Reinicke (1989) and others[10] have identified similar performances for medieval northern France, Flanders and the lower Rhineland; Valencia's irrigated *huerta* also achieved high levels of productivity. Robert Allen (1992) has suggested that the introduction by early modern peasant landowners of small-scale improvements to drainage in the heavy Midland clays fuelled a 'yeoman' revolution in agricultural productivity, while Philip Hoffman (1996) has documented comparable patterns of growth in central and northern France. George Grantham (1993a and 1997) calculates that pre-modern levels of urbanization were 40–60 per cent lower than what the available technology could sustain, and concludes from this that the state of agricultural technology was not a binding constraint on the size of the non-agricultural workforce in pre-industrial times.

The research I have summarized suggests that two major factors were at play in determining the rate of peasant and landlord innovation, namely interest rates and the opportunity costs of trade defined by prevailing transaction costs.[11] As discussed below, however, real interest rates are determined by investment risk and investment opportunity (market size), both of which are a function of transaction costs. We can therefore say that the principal reason why investments in pre-modern agriculture were not more sustained and why productivity experienced frequent setbacks, was the high level of transaction costs in pre-modern societies due to political fragmentation, co-ordination failures, and upheaval and warfare.[12] A further conclusion is that, in the longer term, population density was positively correlated with agricultural productivity as argued by Ester Boserup (Boserup 1965). As might be expected given the high cost of transporting bulk foods and the benefits from higher population densities in terms of specialization and economies of scale in infrastructure, the highest rates of medieval agricultural productivity were found in regions such as north-central Italy, Flanders, Île-de-France, Artois, and Norfolk that also had the highest demographic density in Europe at the time.

Neither conclusion implies that bottlenecks to production causing demographic expansion to stall did not arise; it is clear that a slowdown of this kind was taking place in parts of Europe from the late thirteenth century. What they do is to shift the explanatory focus in accounts of pre-modern economic growth and of its absence from the balance between population and resources (as in the neo-Malthusian model) and the structure of land ownership (as in Brenner's model) to the complex relation between agrarian production and markets.

One of the most misleading aspects of the model we have been criticizing is its overwhelming concern with grain production. While grain as the European staple food was evidently the most salient pre-modern product in terms of volume, it was far less important by value and commercialization (much being consumed directly by the producers). Until quite recently, however, this fact was not recognized, and the sectoral bias in favour of agricultural staples ignored the substantial occupational alternatives faced by rural producers, which included wool production (which accounted for up to a third of rural GNP in early fourteenth-century England), Mediterranean tree crops, livestock meat, dairy and leather production, and most crucially, various forms of by-employment or 'Z-goods' in the manufacturing and service sectors (Hymer and Resnick 1969). It could be argued that the bias reinforced the belief in a 'general crisis', for it led historians to ignore the perceptible increase in some parts of Europe of rural and small town by-employment in the decades before the Black Death, an increase that implies that the price of basic foods relative to manufactures and to raw materials like wool was stable or declining.[13] By excluding activities that raised disposable incomes and stimulated agrarian specialization, the post-war models of the feudal economy overestimated the welfare effects of harvest and supply crises before the Black Death.

Single-minded concentration on cereal production also led post-war historians to ignore or misunderstand the importance of domestic trade and markets,[14] and to assume that since 'average' peasants owned their means of production and could meet their food consumption needs off the land, they would only trade under some kind of 'extra-economic' compulsion. Markets were foisted on the peasantry by feudal lords and by Church and state who needed to monetize the feudal surplus; medieval towns were both parasitical consumers of the feudal surplus and 'islands in a feudal sea'. Under normal circumstances, peasants avoided markets because production for the market was subject to greater risk, that is, to greater income volatility. These arguments are wrong both in theory and in practice. In theory, income volatility can be overcome by diversifying output; however, markets do the job better than an isolated producer because they pool the output from a large number of farms and stimulate specialization which increases productivity. There is therefore in principle no reason for peasants to avoid markets, although the existence of market inefficiencies might recommend some caution (or to put it differently, the extent of specialization is a function of market efficiency). In practice, product markets (and to a lesser extent land, labour and credit markets) were ubiquitous under feudalism, and towns played important roles as centres of consumption, industry and trade in stimulating agrarian and manufacturing specialization. Although these facts have long been accepted for the more urbanized and less feudal regions of Europe such as Flanders, parts of Iberia, southern France and Italy, similar patterns are being discovered in economically less-developed countries such as England, where the period *c.* 1086 to 1348 witnessed rising commercialization, a tripling of the rate of urbanization and perhaps a tenfold increase in per capita coinage in circulation (Miller and Hatcher 1995; see also Britnell 1993). Even in the least urbanized, most feudalized corners of Europe, intensive Smithian growth was clearly being achieved, and towns played an important part in the process.

In sum, post-war models of the medieval or feudal economy underestimated the productive potential and performance of agriculture. Agrarian practices developed for the most part before the mid fourteenth-century crisis could raise output and productivity considerably above the demographic 'ceiling' reached around 1300. Many of the potential gains in productivity had still to be exhausted by the eighteenth century. The major influence on the rate of innovation was the cost of trade broadly defined. Ease of access to structured and competitive markets was the main precondition for growth. Medieval societies, which appear to have regulated their size in response to economic opportunities, did not exploit their technological potential to the full before the Black Death largely for lack of adequate incentives. In most cases, the barriers to trade and therefore the opportunity costs of innovation were simply too high.[15]

2 Outline of a new model of the feudal economy

A new model of the feudal economy must incorporate the recent findings I have just summarized; it must avoid the tautological appeal to trade that causes trade;[16] and it must offer a parsimonious explanation of why regional economies performed differently over long stretches of time. What follows is a brief sketch of what this model might look like.

In the feudal or tributary mode of production, most rural producers owned their means of production and sold a proportion of their produce on the market.[17]

Feudal lords (which included towns with jurisdictional prerogatives over their hinterland) extracted a surplus from the peasantry upon the basis of a decentralized system of legal compulsion backed by military threat; the surplus was perceived directly as rent in cash, kind or labour, and indirectly through levies on trade and the provision of justice. Although the relative share of income from each source varied over time and space, the share from rights of jurisdiction (which included compulsory labour services) was always substantial. Therefore, the principal threat to feudalism did not come from trade; up to a point feudalism thrived on trade (Britnell 1993).[18] But if feudal lords did not exclude markets, they regulated and taxed them for income. The main obstacle to growth in the feudal economy was thus the cost of trade, which was defined mainly by institutional regulation and tariffs and (to a far lesser extent) by developments in transport technology. Within the boundaries of a lord's or city's jurisdiction, markets were by and large competitive, with the exception of the market in food supplies which towns often attempted to regulate; up to a point, feudal decentralization could support both extensive and intensive growth.[19] Yet the lords' and towns' main purpose in stimulating trade was to maximize rent streams from their fiscal and jurisdictional rights, and those rights were a fundamental aspect of their social and political powers. In other words, 'free trade' would have both reduced feudal and urban revenue, and challenged the jurisdictional superiority of lord over peasant and town over country. Consequently, strong feudal jurisdiction was incompatible with long-run economic growth. Not surprisingly, agricultural innovation appears to have been inversely correlated with the intensity of seigniorial rights (Campbell 1997b: 244–5; Verhulst 1985; Verhulst 1990: 25), and rural industrial growth was inversely correlated with the jurisdictional powers of towns (Epstein 2000). The fundamental constraint in the feudal economy was not technological inertia, but the market monopolies and other co-ordination failures arising from political and jurisdictional parcellization.

In principle, therefore, the feudal economy could develop in two opposite directions. Either it maintained or intensified the parcellization of sovereignty – a direction taken for example by the Polish Commonwealth following the collapse of the monarchy after the mid-seventeenth century, and to a lesser degree by Spanish Naples in the same period – or it could evolve into more centralized and politically integrated states, as occurred more or less rapidly elsewhere. In most of western Europe, the use by feudal lords of their extra-economic powers of coercion to tax and monopolize trade, which maintained the feudal economy at a permanent sub-optimal equilibrium, was counterbalanced by the same feudal elites' strategy of military expansion and territorial integration. Although the primary aim of feudal territorial expansion was to broaden the lord's political and economic base, it also benefited the economy more broadly because it increased jurisdictional integration and reduced transaction costs within the new territory (Olson 1982). As discussed below, state formation lowered pre-existing seigniorial dues, overcame co-ordination failures (prisoners' dilemmas) between rival feudal and urban monopolies, systematized legal codes, weights and measures, and reduced the ruler's opportunities and incentives to act autocratically as a 'stationary bandit' against his subjects. State formation was thus a major cause – possibly *the* major cause – of market integration and Smithian growth.

Economic development in the feudal system was therefore the outcome of two countervailing forces, the one pressing for military and jurisdictional decentralization, the other for increased political and jurisdictional centralization. In the long run, the latter won out, lowering transaction costs and stimulating commercialization and specialization. The 'prime mover' and 'contradiction' within the feudal mode of production lay in relations between lords, peasants, markets and the state.

3 The late medieval crisis

If one accepts that population growth offers a crude indirect measure of economic growth, as the research I have summarized implies, the evidence of an economic slowdown in many parts of early fourteenth-century western Europe is hard to gainsay. But if, as has been suggested, demographic difficulties reveal the operation of preventive rather than positive checks, what was causing economic opportunities to contract?

It was pointed out previously that neither the demographic slowdown nor the increasing incidence of famines prove that the population was outstripping available resources, and it was suggested that the increased volatility of grain prices, the socially unequal exposure to famine, and the highly variable patterns of demographic change observed around the turn of the fourteenth century were the effect of institutional bottlenecks to specialization through trade.[20] Where opportunities for agricultural intensification and specialization were being foreclosed and the costs of transporting grain to meet local shortages rose too, the incidence of famines and price volatility rose; societies responded either by deferring marriage and procreation, or (where serfdom did not tie peasants to the land) by migrating. The rising incidence of feudal warfare was particularly disruptive, less because of the destruction it wreaked than because it was associated with higher taxes, distraint and purveyances of foodstuffs to supply armies, disrupted trade (owing both to warfare and to higher fiscal exploitation), and higher and more volatile prices.[21] On the other hand, where institutional and market conditions were more stable, the population continued to expand. Thus in central and southern Castile, for example, the thirteenth-century *reconquista* opened up unsettled lands that immigrants were too few to populate fully; not surprisingly, in this area the symptoms of economic crisis (stagnant or declining population, volatile and rising prices, land fragmentation) were generally more muted. The region's main economic problems arose from a lack rather than an excess of population.[22]

We have seen that the economic slowdown was due neither to primitive technology nor to peasant conservatism, but resulted from increasing competition between feudal lords – including towns that possessed significant jurisdictional rights over the countryside, as in parts of Italy, Flanders and possibly Catalonia – for the profits of trade, for stable food supplies, and for territorial enlargement. The slow build-up of royal, seigniorial and urban levies during the thirteenth century, and perhaps more seriously, the increased incidence of feudal and urban warfare from the last two decades of the thirteenth century, raised the risk threshold of specialization and reduced incentives for agricultural innovation. These bottlenecks did not occur everywhere to the same degree, which explains why in some areas the population kept on growing; but where and when an economic slowdown did occur, it was less a technologically determined 'agrarian crisis' than an institutionally induced 'crisis of distribution'.[23]

Although there is considerable disagreement over the effects of the 'crisis' and of the pandemic shock caused by the Black Death, most historians agree that it marked a watershed in the transition to capitalism.[24] For Brenner (1982), the development of 'agrarian capitalism' required the expulsion of the self-sufficient and market-averse peasantry from the land. This process occurred only in England; elsewhere, the 'crisis' actually reinforced the feudal mode of production based on an independent peasantry or on serfdom. According to Wallerstein (1974) and, more ambiguously, to Braudel (1982–84), the crisis set the stage for the transition to a more vaguely defined 'merchant capitalism' and to a 'capitalist world-system' with western Europe at its core. Both interpretations assume that the transition to capitalism was set in motion by factors external to feudalism itself – as indeed follows logically from the assumption that feudalism possessed no internal dynamic for growth. Brenner sees the *deus ex machina* as being the balance of class power determined by historically contingent national features; for Braudel and Wallerstein, the overseas discoveries offered the external markets needed to pull the medieval economy out of under-consumptionist stagnation. The most frequently heard answer to Maurice Dobb's old question whether there was a 'prime mover within feudalism bringing about the transition to the capitalist mode of production' is a clear and resounding 'no' (Dobb 1946).

The economic dynamic of feudalism is better seen as the result of two endogenous forces, market production and political centralization. In this context, the Black Death was an autonomous or exogenous phenomenon, but it was not the all-important outside shock that bounced the feudal economy out of its 'low-level equilibrium trap' (see B. F. Harvey 1991 and Herlihy 1997 for this view). Even without the epidemic of 1347–50, increasingly powerful political and economic forces had been pressing since the late eleventh century for territorial and jurisdictional simplification. These pressures were coming to a head during the last decades of the thirteenth century, with the outbreak of 'state warfare' in the British Isles, Iberia, Flanders, southern Germany, and Prussia; the two Hundred Years wars between England and France and between Catalonia-Aragon, Sicily and Naples were merely their most salient manifestations. War required taxation, and taxation required forms of political consensus-building, of state sovereignty, and of administrative resources that were in many ways quite new (Genet 1995). Even without the shock of the plague, inbuilt pressures for political centralization would, over time, have provided the benefits sketched above, lowering transaction costs, improving incentives for trade and specialization, and slowly raising the economy to a higher growth path. However, by shifting the bargaining power between land and labour so rapidly and dramatically, the fourteenth-century pandemic turned an evolutionary process into a process of Schumpeterian 'creative destruction' driven by political struggle.

With the support of social groups such as the wealthier peasantry, whose bargaining powers were strengthened by the shortage of labour, and the urban elites, both of whom stood to gain from lower feudal levies and weaker feudal jurisdictional monopolies, aspiring rulers increased the jurisdictional integration of their territories, made markets more competitive, stimulated commercialization and set the stage for the long sixteenth-century boom. The extent and effectiveness of jurisdictional integration were, however, shaped by institutional and political differences between states; these differences also set the framework for further integration. To the extent that jurisdictional integration defined the basic incentive structures within regions, the late medieval crisis both caused greater integration within politically bounded regions and defined the institutional parameters for subsequent economic divergence between regions.

Much of the debate on the late medieval economy has focused on the demand side, especially on the extent to which changes in the bargaining power of lords and labourers improved the standard of living of the poor. Despite significant regional differences in the extent of income distribution and in its effects on patterns of consumption, individual welfare generally increased. Rising consumption is well-attested for meat, cheese, butter, beer and, in Mediterranean countries, for wine, olive oil, fruit and vegetables; probate inventories, dowries, and archaeological excavations show marked increases in the use of cheap cloth, crockery, wooden utensils and suchlike. The description of the late middle ages as the 'golden age of the peasant and labourer' is by and large correct.[25]

However, a consequence of the neo-Malthusian and neo-Marxist focus on grain production has been to divert attention from developments in supply structures that gave rise to market deepening (an increase in the volume, number and quality of commodities exchanged) and market widening (an increase in the geographical size of markets). Market deepening entailed three related phenomena: first, the previously mentioned increase in *per capita* consumption of already commercialized goods with higher elasticity of demand; second, an increase in the traded *proportion* of total output, that is, greater 'commercialization', as reflected in the development across late medieval Europe of rural cloth and metal industries; third, an increase in the traded *range* of consumer goods. These processes, which were at the same time social, technological and institutional, show striking structural similarities with the 'industrious revolution' of the seventeenth century, whose most distinctive feature was the increase in labour inputs in response to a growing range of consumer goods (de Vries 1994; see also Goldthwaite 1993).

One reason why real demand appears to have increased during the late middle ages is that the Black Death reduced the proportion of un- or under-employed in the population and labour participation increased (Bridbury 1973). Several scholars have suggested that more unmarried women were employed in the urban service sector, particularly in the production and petty trade of clothing and food; others that the growth of rural manufacture required greater labour inputs by children and women. The apparently increased concern by urban craft guilds to exclude or delimit women's work was to some extent a reaction to women's greater opportunities for work and bargaining power (Goldberg 1992; Poos 1991; Howell 1986a; Wiesner 1986; Knotter, in this volume). In agriculture, the diffusion of crops such as rice, sugarcane, oil and wine in southern Europe, hops in northern Europe, and woad, madder and flax across the continent helped distribute labour inputs more evenly during the year, making it possible to cultivate the same amount of land for a higher output with less labour.[26]

Gains in average labour productivity were matched by institutional and technical changes that stimulated specialization. If the average per capita value of trade increased after the Black Death, as the preceding argument implies, transaction costs at the margin would also rise; unless more efficient systems of distribution had been devised, therefore, most benefits of more trade would have been lost. In fact, several institutional changes did occur which lowered transaction costs, in most cases deliberately so, even though the process was largely driven by the increased jurisdictional integration of territorial and emerging national states. The most immediate effect of a territory's jurisdictional integration – which was technically a form of customs union – was to reduce feudal and urban tariffs, raise domestic competition and cause domestic prices to deflate, particularly for cheaper, bulk commodities like grain for which the marginal impact of tariffs was high (Daviso di Charvensod 1961; Bergier 1963: 175–80; Zulaica Palacios 1994: 45, 56).

Large gains were also made by changing the way trade was organized. The late middle ages witnessed possibly the most wide-ranging attempts in Europe before the eighteenth-century and Napoleonic reforms to integrate money and coinage and to standardize measurements. While monetary agreements between independent lords and towns were not unknown during the twelfth and particularly the thirteenth century, monetary unions flourished after 1350 in Alsace, Swabia, Franconia, in the southern Rhineland and the Netherlands, and elsewhere in south-western and western Germany, in reaction to the monetary disintegration that followed the fall of the Hohenstaufen (Wielandt 1971: 664, with references). In the regional states of Italy, coinage by individual city-states was supplanted by that of the dominant city, Milan, Florence or Venice. In France, the royal silver *blanc* struggled for hegemony over monetary regions that had themselves only recently emerged out of feudal fragmentation. Inasmuch as political fragmentation gave rise to co-ordination failures and competitive devaluations, political integration may have reduced the incidence of monetary debasement.[27] Use of gold coinage, mainly for large internal and international payments and therefore less susceptible to local abuse, became more widespread. In areas of Hansa commercial influence gold coins account for one-fifth of all hoards in the fourteenth century, but the proportion rises to four-fifths in the fifteenth (Sprandel 1971: 354). In the course of the fourteenth century the Florentine florin and the Venetian ducat established international benchmarks for national gold currencies; only England, the fifteenth-century Rhineland principalities, and briefly France produced gold coins of a different standard (Spufford 1988: 319–21).

Unification of measurements was more difficult to enforce. The proliferation of local measurements was not simply a time consuming nuisance and a constant cause of commercial friction; it was also a primary source of fraud. Since measurements were also one of the most visible signs of jurisdictional sovereignty, their regulation and where possible simplification was of both economic and symbolic importance. Efforts to establish common 'regional' or 'national' measurements increased after the Black Death under very diverse political, institutional and economic circumstances. Even in England, where attempts to unify the country's measures went back for centuries, the enforcement of common national standards became a matter of growing concern during the fourteenth century (Zupko 1977: chapter 2; see also Held 1918; Epstein 1992: chapter 3; Wielandt 1971: 678).

The sharp rise after 1350 in the number of seasonal and annual fairs specializing in regional and inter-regional trade, which may also have contributed to the emergence of a trans-Alpine network of petty traders (Fontaine 1996), provided an institutional backbone to market integration (Epstein 1994). Localized demographic shocks also stimulated the rise of more integrated labour markets for unskilled labour, particularly for seasonal migrants between uplands and lowlands (Viazzo 1989) and between differently specialized lowland regions (Epstein 1998c); it seems likely that rural hiring fairs emerged or were developed further to co-ordinate these labour flows (Penn and Dyer 1990). The period also saw the emergence of regional and inter-regional agreements between specialized master artisans and of journeymen associations, and the establishment of technical entry-tests for masters who were no longer locally trained (Reininghaus 1981; Fourquin 1979: 286; Epstein 1998b); in Germany, territorial lords acted increasingly as mediators between iron miners, and brokered industrial alliances that benefited from economies of scale in production (Sprandel 1969: 310).

A well-established and more circuitous though possibly more effective way of lowering tariffs that was extremely popular among towns and large trading companies (such as the *Ravensburger Gesellschaft* and the Augsburg Walser) was to seek toll exemptions in the communities they traded with most frequently. These agreements differed from standard merchant-company franchises by being restricted to specific communities within a state, rather than being applied indiscriminately to a whole country, possibly because states were increasingly loath to jeopardize valuable taxes but also because patterns of trade and urban hierarchies were becoming more settled and predictable (Bergier 1963: 176; Epstein 1992: chapter 3; Kleineke 1997). Of equal importance was the disappearance from use in the course of the fifteenth century of the law of reprisal, whereby governments granted individual creditors the right to seize the goods of a debtor or of the latter's countrymen. Reprisals, which were seldom effective and were highly damaging to trade, were effectively an admission of political and judicial failure. As legal systems became more established, commercial laws more sophisticated, and state jurisdictions less contested, individual responsibility replaced collective liability.[28]

While attempts to enforce a single jurisdiction were seldom wholly successful, contemporaries would not have expended so much effort on them if they had not made a substantial difference. Evidence of improvements comes from increased integration in the market for grain, which led to lower prices (see figure 2.2 below) and reduced price volatility (figure 2.1 above) (Unger 1983; Tits-Dieuaide 1975: 255–6; Poehlmann 1993; Epstein 2000).

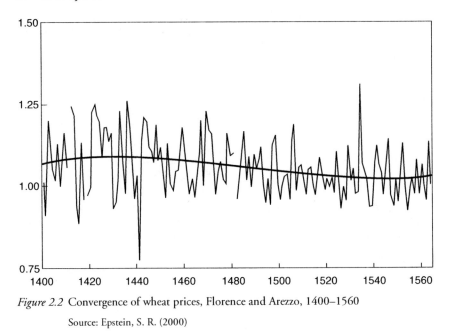

Figure 2.2 Convergence of wheat prices, Florence and Arezzo, 1400–1560

Source: Epstein, S. R. (2000)

But the most significant benefits of market integration occurred in rates of investment, productivity and technological innovation. The most striking development after the Black Death was the collapse in public and private interest rates. The Black Death caused a major break of trend in interest rates across Europe and inaugurated a long-term, albeit slower, decline in the cost of capital that lasted up to the eighteenth century. Interest rates paid by larger monarchies dropped from 20–30 per cent before the Black Death to 8–10 per cent in the early sixteenth century, and from 15 to 4 per cent in the more advanced Italian, German and Netherlandish cities over the same period; rulers became more reliable, lenders were less vulnerable to expropriation and financial instruments became more sophisticated (figure 2.3).

The decline in the expected rates of return or cost of capital for individuals was equally striking. Rates of return in England declined from 9.5–11 per cent (the prevailing rate between 1150 and 1350) to 7 per cent in the half century after the Black Death and to a mere 4.5 per cent by the late fifteenth century; proportionally similar gains occurred elsewhere in Europe (Clark 1988).[29] By 1450, Europeans were enjoying a huge 'free lunch' consisting of a more than doubling in the amount of capital available per person (figure 2.4).[30]

Although the reasons for the decline in interest rates have not attracted much discussion, it appears that several of the factors examined previously contributed to the change and, by mutually reinforcing each other, produced the extraordinary size and rapidity of the gains. These factors were a decline in commercial and institutional risk; increased opportunities for investment as market barriers declined; and an increased range of consumer goods, which raised the individual propensity to save.

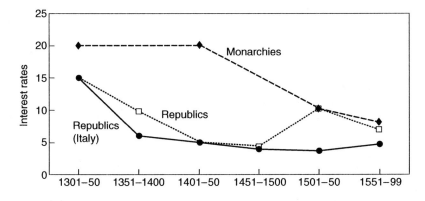

Figure 2.3 Long-term rates of interest on European state debt, 1300–1600

Source: see figure 2.2

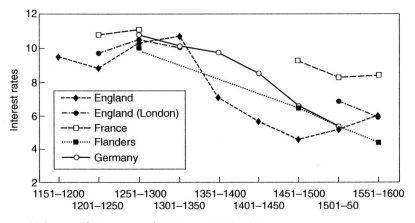

Figure 2.4 The cost of private capital in Europe, 1200–1600

Sources: Clark (1988: 273–4) (figures for England are the average of perpetual rent charges and rent/price ratio on land); Keene and Harding (1987)

After the Black Death, investments became safer; opportunities for investment increased; and it became worthwhile to invest because there was more to spend the profits on.

The declining cost of capital made a vital contribution to the most significant long-term effect of market integration, namely more investment and specialization. These effects can best be tracked through changing patterns of urbanization, which reflect both the division of labour between 'town' (where the industrial and service sectors were concentrated) and 'country' (where the primary sector predominated) and the degree of specialization among towns.

Rates of urbanization generally increased after the Black Death as marketing and distribution systems improved: more people lived in towns because they could be supplied more easily with food, and because more efficient labour markets allowed them to move more quickly to the countryside at harvest time when demand for agricultural labour peaked.[31] However, most gains in urbanization occurred in the less-advanced regions of southern and north-western Italy, and in other formerly backward economies such as Castille, Holland, southern Germany and England. By contrast, after 1350 urbanization in Flanders, Tuscany, Sicily and Catalonia – which had reached peaks of 30 per cent and above before the Black Death – stagnated or declined, perhaps indicating that these regions had attained some kind of structural limit to urban growth (Stabel 1997; Hoppenbrouwers 2000; Sanchez Leon 2000; Scott and Scribner 1996; Bridbury 1962; Epstein 1998a).

The increased proportion of town dwellers was matched by the development of more clearly defined urban hierarchies organized by activity and function within regions or across several regions; England may have been unusually precocious in developing a rudimentary national urban system (Galloway 2000). Although urban hierarchies at the beginning of the sixteenth century appear retrospectively to be strictly regional and 'medieval' (de Vries 1984a), they were in fact largely the outcome of the late medieval crisis. They occurred because of changes both to economic and administrative functions. Like the development of 'national' urban hierarchies in the seventeenth century, the rise of regional hierarchies during the late fourteenth and fifteenth centuries was hastened by political centralization, which weakened traditional urban economic prerogatives, reduced barriers to trade between towns, and concentrated an unprecedented volume of administrative and fiscal resources within newly designated regional and national capitals (Chittolini 1987; Chevalier 1982; de Vries 1984a). Sharper urban hierarchies were also the effect of increased urban competition and larger markets that gave rise to economies of scale and agglomeration, such as the tendency towards concentration of the more specialized cloth industries and the fission of craft guilds into more specialized organizations (Fourquin 1979: 282–3; Persson 1988).

Market deepening and widening also intensified Ricardian specialization based on absolute and comparative advantage. A salient instance of this was the development of a pan-European cattle trade after 1400 (Blanchard 1986; Sivéry 1976: 604–5), and similar albeit less far-flung trade networks developed for metals (copper, iron, tin and silver), salt and grain (Kellenbenz 1986). Even so, because of pervasive fiscal, monetary and linguistic barriers to trade and factor mobility *between* states, compared with rising jurisdictional integration *within* states, domestic specialization was the easier option. Political barriers to trade could be overcome only in part by means of cheap water transport, and maritime regions such as Holland and Sicily were highly unusual examples of strongly export-oriented economies (Blockmans 1993; Epstein 1992). The weaker synchronicity of epidemics across Europe during the fifteenth century compared with the second half of the fourteenth (Del Panta 1980: 118) and the considerable discrepancies in the timing of demographic recovery (which range from the 1440s in Italy and Flanders to the 1490s in England and parts of France) support the view that the European economy was becoming increasingly regionalized.

Despite the rise of proto-national states in Castile, Burgundy and France, the economic landscape of Renaissance Europe remained obstinately regional: differences between northern Italian territorial states were probably less significant than those between many nominally unified, but in fact economically and institutionally more fragmented, regions in Castile and France.[32]

The strong growth of rural and small-town manufacture, particularly of the linen, wool and fustian industries, after the mid-fourteenth century in Italy, Catalonia, Germany, Flanders, England and France is strikingly similar to seventeenth-century 'proto-industrialization'. This similarity has been explained as a quasi-Malthusian response to demographic decline leading to higher rural living standards and stronger demand for lower-quality cloth (Hohenberg and Lees 1985). However, changes in supply structures, particularly a weakening of the major institutional obstacles to manufacture outside the great towns, were probably as or more important. Since town crafts and feudal lords – particularly the former – were unwilling to let rural manufacture develop outside their control, rural industry required a loosening of such institutional vetoes to flourish. These preconditions arose during the late middle ages and again in the seventeenth century, when states launched political offensives on traditional urban and feudal monopolies and prerogatives which made it easier to set up new industries.[33] Institutional restrictions applied mainly to the wool and fustian sectors, however, and small towns and villages found it easier to develop the less-skilled linen and hemp industries which became very popular after the Black Death (Holbach 1994: 47–208).

Increased regional trade and labour market integration – particularly the increasingly mobile masters and tramping journeymen – compensated for declining population in accelerating the rate of technological diffusion. Higher rates of investment spurred by rising demand and declining real interest rates stimulated the invention of new products and the refining and diffusion of existing ones. Improvements to consumer goods include the mass diffusion of linen underwear (with unquantifiable benefits for public health) (Heers 1976); the creation of transportable hard cheese (caciocavallo and parmesan) and of *maccheroni* pasta in Italy (Epstein 1992; Sereni 1981: 323–5); the invention of herring and pilchard preservation in north-western Europe (de Vries and van der Woude 1997a; Kowaleski 2000); the transformation of glass into a middle-class commodity (glass panes became a common sight in the homes of the wealthier bourgeois, and the first plantsman's glass-house made its appearance in the Low Countries during the fifteenth century; see Fourquin 1979: 293); and the production of quality wines identified by their place of origin (Melis 1984; Fourquin 1964: 89–90). The popularity of linen clothing and thus the abundance of rags also made it feasible to produce higher-quality, more-durable paper, a prerequisite for the diffusion of printing. Other better known inventions and innovations include the compass (Kreutz 1973) and the rediscovery of the astrolabe; the diffusion of double-entry book-keeping, of letters of exchange, and of commercial correspondence as merchants made increasing use of foreign agents rather than travelling themselves; increases in the size and efficiency of traditional furnaces, which turned ceramics from a luxury good into a commodity; the diffusion of the 'indirect method' of smelting, the invention of the blast furnace in the fifteenth century, and the improvements in underground drainage that made possible deep-shaft mining;[34] improvements to the water lock for inland navigation (Henning 1991: 457); and gunpowder, portable guns and movable cannon.

Social, political and economic upheaval and increased artisan mobility stimulated cross-fertilization between industrial sectors and economic regions to an unusual degree. Examples include the spread of quality glass production from Venice to Bohemia, the diffusion and improvement of the thirteenth-century Saxony spinning wheel, and the transmission from the Mediterranean to northern Europe of the two- and three-masted cog or carrack and carvel – a process that by the late fifteenth century had given rise to 'the first truly European vessel, ending a major division in the Continent's maritime technology that had persisted since the early Middle Ages' (Friel 1995: 169; Unger 1980); the 'cartographic revolution' that brought together the distinct traditions of portulan charts, 'imaginary' world maps, and 'empirical' local and regional maps (P. D. A. Harvey 1991); the technical cross-fertilization between metallurgy, goldsmithing and engraving that produced spring-driven clocks and watches and movable type; the increased application of water power for metal-working, for spinning (as in the spinning mill that made the fortunes of Bologna's silk industry (Poni 1990), and for grinding raw materials like woad and Sicilian sugarcane (Epstein 1992); and the combination of European peasant and urban with Arab dyeing techniques, including the increased use of alum mordant (Ploss 1973: 35, 42). Although technical diffusion and cross-fertilization were easier to achieve in manufacture and trade than in agriculture, there was also a noticeable increase in the diffusion of agricultural best practice during the fifteenth and early sixteenth centuries in the Upper and Lower Rhineland and the Low Countries. In most cases innovation appears to have been instigated by the peasantry (Bentzien 1990: 105–30). Plants of Islamic origin such as indigo, rice, spinach, sugarcane, artichokes, and probably eggplant, that had been little more than garden curiosities before the Black Death became more widely accepted and spread across the western Mediterranean (Watson 1983).

The increased diffusion of practices and ideas in the spheres of production and trade bears more than a passing resemblance to the accelerated circulation of practices and ideas in the spheres of ideology and representation that historians call the Renaissance. This is not the place to address the debate recently revived by cultural and economic historians on the relationship between the world of ideas and their material context (Goldthwaite 1993; Jardine 1996; Grafton 1997). It is nonetheless significant that historians increasingly use the metaphors of commerce, circulation and consumption to describe a phenomenon that had previously been defined in strictly intellectual and idealistic terms. The evidence we have reviewed suggests that the worlds of production and ideas were facing similar stimuli and pressures to be open to the new, unusual and unexpected.

4 From late medieval crisis to early modern growth

The late medieval crisis is best understood as an exogenous demographic shock which triggered a process of institutional 'creative destruction' that raised the west

European economy to a higher growth path by aligning incentive structures more closely with the exploitation of technological potential. Higher disposable income among the lower classes raised demand for better and more varied food and manufactures; increased state taxation to fund expansionary warfare may also have raised aggregate demand, although it is unclear to what extent states were simply appropriating a larger share of the feudal surplus (Ormrod 1995). But the most significant effect of the demographic shock was sharply to accelerate the process of political centralization inherent to the feudal-tributary mode of production. Ultimately, political centralization underlies all the major institutional changes to market structures previously described. Centralization lowered domestic trans-action costs, intensified economic competition between towns and strengthened urban hierarchies, weakened urban monopolies over the countryside, and stimulated labour mobility and technological diffusion. However, centralization and territorial integration were strongly contested by the more powerful feudal lords and towns; the extent of territorial integration was therefore determined by the balance of power between the four major political coalitions: central rulers, feudal lords, and urban and rural elites. The key to the different economic performances in late medieval and early modern regions can be found in the political economy of state formation and markets (above, note 20).

Although maritime trade and the overseas discoveries have often loomed large in explanations of the late medieval recovery, their effects appear to be on the whole rather marginal. The European discoveries played virtually no role in bringing the demographic crisis to an end. With the exception of England, Europe's demographic recovery mostly dates several decades *before* the great overseas expansion (the implications of Portuguese explorations of the 1430s were fully understood only several decades later). Indeed, rather than a radical break with an obscurantist medieval world, the maritime discoveries of the 1490s are now seen as very much a continuation of, and building upon, technology and information that had developed between the Mediterranean and the North Sea during the later middle ages. More-over, against the suggestion that a fifteenth-century 'bullion famine' caused 'appalling direct effects on trade',[35] the sharp secular decline in interest rates between 1350 and 1500 shows that capital was not in short supply, and implies that American bullion, which began to augment European silver supplies significantly only from the 1530s, was neither necessary nor sufficient to sustain the European recovery.

Similar comments apply to the effects of maritime trade within Europe. Long-distance maritime trade during the demographic crisis contracted relatively to trade overland or by sea within individual regions and began to expand significantly only after populations had begun once again to expand.[36] Foreign trade was hit by endemic warfare (van der Wee and Peters 1970; Munro 1991), which however was a structural rather than accidental feature of the period; it also declined because competition by rural and small-town cloth industries forced established urban industries to specialize in higher value-added products with smaller overseas markets. The relative buoyancy of middle-range shipping between 1350 and 1450 was aided by the development of larger transport ships and of insurance based on value rather than weight, which lowered transport costs for cheap agricultural goods (Unger 1980;

Melis 1964). The size of maritime trade was nonetheless minuscule compared with trade overland in this period; in fifteenth- and sixteenth-century Sicily, whose exports of grain, silk, sugar and lesser agricultural products made it one of the most open economies of pre-modern Europe, foreign trade accounted for no more than 15 per cent of GNP (Epstein 1992).

Finally, one may question Braudel and Wallerstein's opinion that merchant capitalism associated with long-distance trade and urban entrepôts was an independent source of growth. The point can be briefly illustrated with two late medieval examples, Tuscany and Holland. Tuscany before the Black Death was among the most developed economies in Europe, testified by a population density of 60 inhabitants/km², a rate of urbanization of up to 40 per cent, and an industrial, commercial and financial metropolis of over 100,000 inhabitants. Holland by comparison was an under-populated and under-urbanized backwater. A century later, the economy of Tuscany was stagnating and Florence was quickly sliding down the urban ranks, whereas Holland was being transformed into one of the most advanced, urbanized and commercialized economies of Europe (Epstein 1991; Blockmans 1993).

Holland's main advantage over Tuscany was not its ease of access to the sea. The relative decline during the later middle ages, along with Tuscany, of advanced maritime economies such as Catalonia and Flanders goes to show that easy access to maritime trade and well-established mercantile and industrial communities did not offer a permanent comparative advantage. What allowed late medieval Holland to respond rapidly and imaginatively to the new economic opportunities at the crossroads of the North European overland and maritime trade and fishing industry, was its unusual degree of institutional flexibility born of weak seigniorial and urban jurisdictional powers. New towns could spring up and rural manufacture could flourish under weak monopolies and an absence of vested interests. In Tuscany, by contrast, where Florence's conquest of Pisa of 1406 had given it direct access to the sea, the Florentine elites deployed their unrivalled political authority to divert rent streams from their subjects and the region's economy never recaptured its medieval heights.

This comparison also raises the broader question of what caused pre-modern economies to diverge. The pessimistic answer is that the long-run stability in per capita cereal consumption everywhere in Europe outside England proves that, in fact, economic stagnation was the norm, and that early modern England is the one exception that proves the rule. The pessimists presume that pre-modern European economies outside England were fundamentally similar and imply that historical (political, social and institutional) differences did not make much difference, thus leaving the English 'exception' an unexplained mystery (van Zanden, in this volume). The more optimistic line pursued here is that measures of economic growth based strictly on cereal consumption underestimate per caput and GNP growth. First, they do not allow for increased consumer utility caused by better and more diverse food and by declining price volatility, to which the rise of more integrated markets during the later Middle Ages made a major contribution. Second, they ignore the fact that most pre-modern growth occurred in the manufacturing and service sectors rather than in cereal production, even though the precise gains cannot be measured very accurately.

The optimists therefore take evidence of some pre-modern growth to ask why there was not any more. They emphasize regional diversity and consider its causes a puzzle to be explained. While this chapter has dwelt mainly on the common features of the late medieval crisis, it has also indicated how the political economy of the crisis could set regional economies on diverging paths. The answer does not lie, as Brenner has claimed, in whether the peasants or the landlords ended up with full ownership of the land. Peasants were quite capable of raising land and labour productivity if given the opportunity, as was previously shown; on the other hand, landlords were quite happy *not* to embark on capitalist specialization if the incentives to do so were poor, as pre-modern Italy's 'failed transition' clearly shows (Epstein 1998c). Market structures, not property rights to land, dictated regional growth paths; but market structures were the institutional outcome of complex social, economic and political struggles between sovereigns, feudal lords, cities and rural communities whose outcome was regionally diverse. The balance of power determined the extent to which income was redistributed, domestic transaction costs were reduced, gains from specialization could be claimed, low-cost rural industries were allowed to develop, and the price of urban food supplies could be stabilized. Thus, although inter-regional trade and migration stimulated some regional economic convergence, domestic political and market structures were more important for economic performance in the long term.

Notes

This chapter appears in slightly revised form in Epstein, S. R. (2000) *Freedom and Growth. The Rise of States and Markets in Europe, 1300–1750*, London: Routledge.

1 See especially Grantham (1997). For evidence of high levels of productivity in pre-modern agriculture, see Allen (1992); Overton (1996); Hoffman (1996); de Vries and van der Woude (1997a).

2 It has recently been suggested that yields on English lordly demesnes of the kind assessed by Postan and Titow were lower than on peasant lands (Campbell 1997b: 238, 244–5); Winchester yields were in any case low by contemporary standards (Campbell 1995: 555–7). The lack of a clear trend in demesne yields cannot therefore be extrapolated to trends in output from peasant lands. For the suggestion that peasants were frequently more rather than less innovative than lords, see Langdon (1986); Derville (1987); Bentzien (1990: 129–31); Campbell (1997b).

3 Tits-Dieuaide (1987: 534–6) makes the same point for the period after 1400. However, her data do not include any figures prior to the Black Death and have not been detrended; although her general conclusion is thus correct, her estimates of price volatility are inaccurate.

4 This argument does not exclude that in some circumstances, local shortages could lead indirectly to higher rates of mortality, as Postan and Titow (1959) tried to demonstrate by correlating the rising number of heriots (entry fines to peasant tenures, which they assumed to be triggered on a peasant's death) with grain prices, particularly during the great famine of 1315–17. However, heriots were also exacted on distress sales of land, so they are better seen as evidence of a failure in entitlements (B. F. Harvey 1991; Smith 1991).

5 Jordan (1996). Postan (1973: 213) took the crisis of 1315–17 as marking the beginnings of late medieval decline.

6 See Sen (1981); Ravaillon (1987); Cotts Watkins and Menken (1985); Livi Bacci (1990); Walter and Schofield (1989); Fogel (1994). For pre-Black Death examples, see Berthe (1984: 272–3, 315–17, 320–1).

7 For evidence of peasants migrating to Italian cities during early fourteenth-century supply crises, see Pinto (1995: 49–50).

8 Malthus did, of course, also argue that populations could apply preventive checks to maintain a homeostatic balance between population and resources, but most postwar medieval and early modern historians preferred more dramatic hues to their stories. Homeostatic models are notably neutral as to the precise equilibrium point between population and resources that will be maintained. The revisionist argument sketched previously suggests that pre-modern populations left a significant margin between the resources they could theoretically produce with the technology at their disposal, and what they actually required for demographic survival and reproduction. In other words, deliberately or not they remained below their technological 'ceiling'.

9 See Razi (1980); Herlihy (1982); Leverotti (1989). Smith (1991: 60–5) discusses the evidence for the operation of nuptiality and natality, rather than mortality, as the main check on population growth before the Black Death. Although the positive correlation between social status and family size could reflect a lower probability of child survival in poorer families owing to malnutrition, worse heating and lodging conditions, etc., poor peasants could have overcome these disadvantages by increasing their crude birth rate. While evidence of preventive checks among the peasantry is far from conclusive, if we are to take seriously the claim that they responded in economically rational ways to price signals (see below), we must also assume that they would be aware of the penalties of excess natality.

10 Glick (1970); Persson (1991); Day (1999).

11 John Langdon (1986: 172–253) has shown that English smallholders who faced higher average rents than large peasants substituted horses for oxen more rapidly than large-scale tenant farmers and feudal landlords. Since they needed proportionally more cash than their wealthier neighbours, they engaged more in trading activities in which more costly but faster horse transport was advantageous.

12 'The central problem of medieval agriculture was not that methods of raising and maintaining productivity levels were unknown but, rather, that there were insufficient incentives to encourage their adoption outside a few favoured localities' (Campbell 1995: 544).

13 Bridbury (1982: chapter 1); Bailey (1988); Sivéry (1976: 607); Comba (1988); Mainoni (1994); Wolff (1976); Fourquin (1964: 115 and n. 289); Gual Camarena (1976).

14 This bias is visible both in Postan's work (1973) and in Brenner's insistence (1985) that towns were purely centres for the organization of the long-distance luxury trade and for the consumption of the feudal surplus. Paradoxically, Dobb (1946: chapter 2), with far less empirical evidence at his disposal, took a far more sophisticated position. His intuitions on the role of 'petty commodity production' have been developed more recently by Rodney Hilton (1985, 1992), who has had an important influence on the recent revival of interest in small towns, markets and commercialization in medieval England.

15 These conclusions appear to follow in the tracks of recent 'commercialization' or neo-Smithian revisionism, which has been particularly active among Anglo-American medievalists. This group of scholars tends to maximize the cumulative impact of commercial change, to suggest that welfare levels were not severely eroded by 1300, and to imply that the early fourteenth-century mortality crises were temporary and reversible setbacks (Bailey 1998). However, the commercialization thesis has two weaknesses. First, the assumption that medieval peasants behaved like modern Kansas farmers glosses over the most interesting part of the story, which is how incentive structures changed over time. Second, a strictly Smithian model of growth is unable to explain why some areas were more commercialized and technologically advanced than others. Significantly, attempts to address these differences within the commercialization framework appeal to exogenous institutional factors such as the extent of seigniorial controls. The recent reformulation of

Pirenne's thesis that growth was driven by urbanization and access to water transport (Grantham 1997) raises the question of what drove urbanization in the first place. There are enough examples of successful towns that did not have direct access to water transport and conversely of coastal areas that did not develop strong commercial emporia to suggest that the simple opportunity for engaging in trade was hardly enough to determine its emergence and success. The commercialization model describes growth but does not explain it.

16 Above, n. 15.

17 The definition of the peasantry as a class producing jointly for subsistence and for the market is preferable to essentially arbitrary definitions based on farm size, tenurial relations, imputed behavioural patterns, etc.

18 The main long-term threats to the feudal mode of surplus extraction lay elsewhere. First, the development of a class of wage labourers that was no longer tied to its means of production undermined feudal coercion because it could credibly threaten to migrate, and forced lords to compete on the market for labour rather than rely on compulsory labour services. Second, state centralization – the transfer of sovereignty over feudal means of coercion from subordinate lords to higher territorial authorities – transformed feudal rights of jurisdiction (which sanctioned the decentralized feudal mode of coercion) into fiscal or property rights over commercial transactions (which sanctioned the state's jurisdiction over trade). The transformation of decentralized feudal immunities into state-sanctioned and redeemable claims to fiscal rights changed the legal and economic base of the feudal class into a commodity that could be bought and sold to the highest bidder. Financial capital rather than social status became the elites' new coin of exchange. For the state, the issue whether to sell these income streams to the highest bidder or to get rid of them altogether became increasingly a financial and fiscal rather than a political matter.

19 Capitalism is defined as a system in which the majority of producers work for a wage, which is set competitively through markets, and the owners of capital stock compete on the market for profits based on marginal cost rather than for politically sanctioned redistribution. On this definition, the economy of pre-modern Europe at least up to the seventeenth century was largely feudal-tributary and not capitalist.

20 An institutional interpretation of this kind explains better than technological factors the marked regional and local differences in demographic performance, for the simple fact that the strength and effects of institutional bottlenecks were subject to greater local variation than technology.

21 The economic consequences of late thirteenth- and early fourteenth-century warfare are particularly well studied for England, where however, by contrast with most other European countries, the higher nobility sided with rather than against the monarchy. See Maddicott (1975) (who at pp. 70–5 qualifies the 'Postan thesis' along lines sketched here); Prestwich (1972); Harriss (1975); Miller (1975). Mate (1982) suggests that large land-owners could protect themselves more easily against such pressures than smallholders. Bailey (1998) links high price volatility to frequent disruptions to food distribution; see also Zulaica Palacios (1994: 81–2); Epstein (1999). On the other hand, the very nature of these disruptions to trade would have tended to keep supply crises rather localized (Berthe 1984: 240 for Navarre).

22 Mackay (1977); see also Sesma Muñoz (1995) for economic expansion in southern Aragon.

23 Conflicts over access to land, pastoral rights and scarce water resources also intensified between rural communities; rural banditry may have increased. See Berthe (1984: 258–65).

24 The views of Le Roy Ladurie (1966), who observed no fundamental discontinuity between the economy of 1300 and that of 1550, are in a clear minority.

25 Abel (1935); Dyer (1989). This view contrasts with that for which the shift in factor prices and bargaining power from land to labour after the Black Death led peasants and labourers to decrease their work effort rather than increase consumption of marketed goods (Postan 1973). This hypothesis (which postulates a 'backward bending supply curve of

labour') also appears to underlie Wallerstein's argument that the economic crisis could only be ended by opening up new external markets (the 'discoveries'), and Brenner's argument that peasants had to be deprived of land ownership to get capitalism on its feet. Evidence for decreased effort in response to rising real wages comes from two sources, namely an increase in the number of religious holidays and complaints by English landlords that wage-earners were unwilling to stay long in a job. Both types of evidence are ambiguous, however, since there is no proof that the increase in enforced religious leisure was demanded by the workers themselves, and the alleged unwillingness to work by English labourers could equally be seen as the refusal to be locked into long term contracts at a time when labour was extremely scarce and sought after (Penn and Dyer 1990).

26 See Watson (1983) for labour intensive Mediterranean crops of Islamic origin.

27 Cipolla (1963). Kindleberger (1991: 167–9) makes the similar point, that political fragmentation and the lack of effective central authority in the Holy Roman Empire exacerbated monetary devaluation during the *Kipper und Wipperzeit* of 1619–23. The implication that political centralization was making late-medieval states financially more reliable finds support in developments in interest rates discussed below.

28 This important issue awaits a modern, comparative study. The law of reprisal attracted the interest of nineteenth-century legal historians; see de Mas-Latrie (1866); Astorri (1998) (reprisals were being phased out by Florence in the early fifteenth century); Timbal (1958: 137) (reprisals fell out of use in France in the early sixteenth century).

29 Clark's data are based on returns from a low-risk investment like land or housing and therefore represent a lower bound. However, the interest-rate premium charged in England for more costly and risky investments like grain storage declined proportionally, from 20 per cent in 1260–1400 (McCloskey and Nash 1984) to 7.23 per cent in London in 1770–1800 (Clark 1988: 275–6). This corresponds to a gain of 64 per cent that is virtually identical to the decline in interest rates on land.

30 Clark's data are confirmed by the trend in life annuities and perpetual rents in London, which nearly halved from 11 per cent around 1300 to 6 per cent around 1515–30 (Keene and Harding 1987). My thanks to Derek Keene for sharing these figures.

31 See Grantham (1993a) for a discussion of the constraints on urbanization and labour mobility.

32 For a fuller theoretical discussion, with references, see Epstein (1992: chapter 3).

33 For the analogy between late medieval and seventeenth-century developments, see Kellenbenz (1963); Thomson (1983); Epstein (1998c). Overviews of the proto-industrial literature on the early modern period can be found in Ogilvie and Cerman (1996). Note that where urban powers were extensive, feudal jurisdictions could act as protective barriers to urban encroachment and vice versa. For developments in the late medieval cloth industry, see Holbach (1994); Bridbury (1982); Carrère (1976); Epstein (2000).

34 Sprandel (1969: 311–12) estimates that annual iron output increased from 25–30,000 tons in 1400 to 40,000 tons in 1500.

35 See Spufford (1988: chapter 15) for a summary of the literature (p. 358 for the quotation). Sussman (1998) points out that Europe could not suffer a balance of payments deficit with the Near East (as is well known it did) and bullion shortage simultaneously; in any case, money supply conditions varied significantly between regions, implying that the European bullion market was not integrated.

36 This was the significance of the debate between Cipolla, Lopez and Miskimin (1964) on the late medieval 'crisis'. The former were concerned with long-distance trade and were therefore more pessimistic; the latter observed rising shorter range trade and was therefore moderately optimistic.

3 The energy basis for early modern growth, 1650–1820

Paolo Malanima

While the evolution of energy consumption in Europe from the nineteenth century is relatively well known, information for preceding centuries is, on the other hand, scarce. There is general agreement among scholars about the main sources exploited then. What is lacking is an attempt to quantify their importance. In the following pages we shall try to provide that measurement and to connect the changes in the European energy system to the population increase from the second half of the seventeenth century onwards.

A relation always exists between energy consumption on the one hand and the movement of population and production on the other (cf. Cipolla 1962). This connection has been repeatedly demonstrated for the nineteenth century, the 'age of coal', and the twentieth, the 'age of oil'. It would be of interest to investigate the same interdependence during the previous change in the European energy system that took place from the second half of the seventeenth century. This was the first of the three long phases of growth in both population and production, which together articulated modern growth: from 1650 to 1820, from 1820 till the end of the century, and then from the end of the nineteenth century onwards. During this first phase – and unlike the second and the third – exploitation of new kinds of fuel was of only marginal importance. Instead the diffusion of new agricultural products and practices was crucial.

In this contribution we first seek to single out the energy resources in pre-industrial Europe and to evaluate their relative importance (sections 1–2). An examination of the relation between energy consumption and population increase from 1650 to 1820 then follows (sections 3–4).

1 Energy sources and energy consumption in the eighteenth century

The reconstruction by Fernand Braudel in *Civilisation matérielle, économie et capitalisme* (1982–84 Volume 1: chapter 5) may be a good starting point for working out some quantitative estimates of the level of energy consumption in Europe during the eighteenth century.[1] In Braudel's view sources of power were, in order of importance: draught animals, firewood, water, men, wind. To measure energy consumption, however, we have to replace quantities of power, as presented by

Braudel, with the energy consumed by the converters he singled out.[2] While it is impossible to obtain completely reliable data, probable magnitudes are not out of our reach. Following Braudel we then only have to substitute:

1   For draught animals, the fodder they consumed (considering animals as machines and fodder as their fuel);
2   For the power of firewood, the quantities of the same actually utilized by men;
3   For water and wind, the work actually done by mills and sails;
4   For the men, the energy they consumed in food.

These four items are economic resources, i.e. resources whose exploitation involves some cost – the non-economic, such as solar light, are not included in our calculations of energy consumption. They are the primary resources, i.e. economic resources not yet transformed from their natural state. Their combination formed the European energy system, i.e. all of the energy sources used in a particular environment, together with the technical knowledge needed for their exploitation: a system made up of coherences and interrelations we seek to uncover here. All other sources derive from these primary ones in any *ancien régime* economy, as in our developed world every source is a transformation of the main primary sources: oil, coal, natural gas, hydro-electricity, and nuclear power.

Gunpowder has not been included among these pre-industrial sources, just as military uses of energy are not included today. We might consider including manure and other nutrients, such as the nitrogen fixed by leguminous crops. In the calculations presented here these nutrients are excluded as secondary sources. They either result from a transformation of food, as with manure, and are therefore already present in the figures as food calories; or, as with nitrogen from legumes, they are a component of food, and so already included in what animals and men eat.

Quantitative information on these sources is relatively scarce. To define their weight, however, we may turn to many studies of agriculture, technology, and material culture. We try, first, to present some minimum and maximum consumption values and to establish some average figure for this European energy system. Next, it will be possible to distinguish among different geographical areas for which we have information. The goal is to determine how much energy a single person could exploit every day in pre-industrial Europe.

Draught animals

The crucial importance of draught animals in the European energy system is well-established. Dry agriculture as in Europe would not have been possible without oxen and horses. Their large numbers distinguishes European agriculture from that of the rest of the world. We know very little about their physical features, their working time and their food. But from what is known of their weight, size and physical effort, we can assume their daily intake of food to vary between 15,000 and 25,000 kcal. So we should take 20,000 kcal as a reasonable average.[3] As to the ratio of draught animals – only draught animals! – to the total European population, Braudel, using data concerning France at the end of the eighteenth century, suggested a figure of 14 million horses and 24 million oxen; about one draught animal for every four humans. This would mean, with a food intake of 20,000 kcal a day for this biological 'engine', about 5,000 kcal per capita. The average figure proposed by Braudel seems to be supported by what we know of the ratio of animals to men. Only rarely in pre-industrial societies could this ratio climb to one animal for every three humans, which would mean a per capita energy consumption of 6,000–6,500 kcal per day. Draught animals were not, however, evenly distributed across Europe. There were relatively more of them in northern Europe. Here, on the other hand, oxen were usually not employed in agriculture, and horses were really the only sources of power. Oxen were used as sources of food and raw materials. Sometimes draught animals could be more numerous in the south than in the north. But in terms of yield, the power actually exploited was higher in the northern regions than in the south, given the greater efficiency of horses as agricultural energy converters: two horses were more powerful than three oxen.

Fuels

In the use of fuels the difference between northern and southern Europe is still wider, mainly as a consequence of the climate. In countries such as Sweden and Finland a daily consumption of more than 8 kg of firewood per capita – only as fuel, industrial uses included[4] – was not unusual. In northern France, Germany, the Netherlands and England it was lower, but still substantial: about 4 kg a day was common.[5] From the end of the sixteenth century firewood was gradually replaced by fossil fuels in England and Holland. In terms of per capita calories, however, fuel consumption remained more or less the same as before until the second half of the eighteenth century, the equivalent of about 4 kg of firewood. In the Mediterranean regions the average consumption of fuel was much lower. In central and southern Italy firewood consumption amounted to around 1 kg, not unlike it is today in some less developed areas of the world. Assuming an average caloric content of 3,500 kcal per kg that is usual for the kinds of wood available on the continent, the European minimum could be 3,500 and the maximum 30,000 kcal per capita per day.

With the exception of coal and peat, water and wind driven machines such as mills and ships were the only non-biological resources in these pre-industrial European economies. They did not depend, as did other sources, on the soil. While they represented a central element of the European pre-industrial energy system, their importance in terms of energy supply was relatively low. We know that in pre-industrial Europe a ratio existed of about one mill powered by either water or wind for every 250 people (Braudel 1982–84 Volume 1; Makkai 1981; Reynolds 1983). More or less every village had its own mill. Assuming an average power at the water-wheel or windwheel of 5 hp and a working time of 8 hours a day, we reach the figure of about 25,000 kcal per day per mill. If we divide this figure by the average number of persons depending on one mill, we can conclude that the mean mechanical energy supplied per head was, all considered, relatively low: 100 kcal per day. Even if we add to this the consumption of wind per capita by means of sails – about 50 kcal per

Table 3.1 Energy consumption in eighteenth-
century Europe (kcal/day/capita)

	Minimum	Maximum
Fuel	3,500	30,000
Fodder for animals	4,000	6,500
Food for men	2,000	4,000
Water and wind	100	700
	9,600	41,200

capita per day – and we take into account the highest possible estimates for mills, the conclusion is that the role of water and wind energy was relatively limited: between 100 and 700 kcal per day per capita. It was low but not negligible, however, if we consider the limited availability of mechanical energy before the steam engine.

Human energy

In regard to human energy we are relatively well informed by studies on food consumption in early modern Europe. We know that food intake, the fuel of this 'organic machine' that is the human body, was as it is today, usually between 2,000 and 4,000 kcal a day.

Putting together these quantitative elements to establish a minimum and maximum figure we arrive at a range between a little less than 10,000 kcal and more than 40,000 per capita per day (table 3.1). Since the early modern economies were probably closer to the lower margin of this range than to the higher, we can reasonably assume an intermediate consumption of 15–20,000 kcal per capita per day. Thus the annual consumption of Europe's 150 million inhabitants, around 1750, could be estimated at between 82 and 109 million Toe (at 10 million kcal). To provide a rough idea of what this means, we should keep in mind that nowadays the annual European consumption is about 2.7 billion Toe and that world consumption reaches 11 billion Toe.[6] On average, today's energy consumption in the world comes to about 50,000 kcal per capita per day; in Europe it is more than 100,000, in the US and Canada more than 200,000.

2 North and south

To narrow the range between the maximum and the minimum and to define the differences in space, we can reconstruct the more specific levels of energy consumption in some European regions between the beginning of the eighteenth century and the middle of the nineteenth. Reliable calculations are possible for the Netherlands, England, France, Sweden together with Finland, and Italy (table 3.2).[7]

Only for England is it possible to establish the evolution of energy consumption during the eighteenth century. For the other countries the available information does not allow developments over time to be established. Our data do allow, however,

Table 3.2 Energy consumption, 1700–1850 (kcal/day/capita)

	Fuel	Animal	Men	Water/wind	Total
England (1700)	10,580	2,000	2,500	550	15,630
Netherlands (1700)	12,600	2,500	2,500	200	17,800
France (1780)	7,300	3,700	2,500	200	13,700
Sweden/Finland (1800)	28,000	6,100	2,500	100	36,700
England (1800)	25,600	2,000	2,500	650	30,750
Italy (1850)	6,140	3,500	2,500	440	12,580

Note. Oxen are not included among the draught animals in England and the Netherlands, because they were rarely used as such in these countries. They are included, on the other hand, for Italy and France. For Sweden and Finland we follow the estimate proposed by Kander (1998), who followed a method similar to the one used here and who has included oxen, but not cows.

Sources: England: Collins (1993); Wrigley (1988); King (1696); Thirsk and Cooper (1972); Hatcher (1993); Mitchell (1975); the Netherlands: de Zeeuw (1978); Unger (1980); van Zanden (1993b); Gerding (1995); Mitchell (1975); France: Braudel (1982–84, vol. 1); Lavoisier (1988); Sweden and Finland: Kander (1996); Myllyntaus (1996); Mitchell (1975); Italy: Bardini (1998); *Sommario di Statistiche Storiche, 1861–1955*, Rome: ISTAT, 1958.

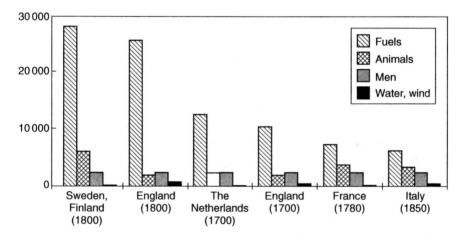

Figure 3.1 Energy consumption in Europe, 1700–1850

establishment of variations over space. If we rank these European regions according to the relative importance of their energy consumption, the result is sufficiently clear: the highest levels are reached in northern Europe (figure 3.1). From north to south the levels of per capita consumption diminish. In an extreme southern region like Sicily, daily energy consumption per capita did not exceed 5,000–10,000 kcal. An ordinary peasant could get the energy he needed from food, from about 0.5 kg of firewood every day, from the services of a mill and, rarely, indeed very rarely, from the use of some animal. In Scandinavia, at the same time, numerous horses allowed the

Table 3.3 Biomass production

	Productivity per unit of surface (gr/mq/year)	Biomass per unit of surface (kg/mq)
Temperate forest	1200	30
Mediterranean bush	700	6

Source: Whittaker (1975: 224)

transportation of significant quantities of firewood. This demand for wood was easily met by the high productivity and density of forests. At the same time a rich fodder production supported a relatively high number of animals. Food for human consumption was also more plentiful because of the higher yields of cereals and the widespread breeding, which allowed a richer daily ration – particularly in animal fats. The difference between levels of energy consumption in the far north and the deep south could amount to as much as a factor five.[8]

We know that normally the human body consumes about 16 kWh (or 13,760 kcal) every day. In part this consumption is covered by food, which accounts for 3.5–4 kWh (or 3,000–3,500 kcal). The rest is a free gift from the sun. Where solar radiation is poorer, man must resort to costly sources of energy. Economic activities must then fill the gap between solar radiation and energy needs. We should remind ourselves that solar radiation, in Mediterranean countries during the month of June amounts to 7.5–8 kWh/m² but in northern Europe to a mere 4.5–5.5 kWh/m². An inverse relation thus exists in pre-industrial societies between solar radiation and economic energy consumption. As population density increased in the north, during the late middle ages and early modern times, its inhabitants were forced to resort to an ever more complex energy system. This could be achieved thanks to the higher density of biomass, i.e. of carbohydrates (either edible for men or not) in northern Europe. Therefore the south is not necessarily favoured in comparison with the north, because radiation in southern regions is often accompanied by an aridity of the soil and a scarcity of biomass.

To extract energy from the land always requires more of an effort in the south than in the north. In northern regions the consumption of firewood may be higher, but forests are denser. Moreover, it is easier to breed animals able to carry lumber because, thanks to the wet soils, fodder production is higher than in the south. Heavy soils are harder to cultivate, but because of frequent rains their productivity is higher than southern soils. In northern environments it was even possible to breed larger numbers of oxen, not as sources of energy but as sources of 'secondary' food such as milk, cheese, meat, a relatively expensive way of producing energy in comparison with cereal cultivation. The decreased radiation was, so to speak, counterbalanced in the north by the increased biomass thanks to the greater availability of water. The biomass production in the two extremes of Europe's environments, the temperate forest on the one hand and the Mediterranean bush on the other, underscores the wide difference among the various European habitats (table 3.3). In the south more sun, in the north more biomass. Or to put it in a different way: while in the north the limiting factor in the energy system is solar radiation, in the south it is the volume of the biomass.

Because of this strong influence of climate on energy consumption in the pre-industrial world, today's connection between the level of exploited energy and income was not so obvious then. In 1820 Sweden had more or less the same per capita income as France and Italy; Finland had about 40 per cent less (Maddison 1995). Nonetheless, energy consumption was widely different. Incomes in the Netherlands and particularly in England were much higher than those in Sweden and notably in Finland, even if Dutch and English energy consumption was lower. A comparison between energy and income should preferably be executed on the basis of mechanical energy alone, which is more directly connected with the level of the economic activity. However, to disentangle mechanical energy from the rest is far from easy for a pre-industrial energy system. Was food, for instance, not simultaneously a source of heat and of mechanical work?

3 The carrying capacity in 1600

Around 1800 most energy had to be extracted from the soil. It has already been shown that wind and water energy did not account for more than 5 per cent of the total energy budget. The other sources that did not originate directly from the cultivation of the soil were fossil fuels, mainly coal and peat, which were widely used only in England and the Netherlands. Elsewhere in Europe they were almost unknown. Coal consumption across Europe was about 13 million tons, 11 million or 85 per cent in England alone. On the whole this consumption was equivalent to 9.1 million Toe a year. If we add to this the 820,000 Toe of peat consumed in Holland we reach 10 million Toe of fossil fuels for the whole of Europe. Because energy consumption, as we saw, can be estimated at around 100 million Toe, fossil fuels accounted for 10 per cent of total consumption. The rise of fossil fuel was the main innovation of the new energy system under construction in early modern Europe. We could add the other, traditional, non-organic sources of energy, namely water and wind, to reach a proportion of possibly 15 per cent.

All other energy sources came from the soil. In these sources too, however, some innovations occurred. A comparison of the main primary converters around 1600 and around 1800 will make this clear (table 3.4). The table strongly suggests a transition between two different energy systems, from the medieval to the modern. The introduction of fossil fuels was clearly not the only feature of the new energy system. An important change in energy converters was also taking place.

Indeed, if the only innovation had been the introduction of fossil fuels, the possibilities for expansion of the new energy system in the nineteenth century, and thus of the economy as a whole, would have been very limited. The influence of coal on the agricultural world was, in fact, low or non-existent. Even the transformation of heating in mechanical energy with the steam engine, which was the main accomplishment in the use of fossil fuels, would have been of very little importance. Steam tractors never made a serious impact in agriculture. The advance in the use of the fossil energy in the primary sector took place only in the twentieth century. The

Table 3.4 Main organic energy converters in 1600 and 1800 (primary converters)

Converters (1600)	Converters (1800)
Fuel	
Firewood	Firewood
	Coal
	Peat
Food for men	
Wheat	Wheat
	Potatoes
	Maize
Fodder for animals	
Forage	Forage
Oats	Oats
	Leguminous crops

possibilities, therefore, of increasing production in the secondary sector would in the long run have been extremely limited without an accompanying increase of productivity in the primary sector. The importance of the synergetic effects between agrarian and industrial changes in the first phases of the economic development has been repeatedly stressed.

During the eighteenth century the creation of a new energy system was in progress in the secondary sector, with the passage from traditional fuels to fossil fuels (cf. Wrigley 1988). But at the same time a new energy system was introduced in the primary sector. To simplify: while the first change allowed intensive growth, i.e. more goods per capita, the second allowed a kind of extensive growth, i.e. increase in population with stable per capita production, which took place simultaneously. Together they created nineteenth-century economic growth, which was extensive and intensive at the same time. To clarify this transition and to assess its importance we have to compare the traditional and the new energy system, leaving aside for the moment water, wind and fossil sources.

The old energy system became established in Europe during the late middle ages, replacing the ancient Mediterranean system. Its novelty was most obvious in two features: the introduction on a large scale of animals, and more specifically in northern Europe of horses; and the relatively wide use of water and wind power.[9] It was the establishment of this new energy system that enabled the medieval economy to grow, both in the Mediterranean and in the north. By the end of the thirteenth century this system had more or less exhausted its potential. With the exception of the introduction of gunpowder, which was on the whole of little direct influence on the economy, only an extensive diffusion of this system took place after the thirteenth century.

In agriculture, in industry and in commerce the energy basis then remained more or less unchanged for three centuries. Even in the energy yield – the ratio between energy output and input – progress was, all things considered, negligible. Changes in agriculture were marginal until the seventeenth century. No new types of cereals were

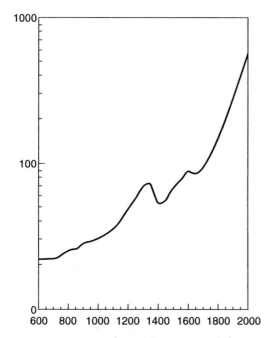

Figure 3.2 European population, 600–2000 (excluding Russia)

introduced on a large scale until 1600. In mills and ships the efficiency increased, but their role in the European energy budget remained modest. With animals, after the thirteenth century progress was marginal. The diffusion of the fireplace and of the stove added little to the efficiency in the use of fire. As a consequence, the increase in population slowed down during this long period. The plague was an external factor that certainly contributed heavily to this demographic stagnation, but cannot by itself explain it completely (Herlihy 1997). Together with the frequent epidemics, the relative shortage of energy, particularly in the form of biomass edible for men, constituted a restraint on growth. Energy availability was from 1300 to 1600 the limiting factor in Europe's economic system. Population figures, between the increase from the tenth century to the stabilization after the fourteenth century and until the second half of the seventeenth, were going through exactly the sort of S-shaped logistic curve that scholars of ecology associate with a saturation of the energy supply in a particular habitat (figure 3.2). In relative terms, i.e. by means of a logarithmic ordinate, this logistic curve may better be appreciated than by means of absolute values.

Data on European demography show an increase of about 10 million people, between 1300 and 1600 and only a little more between 1300 and 1700. If we take the uncertainty of late medieval data on population into account and the possible margins of error, this stability appears much more than a simple assumption.[10] To sum up we could say that the ceiling of 100 million inhabitants consistent with the

Table 3.5 Per capita energy consumption from organic sources, per day and per year (kcal)

Sources	Per day	%	Per year
Food for men	3,000	20	1,095,000
Firewood	7,000	47	2,555,000
Fodder for animals	5,000	33	1,825,000
Total	15,000	100	5,475,000

level of the medieval energy system was reached at the end of the thirteenth century, and that for three centuries afterwards no further progress took place.

To clarify the relation between men and energy, let us take the data concerning the three main organic sources of energy then in use (human food, firewood, animal fodder) and try to evaluate what ecologists call the 'carrying capacity' of the habitat, i.e. the possibility of the habitat to support the energy needs of a particular species (table 3.5). This calculation, already difficult for other animal species, is certainly much more difficult for human societies, given their more sophisticated adaptation to the environment. We can, however, identify at least the magnitude of the problem. If we accept the rough value of 15,000 kcal per capita per day, annual consumption should be about 5.5 million. Probably the real consumption was higher than this, rather than lower. All three sources are different forms of carbohydrates. The problem that the energy system has to solve is to arrive at the right combination of three derivatives of carbon that humans have to burn in different ways to survive. Since the three sources of energy all derive from the soil, the problem is really that of the best mode of exploitation compatible with the varying possibilities of different types of soils. How much land did a European inhabitant need, let us say around 1600, to meet his needs for food, for heating, for mechanical power in agriculture, within the limits of the energy system?

As to food we are comparatively well-informed. We know that the two primary sources were cereals – wheat and minor crops – together with drinks, such as wine and beer. These were the main carbohydrates and accordingly the main sources of human energy consumption. To these were added a few breeding products, such as meat, milk, cheese, all sources of proteins and fats. The latter products were, however, of minor importance and, so to speak, were a transformation of animal fodder, in other words a 'secondary food'. As far as the energy budget goes, they have already been included in fodder, the other energy source, which will be discussed later. The consumption of fish contributed only marginally to the level of protein intake.

Concerning cereals we have much data on both agricultural productivity and wheat consumption. We know less about minor cereals such as barley, rye, oats. European yield-ratios (output per unit of seed) were in the range of 3 to 8, or between 4 and 9 quintals per hectare. Because our information usually concerns the best lands and wheat crops, which had a higher yield than the other cereals, we could assume as a European average, a yield per seed of 5 and per hectare of 6. We know that in northern Europe these levels were often exceeded, while in the south yields were often lower. We also know that the average European consumed between 500 and 800 grams of cereals every day. The figure was probably a little higher in the north than in the south. So annual consumption amounted to about 250–80 kg. If we assume as product per hectare 6 quintals and subtract the 120 kg of seed needed to produce this, the result is that around 1600 to meet his daily consumption requirements a European inhabitant needed between 0.5 and 1 hectare. Therefore we can assume 0.8 hectare per capita. This average diminishes as we move north and increases as we move south. A distinction among several different regions with different levels of productivity would certainly be of great importance. But since we are trying to establish the magnitude in the relation between men and resources, our rough calculation may suffice.

For northern and central Europe we have noted that the daily consumption of firewood was about 4 kg, or 1.5 tons annually (Braudel 1982–84 Volume 1: chapter 2; van der Woude, Hayami, de Vries 1990: introduction; Malanima 1996a: 52–5). Given the average productivity of the forests, the average inhabitant used the product of 0.5–1 hectare to meet his or her needs. Since in southern and especially Mediterranean Europe firewood consumption was about half this quantity, less forest was needed in those areas. But the production of wood was also lower here, because of the lower density of the biomass of southern forests. Therefore we are forced to conclude that in southern Europe too, every individual required the same 0.5 hectare of woodland to meet the needs of firewood. Perhaps this calculation is too low. We know, on the other hand, that in the European pre-industrial economies, as much as in contemporary backward economies, the wide use of agricultural remains, particularly of prunings and threshings, as sources of fuel, would limit to some extent the demand for forest wood.

As concerns draught animals, our information about the land necessary to produce fodder is indecisive. There were, as far as we know, important differences related to the type of animal (horse or ox), their size, their work, and to the variable productivity of the land cultivated for fodder. Again, fodder production per hectare in southern Europe was lower than in the north. But then animals were less numerous in the south as well. Forests were exploited as a source of fodder for animals. In southern Europe the leaves of fruit trees made an important contribution towards the food supply for animals. Straw, a leftover from the harvest, was another important source of nourishment. Oats cultivated on arable land, especially in regions where horses dominated, were another basis for animal breeding. At the same time, necessary as animals may have been to humans as sources of mechanical force, of breeding products and of dung, they were also competing with humans for the products of the soil. Their space was always restricted and sometimes in fact insufficient.

In the eighteenth century it was estimated that a horse or an ox ate about ten times its weight during the year. For an animal of 300 kg this means 3,000 kg (Toutain 1961: 143). To meet this consumption a surface of 1.5–2 hectares of natural meadow or fallow land was necessary. We might estimate that the average production of animal energy available per human individual, i.e. the fuel of the animal 'machine' available for exploitation, demanded about 0.5–1 hectare of natural meadow. With the introduction of leguminous crops, still almost unknown at the beginning of the seventeenth century (Ambrosoli 1992), the space needed for each animal could be reduced. As with firewood and cereals, northern Europe was able to produce more fodder per unit area and therefore exploit a larger number of animals, while the south produced less fodder and thus had fewer animals available.

If we now calculate the space any European needed in 1600 to meet his or her energy demands, we come to a figure of about 2 hectares. It may have been a little more, if we take into account some unavoidable waste and the presence of animals, such as oxen in the north, and sheep exploited as source of food and not of mechanical energy.

So was Europe's carrying capacity in 1600, at an estimated 500 million hectares excluding Russia, able to support a population of 90 million inhabitants within the limits of the energy system then operating? Or, given a mean density of 18 inhabitants/km^2, was this population really making demands that exceeded the capacity of the habitat?

With an average need of 2 hectares per capita the total need amounted to less than 200 million hectares. Even taking into account about 25 per cent of unproductive land (today it is 20 per cent), and allowing for an underestimation of the per capita needs of productive space, the only possible answer is that the carrying capacity was more than sufficient. Every European was supported by an average of at least 4–4.5 hectares of productive land. So the provisional conclusion we can draw from these calculations is that there was no problem of exceeding carrying capacity.

But averages do not tell the whole story. We know, for instance, that in 1600 in several regions of Europe the demographic density was very low. This was the case especially in Scandinavia and in the east. If we exclude these regions from our calculations, the picture changes significantly. Let us concentrate on the central area of Europe, including Italy, France, Germany, Belgium, the Netherlands, England and Wales. In this central band of the continent, comprising 140 million hectares, population levels reached 55.6 million inhabitants in 1600. The average density was 40 inhabitants/km^2. From the available information, however uncertain, about soil utilization, we know that 25–30 per cent of the area was unproductive because of mountains, hills, or marshes (table 3.6). Assuming an unproductive share of only 25 per cent, the productive soil drops to 105 million hectares. Even with the modest estimate of two hectares of productive soil per individual to meet everyone's energy needs, we would need about 110 million hectares. This obviously means that carrying capacity was hardly sufficient, perhaps even insufficient to meet per capita needs in this part of Europe. Only to meet the demand for wheat, a population of 55.6 million required 45 million hectares instead of the 35 which was presumably available in arable. This means that the optimal equilibrium was under severe strain as a consequence of demographic pressures and the accompanying reduction of meadows and woodlands.

We know that in this central area of Europe it became necessary, from the middle of the sixteenth century, to increase imports of cereals, animals and firewood from the less-densely inhabited regions of eastern Europe, Scandinavia and the Middle East. Differences in the distribution of productive factors and demand directed flows of

Table 3.6 Soil utilization in Italy (1600), France (1600), and England/Wales (1689) (in million ha and %)

	Italy	*%*	*France*	*%*	*England*	*%*
Unproductive	8	26	12	27	5.8	30
Wood and meadow	15	48	22.6	51	8.6	44
Arable	8	26	9.4	22	5	26
Total	31	100	44	100	19.4	100

Sources: Italy: Malanima (1998: 59); France: Braudel (1982–84 volume 1: chapter 2); England: King (1696).

goods from the periphery to the centre. These imports, while they helped meet energy needs in some regions, did not fundamentally alter the relation between men and resources in the core area.

It is probable that the difficulties in meeting energy needs in the central area of the continent became greater still during the second half of the sixteenth century and the first half of the seventeenth because of the decline (even if limited) of the external flow of energy from the Sun during this so-called Little Ice Age. The temperature decreased about 0.5–1 degree Celsius on average (Le Roy Ladurie 1967: chapter 4; Pinna 1984: 165–83). We also know that a modest decline took place in the level of wheat ratios. The biomass per hectare fit for human consumption was reduced. The equilibrium between energy resources on the one hand and the increasing population on the other was becoming more and more difficult to maintain within the dominant energy system.

In fact, it would have been impossible for the central area of Europe to support a further increase in population without some changes. In 1800, with 83.5 million people, at least 167 million hectares would have been necessary, much more than the total area of this central band of the continent, even if unproductive soils are included. To establish a new equilibrium between energy and humans the carrying capacity had to grow and 1.5 hectares or less had to suffice to support the per capita energy needs, instead of two or more. If before 1 hectare produced on average 2.75 million kcal/year, now the same hectare had to produce more than 4 million.[11] Thus, an intensification was necessary in terms of energy per unit of land.

4 A new energy system

Several forms of intensification actually did take place from the second half of the seventeenth century, especially in the central, more densely populated areas of Europe. It was the start of the early phase of modern European economic growth. A new energy system was developing. The elements of this energy system have already been discussed. Their analysis in terms of energy, however, makes it possible to attain a more comprehensive view of their development and of their effects on the economy.

The emergence of the new system was associated with the growth of population during the final decades of the seventeenth century. In part at least this was a result of the disappearance of the plague. Another reason for the population rise undoubtedly lay in the improved equilibrium between people and resources, as a consequence of the demographic decrease or stability in several parts of Europe during the first half of the seventeenth century. The preconditions were in place for a demographic recovery. Europe's population, without Russia, increased from 90 to 150 million inhabitants between 1600 and 1800, or by 66 per cent. Population density rose from 18 to 30 inhabitants/km². In the central area, between Italy and the Netherlands, the most densely populated of the continent, the increase was about 50 per cent, and the average density reached 60 people/km².

No doubt, population increases constitute a powerful incentive to intensify energy production. An increase in carrying capacity is, however, not an automatic solution to the energy problems.[12] The supply of energy, for instance, can remain unchanged, causing living conditions to worsen year after year. A deadlock of stagnation may ultimately be reached, with a low equilibrium between population and resources. This kind of equilibrium is to be sure more frequent than development towards higher levels. Technical possibilities of meeting population increase are not always to hand, as technological evolution is not merely a function of demography but also of many other elements independent of demand. The trajectories followed in the solution of technical problems, as well as chance, also have a role to play.

In Europe, however, a developmental process was already underway that led to a new energy system that would be able to raise the carrying capacity and allow, in the long run, the establishment of a new and higher equilibrium between population and resources. We shall briefly list the innovations here, quantifying whenever possible their contribution to the energy consumption in Europe. In particular we shall examine that central area of the continent where these innovations had a greater impact. We should remind ourselves again that any attempt to quantify will provide only a rough idea of the direction of the changes in progress. It will nonetheless be useful to establish the magnitude of the process.

An increase of biomass through the extension of arable lands is always the first reaction when a population increases. For any animal species the increase is met at first by the search for new land. New kinds of adaptation to the habitat are tried only when this solution proves impracticable. Accurate quantitative information on this long process is available only for particular regions of eighteenth-century Europe. New soils were cultivated at the expense of forests and, quite often, marshes. Land reclamation advanced in several areas. The impression we get from the dispersed quantitative information concerning Italy, France and some areas of Germany is that the cultivated area increased by about 10 per cent (Caracciolo 1973: 544; Toutain 1961; Abel 1966: chapter vii). If it were also possible to calculate the conversion of fallow lands to cultivation, this increase would certainly be higher. If the energy needs of the 83.5 million inhabitants of this core area, with their daily per capita consumption of 15,000 kcal, amounted to about 46 million Toe a year, this extensive process could account for 1.5–2 million Toe.

This solution was the simplest attempt to meet the increasing needs. Other solutions were more important. When arable land is increasing at the expense of a forest, no increase of biomass is actually achieved. Usually it will lead to a decrease in terms of useful calories. The conversion merely results in a change of the kind of carbohydrates consumed: from firewood to food. By implication, the increase of one resource occurs at the expense of the other. The exploitation of coal and peat could make this conversion less of a problem, limiting the need for firewood. This is to some extent what happened. If the 83.5 million inhabitants of the central area we are examining had to resort solely to woodlands for their fuel consumption, calculated at 21 million Toe, they would have needed 44 million hectares of woodland in 1800, or a little less than one-third of the area available to them. Because coal and peat accounted for 10 million Toe, it would have been possible to do without some 45 per cent of the forests. But as was shown earlier, only in England and the Netherlands was there significant consumption of fossil fuels. In other areas the forests continued to provide the bulk of fuel supply. Thus the transition to fossil fuels contributed only modestly, and in only a few regions, to savings on the area of woodland that was needed. At the beginning of the nineteenth century forests in Europe covered about one-third of the total area. Everywhere the alarm was raised about their further reduction. Only at the end of the century did woodlands begin to increase again. So in general firewood continued to be the basis of heating and cooking. In a very few regions new fossil fuels also allowed mechanical energy per capita to increase, preparing the way for the intensive growth which was beginning.

In cereal production major innovations occurred which affected both the yield per hectare of the traditional crops and the diffusion of new crops. The rise of the leguminous crops increased the energy intake in the soil in the form of nitrogen, contributing to an increase in yields. We know that at least in central and northern Europe yields per hectare rose to about 7–7.5 quintals (Chorley 1981). In southern Europe, with the exception of some parts of northern Italy, yields remained lower. With a yield of 6 quintals the 83.5 million inhabitants of the central band of Europe needed about 0.8 hectare per person; with a yield of 7.5 it dropped to 0.65 hectares.

The increased growing of potatoes, maize and, to a lesser extent, rice, was another step towards the reduction of acreage per capita. With these new converters the possibility of capturing carbon, which is the main 'fuel' for biological engines, increased considerably. In terms of calories, potatoes and maize yield at least twice as much as the traditional cereals. It is important to note that coal, rice, maize, and potato were already known in Europe for a long time: maize and potato since the sixteenth century, coal and rice even longer. Population increase now promoted their diffusion on a much larger scale than before. From a Darwinian perspective maize and potatoes are mutations. The probability of mutation was now combined with the increasing demand for energy sources, leading to their introduction on a large scale.

How important was the contribution of these new vegetable converters in terms of energy? A cautious calculation of their production in kcal/hectare would suggest a 100 per cent increase compared to the traditional crops. In the first decades of the nineteenth century the new crops were equally distributed in the six countries under examination: potatoes in the north and maize in southern France and northern Italy occupied more or less the same area of more than 2 million hectares each. When rice is included, something like 5 million hectares on the total arables of the core area of about 42 million was planted with the new crops (data in Mitchell 1975). As a result, the arable land used to produce human food decreased from 0.65 to 0.6 hectares per capita. By implication, the productivity of every unit of soil in energy terms increased.

Table 3.7 Trend in productive space per capita to meet
energy consumption in 1600 and 1800 (hectares)

	1600		1800
Forest	0.5	⇒	0.3
Meadow	0.7	⇒	0.6
Field	0.8	⇒	0.6
	2.0	⇒	1.5

Table 3.8 Direction of changes in carrying capacity and population
in England, the Netherlands, Belgium, Germany, France, and Italy
(1600–1800)

	1600		1800
Total area (million ha)	140	⇒	140
Inhabitants (millions)	55.6	⇒	83.5
Total productive space (million ha)	105	⇒	115
Space per capita (ha)	>2	⇒	−1.5
Total necessary space (million ha)	111	⇒	125

Less land was also needed for the production of fodder. It has been calculated that
in eighteenth-century France the transformation of pastures into artificial meadows
by means of clover, lucerne and sainfoin enabled an increase of 50 per cent in forage
production (Toutain 1961: 143). Around 1800 meadows covered about a quarter of
France's total land area. The same progress had been made in the production of oats
as in the production of other cereals: an increase in yield per seed of 1–2 percentage
points. So even in the production of carbohydrates for animals the need for land was
declining.

Although the trend is clear, it is hard to quantify these changes. Estimates provide
only a general impression of the direction – not the real values – of the development
we have so far tried to describe (table 3.7). All this could be summed up with the
conclusion that under the old energy system each individual needed at least 2 hectares
of land, while under the new system the figure had dropped on average to at most
1.5 hectares. So, while it is impossible to arrive at definitive figures, we have a fair
indication of the direction of the changes in progress across these two centuries
(table 3.8). It seems that imports of energy from abroad, particularly in the form of
cereals, had the effect of filling the gap in years of famine, rather than supporting the
ordinary energy needs. The data on energy in any event suggest that, at least in
the decades from 1750 to 1820, growth originating in the transformations within the
energy sector was, all things considered, perhaps smaller than the rate of demographic
increase. Per capita energy consumption may have diminished.

We know that agricultural prices more than doubled all over Europe from 1740 to
the first two decades of the nineteenth century. Firewood prices increased even more.
Famines began to reappear everywhere from the 1760s and became particularly

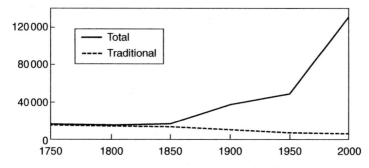

Figure 3.3 Energy consumption in Europe (per capita in kcal)

devastating during the Napoleonic period. Wages increased very little in nominal terms and lost ground in real terms. Living conditions worsened everywhere. Calorific intake declined. In late medieval and early modern Europe the worsening of living conditions was often accompanied by a decline in population, as a consequence of epidemics and famines. Demographic crises then re-established the balance between energy sources and people with the reduction of human biomass through a rise in mortality. At the end of the eighteenth century the human biomass decreased in equal measure: not so much through a rising death-toll as because of the decrease in people's weight and height. Anthropometric studies have recently revealed the effects of worsening economic conditions on stature. As far as we know the average European lost about 5–10 centimetres between the last decades of the eighteenth century and the first two of the nineteenth (Komlos 1996 and 1993). In England, because of the strong growth in the agricultural production in the age of the Agricultural Revolution, and because of the increasing use of coal for heating and industrial activities in the age of the Industrial Revolution, people continued to grow in stature. In England too, however, per capita income increased only slowly: the rate of English per capita GDP growth was one-third of the estimate traditionally accepted (Crafts 1985). There is serious doubt whether European industrialization really began in England at the end of the eighteenth century, or not until after 1820, when GDP per capita rate of increase became stronger and more continuous.

If the data presented here are correct, the change in the energy system may be sufficient entirely to explain the contemporary population increase. The impression is that the new system, which emerged slowly from the second half of the seventeenth century, was able to remove the obstacles towards economic and demographic growth. The first phase of modern economic growth, supported by the new energy system, then ended with the slowdown from the late eighteenth century to the second decade of the nineteenth. A new, and faster phase of growth began only after 1820. This first phase, however, enabled the extensive growth and agricultural advances, without which the establishment of the new energy system still dominant today would not have been possible. Only since the second half of the nineteenth century have the traditional sources of energy lost their role as the main suppliers of energy to fossil fuels, which then became the only primary sources (figure 3.3).[13]

Notes

1   I discussed these problems more widely in Malanima (1998, chapter 1), Malanima (1996a) and (1996b). See also Bairoch (1983) and (1985). Bairoch's results are not very different from those obtained in the following pages, even if with different methods. For a general overview on the problems of energy consumption in the long run, see Caracciolo and Morelli (1996).

2   While power is the capacity for exerting force in a given unit of time, we are interested in the work actually done by the energy employed. Therefore we have to calculate how much energy was really utilized by the sources of power then prevailing.

3   Smil (1994: 76 ff). We assume that an average animal (horse or ox) weighing, as in the pre-industrial world, 300–400 kg, and subjected to relatively heavy agrarian labour, consumed about 11 forage units corresponding to 10 kg of dry substance – hay, for instance – every day.

4   Only industrial use as fuel is included; the use in building industry is, however, excluded.

5   See, in particular, van der Woude, Hayami and de Vries (1990: Introduction). I tried to collect information on firewood consumption in several regions of Europe in Malanima (1996a: 53–4). Firewood transformed into charcoal is included in the average estimate.

6   Traditional sources of energy included in both estimates.

7   I use here (but not in table 3.5) a low estimate of 2500 kcal from food to avoid duplications deriving from the energy used by mills, and then already included in flour, and from breeding products, whose energy is in part included in fodder. Cattle were more plentiful in the north, but since oxen were hardly used in agriculture, the number of draught animals was sometimes higher in the south. Energy actually exploited was, however, generally higher in northern regions because of the higher power of horses compared with oxen.

8   For a comparison: in 1993 energy consumption per capita per day was in Italy 77,000 kcal, in Sweden 125,000, and in Finland 131,000.

9   Another distinction between the ancient and medieval energy system was the absence of slaves in the second.

10 Recently, for example, a new estimate was proposed for the Italian population in 1300: 12.5 million inhabitants instead of the traditional figure of 11 (del Panta *et al.* 1996). If we generalize this increase of 13 per cent to the European population as a whole (Russia excluded), the result for 1300 becomes 91 million, instead of 70. In 1600 European population is estimated at 89 million. So a decrease would have taken place from 1300. Let us remember that the history of the Italian population is better known than that of other European regions, where we have more or less reliable data only from the late middle ages.

11 Naturally considering here an average energy content of firewood, fodder and cereals together.

12 As may be suggested by anti-Malthusian views like those proposed by Boserup (1965).

13 The graph is based, for fossil fuels, on Etemad and Luciani (1991). See also Malanima (1996a: 126) for the importance of traditional energies in Europe during the nineteenth and twentieth centuries.

4 Early modern economic growth

A survey of the European economy, 1500–1800

Jan Luiten van Zanden

During the last thirty years, a fundamental shift has occurred in our views of the early modern economy. This shift hinges on the interpretation of the Industrial Revolution. Economic historians of the 1950s and 1960s stated that it was the single most radical break in the economic history of western Europe, the dividing line between a stagnant agrarian economy, dominated by Malthusian forces, and a dynamic industrial society, driven by the unbound Prometheus. The pessimistic work of German and French historians writing in the tradition of Wilhelm Abel – with their emphasis on the decline of real wages and the increase in poverty in Europe between *c.* 1500 and *c.* 1800 – underwrote his interpretation of the Industrial Revolution as the great divide (Abel 1935). Leroy Ladurie's *histoire immobile* (1977) is the most consistent interpretation of this stagnationist view. He described the French economy between *c.* 1320 and 1700 as characterized by a permanent production ceiling, which it was unable to break through until the middle of the eighteenth century.

In the 1970s and 1980s this picture of the Industrial Revolution, and of the stagnant economy that supposedly preceded it, came under attack from several sides. Attempts to quantify the growth of output and productivity in Great Britain and France in the eighteenth and nineteenth centuries indicated a gradual acceleration of industrial growth, not a clear-cut 'revolution'. Especially the work of N. F. R. Crafts (1985), who revised Deane and Cole's estimates of British economic growth, had an enormous impact on the interpretation of the Industrial Revolution. Recent attempts to test Alexander Gerschenkron's hypothesis concerning the patterns in the development of the Industrial Revolution in Europe have also reinforced this new interpretation: discontinuity (the 'big spurt') is not the typical pattern of industrialization in the various European countries (Sylla and Toniolo 1991).

Moreover, economic historians of the early modern period began to point out that in almost every respect the industrialization of the late eighteenth and early nineteenth centuries was preceded – and made possible – by structural changes that took place during preceding centuries. The development of urbanization and international trade networks (de Vries 1984a), of agricultural productivity, proto-industry (Mendels 1972), of national patterns of specialization (Kussmaul 1990) and labour markets (Lucassen 1987 and 1991), all testify to the fact that this was a very dynamic period, when the basis was laid for the industrialization of western Europe after *c.* 1780. This 'revolution of the early modernists', as Jan de Vries called it, has resulted in a much more optimistic interpretation of economic growth during the centuries before the Industrial Revolution, of which the work of Gunnar Persson is perhaps the best example. In his book on 'pre-industrial economic growth' Persson (1988) states that growth had been more or less normal to the European economy at least since the late middle ages. He was also probably the first explicitly to criticize the stagnationists of the 1950s and 1960s.

In this chapter the various interpretations of economic growth prior to Kuznets' concept of 'modern economic growth' are tested against new evidence of long-term economic development in this period. Various approaches are used to try and find out how much growth there was in Europe between 1500 and 1800. First, the evidence on changes in the size and composition of Europe's population will be reviewed. Second, recent estimates of the growth of gross domestic product (GDP) in six European countries will be compared, which will result in an estimate – albeit highly tentative – of the development of per capita GDP in Europe in this period. Finally, available data on the long-term evolution of a number of sectors are discussed, which seem to confirm the evidence from the country studies. In almost all of these studies it is stressed, and should be stressed again here, that it is very difficult to quantify economic growth in this period, due to a lack of reliable sources and of basic studies in this field. All the estimates are very tentative and may be revised in the future. However, one way to check the findings of the various studies is to compare them with one another and with (qualitative) data of the historical pattern of international differences in economic development. The more improbable results can thus be eliminated, as I hope to show.

In undertaking this exercise, I try to respond to the call by Fernand Braudel, who in his stimulating *Afterthoughts on Material Civilization and Capitalism* (1977: 116–17), has set the task for historians 'to chart the growth of the early modern economy by means of "modern methods of national accounting"'. As Braudel suggested, one of the aims of such an enterprise is 'to grasp . . . the reasons for the change in growth rates that appeared simultaneously with mechanisation'.

1 Population growth and urbanization

Some of the most reliable (and certainly some of the most widely used) data on the long-term development of the European economy concern the size of the population and the urbanization ratio. The value of these two indicators for the measurement of economic change is obvious. The growth of population over the long term indicates an increase in the number of people who need to make a living, and is as such an early indication of an increase in economic 'prosperity' – although, of course, population growth can be accompanied by a fall in income per head under certain particular circumstances. Urbanization, moreover, points to an expansion of urban-based employment in the industrial and service sectors. Obviously, this relationship is not always entirely straightforward: rural population growth can be caused by the expansion of proto-industry, which means that the structural transformation of the economy could in theory be accompanied by a fall in the urbanization ratio.

Especially in the eighteenth century, when non-agrarian employment in the country-side became increasingly important, the relation between urbanization and economic development became more complex.[1] But broadly speaking, and certainly before 1700, population growth and a rise in the urbanization ratio indicate expansion in the early modern period, while a drop in the population and a fall in the urbanization ratio are signs of economic decline.

The broad outlines of demographic development in Europe are well known: strong growth during the sixteenth century, followed by a demographic depression in most European countries beginning in the first half of the seventeenth century (around 1620 or 1650) and ending in the first half of the eighteenth century, after which there is renewed expansion throughout the second half of the eighteenth century.

Thanks to the work of Jan de Vries (1984a) on European urbanization between 1500 and 1800, reliable estimates are now available for the size of the population and for the urbanization ratio in Europe at this time. In table 4.1 the following data are set out: the growth of total population (1500 = 100); the development of the urbanization ratio (defined as the proportion of the population which lived in towns of 10,000 inhabitants and more); and a 'development index', in which both indicators (population and urbanization ratio) are weighted into a single figure. In the calculation of this index it is assumed that a growth of 4 points in the urbanization ratio (e.g. from 6 to 10 per cent) is of equal importance as a doubling of the total population. The justification for this somewhat arbitrary weight is that, calculated in this way, the increase in the urbanization ratio in Europe between 1500 and 1800 has about the same effect on the development index as the doubling of the European population which occurred in the same period. Different 'weights' do not, in fact, give a fundamentally different picture because there is quite a good correlation between increases in the population and rises in the proportion which lived in towns. It should also be emphasized, incidentally, that the development index, with 1500 as a base, does not measure regional differences in *levels* of development (these are perhaps best approached via variations in the urbanization ratio) but merely suggests how a given country has developed since 1500. Figures of total population reveal a doubling of the population of Europe as a whole (table 4.1). Growth was especially high on the margins, in thinly populated regions such as Scandinavia, the British Isles, Portugal and Switzerland. Of the more heavily populated regions, with relatively high degrees of urbanization, only the Netherlands grew significantly faster than the European average. Southern Europe – Italy, Spain, France – clearly lagged behind the rest of the continent in this era, which was also true for thinly populated Poland. Belgium, Austria and Germany, on the other hand, display more or less average levels of population growth.

The shift that took place in the pattern of urbanization is now well known, thanks to studies by de Vries (1984a), Hohenberg and Lees (1985), and Reher (1990). The urban centres of southern Europe declined in importance during the seventeenth century. At the same time, there was a marked growth in the urbanization ratio in the Northern Netherlands and in England, followed in the eighteenth century by major urbanization in Scotland. The urban centre of gravity of Europe thus shifted from northern Italy in particular, to the areas around the North Sea. In the rest of Europe

Table 4.1 Population, level of urbanization and 'development index', 1500–1800

	Population (1500 = 100)				Urbanization (per cent)				Development index* (1500 = 100)			
	1500	1600	1700	1800	1500	1600	1700	1800	1500	1600	1700	1800
Scandinavia	100	147	193	333	0.9	1.4	4.0	4.6	100	160	272	426
England + Wales	100	169	208	354	3.1	5.8	13.3	20.3	100	237	463	784
Scotland	100	125	125	200	1.6	3.0	5.3	17.3	100	160	218	593
Ireland	100	140	280	530	0	0	3.4	7.0	100	140	365	705
Netherlands	100	158	200	221	15.8	24.3	33.6	28.8	100	371	645	546
Belgium	100	114	143	207	21.1	18.8	23.9	18.9	100	57	213	152
Germany	100	133	125	204	3.2	4.1	4.8	5.5	100	156	165	262
France	100	116	116	165	4.2	5.9	9.2	8.8	100	159	241	280
Switzerland	100	154	185	262	1.5	2.5	3.3	3.7	100	179	230	317
Italy	100	125	127	170	12.4	15.1	13.2	14.6	100	193	147	225
Spain	100	119	110	154	6.1	11.4	9.0	11.1	100	252	183	279
Portugal	100	110	200	290	3.0	14.1	11.5	8.7	100	388	413	432
Austria	100	123	131	226	1.7	2.1	3.9	5.2	100	133	186	314
Poland	100	136	112	172	0	0.4	0.5	2.5	100	146	125	235
Europe	100	127	132	199	5.6	7.6	9.2	10.0	100	177	222	309

* See text

Source: Calculated from de Vries (1984a: 30, 36), as explained in the text.

the urban population rose significantly, but the urbanization ratio remained at a relatively low level in Scandinavia, Poland, Germany, France and Austria (table 4.1).

The development index clearly brings out this pattern of diverging trends among the various regions of Europe. On the one hand, we can distinguish a region of growth around the North Sea. England and Wales stand out most clearly in this process. They developed considerably faster than the European average throughout the entire period 1500–1800, although until 1700 their overall development was still exceeded by the rising population and urbanization ratio in the Netherlands. In the eighteenth century, Scotland (with its significant urbanization) and Ireland (with a strong growth in population) were also remarkably dynamic. Belgium, on the other hand, traditionally the industrial and commercial centre of north-western Europe, lagged behind, largely because of the decline in the urbanization ratio in the sixteenth century, the result of the Spanish reconquest after 1580. Finally, Scandinavia also exhibited a higher than average development, due to the solid growth of the population in this still almost empty region. The Scandinavian urbanization ratio, however, remained far below the European average.

In contrast to the dynamism of the area around the North Sea, the countries of southern Europe show a clear and protracted stagnation. In the sixteenth century the increase in the development index for Italy and Spain still exceeded the European average. Portugal even briefly topped the list in 1600, thanks to the ferocious growth of Lisbon. But the seventeenth century was dramatic for these countries: the development index for Spain and Italy declined (as did that of Poland), largely due to a decline in their urban populations. Portugal too saw its urban population fall markedly over the long term after 1600.

Between the two extremes of stagnation in southern and eastern Europe and the dynamism in the North Sea zone, we find several countries that developed more or less in line with the European average: Switzerland, Germany, France and Austria. In this central area we find modest urbanization and a moderate growth in the population.

This pattern, which can be derived from relatively reliable data on the size and composition of the population, will recur in various places in this chapter. Almost always it will turn out to be England that displays the most consistent and impressive growth, while the Netherlands, whose rise in the sixteenth and seventeenth centuries was perhaps even more impressive, fell into relative decline in the eighteenth century. With almost the same regularity, the relative stagnation in southern and eastern Europe will be evident.

2 The development of GDP: country-by-country estimates

Economists and economic historians who analyse long-term processes of economic growth and development almost always make use of estimates of the development of GDP per capita, derived from National Accounts. A large number of studies is now available dealing with the growth of GDP in nineteenth- and twentieth-century Europe. Though most sets of data for the nineteenth century, and especially for the period before 1850, contain substantial margins of error, they nonetheless allow a relatively accurate picture of long-term economic growth. Thanks to the pioneering work of Angus Maddison (1994: 194–200) we are now able to estimate international differences in GDP per capita throughout Europe at the start of the nineteenth century.[2] The results of this comparison confirm that the UK had the highest GDP per capita but also shows that international differences in GDP per capita seem in general to have been rather small. Economies as diverse as Sweden, Italy, Germany, Denmark, Austria, Belgium and Spain had almost identical levels of GDP per capita (at about 60–75 per cent of the UK level) and the gap between the richest and the poorest country – the UK and Russia – is a mere 60 per cent (as a percentage of the UK level) (see also the final column of table 4.3).

The Maddison estimates for 1820 have been used here as the starting point for an inquiry into economic growth in the period before 1800. The relative levels of GDP per capita in 1820 are used to render comparable a number of recent attempts to quantify economic growth between 1500 and 1800. These studies have continued the work begun by Deane and Cole (1962), who already produced estimates of the economic growth of Great Britain in the eighteenth century. In France, Toutain and Marczewski have come up with several, albeit highly controversial, estimates of production in the eighteenth century. The debate which they have provoked has generally led to a downward adjustment of Marczewski's very high growth figures, but no consensus on the pace of economic growth in eighteenth century France has yet emerged. For this reason I have refrained from including French estimates in the analysis which follows.[3]

Recent research got underway with the publications of Graeme Snooks (1990, 1992, and 1993) on estimated national income in England, based on data from Domesday Book (1086). Snooks ingeniously fills out the data from this venerable source, which gives detailed information on 'demesne income', with estimates of income from outside the 'demesne' sector, such as that generated by towns. Snooks provides some fairly conservative figures; he assumes, for example, that the consumption of farmers was on a subsistence level. Snooks then combines his estimates of total income and income per head in 1086 with Crafts' revision of Deane and Cole's estimates for 1688 and onwards, and finally makes several (unspecified) estimates for the intervening period. The result is a set of estimates of economic growth between 1086 and 1688 which are astonishingly high: an average growth rate of 0.29 per cent/capita per year over a period of 600 years, leading, according to Snooks, to a quadrupling of real income per head over the whole period. In some of the component periods – especially in the first half of the sixteenth century – he even finds annual growth rates higher than 1.5 per cent/head. These results mean that growth between 1086 and 1688 were almost equal to those of the eighteenth century (1688–1760: 0.31 per cent/capita per year); the pace of growth in the first half of the sixteenth century would only just be matched by that between 1830 and 1870.

Snooks' optimistic results have met with a great deal of scepticism.[4] There is an almost general objection to his 1086 level, which is probably underestimated, and to the fact that he does not clearly explain how he has apportioned the overall growth between 1086 and 1688 to the various centuries. Neither is it clear how he solves the problem of price changes between 1086 and 1688, and here too there is insufficient explanation of the method he has used in his calculations.

In a recent paper Mark Overton and Bruce Campbell (1997) have produced estimates of the performance of English agriculture in the period 1086–1871 that allow a reassessment of Snooks' estimates. Starting from data on population, food consumption, yields, imports and exports of agricultural products and the development of arable acreage from a large number of different sources, Overton and Campbell were able to construct detailed series of estimates of the total output of grain and potatoes in England across no less than eight centuries. The resulting estimates of the development of output per head of the agricultural population show a long-term stagnation in labour productivity between 1086 and 1600 – with some significant swings – followed by a strong increase in labour productivity between 1600 and 1800 (table 4.2). These estimates can be used to make some crude assumptions about the development of GDP. Two scenarios have been constructed:

1   An optimistic scenario: the increase in labour productivity in the rest of the economy was twice the rate of growth of labour productivity in agriculture;
2   A pessimistic scenario: the growth of labour productivity in the rest of the economy was the same as in agriculture.

In order to calculate one series of GDP from both series of the development of labour productivity in the two sectors (agriculture and the rest of the economy), we need to infer certain weights. Two sets of weights were found: for 1700, when the

Table 4.2 Estimates of the development of the output per head of the agricultural population and of GDP per capita in England, 1086–1800 (indices 1800 = 100)

	1086	1300	1380	1520*	1600	1700	1800
Labour productivity per head of agricultural population	43	41	45	41–5	39	64	100
GDP per capita							
Optimistic scenario							
Weights 1700	31	29	32	28–32	27	46	100
Weights 1800	23	22	24	21–5	21	41	100
Pessimistic scenario:							
All weights	47	45	49	45–50	43	64	100
Crafts						76	100
Snooks	13			20	54	76	100
Preferred				50–4	48	76	100

*Interpolated.

Sources: Crafts (1985); Overton and Campbell (1997); Snooks (1990, 1992 and 1993).

share of agriculture was 37 per cent, and for 1800 when it had declined to 26 per cent (Crafts 1985: 16–17). In the pessimistic scenario both weights give, of course, exactly the same increase in GDP per capita. This implies that the decline in labour productivity in agriculture in the sixteenth century 'automatically' results in a (slight) fall in GDP per capita. That, however, seems unlikely, because the sixteenth century was a period of rapid growth of industrial production and international services, but it is not immediately obvious how the series can be adjusted for this anomaly.

The comparison between the two scenarios and the Snooks' estimates immediately makes it very likely that the latter must have overestimated growth (table 4.2). Therefore, I shall make no further use of his figures in this study. A comparison between the two sets of weights shows that the further back in time one chooses a set of weights, the lower the measured growth rate will be (the famous Gerschenkron effect – see Crafts 1985: 18–26). More surprising, perhaps, is the fact that Crafts' estimates, which have become the consensus view, may seriously underestimate growth in the eighteenth century. In order to arrive at the Crafts series, we would have to assume that the increase in labour productivity in the rest of the economy (i.e. industry and services) was actually slower than in agriculture. However, because productivity growth in agriculture in the eighteenth century was very rapid indeed, and the estimates of the growth of total output of agriculture between 1700 and 1800 of Overton/Campbell and Crafts are almost the same (75 and 70 per cent respectively), I have retained the Crafts series for this period. The bottom line of the table shows the preferred series of estimates. For the eighteenth century this series is based on Crafts' figures. For the period before 1700 I have opted for the average between the pessimistic and the optimistic scenario with the 1700 weights.

Several recent studies on economic growth in various European countries have employed the traditional methods of estimating the long-term development of production and income. As part of the ongoing debate on the development of the

Table 4.3 Estimates of the development of GDP per capita in six European countries, 1500–1800 (UK in 1820 = 100)

	1380/ 1450	c. 1500	c. 1570	c. 1650	c. 1700	c. 1750	1820
UK	46	45–9*	45*	54*	68	81	100
Netherlands	–	60(64)	60(64)	98	97	95	89
Belgium	–	55(49)	65(57)	63	66	72	74
Italy	89	75–6*	62–6	71	71	62–6	62
Spain	–	–	55–61	49–62	50–6*	51–3	61
Poland	–	51–60	48–56	48–55	40–6	34–7	46
Unweighted average	–	57–60	55–8	63–7	65–7	66–7	72
Coefficient of variation	–	0.17**	0.14	0.25	0.25	0.29	0.26

Bracketed figures are original estimates of Blomme, Buyst and Van der Wee (1994), and van Zanden (1993b).
*Interpolated
**Without Spain

Sources: Yun (1994b); Malanima (1994); Blomme, Buyst and Van der Wee (1994); van Zanden, (1993b); Topolski and Wyczanski (1982). Population: de Vries (1984a: 36). 1820: Maddison (1984); and table 4.2.

Dutch economy in the seventeenth and eighteenth centuries, I myself have attempted to outline the shape of economic growth in the Dutch province of Holland for the period 1500–1800. In a number of studies, serial data on production in the most important sectors of industry, agriculture and the services were used (van Zanden 1992 and 1987). But it has to be acknowledged that it was proved especially difficult to quantify the 'growth spurt' in the period 1580–1650, because it was accompanied by the rise of all sorts of new branches of trade for which we have insufficient quantitative material available. Therefore my estimates for the period before 1650 leave room for doubt.

Jan Blomme, Erik Buyst and Herman Van der Wee (1994) have produced a similar study of the provinces of Brabant and Flanders in the period 1500–1800, in which they restrict themselves to estimates of the production of commodities; their contribution thus neglects the vitally important commercial sector. Paolo Malanima (1994) has carried out comparable research on northern and central Italy in the period 1400–1800, in which he processed data on the development of nominal and real wages alongside contemporary estimates of income and production. In a recent extension of this research he has added estimates for GDP per capita during the first half of the fifteenth century.[5] Finally, Bartholome Yun (1994b) has combined existing estimates of the absolute level of production and consumption in Castile with estimates of their development over the period 1580–1800, using for his calculations an impressive array of statistical data. Yun arrives at two sets of estimates, which are included in table 4.3, as minimum and maximum values.

The ultimate aim of comparing the growth of GDP in these countries is to arrive at an impression, if nothing more, of the development of the European economy as a whole. However, the question is then whether these five countries are properly representative of Europe. On the one hand, the more dynamic countries seem to be over-represented, as both England and the Netherlands are in the sample. But on the other hand, the stagnating regions of southern Europe (northern Italy and Castile) are also included. France and central Europe are, however, totally absent. To compensate for this, we used the results of research by Topolski and Wyczanski (1982: 132–3) on the development of agricultural production in Poland between 1500 and 1800. They estimate that per capita output in Polish agriculture fell by around 33 per cent between 1570 and 1800. In order to convert their detailed figures into estimates of GDP per capita, the following assumptions were made:

1   GDP per capita in Poland in 1820 occupied a middle position between that of Russia and that of Czechoslovakia (and stood at 54 per cent below the British level);

2   Levels of agricultural production are taken from Topolski and Wyczanski (1982); population figures are from de Vries (1984a: 36), whose estimates in fact run parallel with those used by Topolski and Wyczanski;

3   Estimates of the development of non-agricultural production per capita are based on the evolution of the urbanization ratio according to de Vries (1984a: 30);

4   Finally, it is reckoned that the share of industry and services in GDP in 1800–20 was at least 20 per cent and at most 33 per cent; this produces two estimates of the development of GDP per capita which are both included in table 4.3.

One problem with this comparison is that five of the relevant studies relate only to a part of the country involved. Yun studied the Kingdom of Castile, which in 1800 made up about 70 per cent of the population of Spain. Overton and Campbell restricted their research to England, which in 1800 represented about 50 per cent of the population of the UK. Malamina discussed central and northern Italy (Lombardy, Tuscany, Liguria and Piedmont) which together included about 60 per cent of the Italian population. The region of Flanders and Brabant studied by Blomme, Buyst and Van der Wee (1994) likewise represents about 60 per cent of the Belgian population (in 1800). Finally the share of the total Dutch population represented by Holland, the province studied by the present author, grew from about 30 per cent in 1500 to 40 per cent between 1620 and 1800; its share of Dutch GDP was probably much higher – perhaps as much as 50 per cent in 1800.

With the possible exception of Yun, all these authors have focused on the more developed parts of their respective countries. For the Netherlands and Italy in particular, it may be assumed that productivity and income per capita in these regions were higher than the national average. But because this bias occurs in five of the studies (Poland is the exception) and because it is impossible to determine the magnitude of the bias, no attempt has been made to correct differences between the countries. In other words, the 1820 'benchmark' levels, which relate to whole countries, have been combined with the estimates of the development of GDP per capita in five regions (plus Poland), without allowing for the fact that these regions probably had a somewhat higher GDP per capita than the countries they represent.

Table 4.3 sets out the results of the comparison of the development of GDP per capita in the six countries/regions. One may well ask, though, what are we to make of these figures? The table invites two possible interpretations, which I shall call 'minimum' and 'maximum'. According to the 'minimum' interpretation, the estimates are a reflection of the view held by experts on the long-term development of the countries concerned. In the case of Spain – where recent years have seen a great deal of innovative quantitative research on the early modern economy – this view seems sound. In the cases of Italy and Poland too, the view that long-term stagnation was involved accords with a *communis opinio*. However, for the three countries around the North Sea, where the issue is the measurement of the degree of economic growth since the sixteenth century, the situation is not so clear: there neither is nor was an accepted view of the degree to which GDP per capita rose in these countries. However, it does seem to be widely accepted that it did increase significantly, especially in England and the Netherlands.

According to the 'maximum' interpretation, these estimates give a convincing picture of the long-term growth of the various countries. In view of the quality of the source material used, my opinion is that such an interpretation is only acceptable in the case of Spain. Of all the work presented here, only the Spanish research (for the sixteenth and eighteenth centuries) is based on a large quantity of statistical source material which is reliably processed and actually permits no other conclusions than those which Yun has drawn from them. However, according to both Malamina and Yun, the close correspondence between the results of Italy and Spain should increase our confidence in the Italian results as well. The Spanish and Italian estimates can then be used to calibrate those of the other countries.

Northern Italy was undoubtedly the most prosperous part of Europe in the sixteenth century, while Spain, more agricultural and less urbanized, probably had an income per head below that of Belgium (Flanders/Brabant) and the Netherlands in 1570. The long-term development of the Belgian economy between 1570 and 1820 seems to fit the picture of Spain and Italy. Nonetheless, these Belgian figures display some anomalies. A comparison of the Blomme, Buyst and Van der Wee figures for Belgium with those constructed for Holland, suggest that GDP per capita in sixteenth-century Holland was already much higher than in Flanders and Brabant. This is very unlikely: only after 1580 did the centre of economic activity shift from the Southern Netherlands (i.e. Antwerp) to Holland (i.e. Amsterdam). All the available evidence suggests that before 1580 the Southern Netherlands were (with Italy) the most developed and the wealthiest part of Europe. This anomaly can be explained as follows. In my view, by concentrating on commodity production, Blomme, Buyst and Van der Wee underestimate the decline in GDP after 1580 that resulted from the shift of international trade and banking to Amsterdam. In view of this, their estimates of the development of GDP should be adjusted to take into account the sharp decline of (international) services after 1580. Next, the Holland figures have been re-estimated to bring them into line with the figures for Belgium and Italy, taking into account the fact that growth rates for the period before 1650 were probably under-estimated in my original study.[6] These corrections in fact have no influence on the final outcome – the estimates of the development of GDP per capita in Europe – because they largely cancel each other out. However, they do serve as a reminder that margins of uncertainty have constantly to be borne in mind.

The Polish figures raise no problems: they are consistently well below the European average and around 1570 still lie below the Spanish figure, as would be expected. Poland's economic decline in the seventeenth century cannot have been much greater than these figures suggest, however, because Polish GDP per capita in 1570 would then come above that of Spain. Only the estimate of GDP before 1570 seems to be on the high side.

Finally, the new estimates for England based on the Overton and Campbell study of agricultural productivity fit into the general picture of European economic growth much better than Snooks' figures. According to Snooks' series, England was considerably poorer than Poland at the beginning of the sixteenth century (its GDP per capita was only about a third of the Polish level), which seems very unlikely. Once again we have to conclude that the Snooks series overstates growth. Perhaps my new series of estimates gives an overly favourable picture of growth in the seventeenth century – it seems rather unlikely that GDP per head in England in 1650 was only about half the Dutch level. The ratio between the two countries in 1700 is consistent with the contemporary estimates made by Gregory King, as well as with the results of other research (de Vries 1984b: 153–60). I therefore suggest that English growth in the seventeenth century is probably over-estimated (and under-estimated in the sixteenth century).

The results of this comparison can now briefly be summarized. Long-term stagnation is revealed on the periphery, i.e. Italy, Spain and Poland. Between 1500 and 1750 GDP per capita in these countries first fell, while later on a mild recovery set in, at least in Spain and Poland. Only in Spain, however, was GDP per capita possibly somewhat higher in 1820 than in 1570. Compared with the stagnation of southern and eastern Europe, the countries bordering the North Sea show relatively gradual (Belgium) or rapid (England) growth in the early modern period. These estimates suggest roughly a doubling of GDP per capita in England between 1520 and 1820. My calculations for Holland imply a more modest rise of only about 50 per cent for the same period; the increase in Belgium was probably smaller still.

The general picture which emerges from these data can again be looked at in two ways. It is clear that, in the long run, population growth was more than compensated for by the increase in production. In 'Europe', i.e. the average of these six countries, production per capita between *c.* 1500 and *c.* 1820 increased by an average of some 25 per cent. Almost 10 per cent occurred after 1750. Overall, the population in these six countries increased by 91 per cent between 1500 and 1800 (see table 4.1). To judge by these data, the Malthusian pessimists, who saw a growing tension arising between population and resources, were therefore wrong. The growth of population was clearly matched by a somewhat larger increase in output. However, the optimists' claims are only partly confirmed: economic growth, in the sense of growth in per capita production, was not normal in western Europe. Rather, it should be considered an exception to the rule, certainly before 1700. In Holland there was just one 'growth spurt' in a period of three hundred years, and this was probably also the case in Belgium. Moreover, growth in Holland was partly achieved at the expense of Flanders and Brabant, where the economy declined simultaneously with the rise of Holland. On balance, growth was very modest indeed in these six countries, taken as a whole: on average GDP per capita increased by a mere 25 per cent over a period of three centuries and this growth was mainly due to the inclusion of the most dynamic parts of Europe (England and Holland) in our sample.

Another conclusion is that overall differences in the level of economic activity within Europe were small. The gap between the richest regions (Flanders and northern Italy) and the poorest (England or Poland) in about 1570 was at most 30 per cent of the level of the richest and probably even smaller than that. Differences did increase sharply during the seventeenth century as a result of the rise of Holland and the decline of Poland and Spain, but this was compensated to some extent by the rise of England and the decline of northern Italy and Flanders relative to the 'European average'. In the second half of the eighteenth century international disparities seem to reduce slightly, due to the increase in GDP in Poland and Spain (and to stagnation in Holland). In 1820 the distribution around the mean was even smaller than in 1700 or 1750, although at that time England was certainly running increasingly ahead of the continental countries.

3 GDP estimates: a sectoral approach

Two recent studies, the paper on English agriculture by Overton and Campbell (1997) and the book by Hoffman (1996: 134–6) on growth in the French country-side, arrive at identical conclusions concerning the development of agricultural output per capita in the early modern period. Although Hoffman (1996: 36) stresses the possibilities for growth in a 'traditional society', he finds that overall output increased by about the same rate as population (which is similar to the results of the 'pessimist' studies by Goy and Le Roy Ladurie). Overton and Campbell (1997) arrived at the same conclusion: between 1300 and 1800 food supply per capita remained basically the same and the increase in labour productivity in agriculture was largely the result of the growth of non-agrarian employment and demand. This is in complete accordance with the hypothesis developed by Wrigley (1987) about the long-term stability in food consumption between 1500 and 1800 in both countries. This hypothesis is also accepted by de Vries and van der Woude in their study of the Dutch economy between 1500 and 1815.[7] Finally, in his study of pre-industrial Germany, Henning (1974) also assumed that per capita output of food remained basically constant in this period.

These studies all suggest that in the core region around the North Sea the growth of agricultural output was probably as rapid as the increase in population numbers. In the rest of Europe this may also have been the case. However, there are some signs that the consumption of agricultural 'luxury' products – especially of meat – declined in per capita terms in large parts of Europe. Abel has already analysed this process as the result of the general fall in living standards in large parts of Europe between the 'golden age of the craftsman' (fifteenth century) and the 'crisis of mass poverty' at the end of the eighteenth century (Abel 1935: 226–42). Perhaps in certain parts of Europe per capita demand for foodstuffs even declined. Summing up, it seems that the output of the agricultural sector between 1500 and 1800 at best kept pace with population growth.

In industry and international trade, the growth of production was much more rapid. This can be demonstrated by looking at some estimates of the growth of two dynamic sectors: international trade and iron production.

To map the development of international trade, it is best to turn to data on the size of the merchant fleet. Romano has published what are probably fair estimates of the size of the European merchant fleet in 1780, which can serve as the starting point for our purposes. The total European fleet in 1780 amounted to around 3,372,000 tons; over a third was British, with France a good second and Holland in third place.

There are hardly any figures for the beginning of the period, on the other hand.[8] It is significant that the Venetian merchant fleet in the fifteenth and sixteenth centuries is estimated at between 15,000 and 20,000 tons (Lane 1966: 5–20). With this fleet, which is very small indeed by eighteenth-century standards, Venice dominated international trade in the Mediterranean. The Dutch merchant fleet, which similarly dominated the trade of north-western Europe around 1500, has been estimated at 40,000 tons (van Zanden 1987: 587). Vogel's (1915) estimate of 60,000 tons for *c.* 1470, seems to be on the high side, but it must be borne in mind that the economy of Holland went through a deep depression between 1470 and 1500, which may have caused the size of the fleet to shrink. Vogel thinks that around 1470 the Hanseatic towns of Germany may also have had a fleet of 60,000 tons. The first estimate of the size of the English fleet dates from 1582, and totalled 33,000 tons (Wilson 1977: 129). In view of the rapid growth in international trade in the England of Elizabeth I it is likely that the figure for 1500 would have been significantly lower. If we add to these figures rough estimates for France, Portugal and Spain, we can very tentatively reckon the total European merchant fleet around 1500 at between 200,000 and 250,000 tons.

For *c.* 1600 Braudel quotes a figure of from 600,000 to 700,000 tons. According to Vogel (1915), who is probably the original source for this estimate, this would include an estimated 60,000 tons for England, more than 200,000 for Holland, around 100,000 tons for Germany and 80,000 tons for France. The remaining 200,000 tons would thus be distributed between Italy, Spain, Portugal and Scandinavia, which is not implausible. We have similar information for the years around 1670. At that time the four great seafaring nations combined would have had over 700,000 tons cargo space at their disposal: over 400,000 tons for Holland, 126,000 for England, 104,000 for Germany, and in France, where estimates vary, between 80,000 and 150,000 tons.[9] If we assume that the proportion of the total fleet represented by these four was about the same as it was nearly two hundred years later (1780), then the total European fleet in around 1670 can be estimated at between 1 and 1.1 million tons.

The estimates from these various sources are set out in table 4.4. The figures clearly reveal the impressive growth of the merchant fleet. During the sixteenth century the size of the fleet doubled per head of population, and did so again in the eighteenth century (1670–1780). During the intervening 'crisis' of the seventeenth century growth was less spectacular, but it was still positive, due to the strong growth of the

Table 4.4 Estimates of the growth of the European merchant fleet, *c.* 1500–1780 (in thousand tons)

Year	Total fleet (thousand tons)	Tonnage per thousand inhabitants			
c. 1500	200–250	3.2–4.0			
c. 1600	600–700	7.7–9.0			
c. 1670	1,000–1,100	12.8–14.1			
1780	3,372	30.7			
Year	Regional/national share (per cent)				
	Southern Europe	The Netherlands	Great Britain	France	Hanseatic towns
c. 1500	40?	16	10–12	?	20?
c. 1600	25?	33	10	12	15
c. 1670	20?	40	12	8–14	10
1780	15	12	26	22	4

Sources: Romano (1962) and the text.

Dutch fleet. At the same time the regional pattern changed profoundly: the southern European share declined steadily, as did that of the Hanseatic towns. In the sixteenth and seventeenth centuries it was Holland that profited most from the growth in international trade. Contemporaries were of the opinion that the Dutch merchant fleet around 1670 was larger than that of the rest of Europe put together (though this is not entirely confirmed by our estimates; see Wallerstein 1980: 46). In the century after 1670 England and France in particular gained ground, while the Scandinavian fleet also expanded substantially. A striking illustration of the expansion after 1670 is that the Dutch share of the fleet fell from 40 to 12 per cent, while the absolute size of their fleet remained virtually the same. A comparable process of stagnation whith absolute levels remaining more or less constant had taken place in Venice and Genoa in the sixteenth century. The size of the Venetian fleet even increased over the long term (from around 20,000 tons in 1450 to 60,000 tons in 1780), but while it had dominated the Mediterranean around 1450 it was of only modest significance around 1780.

There are various estimates of the long-term development of the European iron industry, but they are not in complete agreement. Goodman and Honeyman's estimates (1988: 172), largely based on the work of Pounds and Parker (1957: 27), show a slow growth during the seventeenth century and a doubling of production in the eighteenth century. This would suggest that, on balance, production per head increased by almost 40 per cent (table 4.5, column 1). Sprangel's (1969) estimates for *c.* 1500 and *c.* 1750 indicate a much stronger degree of growth, in fact a four-fold increase (table 4.5, column 2). It is not possible to compare these figures directly (this would lead to an extremely steep increase in production per head in the sixteenth century: see table 4.5, column 3), but both studies do indicate that production per head must have risen substantially over the long term. Between 1500 and 1790 it probably more than doubled, perhaps even trebled.

Table 4.5 Estimates of the development of production in the iron industry of Western Europe, 1500–1790 (in thousand tonnes)

	Total Goodman and Honeyman	Total Sprangel	Total kg per capita	Great Britain	Sweden	France	Germany
c. 1500	–	40	0.65	1	5	12	5
c. 1600	125	–	1.6	17	7*	–	–
c. 1700	165	–	2.0	24	28*	25	30
1740–50	–	145–80	1.5–1.9	27	40*	–	–
1790	335	–	2.2	80	50	140	50

*Based on data of exports of iron.

Sources: Total from Goodman and Honeyman (1988: 172); corrected to exclude the Russian Empire with Pounds and Parker (1957: 27); total from Sprangel (1969); Great Britain: Riden (1977); Sweden: Nijman (1991: 231); France and Germany 1500: Mulhall (1898); 1700 and 1790: Pounds and Parker (1957: 27). Population: de Vries (1984a: 36).

The growth in iron production was concentrated in a few specific regions. In England there was a rapid expansion of the industry in the sixteenth century, followed by a period of more gradual growth. In Sweden the expansion took place in the seventeenth century, under the influence of Dutch merchants who effected a major modernization of the Swedish iron industry using technical expertise developed in Liège (Nijman 1991: 231). The pace of growth increased throughout Europe in the eighteenth century; probably only Spain experienced a fall in iron production during this period (Pounds and Parker 1957: 24). Important innovations in the British iron industry, where coal became the main fuel, were responsible for an enormous growth in iron production in that country. But in France too, and to a lesser extent in Germany where these innovations were barely applied, production increased very rapidly. In the eighteenth century France was actually the largest iron producer, although production per head remained below that of England and Sweden.

It is far from obvious that the growth of the iron industry is typical of European industry as a whole. Unfortunately, however, it is impossible to find the necessary data for other branches of industry, where production may have increased even more sharply. These would largely have been relatively new industries, such as printing, paper making, sugar refining, the tobacco industry, the silk industry, the cotton industry, diamond cutting, and the distilling of gin. The supply of industrial products at the end of the eighteenth century was much richer than at the beginning of the sixteenth century, due to the rise of all sorts of new industries which swelled the market with new products – from coffee, tobacco and sugar to carriages, musical instruments and wigs. At the same time, ship-building and other maritime industries – from anchor smiths to rope makers – must have profited from the huge growth of the international merchant fleet.

Dramatic growth was also evident in the mining of coal, driven by the increasing scarcity of wood as a fuel and by the growing demand for energy. Estimates of the output of British mines reveal a spectacular rise from 210,000 tons in 1551–60, almost 3 million tons in 1681–90, to more than 10 million tons in 1781–90 – an increase by a factor of 49 in 230 years (Wilson 1977: 124). Similarly, in the mining region of Liège total output increased from about 25,000 tons in 1510 to more than 500,000 tons in 1812 (Unger 1984: 237). On the Continent the growth of the coal mining industry was generally less spectacular than in Great Britain, but it was nonetheless very significant. However in most cases coal replaced a declining supply of wood, which makes it difficult to interpret this trend as a clear sign of economic growth (Wilkinson 1973; also Malanima in this volume).

In contrast to these growth sectors – the new industries, those linked to the commercial sector and those linked to the British Industrial Revolution (coal and iron) – there were of course the more 'traditional' sectors, which experienced a much less rapid expansion. In the seventeenth and eighteenth centuries beer brewing was a declining industry almost everywhere in western Europe, as a result of the rise of alternative beverages such as coffee, tea and gin. In Belgium the estimated annual beer consumption per capita declined from 156 litres in 1610–15 to 108 litres in 1760–65 (Blomme, Buyst and Van der Wee 1994: 20). According to Richard Yntema (1992: 128), the decline was even more dramatic in Holland; from 301 litres per capita in 1622 to 38 litres in 1795! The meat industry must also have lost much of its significance, due to the fall in the consumption of meat. It seems, however, that the list of industries in decline is much shorter than the list of expanding ones. Perhaps the iron industry, with more than a doubling of production per head between 1500 and 1750, is after all typical of industry as a whole during this period, but this cannot be more than an educated guess.

In short, agricultural production per head remained at best stable, whereas production in industry and in international trade increased markedly. To judge by the development of the merchant fleet and that of iron production, there was at least a doubling, perhaps as much as a trebling, of non-agricultural production per capita, but both industries were probably more dynamic than the rest of the non-agricultural sector. If we assume that around 1800 between 40 and (at most) 50 per cent of European GDP consisted of non-agrarian production (e.g. Henning 1974: 20) the increase in non-agricultural output would have meant a rise in GDP per capita of 15–35 per cent between 1500 and 1800. Using more pessimistic weights would give even smaller estimates of the increase of GDP per capita. This result is very much in agreement with that of the country-by-country estimates.

4   The character of early modern economic growth

Economic growth was not a normal condition in Europe between 1500 and 1800. On the contrary, stagnation seems to have been the norm. The dynamism of England, of Holland in the seventeenth century, and of Belgium in the sixteenth century (and perhaps again in the eighteenth century), were to a large extent the exceptions that prove the rule. Given the doubling of the population of Europe in this period, the estimates of growth presented here imply an increase in GDP of 130–160 per cent and an annual growth rate from 0.27–0.31 per cent with an average annual population increase of 0.23 per cent. Per capita growth over the very long term (1500–1800) must therefore have been in the order of 0.04–0.08 per cent annually.

However, such general European growth figures are misleading because they hide substantial regional differences in economic development. Large areas of Europe (such as the southern and eastern parts) were characterized in this era by long-term stagnation, i.e. by the absence of any growth at all. The estimates in table 4.3 suggest that Poland and Italy were poorer at the start of the nineteenth century than they had been in the sixteenth century, and that growth in Spain was so slight as to be almost negligible. Only the countries surrounding the North Sea – England, the Netherlands, Belgium and perhaps northern France and the west of Germany – experienced a rise in per capita income. Even in these countries, however, economic growth was not 'normal'. In Holland per capita GDP increased markedly only between 1580 and 1650, after which a process of stagnation set in that lasted for more than 150 years. Moreover, even this 'growth spurt' of the Dutch Golden Age was achieved in part at the expense of the economy of the Southern Netherlands, which suffered a decline during the same decades.

Within this general pattern, the great exception was England. Every century saw an increase in the English population, in England's urbanization ratio and, with the possible exception of the sixteenth century, in English GDP per capita. This continuing expansion emerges with equal clarity from data on the growth of the merchant fleet and of iron production (which was largely concentrated in England). There can be no doubt whatsoever that the English economy grew at an exceptional rate precisely in the centuries leading up to 1800. Ironically, English growth in the two centuries after 1800 has not been so unique. It is remarkable that the country which has provided the model for the classical 'Industrial Revolution' – the decisive break between a stagnating agrarian society and a dynamic industrial economy – was in fact characterized by an impressive dynamism in the centuries preceding this 'revolution'. From the figures presented here, it would appear that the 'Industrial Revolution' of the second half of the eighteenth century was no 'accident' as Crafts (1977) would have us believe, but the almost predictable continuation of the exceptionally dynamic development of the British economy in the sixteenth, seventeenth and the first half of the eighteenth centuries.

Characteristically, economic growth during the early modern period was regionally concentrated and closely linked to centres of merchant capitalism. The expansion of Venice, Florence and Genoa during the middle ages had raised the economy of northern Italy to a higher level, but when these cities lost their position as hubs of international trade, economic development stagnated. A similar curve runs through the economy of Flanders in the middle ages, under the impulse of the three cities of Bruges, Ghent and Ypres. The rise of Antwerp in the late fifteenth and sixteenth centuries dynamically transformed the economy of Brabant, but the decline of the city after 1566 ushered in the relative decline of the whole area. The trajectory of the Dutch 'Golden Age' is in many respects similar, and the fact that London was the engine of British economic growth before the industrial revolution is well established (Wrigley 1978). In each of these examples, economic growth was closely related to the fact that the specific city and region either managed to acquire a central position in the international trading network, or was able by virtue of significant innovations to build up its own export industries.

The somewhat pessimistic conclusions of this paper are to a large extent based on estimates of the development of GDP per capita. Labour productivity, which is probably a superior index of economic performance, may have developed differently. It is highly probable that labour supply increased much faster than the population. E. Scholliers has analysed the increase in working hours in parts of Belgium in the early modern period, and he concluded that they increased from less than 2,800 hours in the sixteenth century to perhaps as much as 3,500 to 4,000 hours in the middle of the nineteenth century (Scholliers 1983: 11–18). Kjaergaard (1994: 151) arrived at an identical conclusion in his analysis of the development of labour input in Denmark between 1500 and 1800: 'on a rough average, working hours increased by about 50 per cent during the three centuries'. According to Kjaergaard the average working day was extended by three to four hours and the working week by one or two days. Although the exact magnitude of the increase in labour input is unknown, there is a consensus that working hours of male workers increased and that labour inputs by females and children went up as well. Why this happened is still far from certain. Jan de Vries (1994) sees it as part of an 'industrious revolution' in which households increasingly switched resources (i.e. labour) to market activities in response to the growing attractiveness of buying goods in the market. A more pessimistic view may explain the same phenomenon as the result of the decline in real wages that occurred in the same period, in much the same way as the general increase in real income since the mid-nineteenth century has led to a shortening of the working week (van Zanden 1999). But if we accept that per capita labour input increased by perhaps a quarter or more, this means that labour productivity (i.e. GDP per hour worked) will not have increased at all in Europe between 1500 and 1800.

Once again, this result underlines the pessimistic conclusions of this study: in Europe as a whole economic growth between 1500 and 1800 was very sluggish and it probably did not result in an increase in labour productivity. This attempt at quantification of economic growth before the Industrial Revolution therefore also makes it clear how 'revolutionary' were the economic changes that first occurred in England in the second half of the eighteenth century and were taken over on the European continent after 1815.

Notes

1 This is apparent, for example, in the decreasing level of urbanization in France and Belgium during this period.
2 Older figures of GDP per capita in 1830, produced by Bairoch (1976), give an almost identical picture of international differences in the level of economic development.
3 For a brief review of these estimates, see Riley and McCusker (1983: 290–3).
4 An extreme example is Crafts' review of Snooks (1993) in *Economic History Review* 48, 1995: 210–11.
5 Personal communication from P. Malanima.
6 Thanks to this exercise in international comparison, it now seems likely that in previous publications (van Zanden 1992) I over-estimated the level of GDP in Holland in the period 1500–90 by at least 10–20%.
7 Although they postulate a small increase in per capita demand for agricultural products, the

result of increased demand for inputs from the industrial sector: see de Vries and van der Woude (1997a: 232–4).

8 All estimates and figures refer exclusively to large merchant ships; vessels used in the fishing industry, on inland waters, and in small scale coastal traffic (such as the British collier trade) are left out of the estimates as far as possible.

9 Van Zanden (1987: 587); Wilson (1977: 129); Vogel (1915: 268–333); Morineau (1977: 177).

5 Pre-industrial economic growth and the transition to an industrial economy

Edwin Horlings

It is generally believed that in the course of the eighteenth and nineteenth centuries the economies of Western Europe crossed the threshold to the modern age. In its most extreme interpretation the Industrial Revolution was a transition from an economically stagnant and institutionally rigid agrarian society to a dynamic and rapidly progressing industrial economy (e.g. Rostow 1961: 4–9). There is, however, growing appreciation of the achievements of the early modern economy. In Britain the continuous revision of macroeconomic measurements has resulted in an increasingly gradualist pattern of development to the point of eliminating the traditional notion of revolutionary change at the level of the entire economy.[1] O'Brien (1996) has re-introduced the *longue durée* in order to explain the difference between French and British industrialization. The debate on Dutch modernization has shifted from the nineteenth century to the Golden Age of the seventeenth century. In the 'traditional' interpretation the Netherlands did not industrialize until well into the second half of the nineteenth century, while the preceding period was allegedly characterized by long-term stagnation (van Zanden 1989). The latest view – put forward by de Vries and van der Woude (1997a) – contends that the Netherlands was a modern economy as early as the Golden Age. This would reduce or at least change the significance of nineteenth-century industrialization.

Macroeconomic estimates, however, do suggest that there was a remarkable difference in the speed and composition of economic growth before and after about 1800–50. In the early modern period growth and structural change were minimal, whereas for most countries in Europe and North America the nineteenth century was an age of industrial growth and relative agricultural decline, of demographic transition and rapid urbanization, of huge technological advances, and a steady rise in the standard of living. In other words, the Industrial Revolution still appears to have been a very real historical event.

Yet there is no consensus on either the nature or the causes of the Industrial Revolution. The further back in time the analysis is extended and the more branches and types of activity are included, the more muddled the issues seem to become (see Mokyr 1985b). The basic problem is that we have no generally accepted definition that captures the scale and scope of the economic changes associated with industrialization. Conversely, the nature of pre-industrial growth is equally uncertain. What were the defining characteristics of economic growth before the

Industrial Revolution? And how did the transition to a modern economy come about?

1 The essence of growth

The Industrial Revolution is considered the dividing line between two different types of economy: one industrial or modern, the other pre-industrial or premodern. They are usually distinguished by examining growth rates, with stagnation or slow growth before industrialization and rapid growth thereafter. However, the difference should be defined by the way in which growth was achieved, rather than by growth itself. Time is the essential variable in assessing economic performance. Short-term changes in income or output qualify as mere fluctuations, but significant achievements are made when real per capita income remains stable or actually increases over a long period of time. An economy is most successful when both population and per capita income show sustained growth. The key to understanding the nature of growth consequently lies in the relationship between population and resources.

The tension between population (the desired level of output) and resources (the means of production) has been central to every growth theory since the classical economists. A plain yet invaluable formulation was provided by Malthus and Ricardo who both concentrated on the relation between land and labour. Malthus argued that the population would grow so long as wages were above subsistence level. However, because the amount of land was fixed, population growth would raise the number of workers per unit of land, average labour productivity would fall in response to diminishing returns to labour, and real wages would decline as a consequence. As soon as wages dropped below the level of subsistence, the population would begin to decrease. Ricardo allowed for the expansion of agricultural acreage. Rising population pressure would force the cultivation of previously unused land. However, this new land was of lower quality so the expansion of acreage reduced average productivity.[2]

Neither Malthus nor Ricardo took into account the possibility of gains in productivity. Both assumed a constant level of technology. Productivity did feature prominently in the work of Adam Smith, the founding father of laissez-faire economics. The production process could be made more efficient through capital formation as well as the economies of scale inherent in the division of labour. This was, however, dependent on the extent of the market, which is why Smith propagated economic liberalization. Nonetheless, he too assumed that growth was limited by the amount of food an economy could produce (A. Smith 1986).

If productivity growth is not continuous, diminishing returns to labour and capital will erode the economic surplus and the population will decline (Schofield 1983: 67; Boserup 1983: 186; Simon 1977: 159). A sustained increase in per capita output or food production consequently depends on the unremitting growth of productivity. Even a stable level of per capita production requires steady improvements to the production process.

Continuous growth and structural change are, on the other hand, central to Kuznets's (1966) model of modern economic growth. In his analysis of macro-economic trends Kuznets basically describes the stylized facts of economic

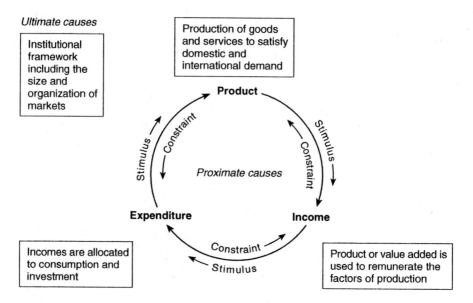

Figure 5.1 A schematic view of the economy

development in the western industrialized world since 1870. In his basic definition modern economic growth is the combination of rapid population growth with a sustained increase in real per capita income. Its principal feature is therefore continuous productivity growth, a function mainly of increases in scale, technological and organisational innovations, and the associated capital formation. A major source of productivity gains was the integration and expansion of markets. Infrastructural improvements and the introduction of new technologies in transport and communication made national and international markets more accessible at lower costs, aided during the second half of the nineteenth century by the liberalization of world trade. Urbanization provided considerable economies of scale. And growth was accompanied and supported by an increase in aggregate demand that was brought about by rising real wages and a long-term decline in income inequality. Modern economic growth thus became a self-reinforcing process.

The remarkable difference in achievement of the premodern and modern economies – virtual stagnation versus sustained growth – does not necessarily imply that we are dealing with fundamentally different economic systems. A schematic presentation of the functioning of an economy shows that the determinants of development can be found at different levels (figure 5.1). The *proximate* causes of growth relate to the cycle of product, income and expenditure. They involve the technology and organization of the production process, the allocation of factors of production (land, capital, labour), and the behaviour of investors and consumers, as well as other basic economic processes. The proximate causes operate in an institutional framework, which comprises producer associations, such as guilds and common lands, public policy, the protection of property rights, and in general the size, integration and maturity of the market economy. Changes in institutions constitute the *ultimate* causes (van der Klundert 1997: 1). The interactions between proximate and ultimate causes determine the nature of the growth process. The economy can be described as a self-organizing system.

There is a constant struggle between the influences that impede the improvement of the efficiency of production, the increase in incomes and equality, the re-allocation of expenditure towards productive investments and high-grade consumer goods – the constraints – and those that encourage productivity growth, income gains and shifts in expenditure – the stimuli. Any economy, regardless of its level of development, has elements that encourage or hinder progress. The balance between the two determines the potential for sustained growth. Technological innovations, exogenous shocks, and other short-term influences merely shift the balance between constraints and stimuli. In the long run the outcome of the interplay between constraints and stimuli at the level of the proximate causes depends on the nature of the environment of ultimate causes in which the cycle of basic economic activities occurs. The low growth estimates for the pre-industrial period suggest that constraints were dominant, whereas stimuli prevail in the modern industrial period. The implicit conclusion is that premodern growth was essentially self-constraining, whereas modern growth is self-reinforcing.

Does this imply that the premodern economy was stagnant or unchanging, a technological dead-end, whereas modernity involves everlasting progress? Was long-term productivity growth impossible before the industrial revolution? The answers will, in turn, raise the question of the nature of the transition. Was it a dramatic revolution or a process of gradual economic transformation?

2 Growth before the modern age

It is theoretically impossible for an economy to remain in perfect equilibrium, completely stagnant and without a change in technology and institutions. Its working depends on the decisions and preferences of a multitude of individual producers, investors, consumers, and so on. The behaviour of the different actors would have to be absolutely consistent and complementary to achieve a 'stationary state'. Even if a situation of perfect equilibrium were somehow achieved, the economy would still be subject to exogenous shocks. Some shocks, such as harvest failures or the discovery of large gold reserves, are virtually unpredictable. However, two phenomena are an integral part of the growth process. Population growth is essentially an exogenous process but to some extent it is related to economic development. And although macro-inventions appear more or less at random, there is a connection between technological progress and economic development (Mokyr 1990 and 1991). Economic change is therefore inevitable.

In the long run of human history the direction of change was probably biased upward. Once it has been acquired, knowledge – of new techniques, methods of production, or forms of organization – is rarely lost completely. Economic experience is preserved and enhanced by on-the-job training and learning-by-doing, while the general body of knowledge has been protected through the institutionalization of scientific research and technological experience in universities, guilds and other organizations, but also by simply writing it down.[3] It would take a tremendous crisis to return a society to an earlier level of development. However, such crises have occurred throughout history. The fall of the Roman Empire, the Spanish invasion of the Americas, and the Black Death of the fourteenth century come to mind. Progress was certainly not guaranteed.

A simple though crude measure for long-term improvement is the rate of urbanization. De Vries' (1984a: 39, 45) estimates reveal a process of steady urban growth in early modern Europe. On average the share of cities in the total population rose from 5.6 per cent in 1500 to 10 per cent in 1800. Even though the percentages and gains were modest and regional differences were considerable, there were only two notable cases of relative urban decline: the Mediterranean in the seventeenth century and the Low Countries in the eighteenth century. Even after this reverse in the upward trend, both regions remained heavily urbanized.

A more revealing indication is provided by research into the productivity of agriculture, the sector 'least likely to succeed' in early modern Europe. Overton (1996: 85, 131–2) demonstrates that the land and labour productivity of English agriculture increased steadily since the middle of the seventeenth century, despite rising population pressure in the eighteenth and nineteenth centuries. Van Zanden (1998: 81, table 7) has constructed a set of rough estimates of agricultural productivity in seven European countries – England and Wales, Belgium, the Netherlands, France, Italy, Poland, and Spain – based on the development of yield ratios. His results show that between 1500 and 1800 agricultural productivity increased everywhere with the exception of Italy.

Finally, we have crude estimates of aggregate economic performance in early modern Europe. Van Zanden's contribution in this volume provides an international comparison of real per capita income in six countries. His calculations suggest an average annual increase of about 0.1 per cent in the period 1500–1820. The differences between the individual economies did not come close to even one percentage point. Relatively advanced economies such as Belgium, Holland, and Britain grew at a very modest rate.[4] Van Zanden concludes that pre-industrial economies were inherently stagnant, even though specific regions – primarily urban centres of international trade – managed to achieve growth.

Growth was thus virtually absent at the highest level of aggregation. But what if the analysis were to focus on a single dynamic region, such as Holland, the south east of England, the city states of northern Italy, or the Paris Basin? Is there such a thing as modern economic growth in premodern surroundings? The first problem is that even from a regional perspective early modern growth proved hard to sustain. However the main objection is that market integration and expansion are vital aspects of modern economic growth. One of its most important features is that regions no longer matter, that growth and productivity gains are national and international until – in the twentieth century – the growth process seems to have become truly global. Stark regional contrasts in the level of economic development – placing 'modern' regions next to 'traditional' ones – should consequently be regarded as characteristic of the premodern economy and a crucial element of the analysis of its development. Individual cities or regions may have experienced a remarkable degree of techno-logical progress, but in the pre-industrial context this growth could not be sustained and its benefits did not radiate to the rest of the economy.

It is difficult to escape the conclusion that regional divergence and near-stagnation dominated the economic landscape of early modern Europe. And yet, growth evidently did occur. The search for the nature of growth in the premodern economy should therefore centre on the constraints on sustained gains in productivity rather than the mere lack of growth.

3 Constraints on premodern growth

There are two ways to increase per capita income or aggregate productivity: by re-allocating the factors of production from low-productivity to high-productivity sectors (compositional growth); or by improving the efficiency of individual branches of the economy (structural growth). Productivity gains can be made simply by re-allocating labour to sectors with a higher level of productivity or by moving capital from low-yield to high-yield investments (e.g. from agriculture to industry, from traditional to modern sectors, or from rural to urban regions) (cf. Lewis 1954). The same is achieved when production shifts towards products with a higher output per unit of inputs.

The potential for compositional growth depends first of all on the diversity of an economy's structure. Flexible adaptation to changes in relative factor and commodity prices requires full knowledge of the market and a wide choice of production techniques. However, in early modern Europe the opportunities to re-allocate labour and capital were limited due to a lack of technological alternatives, a low degree of specialization, and the small size of high-productivity niches. Factor prices would have to undergo considerable relative shifts for an entrepreneur to change his methods of production and factor proportions (Herrick and Kindleberger 1983: 229). Minor fluctuations would merely affect profits. As a result the margins of entrepreneurial behaviour were narrow. In addition, compositional productivity growth is subject to diminishing returns, so that without some form of structural improvement its effects will die out. In reality the two types of growth almost never occur independently, while evidence from the nineteenth and twentieth centuries reveals that compositional shifts accounted for only a small proportion of productivity gains anyway.

Structural growth is determined at two levels of economic functioning. The proximate causes of growth constitute the basic level of process and product innovations. They involve new types of machinery, ideas on firm organization or marketing, demand for new goods and services, and other technological innovations in the widest sense. However, growth occurs within an institutional framework of economic laws, government policy, property rights, and collective arrangements. Where were the constraints to pre-industrial growth located?

The lack of sustained technological progress is sometimes blamed on the mentality of entrepreneurs or even on a difference in economic rationality. The behaviour of premodern producers is often described in terms of risk-aversion (as opposed to profit maximization), leisure preference, and conspicuous consumption (rather than productive investment) (Nussbaum 1968: 248–54; Kerblay 1975: 151). It is, however, unlikely that entrepreneurs acted according to a set of 'irrational' rules specific to the context of the pre-industrial economy. As Gustafsson (1987: 28) rightly points out: 'People who earn low incomes and live in a world of great insecurity have especially great incentives to act rationally!' Investment and innovation in a premodern economy simply involved far greater risks than in the twentieth century. Economic life was highly volatile, especially when agriculture was the dominant form of production. For example, in remote areas peasants were unlikely to change their ways, given that every harvest could mean the difference between life and death.[5] At low levels of income entrepreneurs were hesitant to risk their livelihood by introducing a radically new mode of production. They would have preferred to use the best available and most-appropriate proven technique.[6]

The creation of new technologies and ideas depends to a large extent on the protection of property rights. A dependable system of property rights guarantees inventors a rate of return that reflects the social rate of return and thus encourages further innovation. Without sufficient protection private rates of return will fall short, creating a disincentive to inventors. North (as quoted in Jones 1998: 82) considers the inadequate protection of property rights the main reason for the slow rate of technological change in the pre-industrial era. The rate of progress accelerated from the late eighteenth century on, when substantial legal improvements raised private returns, and became sustained when market forces began to dominate the process of invention (Jones 1998: 83).

Collective arrangements – such as guilds, common fields, or trading practices – could also impede technological innovation. Generally they emerged as a rational solution to the uncertainties of economic life, providing a measure of stability in a highly volatile economy.[7] Yet as European markets expanded and opportunities arose for the use of new techniques and organizations, such institutions became obstacles in the way of change. Their dissolution or adaptation was hampered by the belief that in a context of unrestrained competition, employment would be lost, prices would decline, and the quality of products would deteriorate (de Vries 1976: 41–2). A very real obstacle – at least in the short run – was that all those involved had an incentive to oppose changes that would not benefit the entire group.

The limits of entrepreneurial decision-making are dictated by the institutional framework of economic activity. In early modern Europe these limits were exceedingly narrow due to a high level of risk, the inadequate protection of property rights, and the rigidity of economic institutions. Ironically, a high level of institutional development does not necessarily imply rapid innovation. In a relatively advanced economy the resistance of vested interests to economic change raises the costs of the introduction of new technologies above those for a relatively backward economy without the same institutions.[8] This model has been applied to explain the lag in Dutch technological development after the Golden Age (de Vries 1981: 216–18; also Davids 1995). In addition, economic development is to a large degree path-dependent, which means that institutional and technological choices made in the past define, and hence restrict, the direction of change in the present. O'Brien (1996), for example, demonstrates how differences in the medieval regulation of land rights in Britain and France affected the course of industrialization in the two countries. Institutional rigidity – as embodied in the resistance of interest groups and in path-dependency – consequently creates obstacles to productivity growth because every economic improvement requires additional efforts to break down the barriers to change, which increases the costs of (or lowers the returns to) innovation.

Some constraints to premodern growth can be found in aggregate demand. Its absolute level is usually dismissed as an explanatory variable because there were always wealthy regions and well-to-do social groups to exert a varied demand for goods and services. An alternative interpretation of demand-led growth is that changes in tastes and preferences, or an increase in surplus income to be spent on industrial and other non-essential items, helped bring about the industrial revolution (de Vries 1994; Horrell 1996; Mokyr 1985a and 1988). However, the main shortcomings of preindustrial markets were first a high degree of income inequality and second persistent market imperfections.

With the exception of periods of rapid inflation such as the price revolution of the sixteenth century, nominal wage rates changed little, leaving the cost of living as the main determinant of the purchasing power of wage earners (de Vries 1976: 184–6). Given the steady level of wages, an increase in output per worker aggravated the inequality of the factor distribution of incomes. This inverse relation between growth and equality may have been a function of the relative scarcity of production factors. Capital and land were scarce commodities, whereas labour was in abundant supply. If production were simply intensified by increasing all inputs by an equal percentage, the remuneration of production factors would be biased towards capital and land. Since productivity gains were probably achieved through capital formation or a shift towards capital-intensive industries, such gains would have to result in a significant increase in the inequality of incomes.[9] Although high income inequality was not necessarily harmful to economic growth, excessive income differences could have severe economic effects. With a large part of the population on the brink of subsistence, opportunities for productive investments were restricted to urban markets and foreign trade where demand was sufficiently large. This undermined the possibilities for technological innovation and diverted capital into conspicuous consumption. The demand effects of premodern growth were thus biased disproportionately towards the production of luxury goods rather than the primary goods that accounted for the bulk of output. The inverse relationship between economic growth and income inequality that existed during the pre-industrial period consequently reinforced the demand constraints on productivity growth.

The second dimension of the pre-industrial demand constraint was the quality of market access. Physical obstacles to trade and transport were high. Infrastructural inadequacies created physical barriers between regional commodity markets and – to a lesser extent – factor markets.[10] The bulk of trade consisted of low-value, high-volume products, such as agricultural commodities, building materials and fuel, which incurred high transport costs relative to their value. Moreover, in order to cope with the difficulties of transport and communication, interregional trade relations were maintained by an intricate network of middlemen who added to the costs of distribution. As a result transaction costs were high, communications slow, and volumes of interregional trade comparatively small. There was no 'national' market, even though there always was some degree of trade, capital flow, and migration between regions (proto-industry is a good example). Instead, the pre-modern economy was characterized by large economic variations between small and relatively autonomous regional markets, whose coexistence may be seen as one of the principal features of the premodern economy (van Zanden 1993a: 1–8; also Lewis 1954).

Technological innovation and diffusion were severely hampered by market imperfections. Many process innovations required an increase in the scale of production to offset higher operating costs and repay initial investments, while the introduction of new types of product depended on the level and structure of demand.[11] In both cases the possibility and success of innovations was determined by the quality of market access. Yet this strikes at the very heart of the economic problems of early modern Europe. Transport and institutional barriers, and a lack of aggregate demand weakened the viability of innovations and discouraged entrepreneurs. In addition, owners of capital had little incentive to remove market imperfections by investing in infrastructural improvements.[12] These were low-yielding, high-risk projects with uncertain prospects for profitability. It is not unlikely that the average owner of capital preferred the easier course of putting his money into urban industries, international trade and transport, or agricultural activities in the vicinity of cities. The premodern constraints to growth – the regional concentration of growth opportunities in particular – may have crowded out precisely those investments that could have removed these constraints.

Premodern economic growth can be described as a self-constraining process at the level of the proximate as well as the ultimate causes of growth. Inadequate infrastructure and transport technology created an environment of small and ill-integrated markets at highly varying levels of development.[13] Within each market the opportunities to achieve economies of scale and the viability of technical and organizational innovations were limited by the level of aggregate demand and the quality of access to regional and international markets. The limited extent of the market encouraged the emergence or strengthening of institutions and regulations aimed at controlling (or limiting) competition and reducing overall economic risk, and may also have obstructed the development of an adequate system of property rights. Market imperfections thus acted as a disincentive to invest in innovations. The resulting inability to achieve a sustained increase in productivity imposed a demand constraint on the economy, mainly through the inverse relation between growth and equality. Large regional differences in development, the limited growth potential of individual markets, and the low yield and uncertain prospects of infrastructural investments discouraged entrepreneurs and capital owners from trying to remove market imperfections, especially when more profitable alternatives were available. The absence of sustained productivity growth was therefore inherent in the premodern economy.

4 The tools of growth before industrialization

The pre-industrial economy was unable to achieve a sustained increase in per capita income, but changes did occur and the evidence suggests mild progress in the long run. How then did productivity growth come about before the industrial era?

Population growth is generally seen as an additional burden for an economy apparently caught in a Malthusian trap. Technical change could provide temporary relief, but in the long run demographic growth would undermine itself. However, population growth can also be considered as a force for change. Boserup argues that an increase in population changes the ratio of human needs to natural resources: it raises the demand for goods and services and compels the economy to expand its productive capacity, which calls for a more intensive use of the factors of production. Unless vast tracts of cultivable land are available, an intensification of agricultural production requires a change in technology.[14] However, Boserup's theory focuses mainly on the production of food and it is unlikely that the effects of population growth will be able to outpace the diminishing returns to labour (Lal 1998: 179–81). Gunnar Persson has developed a general theory of the connection between population growth and technological change (read: productivity growth) in the early modern period. Persson maintains that new technologies will only be applied if there is sufficient demand: a change in production methods results from new opportunities provided by population growth rather than from straightforward demographic duress. An increase in population density (possibly accompanied by improvements in transport technology) leads to an expansion in the size of the market, which in turn encourages a division of labour and regional specialization. This then stimulates technical change, because at a higher level of aggregate demand the costs of training and equipment associated with new technologies can be offset. What is more, in Persson's (1988: 17) theory the technological effects of population growth involve an increase in productivity through a saving of inputs rather than the substitution of labour for land as is suggested by Boserup.

It follows that cities were the hot spots of growth in the pre-industrial world. The economies of scale inherent in the high density of population gave rise to an advanced division of labour, specialized production, and low transaction costs. Government, administrative services, financial and specialized distributive services, medical services, and other types of highly skilled labour were predominantly found in cities.[15] The relative success of the urban economy was rooted in the extent of its market. Urban density made for low transport costs and high aggregate demand; cities were generally centres of interregional and international trade; and the majority of people relied on wage labour and was thus compelled to purchase rather than produce the foodstuffs and industrial goods they consumed. Yet cities could not exist or grow on their own account. The relative size of the non-agrarian population depended on the productivity of local agriculture as well as on the possibility of long-distance trade.

The urban monopoly on long-distance trade provided opportunities for economies of scale and specialization beyond the limits imposed by the size of the city or the productivity of regional agriculture. The best recipe for growth was to gain control of a share in world trade by exploiting and enhancing the city's comparative advantages. These could be the specialized production or resource endowments of the hinterland (e.g. wine in France, grain in Poland), the control of international trade routes (the east–west trade of Venice or the Baltic grain trade of Amsterdam), or the conquest of colonies. The drawback of economic expansion based on international trade was that it made urban development highly dependent on the city's ability to maintain a competitive edge over other port cities. The long-term economic strength of a city was ultimately determined by its capacity to remain in control of its trade network and was therefore a military as much as an economic issue (Israel 1989).

So how did innovations spread to other cities and rural areas in the non-integrated economies of the premodern world? One explanation for the diffusion of techno-logical or institutional innovations without improvements in transport and communication is found in the theory of economic density. Ciccone and Hall (1996)[16] have recently examined the relationship between labour productivity and the density of economic activity in the United States, where density is defined as the amount of labour, human capital and physical capital per acre. They argue that an increase in economic density will favourably affect labour productivity because (1) any given technology has increasing returns to density with constant returns to scale and rising transport costs with distance, (2) inter-industry or inter-regional spillovers (or external economies) increase when production becomes physically closer, and (3) a higher degree of specialization in products and intermediate services is made possible. Even though inter-regional diffusion is not explicitly included in their models, an increase in density in one region will almost certainly have had beneficial effects on the surrounding regions as a result of technological spillovers and an increase in aggregate demand.

The best-known density effect of urban growth was that the demand of a large non-agricultural population and favourable terms of trade for arable and livestock products sparked off intensive and highly specialized agricultural production in the surrounding countryside. However, the beneficial effects of urban density diminished with rising distance. Their scope was further limited by market imperfections and institutional obstacles in the pre-industrial economy. In addition, given the promi-nent role of urban agglomerations and the short range of density effects, urban growth would probably have widened the gap between 'modern' and 'traditional' regions.

On the other hand, economic progress was not exclusively an urban issue. Possibly the most controversial element in the development of early modern Europe concerns the rise of proto-industry, which is considered by some as a precursor of the Industrial Revolution. Proto-industry appeared mainly in regions with high population density, low agricultural productivity and low wages (Mokyr 1976: chapter 4; van Zanden 1993a: 6–11, chapter 6; Hymer and Resnick 1969). Where urban demand was low and transport facilities were inadequate, peasants had no incentive to abandon self-sufficiency in favour of specialized market-oriented production. However, rising population pressure made it increasingly difficult for peasants to feed their family exclusively from their small plots of land, while at the same time they needed cash income to pay taxes, tithes and other dues. To supplement their income (and thus relieve the pressure of population growth) they turned to industrial activities (Gullickson 1983: 849–50). Even though population density was an instrumental variable, the emergence of proto-industry was not a matter of technological diffusion. It can best be described as urban–rural trade based on comparative advantage. Merchants supplied capital, linked the rural community to the world market, and provided peasants with a source of income above and beyond the productive capacity of local agriculture. The advantage of the proto-industrial region was that it could operate at very low wages.[17] Proto-industry was thus a solution to the problem of large-scale labour-intensive production in a premodern environment, and in particular to that of access to product and factor markets.

In the long run productivity gains were undoubtedly possible, but the outcome still was decidedly premodern. Growth was slow and intermittent. It was focused on regions with the most favourable market conditions, resulting in a wide variation in levels of development. Its gains were unevenly distributed. And it was based at least partly on the exploitation of the traditional sector by the modern sector. The impact of population growth and the scope of density effects were limited so long as the principal constraints to productivity growth remained in place. A fundamental breakthrough was required to change the way in which the economy operated.

5 Transition to modern economic growth

It is common practice to subdivide the economic development of Western Europe into large segments separated by relatively short periods of revolutionary change. Thus the last millennium has been divided into eras of feudalism, merchant capitalism, and the first and second industrial revolutions, whereas presently we seem to have entered a period of post-modern economic development. Yet when one considers that the basic functioning of (market) economies remained unchanged and that economic progress was possible in the premodern economy, is it still useful to make a sharp distinction between pre-industrial and industrial economies?

Differences in growth rates support the traditional historiographical periodization. Pre-industrial economies grew very slowly (0.1 or 0.2 per cent per annum), nineteenth-century growth accelerated to between 1 and 2 per cent, while the expansion of the industrialized world after 1945 reached unprecedented rates of annual growth (3 per cent or more). The essential difference was, however, related not to the incidence or duration of growth but to the nature and scope of the growth process. Modern economic growth is a comprehensive and self-reinforcing process in which one improvement triggers the other, whereas premodern growth was inter-mittent, regionally concentrated, and basically self-constraining. What caused the transition from one economic system to the other, and was it a radical or a gradual change?

Chaos theory supplies the first part of the answer. The premodern and modern economies can be seen as relatively stable, self-organizing systems. The transition came about when a set of events or developments broke through the self-constraining mechanism of the pre-industrial economy to create a situation of economic instability or chaos. Out of this chaos emerged the new equilibrium of self-reinforcing modern growth (Krugman 1996). Under these conditions the transition must inevitably have been radical.

The most gradualist interpretation would be that the pre-industrial economy slowly but steadily progressed until it reached critical mass and slid smoothly into a pattern of modern growth. The difficulty lies in defining the turning point: did the economy reach a certain level of density or did the scarcity of strategic resources (such as wood) trigger innovations based on substitutes (such as coal)? It is safe to state that gradual change alone cannot account for the dramatic difference in economic performance before and after industrialization. Accordingly, there would not have been an Industrial Revolution without radical innovations.

There is a great deal of evidence concerning dramatic changes, sudden exogenous shocks, and revolutionary improvements to support the radical interpretation. Berg and Hudson (1992: 26) demonstrate that there are plenty of examples of radical change during the Industrial Revolution in Britain. The best-known type of radical change is the introduction of strategic inventions with far-reaching effects on productivity growth, such as Newcomen's atmospheric steam engine in coal mining, large-scale manufacturing based on an efficient division of labour, and the rise of railway transport and steamshipping.[18] Such innovations could reduce the amount of inputs per unit of output, substituted an abundant resource (e.g. coal) for a scarce one (e.g. wood), or had inherent economies of scale, as with new transport technologies.

However, the transition from a pre-industrial to an industrial economy was not simply a matter of introducing new technologies and thus substituting stimuli for constraints. It occurred only when changes in the balance between constraints and stimuli at the level of the proximate causes of growth were supported by improvements in the ultimate causes of growth, such as the removal of market imperfections, political centralization, changes in government policy, and institutional reform. In practice the proximate and ultimate causes were intimately related. Technological innovations could themselves induce institutional change. Examples are the capital requirements of new techniques, the reorganization of labour markets to suit the demands of large-scale manufacturing, and the construction of new roads and waterways to improve the supply of raw materials and the delivery of finished products.

The principal event in the environment of the ultimate causes was the impact of the Napoleonic Wars on the political and institutional landscape of Europe. Napoleon's drive for domination wiped out feudal structures in large parts of Europe, changed the course of state formation (e.g. in Belgium and the Netherlands), and laid the foundation for the institutional framework of industrialization. The British economy seems to have been the obvious exception: its industrialization began at the end of the eighteenth century and the country was not occupied by the French. On the other hand, Britain was actively involved in the wars, which had a considerable impact on industrial production, labour supply, public finance, and international trade. For example, the Napoleonic Wars upset relations in the world market at the expense of some of Britain's main competitors, such as Holland, Belgium and France. But a number of fundamental processes began earlier in Britain than on the Continent, such as political centralization and infrastructural improvement, for example the turnpikes and canal boom of the late eighteenth century. Both in Britain and in the rest of Europe radical innovations occurred simultaneously with the expansion and integration of national and international markets and, on the Continent, with the transformation of political and economic institutions.

The radical nature of the transition notwithstanding, it is self-evident that modern economic growth did not appear out of the blue. The roots of industrialization have been uncovered in preceding centuries, as far back as the late middle ages.[19] As we saw earlier, the pre-industrial economy was anything but static, even if progress was slow. Radical changes may ultimately have been instrumental in bringing about the Industrial Revolution, but their effect on aggregate economic development was less than dramatic. Macro-inventions, technological and otherwise, occurred at random, but the process of invention was also guided by the scarcity of key resources and the rise of new growth opportunities, which made it an integral part of the growth process. The improvement and spread of new techniques and production methods is never an automatic or unconstrained process. They have to be economically viable, while it takes time and money to transmit knowledge, to convince entrepreneurs of the potential benefits of an invention, and to assimilate new techniques and organizations.[20] The innovations and political–institutional changes that would dramatically change the world may appear to have been radical, but their incorporation into the economy as well as the adaptation of economic life to such changes was a slow process.[21]

Remarkably, all the European industrial revolutions in some form or another occurred between roughly 1780 and 1913. Given the considerable international differences in resource endowments and population density, the transition cannot be explained at the level of individual economies. The diffusion of technological, organizational and institutional knowledge was a crucial part of the process. Britain could act as the testing ground for new methods of production by virtue of its excellent infrastructure, stable and centralized government, sound economic institutions, and vast colonial empire. Once improved and, above all, tested, new techniques and forms of organization spread to other countries on the European Continent. More important than mere diffusion was the fact that, rather than to provide a single economy with a comparative advantage, the innovations of the late eighteenth and early nineteenth centuries opened up the world market and, hence, provided all countries with new opportunities to innovate and expand production. Modern economic growth ended the regional concentration of growth and went beyond industrial and national boundaries.

6 Conclusion

Gains in economic efficiency have been made throughout human history. Yet the ability to sustain an increase in both population and per capita income is unique to the industrial era. The nature of growth before and after industrialization is therefore essentially different. On the other hand, it was also argued here that the underlying principles of growth remained unchanged. The economy is a self-organizing system. At a basic level growth or stagnation is determined by the constant and self-reinforcing struggle between forces that obstruct or encourage technological progress (the proximate causes of growth). Yet the balance between constraints and stimuli depends on the institutional environment, most notably the system of property rights and the size and efficiency of the market (the ultimate causes of growth). In the pre-industrial economy constraints prevailed and growth rates were minimal, whereas the modern industrial period was one of sustained productivity growth fuelled by continuous technological and institutional innovation.

The transition to modern economic growth involved revolutionary changes in the political and institutional framework as well as the introduction of ground-breaking technologies. While its deep historical roots and the slow accommodation to new technologies and institutions cannot be denied, the transition was ultimately a fairly radical event. In the long run the nature of growth became fundamentally different. Two elements were of particular importance. The integration of domestic and international markets ended the regional concentration of growth and facilitated the diffusion of innovations. And as growth accelerated new scarcities arose: capital became more easily available, whereas labour – skilled labour in particular – became relatively scarce. The result was a decrease in income inequality and mounting pressure for the introduction of labour-saving technologies.

The distinction between premodern and modern growth was not as extreme as the analysis suggests. The term 'premodern growth' has been used to describe thousands and thousands of years of economic development in all parts of the world, whereas modern economic growth was successfully established only in a limited region of the world economy, the so-called 'western' industrialized nations (including however countries such as Australia and Japan). Here sustained growth has led to high levels of general well-being, a more equal distribution of incomes and wealth, political stability and democracy, liberty, easy access to medical care and education, and so on. Yet, even today there still is a division between 'modern' and 'traditional' centres of production, both between the western world and the developing nations and within the developing economies themselves.[22] The main difference with the pre-industrial era, however, is that in the late twentieth century the world market has achieved a remarkable degree of integration. While allowing the developing nations to import advanced production methods at comparatively low cost, it has also opened up their markets to western competition at unfavourable terms of trade. The success of the West has crowded out the growth opportunities of the rest.[23]

Will modern economic growth come to an end? By emphasizing its sustained nature the definition suggests that modern growth is everlasting. Even so, there is no reason to assume that the self-reinforcing mechanism of modern economic growth cannot break down. First there is increasing concern over rising tensions between resources and population growth, connected with environmental damage, the depletion of natural resources, and increasing demands for a sustainable future. The optimistic view is that the new scarcities will trigger technological progress much like those at the end of the eighteenth century. However with a few exceptions these 'technologies' have no market price, so that there is no immediate economic necessity to develop clean technology, conserve resources, or improve well-being (Smits 1995). Sustained growth creates its own rigidities in that entrepreneurs and even government are unwilling to sacrifice their private returns for the greater good. An equally serious threat is the unbalanced distribution of population growth. The demographic development of the western industrialized world is very much under control, but many Third-World states combine low levels of development with extremely rapid population growth. If modern growth is to be sustainable, economic development will have to be re-defined to take into account its potential environmental limits as well as the worldwide distribution of income and wealth.

Notes

1 The work of Crafts (1985) in particular. Others focus on specific issues – such as female labour or industrial technology – to demonstrate that the industrial revolution was indeed a radical transformation of economy and society (cf. Berg and Hudson 1992).

2 An increase in the pressure on land also led to higher rents, while diminishing returns to labour lowered real wages. Population growth thus resulted in greater inequality in the distribution of factor incomes (Schumpeter 1954).

3 It can be argued that path-dependency derives from the scientific, economic, institutional memory of society, although in technological terms it would be embodied in the existing capital stock.

4 For example, between 1700 and 1830 real per capita income increased at an average annual rate of 0.0 per cent in Holland, 0.1 per cent in Belgium, and 0.3 per cent in Britain. See van Zanden, in this volume; Crafts (1985: 45); Blomme, Buyst and Van der Wee (1994: 91).

5 In McCloskey's (1991: 343) words, 'Peasants were not perhaps rational in every detail; but they were prudent'. The same circumstances that obstructed growth may have enhanced the role of non-economic considerations in economic life, such as religious and cultural practices. It is not inconceivable that such non-economic factors ultimately became a force of their own as a result of the persistence of economic limitations (cf. Lal 1998).

6 The technologies and forms of organization may simply have been inappropriate. In the process of their development, innovations are adjusted to the specific factor proportions as well as social and institutional arrangements of their environment. For example, the urban economy made possible the division of labour and the application of labour-saving, capital-intensive techniques, whereas regions with a large reservoir of cheap and unskilled labour had every reason not to mechanize.

7 Boserup (1965: 81–6). For a theory on the formation of groups in the premodern economy see Olson (1965: 2–16). Persson (1988: 35–41) links the pre-industrial institutional organization of production to the extent of the market. Premodern entrepreneurs could exert noticeable influence on their market: they had to enter into face-to-face negotiations in order to establish the price of goods and services. Institutions limited the power of individuals in order to contain transaction costs and gain some measure of certainty in the outcome of the market process.

8 The theory of the 'penalties of the pioneer': Ames and Rosenberg (1963). See also Gerschenkron's (1962) model of relative economic backwardness.

9 This corresponds more or less to the classical model of income distribution. Cf. Lewis (1954); van Zanden (1993a).

10 Pounds (1985: 427). For migration see Lucassen (1987) and Canny (1994).

11 More precisely, on the income elasticities of the new products.

12 The infrastructural development of the Netherlands provides an excellent example. See Horlings (1995: chapter 7), and Smits (1995: chapter 6).

13 With the exception of world trade, where integration and transport technology were highly developed.

14 In practice this boils down to an increase in the frequency of cropping or a reduction of fallow (Boserup 1965: 12–16, 23–7), but organizational and institutional changes are often included as well.

15 De Vries (1984a); Boserup (1981: 102). It should be noted that this was sometimes not so much a matter of economic opportunity as it was a prerequisite to preserving the quality of urban life (Kuznets 1966: 271–4).

16 Their model is in fact a macroeconomic version of Marshall's work on the economics of agglomeration at the firm level (Ciccone and Hall 1996: 55).

17 Van Zanden (1993a: 8), states emphatically that 'in merchant capitalism, the remuneration of labour power is less than the reproduction costs of labour', particularly because merchant capitalists were able 'to pass along a part of the reproduction costs of labour to the pre-capitalist modes of production'.

18 The classic work on the role of technology in the industrial revolution is still Landes (1969). The importance of improvements in transport to the U.S. economy is demonstrated in Szostak (1991: 289–302). The relationship between economic development and the state of the infrastructure in Britain is discussed in Dyos and Aldcroft (1969: chapters 1–3). See also Deane (1969: 83). The effect of railways on the productivity of French agriculture is examined by Price (1975 and 1983).

19 Cf. O'Brien (1996). The exceptional development of Britain can only be understood when examined in the very long run and with the emphasis on the gradual growth of institutions rather than the radical introduction of new techniques.

20 For a clear description of the problems that confront technological innovation, see Herrick and Kindleberger (1983: 233–8); Jones (1998).

21 For example, it took several decades for the political revolution of the Napoleonic Wars to come to fruition. In the nineteenth century the economic role of government was redefined, which involved an increasing amount of intervention. Political centralization and active intervention were ultimately instrumental in the removal of market imperfections and institutional obstacles. See for example, for the Netherlands: Smits (1995); Horlings (1995); van der Voort (1994). For Belgium: van der Herten (forthcoming). For Prussia and the United States: Dunlavy (1994).

22 This is why Kuznets (1966) paid separate attention to the developing countries in his original work on modern economic growth.

23 On the other hand, the Asian 'tigers' prove that the situation of the developing nations is not altogether hopeless.

Part II
Capital and labour

6 International capital markets and their users, 1450–1750

Ian Blanchard

For successive generations of historians, medieval feudalism has been perceived as a regressive system that created a stable-state, low-productivity economic system, which was transformed only in the sixteenth century by an emergent capitalism. They regarded the regressive nature of the feudal economy as arising from the activities of the dominant landlord class who squandered the surplus they extracted from the bulk of the population, resulting in a lack of investment funds so that the latter could not transform their pitiful existence (Aston and Philpin 1985: chapters 1, 6–7, 10). Only in the sixteenth century, during the Age of Discoveries, was a new world economic system regarded as being created. The evolution of commercial capitalism in western Europe allowed the merchants of that region during the years 1500–1700 to exploit the rest of the world and establish the beginnings of European economic supremacy. This was realized finally in the industrial capitalism of the period from 1700 to the present day (Wallerstein 1974 and 1979). In this chapter it will be my task, therefore, to undertake an investigation into the nature of this capitalist system and to examine the mechanisms that caused major silver (and gold) booms to be translated, through the operations of financial–monetary markets, into fundamental changes in the 'real' economy.

1 The integration of money markets in late medieval Europe

During the later middle ages, European capital markets underwent a major transformation. As population numbers declined from a peak at the end of the thirteenth century, prices fell, per capita incomes increased and real savings levels were enhanced. Base interest rates, measured in terms of the price of land or rather in terms of the price of a perpetual fixed rent charge secured on land, accordingly fell.[1] During the course of the thirteenth-century, western European base rates had fluctuated about a high-level equilibrium of about 10 per cent per annum.[2] Then from *c.* 1300 they steadily declined until almost a quarter of a millennium later in *c.* 1525, they finally settled at a new low level of between 4 and 5 per cent (figure 6.1). As the early modern era dawned, an enriched populace was prepared to lend, on first-class security, at previously unheard-of rates.

Even as rates tumbled, the market also underwent a major structural transformation. As in the high middle ages, money remained cheapest in England and in

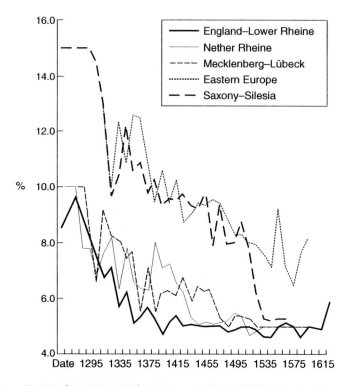

Figure 6.1 Northern European base interest rates, 1265–1635

the lands of the Lower Rhine.[3] Here borrowers, with prime security, who had been able to take up funds in the thirteenth century at 10 per cent, were able to borrow during the later middle ages (*c.* 1400–1525) at between 4 and 5 per cent (Epstein, in this volume). During the fifteenth century, however, this market underwent a process of extension. From *c.* 1460 both south German and upper Rhenish capital markets became integrated with those of England and the lower Rhine and before the century was out even the volatile markets of Basle and its territories were brought within a unitary central-European structure. Nor were the denizens of this market alone in enjoying the benefits of cheap money in the fifteenth century for at this time in the north German lands, extending from Bremen to Lübeck–Mecklenberg, interest rates also converged on those of central Europe. Thus in northern Germany and many lands west of the Erzgebirge, during the later middle ages, money became progressively cheaper. A steadily widening population of potential borrowers and lenders were drawn, moreover, into a unitary market structure wherein by 1500 loans could be arranged, on the production of iron-clad security, at a standard 4–5 per cent rate. In the lands east of the Erzgebirge, the situation was very different. Here in the later middle ages capital markets remained largely un-integrated and although base interest rates declined the pace was in comparison with western Europe a slow one, causing east–west rate differentials to widen.

In each case where integration was achieved, cheap money, in financial centres on the periphery of the pre-existing market network – Frankfurt, Basle and Lübeck respectively – disseminated through trade credit systems, helped effect a major transformation of neighbouring agrarian regimes. The resultant rising incomes and savings levels caused base interest rates to fall in rural areas and led to a secondary transformation in urban capital markets therein, allowing their integration into the primary financial network.

During the high middle ages England and the lands of the lower Rhine had thus formed an oasis of relatively cheap money in a European market where base interest rates of about 10 per cent annually were normal. Two centuries later the market situation had been transformed. Inhabitants of England and the lower Rhine still enjoyed the cheapest money in Europe but now these lands formed only one element in a unitary market structure encompassing much of western Europe where a single rate of 4–5 per cent reigned supreme. Within this unitary market money was cheap and not least amongst those who availed themselves of the new situation were members of the international merchant community. During the later middle ages, as international trade declined (Lopez, Miskimin 1962; Cipolla 1964), they had experienced an increase in the cost of commercial credit and had responded, in England at least, by creating a new financial system to tap alternative sources of funds. There during these years alternative borrowers, such as English agriculturalists, had possessed few ways of improving production and the returns on any money invested in this sector had been small. The interest they could offer on mortgages for agricultural improvement, accordingly, was also low (1.5–3 per cent per annum) and few if any amongst an enriched population had been tempted to put out money on such instruments when they could make a totally safe return of 4–5 per cent.[4] In such circumstances, merchants, able to offer returns above base rate, found few competitors bidding for money in the market place. Funds accordingly flowed from the agricultural to non-agricultural sectors of the economy, providing the basis for an elaborate sales credit system, which was the main source of English commercial finance.[5] The international merchants' financial systems had undergone a process of 'rustication', causing merchants and traders to make only marginal use of exchange facilities.[6] Bill markets in the great commercial metropoli of western Europe were accordingly characterized by a certain thinness, as low and intermittent activity occasioned marked fluctuations about a high median rate.

2 The impact of central European silver

Nor did this situation fundamentally alter during the subsequent half century (*c.* 1525–75). As recurrent population growth resulted in an immiseration of the population and inflationary pressures undermined the value of savings, however, base interest rates edged upwards and sales credit terms shortened. Cash flow problems were precipitated amongst provincial merchants, causing those who had access to metropolitan capital markets to be tipped over on to the exchanges. The balance between exchange and sales credit systems altered in favour of the former but the basic pattern of capital flows from the agricultural sector remained.

That the increased calls upon the facilities of metropolitan exchange markets did not force up interest rates and precipitate crisis conditions therein, however, resulted from equally fundamental changes in exchange dealings, whose origins can be traced back more than half a century. From 1460, a new market structure had been super-imposed upon the old as the great central European silver mining boom ran its course.

Most spectacular in this respect were the effects on regional capital markets of successive booms in 1460–1486/91 and 1516/22–1542/7 in the important Saxon–Silesian mining complex. These resulted in local interest rates falling from the high levels of eastern Europe to the much lower ones prevailing on the central European capital market. Similar downswings in interest rates also occurred within that central European market, although initially at least the impact of successive mining booms was highly localized. The first great Saxon mining boom (1460–86) thus produced extra-regional effects only on the Frankfurt–Cologne money markets. Similarly, the second sub-cycle, which was played out from 1476–92 in the Tirol against a back-ground of Saxon decline, resulted in a decline in interest rates only on the capital markets of the upper Rhine region. During the first production cycle (1460–92) of the central European mining boom, successive sub-cycles thus wrought their impact solely on a local basis. During the second cycle (1492–1526), however, the production elements of a new Tirolean–Thüringian–Slovak mining complex became much more highly integrated. The effects of the resultant boom were accordingly diffused much more widely on the capital markets of central Europe and beyond (van der Wee 1963, Volume 1: 527). Particularly from *c.* 1505/15–1526 money markets throughout western Europe felt the beneficial effects of the silver boom, with interest rates falling to a new all-time low. A new structure had been imposed upon west-central European capital markets. In the east rates continued along that path first established in the late middle ages. In the west the market split into a bipartite structure, for the time being high rates on the markets of the Saxon–Silesian region contrasting with the incredibly low rates prevailing throughout a unitary system centred on the new Tirolean–Thüringian–Slovak mining complex. Nor during the third production cycle of 1516/22–1542/7 was this structure disturbed, although the inter-regional balance of rates therein was reversed. As the Saxon–Silesian complex once more came to the fore at this time, whilst silver production in the Tirolean–Thüringian–Slovak mining complex entered on a path of decline to 1538/42, base interest rates in the former region again fell whilst those in the latter region rose. As central European silver production thus expanded to a peak from *c.* 1505/15–1540, a new bipartite structure had been imposed upon west-central European capital markets. These were characterized by an alternating inter-sectoral movement of rate: first (1505/15–1525) a unitary western European market experienced the benefits of cheap money, then (1527–1538/42) rates therein rose and it was the markets of the Saxon–Silesian region which benefited from readily available and cheap funding.

Because of these changes the financial and commercial systems utilized by the international merchant community were transformed. The great mining boom since its inception had attracted investment funding from the south German merchant banking houses.[7] As the returns from these investments were realized these houses were able, with their new found wealth, to fund with increasing ease the ever growing fixed and variable requirements of their industrial enterprises; underwrite the burgeoning volume of their exchange dealings; finance their growing involvement in international trade; and even satisfy the voracious appetite of the Habsburgs for loans. In relation to the funding of commercial activity the silver obtained from the mines, having been turned into coins at local mints (see for example Schüttenhelm 1984), was available for exchange operations on local money markets. This either allowed merchants in distant centres to take up funds for commercial activity secure in the knowledge that their bills on these markets would be met when they fell due, or made abundant funding available to those proffering bills to finance their trade. In such circumstances money markets where commercial credit could be funded at relatively low interest rates drew trade towards them and effected a realignment of commercial activity in accord with the alternating pattern of central European mining activity.

During the years of the first great mining boom, 1460–86, because of the weak level of activity in the Tirolean–Thüringian–Slovak mining complex, old and new commercial–financial systems co-existed in the west-central European market region. At Bruges and London international trade continued to be financed on the basis of rural sales credits and merchants very occasionally resorted to exchange markets where Italian houses could offer only high-priced commercial credit on the basis of retained trading profits. Further east however, the situation was very different. Here, under the influence of the contemporary mining boom, a new commercial–financial system was forming (figure 6.2).

At this time, it assumed a simple tri-nodal form, linking Cologne–Aachen in the north with Vienna in the east and Venice in the south. Merchants, moreover, were not slow to take advantage of the new situation. Utilizing cheap commercial credits they propagated an active trade involving the exchange of north-western European textiles (predominantly Cologne–Aachen cloths and South German barchants and fustians) for south-eastern European agrarian produce and Italian wares (Amman 1954 and 1953). Nor did this system undergo major structural changes during the second (1492–1526) production-cycle of the Tirolean–Thüringian–Slovak mining complex. In Bruges and London the old ways continued, although particularly during the years 1505/15–1526 the balance of activity within the west-central European region began to shift from these centres towards the new central-European system. Rapidly increasing silver production, within a commercial network where financial and mining operations were becoming more integrated, brought the benefits of cheap money to the existing system of exchanges. In the context of the 1486–92 Netherlands monetary reforms, moreover, there was an extension of that system to incorporate the emergent centre of Antwerp. During this period therefore Antwerp became the western terminus of a major commercial system. Within this system a trade in Anglo–Netherlands textiles now expanded on the ruins of the old Rhenish industry (Dietz 1910–25, Volume 2: 266–7): the merchants of Cologne and Frankfurt carried these wares to South Germany and the Alpenlands through Augsburg, and to the lands of the Hungarian crown through Vienna. Along the way they shared passage with those merchants who traded with Italy, merchants who at Augsburg took passage via the Brenner and occasionally the Rescheneideck Passes to Verona and

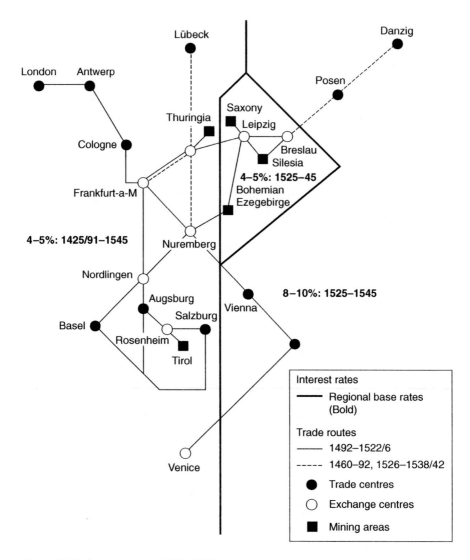

Figure 6.2 Exchange systems, 1460–1545

Venice (Brulez 1962; Pohl 1971: 477–82). North-western European textiles thus continued to be exchanged for south-eastern European agrarian produce and Italian wares, but now these textiles emanated from the Anglo–Netherlands production complex and, as in response to increasing silver production interest rates on commercial paper fell, trade expanded. Within this new west-central European system the fortunes of the merchant-financier was linked, however, to those of the mining entrepreneurs of the Tirolean–Thüringian–Slovak production complex. Each phase of increasing silver production occasioned a fall in interest rates and enhanced commercial activity. Each decline brought about a stabilization in interest rates and commercial stagnation. On these latter occasions, moreover, in the context of the alternating pattern of mining activity, the focus of commercial-financial activity was displaced elsewhere. Thus during the years 1460–1486/91 and 1527/8–1542, as the Saxon–Silesian complex came to dominate central European mining operations, an alternative commercial–financial system, centred on Leipzig (Fischer 1929) and Breslau came to the fore. Merchants at Nördlingen–Nuremberg, who in the period 1492–1526 were active in the trade via Frankfurt to Cologne and Antwerp, during the years 1460–1486/91 and 1527/8–1542 increasingly drew bills on Leipzig or Breslau to finance their trade to the north or east. Along new routes they transported domestic weaponry, metal wares and exotic luxury goods from Italy and the Levant to Lübeck–Hamburg or Posen–Danzig, and returned not only with Baltic wares but also with western textiles trans-shipped through the former centres and destined for either domestic consumption or re-export south.[8]

During the years 1460–1560, therefore, as central European silver output increased during the upswing of the industrial long cycle, western European capital markets were subject to a process of change as a new market structure was super-imposed upon the old. Interest rates oscillated around the prevailing 5 per cent norm in response to production fluctuations in the mining industry. Because of market imperfections however, the timing and incidence of these changes in interest rates varied widely between finance markets, which during the years 1460–1540 continued to be dominated by local specie supplies from an industry characterized by its own developmental pattern. Even as the industrial long-cycle ran its course there was superimposed upon it a pattern of medium-term, resource-related cycles which followed each other at about 30-year intervals and displayed a pattern of spatial displacement of an inter-sectoral character. In the central-European industry, this assumed an alternating form. During the first (1460–1491) and third (1516/22–1542/7) production cycles the mines of the Erzgebirge rose to a position of supremacy. During the second (1492–1522/6), they were displaced by those of the Tirolean–Thüringian–Slovak production complex. Each displacement brought the benefits of cheap money to local finance markets. The Saxon–Silesian mining booms of 1460–1491 and 1516/22–1542/7 transformed conditions on the Leipzig market, whilst Antwerp, as an extension of the Rhenish–Tirolean mining and commercial system, enjoyed the benefits of cheap money predominantly in 1492–1522/6. In each instance merchants responded to the new situation by reorienting trade to avail them-selves of the benefits of cheap money. Whether western European merchants accessed the new systems via Hamburg–Lübeck (in 1460–91 and 1526/7–1542) or Antwerp and the Brabant Fairs (in 1492–1522/6), the availability of cheap money ensured that their trade expanded rapidly to 1540.

A new age had dawned in the provision of commercial credits. The focus of activity had shifted from the Rialto to the marts of central Europe, where abundant supplies of silver from the mines provided the basis for cheap bill finance and an increase in commercial activity. The effectiveness of the new system was revealed when (in 1485–91, 1514 and 1527/8) markets were disrupted and merchants, who were forced back onto older credit systems, were confronted with a 2–3 per cent increase in the cost of bill finance.[9] At these times trade declined. Yet these circumstances were ephemeral in character, interrupting but not stopping the trade boom which, on the basis of cheap credits, continued to 1540.

3 American silver and the European financial markets

From about 1540 however, this whole system began to disintegrate as the focus of international silver production shifted to the Americas and Seville. The central-European market was now eclipsed and began to fragment into atomistic units as there was a return to pre-1505 conditions. Thus during the fourth production cycle (1537/42–1568), which marked the beginning of the downturn of the prevailing central-European production long cycle, the impact of regional mining booms once again became highly localized. Increased Thüringian silver production resulted in falling interest rates on the money markets of the lower Rhine region but not on those of the upper Rhine, where falling Tirolean output caused rates to rise. Rates on both markets, moreover, diverged from those of the Silesian–Saxon mining region. During this production cycle and the next (1565/8–1598), which saw the central-European mining industry move further down the secular path of decline, successive mining booms again wrought their effects on capital markets in an essentially local fashion.

As the focus of international silver production shifted to the Americas, there was yet another displacement of activity; Seville and the fairs of Medina del Campo became the focus of a new financial network in western Europe. Already in the 1530s the foundations of this new system were being laid as the arrival of increasing quantities of gold at the Guadalquivir effected a transformation of conditions at the fairs of Medina del Campo (figure 6.3). Interest rates on both public and private loans fell, reducing the cost of exchange transactions between Spain, Italy (particularly Florence and Genoa) and France (Lyons). Nor was the impact of American specie confined to this primary network, for through the involvement of German houses, such as the Fugger and Welser, Antwerp was drawn into the new system and with it London and Augsburg.[10] Once again, therefore, the focus of commercial credit systems had shifted. Having re-located from Italy to central Europe it now settled in Spain, where the exchange moved to a new tempo conditioned by news of the arrival of the Indies fleet.

From its inception, however, the new system was subject to major changes, which initially altered its structure and ultimately wrought its demise. Even as the Spanish–Netherlands exchanges began to move in response to the new forces that were transforming activity at Medina del Campo, continuing Habsburg intervention on the Antwerp bourse crippled that city's money market. It also resulted in a displacement of activity elsewhere, bringing new life to markets such as London and setting in motion forces that would bring the Piacenza Fairs to the fore in financing transcontinental trade (de Silva 1969).

Yet the effects of the American silver boom were not confined to a geographical restructuring of European capital markets. As increasing supplies of the precious metal were transported to Spain, local money markets were flooded, interest rates fell

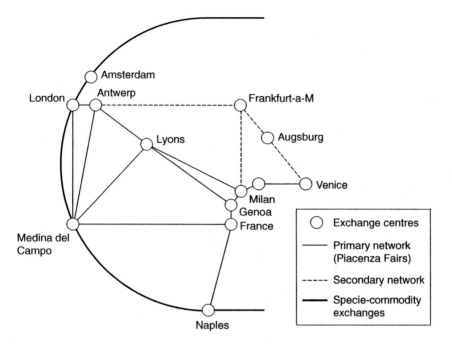

Figure 6.3 Exchange systems, 1540–1740

below the specie export point and supplies of the metal were transhipped elsewhere. A constant, if illicit, stream of specie flowed to Genoa and Italy, Lyons and France.[11] A new age was dawning and henceforth for some two centuries from *c.* 1540, a new trend was superimposed upon the existing pattern of interest rates. From that time lenders attempted to protect their assets by increasing rates in line with regional price increases, and merchants attempting to raise finance for their businesses found a new competitor in the specie exporter, who had to be outbid to secure the money they needed. All over Europe those with money to lend were forced to adjust to a very different market situation.[12] Yet, at least initially from *c.* 1545–75, in most instances they seem to have responded in the same way; interest rates rose in line with prices and enhanced arbitrage margins, 'monetary' rather than 'real' factors exerting a dominant influence on their decision making. Finance costs, including those for commercial credit, rose and from 1550–75 trade declined, ushering in a crisis which marked the end of one age and the beginning of another when Amsterdam and London would reign supreme.

4 The expansion of credit

From 1575, for reasons which are as yet unclear, specie distribution systems began to disintegrate and distinctly different patterns of inflation began to emerge throughout

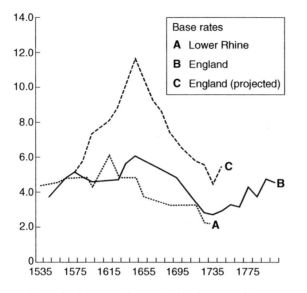

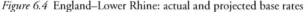

Figure 6.4 England–Lower Rhine: actual and projected base rates

Key: A–B = 'real' interest rates. 'Nominal' base rates deflated by changes in the general price level. C = inflationary adjustment index applied to constant base rate

Europe (Braudel and Spooner 1967). Thus in England and the lands of the Lower Rhine prices, which had risen from 1545–75, continued to increase steadily to *c.* 1640 before falling slowly thereafter. In France, Italy and Iberia the price rise ended much earlier in the 1590s. In each case, however, prices continued to rise after 1575 before there was a downturn at some time between 1595–1645. Such was not the case in southern Germany and the lands of the eastern Europe. Here prices and interest rates fell from 1575 to 1610/20 (Hildebrandt 1992: 58–66, 74) before recovering and passing to a new high in the period 1640–60.

Only in England and the lands of the Lower Rhine was the situation again seemingly different. Here as elsewhere during the years from *c.* 1545–75 prices and base interest rates had risen but thereafter, as prices continued to increase, interest rates actually fell and then stabilized around a 5 per cent norm until about 1645 (figure 6.4). An increasingly rich population with enhanced savings was allowing 'real' interest rates to equilibrate to a new low level. Then from 1645–95 as prices fell, in England 'real' interest rates began to rise, bringing this first phase in the restructuring of its capital market to a close. This, however, was merely an interlude in the long-term evolution of that market, for as the eighteenth century opened a second phase in its development began. Once again, from 1695–1745 'real' interest rates on the English market fell heavily before the pace of decline first slackened and then in *c.* 1800 once more began to increase.

Whilst during the years 1550–1750 'real' interest rates stabilized throughout most of Europe, therefore, in England and the Lower Rhine lands these years witnessed an alternating pattern and secular decline in base interest rates. Initially a slow and then from 1575 a rapid rise in income and saving levels meant that investors were willing to accept a steadily diminishing rate of return on first-class securities. Such changes before the eighteenth century were measured in England in terms of the price of land or rather in terms of the price of a perpetual fixed rent charge secured on land and thereafter in terms of the yield on consuls. From a level of 4 per cent in 1545 'nominal' rates had risen, as a hedge against inflation, to 5.3 per cent (19 years purchase) in 1575 before stabilizing at just below 5 per cent by 1625. At no point however was the rate of increase comparable with that of the general price level, so that by the latter date the 'real' rate of return was less than half (45 per cent) of what it had been 80 years earlier. Subsequently the rate of decline slackened. Then in the years to 1695 'real' rates actually increased. But this was merely a passing interlude and as the eighteenth century opened rates once more tumbled, until in 1730 the 'real' rate of return on land or consuls was a mere third of what it had been two centuries earlier. With rising incomes and savings levels money for investment was becoming in the early modern period progressively cheaper and more available, making England and the lower Rhineland an oasis of cheap money in a European market where traditional 'real' rates continued to prevail.

Throughout most of Europe during the years 1540–1740, therefore, would-be borrowers operated within markets where, in 'real' terms, conditions remained remarkably stable. In England and the lands of the Lower Rhine however, such borrowers sought funds in quite different circumstances as domestic capital markets underwent major changes. The rate that any would-be borrower could offer depended on the efficiency with which he could use the capital. The greater the efficiency, the greater were the returns he could offer investors relative to other enterprises and the easier, accordingly, it became to attract the capital required. Whilst the English market thus looked increasingly attractive to would-be borrowers who either earlier or elsewhere found difficulty in raising funds, it was not only base lending rates which determined whether they would be successful in contracting a loan. Equally important were the activities of others who also required money and the amounts that they could bid for a loan.

Of paramount importance in this context were changes induced by technological change in the economy and in the period under consideration of greatest significance were the activities of agricultural borrowers on the English market.[13] During the years from *c.* 1500–60 English agriculturalists had possessed few ways of improving production and the returns on any money invested in that sector were small (1.5–3 per cent per annum). The interest that they could offer on mortgages for agricultural improvement was also low. In such circumstances funds flowed from the agricultural to the non-agricultural sectors of the economy. Subsequently from *c.* 1527–75, with the integration of the London market into the Seville–Medina del Campo financial network, the balance between exchange and sales-credit systems altered in favour of the former but the basic pattern of capital outflows from the agricultural sector remained.

The 1540s in England as on the Continent, however, witnessed a major transformation of the market as inflationary pressures induced lenders to enhance rates in

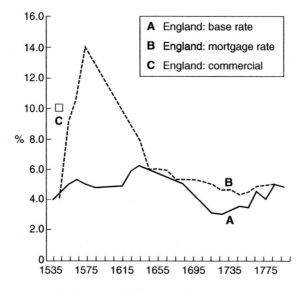

Figure 6.5 England: marginal efficiency of capital

line with contemporary price changes. But in England and the Netherlands, unlike in most of continental Europe, this trend was superimposed on another. Technological change in the English agrarian sector, following some twenty years after similar changes in the lands of the lower Rhine, set in motion a process which by enhancing incomes, from *c.* 1575 caused base interest rates, even in 'nominal' terms, to fall.[14] Agrarian change thus created conditions of cheap money in England and lower Rhineland. It also created a major investment demand for that money. From about 1575 the market situation was transformed as in England at least, farmers and landowners began to offer rates of *c.* 14 per cent on mortgages, reflecting the returns that could be obtained by the first innovators in the new agrarian regime. Such pioneers enjoyed the best of both old and new worlds. They made little contribution to total output, which continued to be dominated by traditional producers. The price level was thus unaffected. However, unit costs for the innovators were reduced markedly and profits accordingly increased, allowing them to offer high interest rates to investors for the capital they required. As more and more farmers, attracted by these profits, innovated, output expanded and prices fell until in the second half of the seventeenth century, with the achievement of total market domination, prices fell towards the new low-cost level and farmers could make only 'normal' profits. Each new producer entering the business thus pushed down prices, profits, the rate of return on capital invested and the rate of interest on mortgages (figure 6.5).

During the initial phase of agricultural innovation, (1560–1610) investment in English agriculture was thus highly profitable, as farmers were able to offer rates of 10–14 per cent to venturers of capital on mortgages for the purposes of agricultural improvement. Nor did this rate fall rapidly as sustained population growth to 1650 allowed the consumption of marginal output whilst acute inflationary pressures sustained 'nominal' prices above their 'real' level. Thus during the years 1560–1650 and particularly from 1560–1610 English agriculture attracted funds from all sectors in the economy. Merchants and manufacturers, whose products were overpriced on international markets and who were unable to compete with the specie exporter for funding,[15] could not make comparable returns in their own enterprises. They thus increasingly deployed their funds either directly or indirectly on the financing of estates for the purposes of agricultural improvement. Tudor and Stuart merchants might, as so often has been suggested, have had a desire to acquire landed status – but it was also a very profitable way of diversifying their investment portfolios. Indeed, the capital markets of England and the lands of the lower Rhine were incomparable in investment opportunities, attracting during the years 1590–1610 funding from central Europe.[16]

Yet the situation was both ephemeral and unstable. Many who had taken up funds in conditions of rising prices from *c.* 1610–40 subsequently, as prices fell, found their previous profit margins were illusionary and got into difficulties. Some, by the exercise of extreme economy, extricated themselves from this difficult situation (Hopkins 1992: 58–66). Others did not and the years 1640–95 witnessed many foreclosures on mortgages, turning merchants into reluctant landowners at a time when the decline in interest rates on mortgage bonds was once more encouraging a counter-flow of money to the non-agrarian sector. Indeed, with the decline in interest rates on mortgage bonds from *c.* 1640–95 and their assimilation with base rates from *c.* 1660, there was a wholesale search for new investment opportunities in the non-agrarian sector of the English economy and beyond (see Ward 1974). Investors, when unimpeded by legal restrictions, thus once more found industry an attractive outlet for their money (e.g. Blanchard 1985). The great mercantile companies attracted a flood of would-be subscribers to take up their shares and, in attempting to secure capital gains by limiting equity issues whilst expanding their business on the basis of bond finance, initiated a frenetic series of 'raids' aimed at opening up these companies to outsiders.[17] Other investors showed a willingness to roll-over short-term bill finance to provide long-term investments in the plantation economies of the New World and thus found another outlet for their funds (see Price 1980; Davies 1957: 316–25 and Davies 1952b). But investment opportunities were limited and as the marginal efficiency of capital fell there began a frenzied struggle to find new investments in a situation which was aggravated by Dutch investors seeking outlets in England – much to the ire of Englishmen seeking ways to place their money.[18] The basic problem was that at the end of the seventeenth century the English and Dutch capital markets were awash with money and investors were accordingly prepared to put out their money on the most speculative of ventures (see Macleod 1986, and Jones 1988 for the general context).

Nor did this situation change as that market underwent a basic restructuring during the early eighteenth century. Those proffering agricultural mortgages were again able at that time to offer a premium over base rate as a second phase of innovation transformed that sector (Overton and Campbell 1991). Yet such was the fall in base rates and the relatively low returns to the innovator that interest rates on mortgage bonds continued to fall from their late seventeenth century level. The amount of funding available for non-agrarian investment was increased again in a domestic market lacking investment outlets and in a situation where overseas investment opportunities were restricted by the continuing existence of bi-metallic premiums on exchange dealings. By the 1720s therefore conditions were again ripe for a new phase of acute speculative activity – the South Sea Bubble (Carswell 1960; Hoppit 1987: 132, 164 and 1986: 47–8). This however was merely a passing interlude in a market, which since the late seventeenth century was beginning to assume a new aspect, for as domestic opportunities failed to materialize investors began to look elsewhere. During the period 1670–1770 Anglo-Dutch merchants, working in co-operation with each other, now showed themselves quite willing to roll-over short-term bill finance to provide long-term investment in foreign agriculture and industry (Newman 1983). Initially observable in the Americas trades, with the removal of bi-metallic impediments to the operation of foreign exchange markets in the 1730s, such investments became characteristic of many branches of European commerce. Bill rates on such foreign bourses as St Petersburg increasingly moved to the rhythm of English base rates (Newman 1992). The second third of the eighteenth century thus saw England and the Netherlands become major capital exporters, alleviating shortages abroad and providing necessary funding for the expansion of foreign industrial and commercial enterprises. By the end of the eighteenth century, in countries such as Russia it had became an axiom of economic policy making that[19]

> the greatest part of our domestic industry was put into movement by the advances that the English make to us and which allow our peasants to be put to work. . . .

Even as Count Strogonov penned these lines, however, the age of which he wrote was passing.

For more than two hundred years, from *c.* 1570 to 1790, conditions prevailing on the London and lower Rhenish capital markets had influenced strongly international financial systems. Initially from 1570–1610/50, these markets had attracted funding from all over Europe to finance the process of economic growth within their respective domestic economies. Then from 1650/70–1790 as these domestic economies grew to maturity and the pace of innovation slackened the flow was reversed. A lack of investment opportunities at home henceforth caused investors to seek new outlets for their funds abroad. Initially slowly but then rapidly with the removal of impediments to the operations of the foreign exchanges in the 1730s, English and Dutch capital exports grew, providing much needed funding for the expansion of foreign industrial and commercial enterprises. During the years 1650/70–1790 a new pattern of Anglo–Netherlands overseas investment had been set but before it was fully realized in the period 1820–1870 the French wars, from 1792–1815, resulted in an interruption to the process. During these years from 1792–1815, the recipient economies themselves began to mature whilst English capital markets felt the baleful effects of government intervention. Signs began to appear that far from maintaining its position as a capital exporter, Britain was again becoming a capital importer, drawing finance during the years 1790–1820 from Russia, Holland and Prussia to fund commerce and industry which was starved of capital by the demands of a rapacious government (Brezis; Newman 1992: 135).

5 Conclusion

The late middle ages had witnessed a complete transformation of capital markets in the European lands to the west of the Erzgebirge. As population numbers declined from a peak at the end of the thirteenth century, prices fell, per capita incomes increased and real savings levels rose. Base interest rates, measured in terms of the price of land or rather in terms of the price of a perpetual fixed rent charge secured on land, accordingly fell from about 10 per cent per annum in *c.* 1300 to 4–5 per cent almost a quarter of a millennium later in *c.* 1525. As the early modern era dawned, an enriched populace was prepared to lend, on first-class security, at previously unheard of rates. Subsequently, from *c.* 1525 to 1635, population numbers again increased. Average per capita incomes across most of west-central Europe fell and real savings levels declined. 'Real' base interest rates, accordingly, initially stabilized then showed a tendency to rise.

From *c.* 1460 however, a new pattern was superimposed upon this stable series of base rates as successive central-European (1460–1560) and American (1530–1640) silver production booms ran their course. Henceforth at those points where the new quantities of specie accessed contemporary European credit systems, interest rates fluctuated about prevailing base rates in accord with changing precious-metal supply conditions. Increased specie supplies pushed down rates but the effect on the local market depended on investment opportunities therein. Thus in Spain during the years 1540–1640, increasing inflows of gold and silver created major inflationary pressures and base interest rates edged upwards. The failure to invest and increase productivity in the export industries, however, led to the emergence of an adverse balance of trade, a fall on the exchanges at Medino del Campo, and an outflow of specie. Recipients of this specie throughout most of Europe underwent a similar experience. Inflows of specie posed major problems for the denizens of those countries to which specie passed. As inflationary pressures pervaded these economies, those involved in the foreign-trade sector experienced an overpricing of their export wares, which threatened to undermine sales. Where they failed to take advantage of increasingly cheap finance to invest and enhance productivity in their industries, export sales diminished, leading to the emergence of an adverse balance of trade, a fall on the exchanges, and an outflow of the specie which had previously flowed in.

Only in England and the lands of the lower Rhine was the situation seemingly different. Here as elsewhere, major silver inflows occurred in the period 1525–35. Prices rose in both the Netherlands (1525–31) and England (1531–35) but in the latter at least, in 1532–35 this did not lead to an overpricing of export wares. Taking advantage of increasingly cheap finance to invest and enhance productivity in the export industries and in their raw material supply systems, export sales continued to boom. Silver stocks were thus retained and the nation experienced acute inflationary pressures (Blanchard, in press). 'Nominal' base interest rates rose as a hedge against this inflation, from a level of 4 per cent in 1535 to 5.3 per cent (19 years purchase) in 1575 before stabilizing at just below 5 per cent in 1625. At no point however was the rate of increase comparable with that of the general price level, so that by the latter date the 'real' rate of return was less than half (45 per cent) of what it had been 90 years earlier. Then in the years to 1695 'real' rates actually increased. But this was merely a passing interlude and as the eighteenth century opened rates once more tumbled until in 1730 the 'real' rate of return on land or consuls was a mere third of what it had been two centuries earlier.

Throughout most of Europe during the years 1540–1740, therefore, would-be borrowers operated in markets where, in 'real' terms, conditions remained remarkably stable. In England and the lands of the lower Rhine however, such borrowers sought funds in quite different circumstances as domestic capital markets underwent major changes. Here an increasingly rich population with abundant savings was willing to accept a steadily diminishing rate of return on first-class securities. The rate that any would-be borrower could offer, depended on the efficiency with which he could use the capital. The greater the efficiency, the greater were the returns he could offer investors relative to other enterprises, and the easier, accordingly, it became to attract the capital required. Whilst the English market thus looked increasingly attractive to would-be borrowers who either earlier or elsewhere found difficulty in raising funds, it was not just base lending rates which determined whether they would be successful in contracting a loan. Equally important were the activities of others who also required money and the amounts that they could bid for a loan.

For two hundred years, from *c.* 1570–1770, conditions prevailing on the London and lower Rhenish capital markets influenced strongly international financial systems. Initially from 1570–1610/50, with unparalleled investment opportunities, particularly in the English and Netherlands agricultural sectors, these markets had attracted funding from all over Europe to finance the process of economic growth in their respective domestic economies. Then from 1650/70–1770, as these domestic economies grew to maturity and the pace of innovation slackened, the flow was reversed. A lack of investment opportunities at home henceforth caused investors to seek new outlets for their funds abroad. Initially slowly and then rapidly with the removal of impediments to the operations of the foreign exchanges in the 1730s, English and Dutch capital exports grew. From 1670–1770 Anglo-Dutch merchants, working in co-operation with each other, now showed themselves quite willing to roll-over short-term bill finance to provide long-term investment in foreign agriculture and industry. Initially observable in the Americas trade, with the removal of bi-metallic impediments to the operation of foreign exchange markets in the 1730s such investments became characteristic of many branches of European commerce. Bill rates on such foreign bourses as St Petersburg or Trieste increasingly moved to the rhythm of English base rates (Newman 1992; Blanchard 1998). The second third of the eighteenth century thus saw England and the Netherlands become major capital exporters, alleviating shortages abroad and providing necessary funding for the expansion of foreign industrial and commercial enterprises.

Notes

1 Base interest rate statistics presented in figures 6.1, 6.4 and 6.5 have been derived from Neumann (1865: 266–73); Habakkuk (1952); van Dillen (1964: 376); Ashton (1959: 187); Mitchell and Deane (1962: 455). The data utilized here make no pretension to either spatial or chronological comprehensiveness.

2 In east-central Europe, which at this time had not felt the full impact of the 'economic revolution' of the twelfth century, the rate was some 50 per cent higher; see Blanchard (1996: 12–14).

3 Henceforth used to describe the Netherlands, Cleves, Jülich-Berg, Speyer, Nassau, and the archbishoprics of Trier and Cologne.

4 Data concerning interest rates on English mortgage bonds discussed below is derived from Travers (1976).

5 See for example Malden (1900); Hanham (1975); Hanham 91985, particularly part II, 109–254). It should be noted that the terms of credit noted by Power (1933: 56–7) are somewhat abnormally generous due to the contemporary depression in the export trade. On an analogous situation relating to Flemish textile producers see von Brandt (1954).

6 Postan (1928) contains much that is relevant to a description of the London money market during the opening decades of the sixteenth century. The picture of the London market in this work has been confirmed and extended through a study of contemporary Anglo-Netherlands merchant account books for the period 1486–1527 undertaken in the context of the ESRC projects HR 8205 and B 0023002/1.

7 Although there is an enormous literature on the history of mining in this period, comprehensive data about investments is not available as yet. Most studies are more concerned with the output rather than the financing of mining operations. For a recent careful survey of the present state of research see Vazquez de Prada (1988), while some scattered data will be found in Vlachovic (1964), Westermann (1971a) and Scheuermann (1929).

8 On the trade at this time to the east, see Lütge (1967); Simsch (1970), and Dersch (1918); central European commerce to Lübeck is considered in Fudge (1995: 164–5).

9 On the place of the 1527/8 crisis in the pattern of international financial disorders see Ehrenberg (1922, Volume 1: 385), whilst particular aspects of the crises of 1514 and 1527/8 are considered in Westermann (1972 and 1971b).

10 For a useful introduction to the activities of the Sevillian Genoese see Pike (1966), whilst Carande (1949) and Kellenbenz (1979) provide considerable information on their activities and those of the Germans on Spanish money markets. The impact of these changes on the London and Augsburg markets is briefly considered in van der Wee and Blanchard (1992: 54–6) and Hildebrandt (1992: 58–66).

11 Gascon (1971: 118–19); Van der Wee (1963, Volume 2: 201–2) and Ehrenberg (1922, Volume 1: 136). This created a pattern of market behaviour which continued into the second half of the century and beyond: Lapayre (1953) and Ruiz-Martin (1965).

12 For another analysis of this situation viewed from a somewhat different perspective see Boyer-Xambeu *et al.* (1986).

13 Data concerning interest rates on English mortgage bonds presented in figure 6.5 below is derived from Travers (1976) and Ward (1974: 166).

14 See on this first phase of technological change in England, Kerridge (1967 and 1969), whilst Van der Wee (1963, Volume 2: 166–76) deals with the earlier changes in the Low Countries.

15 Blanchard (1993). The bullion exporter, able to maintain his position by exploiting regional differentials in the purchasing power of specie, was able to develop an active import trade in primary produce from eastern and southern Europe.

16 Hildebrandt (1992: 73). The relevant sources about these almost unknown investments are quoted by the same authors (1981: 61–76). Because of the legal complexities involved in participation in the mortgage market, described in Holden (1955), it remained largely the

preserve of native investors at a time when the activities of foreigners were predominantly concerned with the shares of the great chartered companies.

17 See for example 'Old' East India Company and the creation of the 'New' and the Darien Companies discussed in Scott (1910–12) and Davies (1952a).

18 On Dutch investment at this time see Wilson (1941: 88–196); Carter (1953a and 1953b), and the exchange between the two authors in the *Economic History Review*, Second Series, 12 (1960) 434–44.

19 *Vneshniaia Politika Rossii. Seriia pervaia, 1801–1815*, Moscow 1965, Volume 4: 108, as quoted in Anan'ich and Lebedev (1990).

7   Labour in proto-industrialization

Big questions and micro-answers

Jürgen Schlumbohm

In comparison with some very large issues, such as 'economic growth' or the 'feudal mode of production', theories of 'proto-industrialization' appear but middle-sized. Still, the concept of proto-industrialization, devised more than 25 years ago by Franklin Mendels (1972, 1981b) seems to owe much to the spirit of the 1970s, fascinated as that decade was by long-term processes and large structures. For Franklin Mendels, proto-industrialization was the first phase of the industrialization process. For Peter Kriedte, Hans Medick and myself, it was a crucial element in the transition from feudalism to capitalism (Kriedte, Medick and Schlumbohm 1981). Since those heady days historiography has moved in a different direction. There is more interest in the specificity of individual cases than in generalizations. Identification of long-term trends now seems more doubtful, when detailed analysis shows that changes took off in many directions at any particular point in time. It may prove fruitful, therefore, to take up the challenge of micro-history and see whether it can lead to a different understanding of pre-industrial economy and society (cf. Schlumbohm 1998).

In this chapter, I do not try to provide an exhaustive survey of the wealth of studies of proto-industrialization carried out over the last twenty-five years, although most of them also deal with the question of labour as well. Rather, I focus on only a small number of problems. Some of these have been particularly prominent in the debates of the last quarter century, others would seem to warrant more attention in the future. To illustrate my discussion, I shall mainly use data from my own research on the rural linen industry around the towns of Osnabrück and Bielefeld as well as from other German-speaking regions.

1   Proto-industrial labour equals rural (semi-)proletariat?

The theories of proto-industrialization, however divergent they may be on other issues, usually agreed that 'in most cases' the labour force of cottage industries was 'at the bottom of the social scale'. It was recruited from the land-poor and the landless, who needed to find an additional or an alternative source of income outside agriculture.[1] However, the difference between smallholders engaged in craft production and a truly property-less rural proletariat was already considered to be relevant in the early stages of the debate (Kriedte, Medick and Schlumbohm 1981: 74–8, 85–7).

Subsequent researchers have been more interested in those characteristics that distinguished proto-industrial workers from a 'true proletariat', and they have laid greater emphasis on diversity than on common features of proto-industrial labour. This seems to be in line with recent trends in studies about labour in contemporary 'Third-World' countries: 'peripheral labour' was – and still is – often only partially proletarianized, not 'free' in the double Marxian sense, as some of them lack personal freedom and others have a stake in the means of production. That is all kinds of inter-mediary forms can be found.[2] If specialists in this field point to worker-peasants in European proto-industrialization as a parallel (Amin and van der Linden 1996), this echoes an earlier meeting between the two fields, for some aspects of proto-industrialization theory were originally inspired by economic arguments about 'growth' and the supply of labour in 'developing countries' (Mendels 1972: 253–5; Kriedte, Medick and Schlumbohm 1981: 22, 28, 38–41, 104, 280). Apart from such occasional borrowing, however, so far there has been little systematic dialogue between scholars from the different specialisms. Closer co-operation might none-theless lead to interesting new perspectives on both their fields.[3]

In some proto-industries the social structure of producers was quite different from what the theory would lead one to expect. This is true, for example, of the coarse linen (*Löwendleinen*) industry in the region of Osnabrück (north-west Germany). There, reports from the eighteenth and nineteenth centuries make plain that all classes of rural society were active in spinning and weaving. A nominative analysis (details in Schlumbohm 1994: 69–72, and 1985) linking the linen sales registered during the years 1809–14 in the market (*Legge*) of the town of Osnabrück to the households of the nearby parish of Belm, as listed in the census of 1812, demonstrates this.

Land-rich peasants usually produced much greater quantities of linen than land-poor or landless producers (table 7.1). On average, the owner of a large farm sold two and a half pieces of linen, each more than a hundred metres long, every year, whereas a propertyless *Heuerling* (tenant labourer) sold only one piece every other year. Correspondingly, the income from the textile industry was five times higher for a land-rich than for a landless household. Smallholders were in an intermediate position, selling slightly less than one piece per year. This notable fact is due to the peculiar character of the Osnabrück linen industry, whose character was preserved until the industry fell into decay in the middle decades of the nineteenth century. All the component stages of the production process were usually carried out within one household, from the planting of flax to the weaving of the finished piece. Of course, land-rich peasants produced much more flax than the property-less *Heuerling* families could on the small plots they rented. Apart from differences between house-holds in their access to raw material, the supply of labour was also crucial. Virtually no persons or households specialized in linen production; it remained a secondary source of income for almost every household in the region. All these families had an agrarian base, either as owners of a small or large holding, or as tenants. The manufacturing of textiles was therefore fitted into the seasonal cycle of agrarian work. Spinning in particular, by far the most time-consuming part of the production process, was performed in winter. Land-rich peasants had larger households than *Heuerlinge* (on average 8.6 against 4.1 persons in 1812). Moreover, the proportion of

Table 7.1 Linen sales by the households of the parish of Belm 1809–14 and 1847–49, by social class

Years	Land-rich peasants	Smallholders	Heuerlinge/Landless
(a) Mean number of pieces sold, per household and year			
1809–14	2.55	0.83	0.56
1847–49	1.64	0.85	0.50
(b) Mean amount of linen (in *Leggeellen*) sold, per household and year			
1809–14	226.6	72.1	46.2
1847–49	127.7	64.6	35.8
(c) Mean income (in *Taler*) earned by linen sales, per household and year			
1809–14	57.39	18.37	11.80
1847–49	24.24	12.53	6.88

Notes
(i) Households which did not sell any linen are included
(ii) 1 *Leggeelle* = 1.22 metre

young adults, either grown-up children or servants, was much higher on large holdings. This labour force was kept busy by a combination of agricultural and textile work, according to the season (Schlumbohm 1994: 71–2, 202, 213–19, and 1983) All this does not mean that textile work was unimportant for the landless households. On the contrary, it contributed significantly to their cash income.

To be sure, the Osnabrück region was a peculiar case: a large majority of property-less *Heuerling* families faced a small minority of peasants owning large impartible farms, who dominated proto-industry as well as agriculture. But in other parts of Europe and under different conditions, wealthy farmers played an equally prominent part in the cottage industry (see for example Isacson and Magnusson 1987: 21–3; Kriedte, Medick and Schlumbohm 1993: 227–32). In Württemberg (south-western Germany), a much more egalitarian society practising partible inheritance, Hans Medick has found that the amount of land owned was a crucial factor in determining a household's chances in the linen industry. This was true though only part of the raw material was produced within the household and locally, so that much of the flax and yarn had to be imported (Medick 1996: 212–21, 229–36, 245–53, 259–63).

Ulrich Pfister, in his book about the hinterland of Zürich (Switzerland) during the early modern period, has compared individual communities with different social, agrarian and industrial structures. In this way he built a model that predicts two different types of relationship between the amount of land held by a family and the level of its proto-industrial activities. Under one set of circumstances, there is a negative linear relationship: the poorer a household is in terms of land, the more it tends to work in rural industry. This is, of course, the classical hypothesis of the proto-industrialization theory. Pfister, however, accepts it only for those cases in which very little capital was needed, i.e. where raw material, tools, etc. were cheap. Spinning is a typical example. In other proto-industries, considerable investments were required. In such cases, Pfister's model (1992a: 266–77, 285–9, and 1992b) predicts a 'curvi-linear relationship': 'The highest share of proto-industrial labour is expected to prevail among the rural middle classes, whereas both farmers and poor households devoid of any investment capacity will record lower proportions of proto-industrial household labour' (Pfister 1992b: 206). Examples are provided by several weaving communities in the Zürich region, as well as some villages near the town of Bielefeld (Westphalia, Germany), where high-quality linen was produced (Schlumbohm 1985: 381–6). It remains open to discussion to what extent Pfister's model can explain the full variety in the social composition of the proto-industrial labour force across regions and branches of industries.[4]

2 Proto-industrialization equals proletarianization of labour?

If the original theory conceded that a rural proletariat was not necessarily a pre-condition for proto-industrialization, it nevertheless tended to suggest that over time a broad class of poor workers emerged in the course of proto-industrial development (Mendels 1972: 252–3; Kriedte, Medick and Schlumbohm 1981: 74–93, 110–11). Some authors have integrated this aspect of proto-industrialization into a broader concept of proletarianization, seen as a dominant trend in the social history of the Western world since the middle ages (see for example Levine 1987 and Tilly 1984).

From a methodological point of view, this can be criticized as a teleological assumption (Quataert 1988: 11). From the perspective of the rich empirical work carried out over the last two decades, it appears at least as an oversimplification (Clarkson 1985: 49–50; Kriedte, Medick and Schlumbohm 1993: 227–32). Even with regard to Franklin Mendels' classical case, it has been argued that 'in the course of the eighteenth century, this so-called pauperization never occurs in Flanders' (Vandenbroeke 1984: 920; cf. however Mendels 1984). In the parish of Laichingen studied by Hans Medick, 'proletarianization' would likewise be a misleading name for the social aspects of proto-industrial growth during the second half of the eighteenth century. While the number of weavers almost doubled, to the point that two-thirds of all households were weavers at the turn of the century, the proportion of those who owned nothing but a part of a house and a garden rose, and the share of the holders of medium-sized real property declined. Nevertheless, in absolute numbers the latter group grew as well; the proportion of those owning more than a house and garden, but less than a medium-sized property remained stable over time. Only one out of seven weavers could be considered as truly poor. A handful of weavers, on the other hand, made their way to the very top of the social pyramid by acquiring large amounts of land, at least by local standards.[5] This looks more like a process of differentiation, and moreover at a modest scale, than proletarianization or even pauperization.

If by the mid-nineteenth century the landless and land-poor households in the Osnabrück *Löwendleinen* industry contributed more to total output than they had done forty years earlier, this cannot be ascribed to advancing proletarianization. Rather, it was the result of a declining participation of land-rich peasants in textile manufacture. Given the decreasing returns from linen production and the rising opportunities for agricultural intensification, the owners of large holdings opted for the latter alternative. In 1847–49, they cut their mean textile output by almost half, to just 56 per cent of what it had been in 1809–14. The property-less *Heuerlinge* had reduced their linen production as well, but with fewer alternatives to make a living in other trades, they still sold 77 per cent of the quantities marketed in the beginning of the century. Smallholders stuck most stubbornly to the manufacturing of cloth, with their mid-century production still at 90 per cent of their former output. In spite of these shifts, a land-rich household continued to sell much more linen than less-endowed neighbours: about double the amount of a smallholder, and more than three times that of a landless peasant (table 7.1) (Schlumbohm 1994: 70, 89–91).

In other regions continued endurance of 'peasant-workers' can be observed, not just during the period of proto-industrialization but also well into the era of factory-based industrialization and even into the twentieth century (Holmes and Quataert 1986). Of course it would not be much use to replace sweeping statements about proletarianization with equally global visions of continuity. Rather, changes over time, in periods of boom and of crisis and both in the agrarian and the industrial context, have to be analysed individually with care.

3 Social inequality or life-cycle mobility?

Once general assumptions about the (semi-)proletarian status of proto-industrial labour are abandoned, the whole concept of social inequality may be called into question. In some regional and local societies of pre-industrial Europe, what seem to be social classes in a cross-sectional perspective, can turn out to be stages in individual life courses. Not only has it been suggested that such a 'cyclical mobility' was a general characteristic of 'peasant societies' on the European continent (Macfarlane 1978a: 29–30), but in some proto-industrial regions an important intragenerational mobility has been observed. Men who started out as weavers gradually acquired more land and ended as propertied peasants. This amounts to accumulation, i.e. a de-proletarianization, during the course of a life.

Ulrich Pfister has uncovered indicators of this pattern in some villages of the Zürich region, though by no means everywhere. According to his model, he expects it to prevail wherever the institutional, social and economic conditions in a particular community allowed saving and investing *in small steps*. A flexible land market was particularly important as a precondition. Pfister goes on to try and explain the fundamental basis of economic behaviour of proto-industrial workers, which had already been a major issue in the theoretical debate. Were they utility maximizers, or were they oriented towards use-value and subsistence, preferring status consumption and leisure to additional income (Kriedte, Medick and Schlumbohm 1981: 41–4, 100–1, 108, 114)? Pfister's answer is that, in general, they were utility maximizers. However, where local social circumstances made incremental accumulation strategies impossible, or where proto-industrial incomes were too low to allow saving, a subsistence orientation would be expected to prevail (Pfister 1992a: 265, 274ff, 302–3, 347, 349, 370–3, 382–6, 389–92, and 1992b: 203, 221–2).

Although Pfister makes the most of the richness of his regional material, the aggregative nature of his data does not allow him to test whether the weavers who later became propertied peasants really saved the returns from their proto-industrial activities, or whether they inherited portions of land (cf. Pfister 1992a: 373–4) in the piecemeal way observed in regions with egalitarian inheritance practices.[6] Only micro-history can provide answers to that type of question. In Laichingen, during the 'golden age' of the linen trade in the late eighteenth century, Hans Medick found many weavers who accumulated considerable wealth, provided they lived long enough to overcome the critical early phases of the family life course. It was not unusual for them to double the amount of property they had inherited. Interestingly, the most successful groups were neither those who, in terms of what they inherited, were the richest nor the poorest, but rather those who started out with a small or medium-sized stock of capital (Medick 1996: 221–8). These results seem to lend support to the theoretical model that assumes that the poor may be unable to earn enough to accumulate significant savings, whereas rich villagers may be too satisfied with their status to be ambitious (Pfister 1992a: 276–80, 384–92).

4 Family labour

One of the assets of proto-industrialization theory may well be that it never adhered to a 'male-breadwinner' notion of labour. In all kinds of sources to do with cottage industries, the work of women and children is just too conspicuous to ignore. Perhaps some variants of the theory went too far in the opposite direction and developed too strong a concept of family labour and the family economy. The proto-industrial family was thought to have been an integrated unit of production, in which all members co-operated on the basis of an intra-family division of labour by age and sex (Kriedte, Medick and Schlumbohm 1981: 41–50, 54–63).

In some cases, this view of the family as a 'miniature factory' (Pinchbeck 1969: 113; Smelser 1959: 56) has been confirmed by subsequent research.[7] Usually however, the component stages of the proto-industrial production processes were divided between rather than within households. The division of labour could be organized much more flexibly in a larger labour pool than in the narrow unit of a family. Especially in the putting-out system, individual cottage workers were typically specialists in narrowly defined tasks, rather than each household involving itself in the full range of the production process. Within a family, several people often did the same work side by side (Knotter, in this volume; Kriedte, Medick and Schlumbohm 1993: 223–4; also 1981: 106–7). In the Krefeld silk industry for example, a master weaver often had several persons weaving but his children only did wheeling while his wife might clean the warp. The warp itself, however, was distributed by the putter-out, who also organized all the other stages of the manufacture (Kriedte 1991: 114–20). According to Pfister's analysis of household lists in the villages of the canton of Zürich, families sought to optimize the earnings of individual members according to their capacities by age and sex, more than they strived for the autonomy of the family economy by undertaking as many steps in the manufacturing process as possible. In fact, in this highly diversified regional economy many households combined a variety of heterogeneous activities, with some members working in agriculture, others spinning wool, yet others weaving silk, and so on. In other families almost everyone did the same kind of work, such as spinning cotton (Pfister 1992a: 350–1, cf. 322, 362–4, 389; also 1989).

In another respect too, families were more flexible than was sometimes assumed in proto-industrialization theory. On the one hand, they did not necessarily keep their children at home until marriage. On the other hand, some proto-industrial households took in servants or lodgers in order to optimize their incomes (Pfister 1992a: 304–14; Tanner 1982: 257–63). This implies that the household as a social unit was not identical with the family as a demographic unit, an observation that has important implications for some versions of the demographic model of proto-industrialization (Kriedte, Medick and Schlumbohm 1993: 223–4; cf. Engelen 1994: 67–8).

5 Relations of production: from structures to strategies

During the early stages of the proto-industrialization debate, it was suggested that economic actors might behave according to a specific logic, depending on the type of relations of production (Kriedte, Medick and Schlumbohm 1981: 94–111). Since then, the focus of interest has clearly shifted away from the construction of typologies to a detailed reconstruction of the complex reality of individual cases. This shift has encouraged a new perspective. Micro-history seeks to deal with the relations between individuals, however unequal they may be, not as reified structures but as connections that are produced, reproduced and changed by continuous negotiation among the actors involved. In this approach, the concept of 'strategies' has become crucial (cf. Fontaine and Schlumbohm 2000).

Although we do not yet have any in-depth studies along these lines of the relations of production in proto-industries, elements and fragments which do exist seem to suggest that studies of this type could bring interesting results. Let us take the relations between rural linen producers and urban merchants in Osnabrück, where the town authorities regulated the market in order to guarantee the quality of the products and to protect the weavers' independence in an open *Kaufsystem*. As the *Legge* (market) ordinance of 1789 stated, some merchants had used credit ties to force many peasants to sell their linen exclusively to them. The danger of a quasi-monopoly appears to have been very real: in the years 1809–14 we find that eight linen merchants accounted for 97 per cent of the Osnabrück linen market. The first five bought 85 per cent of the cloth, the largest firm alone 41 per cent.

How did the small producers respond to this situation? By linking the entries in the register of linen sales to the households in the census list, we discover that most peasants again and again sold to different merchants. Seldom did a rustic weaver sell the four, three, or even two pieces he produced in a year to only one merchant (table 7.2). In the rare cases when a villager brought two pieces to the market on the same day, he would sell them to two different merchants. The *Heuerlinge* acted no differently from propertied peasants. Those who produced just one piece in a year seldom sold it to the merchant who had bought their linen the year before. This was plainly a systematic strategy. The small producers, scattered over the countryside and facing the oligopsony of urban merchants, appear to have striven anxiously to preserve their independence (Schlumbohm 1985: 386–8). Even under the putting-out system, spinners in the Zürich region behaved in a similar manner. Once the

Table 7.2 The linen producing households of the parish of Belm, by the number of merchants to whom they sold, 1809–14

(a) By the total number of pieces of linen sold 1809–14

Number of pieces	Number of merchants (row–%)								Row total (column–%)
	1	2	3	4	5	6	7	8–	
2	5 (35.7)	9 (64.3)							14 (9.0)
3–6	3 (5.5)	11 (20.0)	27 (49.1)	9 (16.4)	3 (5.5)	2 (3.6)			55 (35.5)
7–12	0 (0.0)	3 (6.0)	6 (12.0)	15 (30.0)	11 (22.0)	12 (24.0)	2 (4.0)	1 (2.0)	50 (32.3)
13–18	0 (0.0)	0 (0.0)	0 (0.0)	0 (0.0)	5 (26.3)	5 (26.3)	5 (26.3)	4 (21.1)	19 (12.3)
19–	0 (0.0)	0 (0.0)	0 (0.0)	0 (0.0)	3 (17.6)	2 (11.8)	5 (29.4)	7 (41.2)	17 (11.0)
Total	8 (5.2)	23 (14.8)	33 (21.3)	24 (15.5)	22 (14.2)	21 (13.5)	12 (7.7)	12 (7.7)	155 (100.0)

(b) By the number of pieces of linen sold in one year

Number of pieces	Number of merchants (row–%)				Row total (column–%)
	1	2	3	4–	
2	43 (22.2)	151 (77.8)			194 (51.5)
3	8 (7.8)	54 (52.4)	41 (39.8)		103 (27.3)
4	4 (8.0)	19 (38.0)	20 (40.0)	7 (14.0)	50 (13.3)
5–	0 (0.0)	4 (13.3)	12 (40.0)	14 (46.7)	30 (8.0)
Total	55 (14.6)	228 (60.5)	73 (19.4)	21 (5.6)	377 (100.0)

Note
In table (a) each household is one case, if it sold more than one piece of linen in 1809–14. In table (b) a household is considered as several cases, if it sold more than one piece of linen in several years.

period of a contract (probably a week) was over, they turned to a different employer, rarely if ever continuing to work for the old one.[8]

To be sure, there were many conflicts about price. But if they are studied in a broader context, it turns out that often much more was at stake for the parties involved. When, during the 1750s, the linen weavers in Württemberg refused to sell their cloth at the official price, they were fighting for a fair price setting mechanism, and ultimately even for 'free trade'. They wanted to be allowed to sell their products to whomever they wanted, and to be freed of the fetters imposed by the privileged linen company (Medick 1996: 70–82; cf. Liu 1994: 68–74).

The strategies of the various parties will be better understood if the behaviour of all actors involved in a relationship can be analysed at the same time. If, for example, merchant-manufacturers tried to tie workers to their firm by credit, weavers often sought commissions and credit from several putters-out, even if this violated official regulations. That is also the reason why they opposed the *livret ouvrier* and similar documents, which made control much easier.[9] Institutions matter in this type of analysis: how did actors use them, or in what ways did they seek to reshape or to get round them? Often, more than just two parties were involved: middlemen mediated between producers and merchants, masters between journeymen and putters-out. Spinners, yarn collectors, weavers and entrepreneurs all had their own strategies.

The analysis obviously becomes much more complicated when each actor is observed in the multiplicity of fields in which he operates (cf. Fontaine 1996). In the *Heuerling* system of the Osnabrück region for instance, people were heavily dependent on the land-rich peasants who rented them a cottage with a tiny piece of land, and for whom they had to work whenever they were called upon. Although the poor sought to reduce this dependence by developing social ties with several propertied peasants and by changing from one farm to another, there was a strong element of paternalist subordination in the *Heuerling*-farmer relationship (Schlumbohm 1994: 539f–620; also 1995). In the Osnabrück linen market however, the same persons insisted on their independence in a persistent, almost stubborn fashion. This would seem to suggest that the urban market was particularly important as a place of freedom to those who enjoyed little liberty in their village.

Ultimately, 'economic' strategies should not be isolated from 'social' and 'cultural' aspects of behaviour. Careful analysis of conflicts shows how closely they were inter-related. Sometimes, workers were prepared to accept financial disadvantages if the merchant-manufacturer respected their self-esteem and symbolically renounced his own superior power. On the other hand, once a conflict had broken out, action was often not confined to narrowly defined economic goals; the relation as a whole was at stake. Where paternalist care was neglected or absent, deference could soon turn into violence, and business come to a standstill (Kriedte 1991: 118–24, 259–76, 302–26, 366–79; also 1997).

It might be objected that the sources are insufficient for a detailed analysis of the strategies of workers, merchants(-manufacturers), middlemen, and all the other actors involved in proto-industries. Of course it is true that evidence is always fragmentary. Nevertheless, business archives and account books can yield important clues to everyday transactions between merchants and workers or artisans. In addition, court records, particularly those of the *conseils de prud'hommes*,[10] provide serial information on conflicts. The more they can be contextualised, the more information about each actor that can be assembled, the more they can reveal about patterns of behaviour. It may prove fruitful for future research to rethink relations of production in terms of permanent negotiations between actors who are pursuing their own strategies.

Notes

1 Mendels (1972: 242); compare the discussion in Kriedte, Medick and Schlumbohm (1981: 14–17).
2 A useful introduction to this field is Amin and van der Linden (1996). The quotation is from the editors' Introduction, pp. 3–4.
3 Cf. the special issue of *Jahrbuch für Wirtschaftsgeschichte*, 1998, no. 2 on proto-industrialization, especially Roy (1998), and Kriedte, Medick and Schlumbohm (1998: 16–20).
4 In its original version, the model included a third alternative: under certain conditions, there could be a positive linear relationship between the amount of land held by a family and the level of its proto-industrial activities. The Osnabrück *Löwendleinen* industry was then explicitly used as an example by Pfister (1992b: 205–6).
5 Medick (1996: 191–205). During the early nineteenth century, economic trends tended to be less favourable to weavers (*ibid.* 244–63).
6 Sabean (1990: 16, 189–93, 247–9, 259–61, 300–5). This, of course, was a major cause of life cycle mobility (*ibid.* 256–8, 479–80).
7 In the canton of Appenzell-Außerrhoden (Switzerland) the independent weaver conformed to this pattern, though not the wage weaver (Tanner 1982: 239–63). In the production of *Löwendleinen*, we observed a similar pattern (Schlumbohm 1983: 106–11).
8 Pfister (1992a: 261, 529–30), based on a list of spinners and their employers for one village in 1711.
9 Kriedte (1991: 100–24); Schöttler (1985: 172); Emsbach (1982: 202–3); Delsalle (1985: 111–25); Terrier (1996: 218–22).
10 They were used to some extent already, for example in Delsalle (1985); Schöttler (1985); Terrier (1996); Cottereau (1987).

8   Problems of the 'family economy'

Peasant economy, domestic production and labour markets in pre-industrial Europe

Ad Knotter

Over the last twenty-five years or so the history of the family has advanced from a marginal and rather boring topic in the history and sociology curriculum to a subject of intensive study and debate.[1] Some have spoken of an 'explosion of family history', maybe even in the literal sense that family history has been blown up and fragmented into widely diverging subjects and fields of interests (Ryan 1982). Michael Anderson's *Approaches* (1980) to the history of the family have not only been continued but, in fact, multiplied. Students of the economic history of the family, of family labour, work roles and income, of the history of family structure and family formation, of marriage strategies and demographic behaviour, of emotional and sexual relations, of youth, old age, or in general the life course,[2] all seem to go their own way, only superficially paying attention to the others. Family history has opened a whole new range of topics and questions about the nature and contents of past social change (cf. Hareven 1991), but precisely because of its very success, it has tended to become integrated into other fields of social, economic and cultural history, while at the same time losing its internal coherence.

From the 1970s, there have been attempts to overcome this fragmentation by combining the economic history of the family with other 'family histories'. Several scholars have tried to relate the evolution of the family and of family behaviour to underlying economic parameters: the changing organization of work, labour relations or 'modes of production'.[3] The idea of the rural 'proto-industrial family', with its ascribed social, economic and demographic behaviour has been most influential in this respect. However, in spite of its enormous impact and the ongoing research and debate, the supposed relations remain subject to considerable doubt. The idea of proto-industrialization (the proliferation of rural cottage industry) as a stage in the development of industrial capitalism has been severely criticized, and a uniform relationship with marriage strategies, fertility and population growth has not, as yet, been firmly established. Several studies reflect an urgent need to re-think some of the basic ideas of proto-industrialization.[4] In my opinion, the relative failure of the 'proto-industrial family' as an integral concept was inherent in the way it was originally conceived by Medick and others in the 1970s, as a stage in the evolution of the organization of work, or 'mode of production': the so-called 'family economy', characterized by the co-operative labour of the family as a unit of production (Medick 1976). This idea of the prevalence of such a specific pre-industrial or pre-capitalistic family economy was shared by several others in this pioneering stage of the 'household economics approach' in family history (Anderson 1980, 65–84; also Tilly and Scott 1975, and 1977).

The concept of family economy was introduced in the 1970s into the emerging debates on proto-industry by Hans Medick and, more or less simultaneously, into debates on women's work by Louise Tilly and Joan Scott.[5] Their common idea was that, before industrialization, the household was a co-operative unit of production and labour. Family economy was defined by Medick as 'a socio-economic formation that organizes and combines production, consumption and reproduction through the common labour relations of the family members'. For Medick the proto-industrial family essentially was a continuation of the peasant family. The proto-industrial family was just as much a unit of production and consumption as the peasant family, albeit that its existence was no longer tied to the transmission of property through inheritance but to the possibility of founding a family as a unit of labour (Medick 1976: 299, 303). However important were the effects of this difference in his view, especially on demographic behaviour, the proto-industrial family economy basically evolved directly from the peasant family economy. It was seen as a stage in the evolution from peasant economy to capitalist industrial relations.

Tilly and Scott used the concept of family economy in a much wider sense. In their view, most pre-industrial productive activity, be it in urban craftshops or on the land, was based in a household. Just as Medick referred to the idea of a 'household or domestic mode of production', so they defined family economy by 'the interdependence of work and residence, of household labor needs, subsistence requirements, and family relationships'. While recognizing important differences between craftsmen and peasants, and between families with property and those without, in all cases 'the household was the center around which resources, labor, and consumption were balanced'. Even if peasant families barely subsisted on their land, their life was organized around the property, no matter how small the holding (Tilly and Scott 1977: 12–13). When 'the industrial mode of production replaced the domestic mode of production' (*ibid.*: 63), the pre-industrial family economy gave way to the 'family wage economy', an income-pooling unit dependent on the wage labour by each of its members. In the 1987 reprint of *Women, Work, and Family*, however, Tilly and Scott appeared to have recognized some of the problems of family economy: 'the household economy we depict in the pre-industrial period seems, in fact, to have been more complicated than we suggest. [. . .] Wages seem to have been an important part of life [. . .]. Our model of the pre-industrial family economy [. . .] minimises the extent to which capitalist forms of production and exchange already existed in the eighteenth century'.[6] However, in both Medick's and Tilly and Scott's still-influential original formulations, the majority of parents and children in the pre-industrial or proto-industrial family economy were supposed to have worked together in a unitary household, based in or immediately around their home. As such, the family economy differed fundamentally from the proletarian family wage economy, or – in a later stage – the family consumer economy.

In this essay I intend to review the historiography on the subject and to make an inventory of criticisms of the concept of pre-industrial or proto-industrial family economy. I do not question the argument that the labour of individual historical actors can be understood in terms of family position (daughters, wives, husbands, sons), an argument I value as a major breakthrough in both labour history and family history. However, after some twenty-five years of research and debate, it seems appropriate to reflect once more on the explanatory and analytical value of the concept of family economy and its meaning in the history of European labour relations. By focusing on the interrelationship of 'family strategies', household economics and labour markets, some serious deficiencies of the concept of family economy are brought to light. In the process of adaptation to the opportunities and constraints of resources and employment in specific economic and ecological settings people appear to allocate and co-ordinate their labour within the family in much more varied ways than was originally assumed. Labour markets are important in this process as far as wage labour is concerned. Depending on the degree to which wage labour determines employment opportunities, labour markets will determine family income strategies and the allocation of labour time of individual family members. The way people act and adapt their behaviour to changing employment opportunities can be labelled a *strategy*, defined as a pattern of behaviour consciously undertaken to achieve a specific goal, in this case perhaps simply to gain a living. This strategy is supposed to be related to, or aimed at, the well-being and the cohesion of the family as a social group, however defined; hence 'family strategy'. This, of course, is not to deny 'co-operative conflicts' in family behaviour. Coping with conflicts can also be considered a 'family strategy' based on 'principles that inform bargained inter-dependent decisions'.[7] More than the rather static concept of family economy, the dynamic concept of 'family strategies' presupposes interacting people who actively help determine their own lives and circumstances.

1 Origins of the concept of family economy: Chayanov and his critics

The original formulations in the 1970s of the idea of an historic family economy were highly indebted to the so-called 'mode of production' controversy in economic anthropology and to the idea of the 'peasant economy' as a specific mode of production. The theories of the Russian economist Chayanov were crucial here; his writings clearly inspired Medick as well as Tilly and Scott to formulate their ideas about the peasant, proto-industrial and artisan or, in general, 'pre-industrial' family as a unit of production and the family economy as a stage in the history of labour relations.[8] Their work reflected the contemporary fascination of Third-World sociologists with Chayanov's theories on the Russian peasantry. Many combined the idea of the peasantry as a special social category with structuralist notions about the 'articulation of modes of production', at that time very popular among anthropologists inspired by neo-Marxist structuralism, of Louis Althusser for example.[9]

Admittedly, the structuralism of the concept of the (peasant) household as a 'mode of production' and its 'articulation' has also been challenged in Third World sociology by a view of household economics as a set of intentional strategies resulting in a variable mix of waged and non-waged work (Wallerstein and Smith 1992). There has never been an overall acceptance of the Chayanovian perspective in Third-World peasant studies, as a glance through the *Journal of Peasant Studies* will reveal. Since the late 1970s the debate over Chayanov in that and other journals has acquired the dimensions of what may be called a minor industry, and among much ideological hot air some fundamental criticisms brought forward in this debate may also be singled out as being particularly relevant to the historical use of the concept of family economy.[10] In its pure form, Chayanov's peasant family farm is an isolated unit of production, distribution and consumption. As it is operated by the co-operative efforts of the family, without outside labour, its prevalence presupposes the virtual absence of a market for wage labour.[11] Having no objective measure of real labour costs, the peasant family tends to stress its 'drudgery' below opportunity costs, a tendency Chayanov labelled 'self-exploitation'. The peasant family would prefer working on its own farm even if marginal income from off-farm labour would be higher; in other words, even if more could be earned in alternative occupations. The peasant family balances consumption needs and resources by adding and reducing land according to family size. Differences in farm size and amounts of land owned are primarily explained not by social differences but by the changing composition of the family during the family life-cycle. Inequality within peasant society is cyclical, not structural. The extent of non-agricultural supplementary employments in wage-labour crafts and trades is just a temporary element in the balancing of labour and consumption, not a structural aspect of the differentiation of the peasantry (cf. Chayanov 1966: 101ff). The development of a rural labour-surplus of migrant and other forms of wage labour is analysed in the context of family economy, and not of emerging labour markets or a 'wage economy'.

Criticism of this Chayanovian approach has centred on the tendency for the concept of the peasantry as a unified social category to incorporate many contrasting forms of production and social organization, and to obscure social dynamics. The approach ignores the effects of processes of social differentiation in the countryside and their impact on internal differentiation of work and labour relations of family members on and off the farm, influenced by age and gender. The crucial question is that of the allocation of labour time between work on the farm, off-farm hired work, non-agricultural (supplementary) employments, and leisure. If wage labour and non-agricultural work are structural rather than cyclical or additional elements of the resources of the peasant family, it has to be assumed that the family employs a rational strategy to achieve an optimal allocation of labour time and therefore measures real opportunity costs. This is more likely than, and in fact incompatible with, Chayanov's central doctrine of 'self-exploitation'.[12] The Chayanovian peasant appears to be a kind of ideal-type construct, modelled on the 'middle peasant'. In social and historical reality however, the poor peasant's family is not a co-operative unit of production at all, but structurally dependent on a combination of different resources and occupations of different family members, connecting the fate of the land-poor or landless peasant family with that of other families and the outside world through the operation of a market for wage labour.[13] The poor peasant's family is rather a source of labour supply than a unit of production. With many regional variations and time-lags this seems the more realistic approach for a major part of the rural population in pre-industrial Europe, at least since the seventeenth or eighteenth century, and, for some regions in north-western Europe (especially in parts of the Low Countries and England), even much earlier. There is abundant proof that between the sixteenth and eighteenth centuries, Europe's peasantries had dissolved into very different societal complexes.[14]

2 Peasant differentiation and allocation of labour in the proto-industrial family

In the debate over the proto-industrial family economy, the social differentiation of the rural community and the internal differentiation of work inside the family remain unsolved problems. Originally, work roles of different family members were thought to be characterized by a unified organization of family labour to maximize the productive capacity of the domestic unit. In this view the 'self-exploitation' of the proto-industrial family as a production unit allowed merchants to pay extremely low wages and induced the family to adapt its reproductive behaviour to enlarge its productive potential. In a later contribution to the debate, however, Kriedte, Medick and Schlumbohm (1993: 223–4) seemed to retreat from this cornerstone of their argument, admitting that 'the cooperative division of labour did not invariably occur within the household'. In some interesting analyses of the allocation of labour time in proto-industrial families, the Swiss historian Ulrich Pfister (1991; 1992a: 264–80; 1992b) concluded that the labour of the family was not necessarily as co-operative as it would be in a unit of production, but could also be highly diversified, depending on the social position of the family and on local circumstances. Households exclusively engaged in manufacturing were perhaps more a phenomenon of the transition to industrialization than proto-industrialization as such, he suggested (Pfister 1992b: 222). In the classical period, probably a combination of various employments was more typical, such as female spinning with male wage-labour or a domestic craft and some subsistence farming, in the way of an 'economy of makeshifts' (Hufton 1974) or an 'adaptive family economy' (Wall 1986a). In contrast to Medick's adoption of the Chayanovian concept of 'self-exploitation', Pfister preferred a neo-classical approach of utility-maximizing behaviour (within certain limits): the proto-industrial peasant family aimed at an optimal allocation of its labour time to increase its earnings, flexibly adapting its labour to regional and inter-regional market forces.[15]

Pfister and other researchers clearly showed that rural domestic industries could take variable forms, from individual or co-operative family labour by poor peasants to supplementary employment in rich or middle peasants' households.[16] Kriedte *et al.* were therefore probably right to distance themselves from ideas like, for instance, Charles Tilly's about proto-industrialization as a part or stage of a unilinear and irreversible long-term process of proletarianization. The problem is that, like proletarianization, the proliferation of cottage industry in the countryside is neither a uniform or unilinear process, nor a stage. I do agree, however, with their conclusion that 'extensive involvement in rural industry seems to have required a process of social differentiation, leading to the emergence of a stratum of small peasants or sub-peasants who had to turn to cottage industry to survive' (Kriedte, Medick and Schlumbohm 1993: 229).

In this context their subsequent reference to the concept of 'peasant ecotype' is important. This concept, first introduced by the Swedish anthropologist Orvar Löfgren, has been further developed by Michael Mitterauer (1986, 1992b; also Rudolph 1992: 122) as an alternative to the concept of a uniform peasant family economy. Löfgren's peasant ecotypes were conceived as resulting from flexible strategies to cope with processes of proletarianization, variably exploiting natural resources as these differ in regionally specific ecological settings.[17] Mitterauer's approach seeks to place rural labour relations within and outside the family in the context of the economic and physical specificities of the regional environment, and of 'cultures' of work developed on the basis of these specificities. According to Mitterauer, at least two types of family have to be distinguished in pre-industrial rural societies: those of peasants and those of a 'sub-peasant strata' (in German: *unterbäuerliche Schichten*), or semi-proletarians. The concept of family economy is not applicable to the 'sub-peasant strata'. These clearly cannot be defined as units of production; they are more dependent on supra-regional markets and are particularly influenced by their wage relationship with the peasant strata. As far as proto-industry is concerned, Mitterauer (1992b: 152, 155) argued that a 'pluralism of activities is to be respected in a discussion of the proto-industrial family economy'. The activities of rural lower-class families 'included different kinds of wage work, industrial production, and cultivation of their own plots'. The growth of various types of domestic industry in rural areas was only one of several possible strategies employed by 'sub-peasants' to combat their impoverishment. In many cases, proto-industrialization concerned only the women; in other cases men helped in the textile industry only during the winter months. There were also proto-industrial activities that were performed predominantly by men.

3 Pre-industrial family economy and women's labour

The idea of the family economy as a stage in the history of European labour relations was derived not only from prevailing theories in Third-World sociology but also from earlier writings. Both Medick and Tilly and Scott were able to build on historical work in the field of the history of the family, labour relations and women's work in the German and English speaking countries. The elaboration of the concept of proto-industry by Medick and his co-authors Kriedte and Schlumbohm (1981: 2–5), for example, owed much to nineteenth and early twentieth-century German research on the evolution of home industries by the 'historical school in economics'. It is, perhaps, no coincidence that historians belonging to this school thought of economic history pre-eminently as a phased evolution of industrial organization.[18] Medick also related his Chayanovian conception of the proto-industrial family to Otto Brunner's (1968) influential concept of *das ganze Haus* as a basic institution of production, consumption, and co-habitation, governed by its own rules of internal cohesion. However, in German social historiography, both the economic foundations of this idea and its social and ideological implications now appear highly controversial. H. U. Wehler, for instance, considered it a 'legend', because it grossly underestimated the influence of market forces in peasant and artisan production alike (quoted in Opitz 1994). Claudia Opitz (1994), in her inaugural lecture, argued in favour of an approach of dynamic 'family strategies', against the closed and static concept of *das ganze Haus.*

In their work, Tilly and Scott in essence only reformulated the interpretations of pre-war British feminist historians in Chayanovian terms.[19] Since the writings of Alice Clark, Ivy Pinchbeck and others, the notion of a pre-industrial family-based household economy has been well established in feminist history and sociology.[20] In rural and urban production, housekeeping and productive functions were thought to be integrated, and women were supposed to have an important role in family production. On the basis of this English research, it has generally been assumed that in the family economy, women's work and female subordination differed markedly in the pre-industrial period from what was to follow. The introduction of the concept of family economy by Tilly and Scott allowed feminist historians to give these ideas theoretical support and justification.[21]

However, empirical historical research and reflection on the household economics of pre-industrial English families have increasingly cast doubt on the usefulness of this generalized model. Though neither the first nor the only ones, Peter Laslett (1983) and Richard Wall (1986a and b) were surely among the best-known historians to criticize the idea of family economy and to argue that the pre-industrial family or household often failed to function as a 'work group'. For Laslett, the overriding issue was, again, the degree of social differentiation. Where in consequence of such differentiation there were heads of households who had to go out to work in order to earn or supplement the family living, that is, where a labour market existed, not every domestic unit could have been a work-group: 'The family economy of the poor was not, in itself, a work economy' (Laslett 1983: 543, 547). His and Wall's objection, that 'the family economy appears to exclude the very possibility of wage labour', is reminiscent of the arguments against the Chayanovian construct of a 'peasant economy' as already mentioned.[22] To avoid the dichotomy of family formation based on household labour versus wage labour and to take due account of the varied strategies of those who had to survive on the proceeds of their labour, Wall introduced the concept of the 'adaptive family economy'. This was to prove particularly helpful in the interpretation of household economics in societies where household-based labour co-existed with a wage economy.

In women's history serious doubts have arisen about the supposedly greater sexual equality in the pre-industrial or pre-capitalist economy. It has been argued that female independent participation in urban crafts was, by and large, the preserve of widows, whose position had been reached during their married life. In spite of attempts, such as those of Martha Howell (1986a and b) to push the notion of a 'golden age' of at least urban women's work in the family economy back into the middle ages, most studies of medieval or pre-modern women's work show that their disadvantaged status as workers was a pervasive feature of economic life both before and after 1500: women have generally been clustered in low-skilled, low-status, low-paying occupations. Peasant women as well as urban women lacked equal access to economic resources, and had to accommodate their working lives to the demands of men and family.[23] In an historical overview of women's work and the family economy, Pat Hudson and Robert Lee (1990), while adhering to the model of a preliminary stage of the family production unit, were also highly sceptical of the supposedly higher labour status of women associated with it (see also Berg 1987). The temporal sequence of organizational change from the traditional family economy to the family wage economy as originally suggested by Tilly and Scott was considered to be only of limited use. Instead, they argued, women's work should be examined in the context of 'regionally-divergent gender-specific labour markets and local configurations of female employment opportunities in both formal and non-formal activities' (Hudson and Lee 1990: 33).

These and other criticisms led Michael Anderson (1992: 131) to conclude in a review of family history in Britain since the appearence of his *Approaches*, 'that in much of England it has been a very long time since the majority of parents and children worked together in a unitary household economy, based in or immediately around their own home'. Instead, a large part of the population, who lived close to, or below, the margins of subsistence, had to employ varying 'coping strategies' to obtain the necessary resources, a way of behaving clearly considered by Anderson to be at variance with the concept of pre-industrial family economy. According to Anderson, since medieval times substantial numbers of British labourers had to leave home to hire themselves out to someone else, while their wives engaged in some quite different economic activity. It is also clear that a very high proportion of urban workers' wives were not engaged in the same trades as their husbands.

To sum up. Many analysts of the household economy of the pre-industrial European family have stressed the inadequacy of the concept of the co-operative self-exploiting family economy because it ignores the differentiation of work and labour relations in peasant, proto-industrial and artisan production, and because it underestimates the extent of wage labour and the impact of labour markets in pre-industrial society. Against the structuralist and functionalist notion of a 'household mode of production', based on 'self-exploitation', they have put forward the idea of 'strategies' of the labouring family to cope with processes of impoverishment, to adapt itself to changing resources and employment opportunities, and to (re)allocate its labour time accordingly in the most profitable way. In contrast to a powerful feminist tradition, these strategies did not create inequalities in men's work and women's work, but were built upon existing gendered divisions. All in all, the evolutionary thinking of labour and the family as a phased succession of more or less uniform structures, like the concept of family economy, should be abandoned. A consideration of flexible 'family strategies' is more helpful to understand the spatial and temporal variations in the organization and allocation of labour in the family. In the next sections I examine these issues in greater detail.

4 A medieval wage economy?

A discussion of the incidence and meaning of the peasant family economy in the history of European labour relations can start best from the most extreme position taken by Alan Macfarlane (1978a, also 1978b and 1984), who flatly denied its historic existence in England, at least from the thirteenth century on. Macfarlane deliberately omitted any reference to the work of Chayanov in order to avoid 'becoming involved in the heated debate between Populists and Marxists' (1978a: 15 n. 31), but the model of the peasant economy he chose to disclaim is clearly derived from Chayanov. The core of his argument is that a market economy of independent producers, employing wage labour rather than family labour, was already present in England in the middle ages. To prove this, he focused on the existence of individual ownership and a market for private land sales. His discussion of the extent of wage labour in the medieval English countryside, however, is very limited and, in fact, completely inadequate. His claims are very poorly documented, and servants and hired wage-labourers were arbitrarily lumped together (Macfarlane 1978a: 147–50). There is no account of any dynamics of social differentiation: the incidence of wage labour is deemed enough to prove the existence of a full-blown labour market, even in thirteenth-century England. In a much more sophisticated analysis of family and non-family peasant labour, however, R. M. Smith (1984: 22–38) enlisted evidence of 'an impressive array of scholars' suggesting that in the late thirteenth century 'between 40 and 70 per cent of holdings were too small to absorb the labour of those families resident upon them' (quotes on pp. 23 and 31). He argued that we could not expect to find that the family labour farm *à la* Chayanov was the norm in the more densely populated regions. Rather, there was a potential amalgam of non-paid family and wage-paid non-family labour, so that there were 'relations of production developing through labour markets'. However, in his argument, Smith also lumped in-door service and out-door wage labour together as non-familial labour.

This view contrasts sharply with that of British medievalists of whom Rodney Hilton is perhaps the most outspoken. He painted the medieval English village essentially as a 'peasant economy' in the Chayanovian sense.[24] Servants were exchanged between households, and although there was a 'division between the ploughman-husbandman and the hired labourer', the antagonistic element between household economies was modified by a system of mutual adjustment, only partly operating through the market. Antagonisms in the village were overshadowed by the social gulf dividing peasants and landlords. There was a considerable number of servants living-in, often the younger offspring of other peasant families, who must not be confused with labourers who had their own independent households. Inequality among medieval peasants was determined by several factors with varying force at different times, but generally not by the development of markets for agricultural commodities and labour. The number of labourers with small holdings was determined by cycles of population growth and deprivation, not the development of a stratum of prosperous farmers enriching themselves through the market (Hilton 1977). Not until the fifteenth century, according to Hilton, did developments in the feudal economy allow the 'retention of surplus on the peasant holding', resulting 'in a considerable degree of prosperity in the peasant economy', 'a regrouping of settlement', and 'the appearance of holdings of considerable size'; that is, a structural differentiation of the peasantry (Hilton in Aston and Philpin 1985: 133–5).

Whatever the merits of these conflicting opinions, the increasing social differentiation of the peasantry in the following centuries is a classical topic in British social and agricultural historiography, known as the problem of 'the disappearance of the small landowner'.[25] There are two related questions that arise from the above discussion: first, in what ways did the social differentiation of the peasantry result in the development of rural labour markets; second, to what extent can unmarried, living-in servants be considered to have formed a part of an emerging class of agricultural wage labourers?

5　Farm regions and peasant differentiation after the sixteenth century

There has been a tendency amongst scholars to stress the regional diversification of agrarian systems and rural social relations in this period, as in the authoritative work of Joan Thirsk.[26] The extreme polarization that was once thought to typify the whole of the English countryside was, in fact, typical only of regions of arable (or mixed) farming concentrated in the southern and eastern parts of the country. Here, a class of commercial large-scale farmers, who were already prospering by the sixteenth century, were faced with an increasing number of landless or almost landless cottagers and labourers. Their ranks were swelled by peasants who had been forced to give up their holdings, and by the natural increase of the population. In the pastoral districts in the middle and northern parts of the country, small-scale peasant farming seems to have fared considerably better. No completely landless proletariat emerged there. Instead, population growth led to an increasing number of very small holdings. However, a division into arable and pastoral districts is a very broad generalization. In practice, many smaller farming regions with varied ways of making a livelihood can be identified (Thirsk 1987). There were many areas where a kind of peasant economy persisted through the centuries well into the nineteenth century, as Mick Reed (1984, and 1986/7) argued. Close reading of his argument, however, may reveal that his examples could be more appropriately analysed as 'peasant ecotypes' (as will be argued below).

Both the peasant holdings described by Reed and those in the seventeenth-century pastoral districts were too small to provide a livelihood. Access to common or waste land for livestock pasturage, supply of fuel and other necessities enabled the growth of smallholdings in the pastoral areas in the seventeenth century. Opportunities for small peasant families to supplement their income from non-agricultural sources were often available as well. It was no coincidence, Joan Thirsk (1984b) argued, that these northern and midland areas were to become the heartland of rural industry, and later, of the Industrial Revolution. In an important essay on seventeenth-century agriculture and social change, she compared this seventeenth-century type with the twentieth-century phenomenon of 'worker-peasants' who, until recently, continued their own way of life in various parts of continental Europe, and who have attracted much attention from social anthropologists (Thirsk 1984a: 211).

Contrasting social developments in agrarian regions challenges approaches based on national comparisons, as Robert Brenner's (1985a). This becomes apparent in J. P. Cooper's contribution to the 'Brenner debate', in which he criticized Brenner for underestimating the extent of diversity in the development in France's agrarian regions and social relations. In the grain producing areas in northern France, in upper Normandy, Île-de-France, Picardy and Champagne, there was a great loss of peasant property when holdings were joined into larger farms in the sixteenth and seventeenth centuries, thus making these regions resemble the arable-farming areas of lowland England.[27] The proportion of wage labour in the rural population of northern France in the sixteenth century suggests to have been almost the same as that in comparable parts of England, *c.* 25 per cent.[28] In the southern and eastern parts of France, pastoral farming was more important and farms were smaller. Cooper argued that it would be too rash to take the whole of France to be a peasant-dominated economy in Chayanov's sense. In many ways it was as market-dominated as England, with trends and potentials not qualitatively different (Cooper in Aston and Philpin 1985: 168, 180–1).

In general, a regional approach underlining the variations of labour relations in the countryside during the early modern period seems more adequate than generalizing about a uniform 'pre-industrial' peasant family economy. The Netherlands is a case in point: in the sixteenth and seventeenth centuries a highly commercialized agriculture developed in the coastal provinces in the west and the north, based on specialized farms using wage labour. On the sandy soils in the eastern and southern provinces a more peasant-like economy remained in existence where wage work was much less important.[29] The relevance of Chayanovian concepts to the eastern and southern agriculture in the eighteenth and nineteenth centuries, however, is still open to debate.[30] It is clear that in the east the number of cottagers in the lower strata, who were partly dependent on waged farm labour or industrial supplementary employment, grew markedly in the eighteenth century (although no substantial landless proletariat emerged) (Bieleman 1987: 127–51; Slicher van Bath 1957). Social differentiation in village communities increased as a result of population growth and probably also as a social effect of the increasing market orientation in agricultural production. In the light of this debate on the rural economy in the eastern provinces of the Netherlands, it is significant that Josef Mooser in his study of the more or less similar rural society of adjacent Westphalia in the late eighteenth and early nineteenth centuries was very ambiguous about the idea of a homogeneous 'peasant society'.[31] The book's title *Ländliche Klassengesellschaft* ('Rural Class Society') is programmatic in this respect. Mooser (1984: 25–6) emphasized the social differentiation of the peasantry, however with the important qualification that social divisions were not uniformly based on opposite positions in the labour market. Following the criticisms already discussed, he considered the Chayanovian model of the self-exploitive peasant family balancing labour and resources around the property to be 'a-historical'. Like his British counterparts, he concluded that the family economy of the lower strata can be better understood as an adaptive economy of survival or 'make-shifts', combining several types of resources (Mooser 1984: 73).

6 Servants, family economy and agrarian labour markets

The question concerning the position of servants is very important in the context of the operation of the peasant family farm. In his essay on the developmental cycle of the peasant household, Lutz Berkner argued that servants were hired and dismissed with the phases of the life cycle of the family (Berkner 1972). Servants were employed to bring the labour of the family into balance with the land available for it. In Russia the relative stability of the rural community was achieved by expanding and contracting the size of the farm and redistribution of land (as Chayanov had pointed out). In countries where the institution of service prevailed, it was achieved by the circulation of unmarried youth, who were considered to be members of the host-family. In the early years of marriage servants did the work for which the children were still too young. As the children grew up they replaced the servants or became servants in other households.

Berkner, and in fact all who have done serious research on the topic, understand service as a peculiar institution, part of the agricultural labour force in the peasant family economy, and not necessarily of an agricultural labouring class, like young proletarians.[32] So in any search for evidence of increasing differentiation and the growth of a class of near landless labourers, the issue of service must be resolved. The social position of servants in husbandry in early modern England was analysed in depth by Ann Kussmaul (1981) in a remarkably elegant study. She observed that large and small farmers sent their sons and daughters into farm service, not out of economic necessity, but in order 'to take their places in the economic life of the house-hold' (similar to Berkner's argument) (Kussmaul 1981: 76). While the institution of service may not simply have been a temporary extension of the agricultural proletariat into the household of farmers, it is nevertheless very likely that more labourers than farmers sent their children into service. Increasingly, servants became part of a wage economy, not merely of the family economy. This can be concluded from Kussmaul's argument that the farmer's choice to recruit servants or day-labourers to do the work on the farm varied according to the tightening or relaxation of the labour market, as influenced by population movements, changes in the cost of living, and real wages. The effect of population growth was to create a mass of poor adult labourers in need of wage work. In such a situation, farmers preferred labourers above servants, while in periods of stagnating or declining population and labour scarcity, they were inclined to ascertain of a continuous supply of labour throughout the year by binding youths to annual contracts and by keeping them on the farm (Kussmaul 1981: 100–1). Thus, the composition of the rural labour force was like a 'dual labour market': servants gave farmers a reliable core around which to shape their external labour force according to their needs.

The cycles of change Kussmaul observed were not evenly spread across the country. Because of the pronounced seasonality of work, grain production caused farmers to hire more temporary wage labourers than permanent servants. Animal husbandry used more servants, because the work was more continuous (Kussmaul 1981: 104). In his essay on 'peasant ecotypes', Mitterauer (1992b: 149) differentiated in an analogous way between two main types of rural labour relations: those employing farmhands or servants, and those employing day labourers (*Gesinde-gesellschaften* and *Taglöhnergesellschaften*). Farmhands participated in all activities of family life, day labourers worked on short contracts and were not integrated into the family. Nowhere, he argued, can both types be found in their pure form. Combining these types of labour recruitment with rural ecotypes, he observed a remarkable correspondence between family economies with servants and cattle raising. Different types of grain farming had a mixed composition of the labour force, while viticulture worked predominantly with day labourers.

7 Peasant ecotypes and gender-specific work patterns in agriculture

Even more important to the ecotype approach than the contrast between farm regions using wage labour and those predominantly using family labour, is the emergence of a variety of labour relations within and outside the family in the process of adaptation to different ecological settings. The ecotype approach seeks to combine the perspective of the anthropological research tradition of 'cultural ecology' with social and economic developments. An ecotype can be defined as a pattern of resource exploitation, or ecological adaptation, within a given macro-economic frame-work, resulting in specific regional and inter-regional 'cultural complexes' of social networks, labour relations, cultural norms and perceptions.[33] Both Mitterauer and Löfgren emphasized the regional variety of labour relations under the impact of different modes of ecological adaptation in pre-industrial society. To a large extent, access to natural resources, such as soils of differing fertility, peat bogs or other waste-land, seas, and mineral deposits, determined the development of work and local labour relations. In his research on labour organization and family forms, Mitterauer distinguished four historical ecotypes in Austria that determined the labour organiz-ation in the peasant family: ecotypes based on cattle raising, on arable farming, on viticulture and on cottage industry. While these four types were heterogeneous in themselves, the character of rural families as work-groups and the proportion of wage labour used in and outside the family varied according to different organizational forms, ranging from the isolated peasant family farm to rural activities predominantly based on wage labour, such as forestry or mining.

Of course, many other ecotypes are conceivable. In north-western Europe, ecotypes based on access to the sea are immediately obvious, like different types of fishing and seafaring. In Holland one also finds what Löfgren in his Swedish research designated as 'marginal ecotypes' of coastal villages.[34] As the sea 'represented an open, common-property resource', landless peasants were able to establish themselves as small fishermen, combining their coastal fishing with other activities, such as sea-faring. Löfgren pointed out other aspects in Swedish regions. Population growth and a shift towards a market-oriented agrarian economy in the nineteenth century forced growing groups of landless labourers and peasant smallhoders to proliferate new 'marginal adaptations' to local economic and ecological situations. The ecological setting determined the heterogeneous outcome of what, on a macro-level, appears to be a uniform process of proletarianization: the emergence of day-labourers in grain-growing plains, crofter-fishermen along the coast, cottagers in wood and heathlands, peasant-workers close to emerging industrial centres, and so on. As a consequence of the increasing differentiation in the rural community, varying organizational types of household economies emerged. Löfgren set the *centrifugal* farmstead of the well-to-do landed peasant as an integrated production unit and a focal point for family and non-family labour, against the *centripetal* homestead of cottagers and farm labourers, functioning as a base of operation, at the two ends of the social continuum. If, however, the poor family's labour could be used intensively, for instance in cottage industries, the economic integration of the domestic unit could become stronger (Löfgren 1974: 28–9).

Löfgren detected several structural similarities in the patterns of marginal ecological and economic adaptation. First, they were based upon the exploitation of marginal resources with the use of family labour. Second, there was generally an attempt to keep up some sort of agricultural production, mainly potatoes (hence the nickname 'potato people'). Third, industrial crafts were developed that could form a basis for market exchange. Fourth, these activities were often combined with seasonal wage labour, whether farm labour nearby or migrant labour far away. Löfgren concluded that the households of such poor peasant families, typically engaged in 'occupational pluralism', had to co-ordinate the many short-term activities into a complex annual production or labour cycle with marked seasonal variations within a gendered and generational division of labour (Löfgren 1978: 103).

The gender-specific division of peasant labour was, in turn, subject to considerable local, regional, and class-specific variation. In spite of some interesting discussions on universal biological and socio-cultural determinants of women's work roles in European agriculture (for example, by Mitterauer)[35] women seem to have carried out a wide variety of tasks. The available historical evidence fails to reveal any rigid or inflexible pattern, either over time or space (Lee 1990). First, there is abundant proof (for nineteenth-century Germany, at least) that the modernization of agriculture, associated with the intensification of crops and the diffusion of new technology on the land, required a reallocation of individual labour tasks within the peasant household.[36] Second, the work role of women was correlated with the size of holding and family income: the influence of socio-cultural constraints on female work was necessarily weaker in smallholding and proletarian households (Lee 1990: 57; see also Löfgren 1975). Third, as agricultural change and social differentiation did not develop uniformly, the regional ecotype itself appears to have been an important determinant of the gender-specific division of labour. This was particularly stressed by Löfgren (1975). In his view, varieties in the gender-specific allocation of labour resulted mainly from a flexible adaptation of work roles to ecological and economic conditions. In this context he pointed to the annual labour cycle of marginal peasant ecotypes, based on a plurality of activities during the year. In many regions, the seasonal mobility of the men forced peasant women to perform the presumably male tasks on the farm.

8   Labour cycle and rural labour markets: migrant labour, proto-industry and proletarianization

Löfgren's representation of the poor rural family's labour in an annual cycle has more than just descriptive value. The labour cycle determines how the various resources of the members of the family are combined throughout the year. The poor family's different labour tasks are arranged in such a way as to achieve an optimal allocation of its available labour time during the year. The members of the family cannot choose jobs according to earning differentials or opportunity costs alone, as they would do according to neo-classical economic theory. They have to co-ordinate their labour efforts among themselves and adapt to seasonal variations in labour demand in specific economic and ecological settings.

The analytical consequences of the concept of the annual cycle of family labour become particularly clear in the study of migrant labour in pre-industrial Europe by Jan Lucassen (1987). As each component of the cycle is equally important to generate the collective income fund, he argued, a labour cycle once established tends to become a closed system, unaffected by minor or temporary changes in the labour market. However, more permanent changes in one of its components can lead to a complete restructuring of the cycle itself, sometimes even to the point where the peasant holding has to be abandoned (in which case proletarianization is completed), and migrant labour has to become permanent migration. It is important to note, however, that this is not necessarily the outcome of a restructuring of the cycle: other combinations of work on and off the farm or a reshaping of migration flows are conceivable as well. Again, the point seems to be that there is no unilinear, progressive development of labour relations from peasant to proletarian.

The concept of the labour cycle, because it recognizes flexibility within structural constraints, can thus provide a more complete and dynamic picture of the income strategies of the early-modern rural poor and their interrelationship with labour markets than can the static Chayanovian interpretation of the peasant or proto-industrial family economy. The differentiated nature of these strategies in the rural economies of pre-industrial Europe can be explained more adequately. This will be even more obvious when we look more closely at three aspects of the interdependence of family income strategies and rural labour markets: first, the development of migrant labour and its intersection with rural industry; second, proto-industrialization and the gender division of labour; third, processes of proletarianization.

As becomes clear from Lucassen's study, the sheer extent of seasonal migrant labour in pre-industrial Europe would refute any attempt to ignore the impact of labour markets on the income strategies of the labouring poor.[37] In the context of a discussion of the labour cycle, the relationship of migrant labour with cottage industry is particularly interesting. Although there are instances where both were included in the family's labour cycle, in most cases they seem to have been mutually exclusive. In another context, cottage industry and migrant labour have been differentiated as 'continuous' and 'discontinuous' peasant-worker strategies (Holmes and Quataert 1986). Both Lucassen (1987) and Mooser (1984: 242) observed that in the German 'push' areas of migrant labour in Westphalia, proto-industry was less developed, while in proto-industrial (weaving) areas, migrant labour was virtually non-existent. Spinning, as a female activity, could more easily be combined with male migrant labour (see also van Zanden 1993a: 165). Pfister (1992a: 422–3) reached a similar conclusion for the northern Swiss Alps: the market for agrarian migrant labour in the bordering German areas resulted in relatively little development of proto-industry. In a somewhat different fashion the sizeable migrant labour (of building workers) in the nearby Austrian region of Vorarlberg was progressively replaced by proto-industry in the eighteenth century (Fitz 1985). Only then did the poor peasant's family become a production unit. In other words, labour was becoming 'familiarized' (Mitterauer 1992b: 154–5; and 1986: 234–5).

Migrant labour seems to have been similarly absent in areas with a strong regional demand for agricultural wage labour (Lucassen 1987: 35–9, 48–52). The seasonal nature of most agricultural labour, however, forced families to adopt other kinds of work to complete a full annual labour cycle. This was clearly shown by Gay Gullickson (1986: 58–62) in her research on the French proto-industrial Pays de Caux, north of the textile city of Rouen. She maintained that if work in cottage industries had not been available to supplement harvest wages in this grain growing area, farmers would have been forced to use migrant labour. In her work she gave evidence of the changes in the labour cycle of the people of the Pays de Caux in the eighteenth and nineteenth centuries. The household economy of labouring families was only partially dependent upon the cottage industry. In the eighteenth century there was a large seasonal transfer of male labour from cottage weaving to harvest field work. Spinning was almost entirely a female occupation, and with a ratio of six to ten spinners to one full-time weaver, many more women were engaged in the region's textile industry than men. Therefore female spinners had to be recruited from both weavers' and agricultural labourers' families. In this way the sexual division of labour in the cottage industry meshed nicely with the sexual division of labour in agriculture. The supply of female labour in the textile industry was partly determined by the male agricultural labour market and *vice versa.* In the course of the nineteenth century, however, this sexual division of labour broke down. Weavers were increasingly employed all year round and the interaction of agricultural wage labour and male weaving declined. At the same time, the mechanization of spinning had created a serious unemployment problem for village women. As the demand for agricultural workers and weavers increased, women moved into these traditionally male occupations and even came to dominate the weaving branch of the textile industry. After 1870, when weaving had also been mechanized, cottage industry disappeared completely, resulting in a mass exodus from the Pays de Caux and a severe shortage of agricultural labour (Gullickson 1982, 1986, and 1991).

That spinning as a predominantly female preserve was almost universally used to supplement earnings in rural lower-class families of both textile workers and others has been shown in such diverse proto-industrial regions as the Pays de Caux in France, Northern Ireland, Zürich and Appenzell-Ausserrhoden in Switzerland (Gray 1992/93; Pfister 1989; Tanner 1986 and 1982). The sexual division of labour between spinning and weaving maintained in these areas – implying status and earning differentials as well – once again shows Medick's assumption of a functional interdependence among the members of the proto-industrial family to be an oversimplification. Moreover, in the long run work roles in spinning as well as weaving were flexibly adapted to changing circumstances in labour demand. Research on several proto-industrial weaving areas in the nineteenth century shows a diversification of family work roles in the period of declining cottage industry during industrialization (Quataert 1984 and 1985a; also Rose 1988; Lyons 1989). This may once more be taken as an indication that there was no self-evident tendency for the proto-industrial family to exploit its common labour below opportunity costs, even in extreme situations.

A diversification of work roles and a restructuring of the labour cycle enabled the semi-proletarian rural family to stay on the land, thus preventing a rural exodus. Nevertheless, the dissolution of one of the components of the labour cycle, for example through the loss of the occupation of one of the family members, could induce poor families to migrate, as happened in the Pays de Caux after 1870. Developments in several other French regions can serve to illustrate this effect. For instance, in the Val d'Isère near Lyon the insinuation of the silk industry into rural life in the nineteenth century at first slowed down the pace of the rural exodus and sometimes even reversed it. Small farming households resisted permanent migration by sending one or more members to work in the mills, mostly females who stayed in dormitories. The feminization of the silk industry led to a new sexual division of labour, with the men staying at home to work the peasant plot. Only the loss of female income through the contraction of the silk industry in the last quarter of the century forced these families to give up their peasant holdings and move to the cities (Jonas 1991; Chatelain 1970). In the Stéphanois (the St Etienne region) before industrialization, the timing and allocation of industrial activity in the family was regulated by the timing of the harvest and sowing. Adult males were allocated to agriculture during the season and were otherwise engaged in seasonal metal-working, while women and children were employed in year-round silkmaking, either spinning or weaving (Hanagan 1986, and 1989; also Lehning 1980). However, when agriculture was transformed into dairy production for the urban market, providing year-round work for family members, seasonal employment in agriculture disappeared. Rural dwellers too poor to buy cattle lost an essential part of their income. They preferred to migrate permanently, and so the rural supply of temporary industrial labour also diminished.

As a final test to demonstrate how proletarianization was related to changes in the labour cycle, the much-debated classical English case of enclosures and labour supply in the late eighteenth and early nineteenth centuries is particularly revealing. Here, new research has come up against the dominant, 'revisionist' tradition that started with Chambers's (1952) criticism of Marx's and other social reformers' view of enclosures as implying massive proletarianization, followed by a rural exodus into the industrializing towns.[38] The 'counter-revisionists' argue that enclosure eroded non-wage resources of subsistence available to semi-proletarian families, leaving them increasingly dependent on wages. Before enclosure many families were able to use common and waste land to keep a cow or other livestock, and to hunt and gather for consumption or sale, minimizing opportunity costs of labour by the employment of otherwise underemployed family members, especially women and children.[39] By eliminating non-wage resources, enclosure undermined their productive contributions to family survival. Increased dependence on wages of both men and women made proletarian families much more vulnerable to the vagaries of the seasonal agricultural labour market, as Keith Snell (1985: 138–227) demonstrated. Loss of common rights or allotments forced them to apply for poor relief to replace former non-wage resources in their family's labour cycle. This seems to have been particularly true in southern grain-growing areas, where it was reinforced by the decline of cottage industries. Families formerly employed all the year round were now unable to find employment in agriculture during slack seasons. Labour shortage and rural exodus could only be prevented by the system of outdoor poor relief that was consciously developed to replenish income for seasonally unemployed labourers (Boyer 1990). In the north, it is argued, access to and productive use of the common fields had enabled cottagers to take up some industrial craft. This cottager class with a small stake in the land was particularly hard-hit by the enclosures. Abolition of this part of their resources forced them to give up the craft and trading part also, with a growing social differentiation of the rural community as a result. Some managed to become full-time farmers or traders, others became agricultural or industrial labourers (Martin 1984).

It may be concluded that the need to combine several resources into an annual labour cycle was a pervasive feature of the economics of the families of both the agricultural wage labourer and the small peasant. This determined their economic behaviour much more than the urge to work as a unit of production regardless of 'opportunity costs'. Mainly because of the pronounced seasonal nature of both agricultural and industrial work, early modern social differentiation in the country-side resulted in the emergence of 'sub-peasant strata' of various kinds, dependent on a pluralism of economic activities. Dependence on a single source of income or subsistence would not provide a secure livelihood for a broad range of the rural populace. However, the existence of these 'sub-peasant strata' cannot be equated with the emergence of a modern permanent agricultural or industrial proletariat. Nor did it necessarily develop into such a proletariat. Rather, these 'sub-peasants' constitute social groups or classes in their own right. In this respect some of them can readily be compared to the peasant-workers of the twentieth century (Thirsk 1984a; Holmes and Quataert 1986). The peasant-worker phenomenon has been presented as an alternative to proletarianization, which has, erroneously, generally been viewed as the inevitable outcome of the type of structural developments as described above (see the references in Holmes 1989: 220 n. 5; also Kaschuba and Lipp 1982). The behaviour of worker-peasantries demonstrates that enduring dependence on wage earning and on the forces of a labour market can exist without the creation of a working class. Smallholdings provide subsistence security in the face of the uncertainties of marginal wage employment; wage labour provides cash in the market economy. To achieve these ends, labour has to be co-ordinated among the members of the rural households. The labour of the peasant-worker's family is in a state of permanent reconfiguration. In the long run, peasant-worker groups did have the potential to shift their labour involvements to either side: working-class formation or permanent proletarianization on the one hand, 're-peasantization' on the other (Holmes 1989: 205–7). This description seems also to be fairly accurate for the process of social differentiation in the European countryside before the creation of a permanent proletariat in the nineteenth century. The latter must be regarded as only one of several possible developments (cf. Hoffmann 1972; Kellenbenz 1975: 195–213; Mitterauer 1981).

9 Urban crafts and industries: workshops, households and 'familialization' of artisan production

The idea of a pre-industrial family-based household economy in urban production, integrating productive functions at home, seems to be even more misleading than the idea of a uniform peasant or proto-industrial family economy. Apart from the 'sub-peasant strata', there were indeed many farms that were worked co-operatively by peasant families. Labour in urban workshops, building sites and industries was generally not co-ordinated among the members of the family. The artisan workshop cannot be equated to the peasant family farm in this respect, still less so the numerous married journeymen and wage labourers in early modern towns, whose families, like those of agricultural labourers and cottagers in the 'sub-peasant strata', were by definition not units of production.

The separation of workshop and household characteristically differentiated peasant and proto-industrial worker from urban handicraft labour (Mitterauer 1984, and 1979; Quataert 1985b). The setting up of a workshop and the organization of labour in artisan production was not a matter of individual or family strategies to exploit common property or labour, but of collective guild rules. According to these rules the labour force in the workshop was generally constituted by non-kin apprentices, journeymen, and – in specific industries – female workers, excluding the master's wife and children. Productive functions were performed in the workshop, perhaps close to, but not inside the home. 'Household' and 'workshop' were separate spheres. *A fortiori* this would be the case in trades performed in the open air or in the house of the customer, such as most of the building trades. The non-familial character of artisan labour is further attested to by the fact that sons or daughters hardly ever performed their apprenticeship or service in their father's workshop, even if they were trained in the same trade. This is not to deny that family income was often earned by both men and women, but these earnings were based on individual rather than co-operative labour.

These general observations, mainly derived from Mitterauer's research on Central Europe, are clearly at odds with the use of Tilly and Scott's concept of the family economy in urban handicrafts, as for example in Martha Howell's research on women's labour in late medieval cities of north-western Europe. Following Tilly and Scott she supposed, erroneously, that women's work was part of the family's work, because the family would have had a central role in market production.[40] While admitting that 'the family production unit was not necessarily physically located in the household', she nevertheless maintained that 'it always had the family and its coresidents as its producers' (Howell 1986b: 219). However, Mitterauer's research and that of others show – at least for the German speaking countries – that, if households and workshops were integrated, this was not because of co-operation of family members in the workshop, but because non-kin apprentices, journeymen and servants lived together in the household of the master artisan.

The interconnection of production, consumption and cohabitation of the artisan labour force in the way described above is at the heart of Otto Brunner's influential concept of *das ganze Haus* as it has been employed by numerous Central European social historians to characterize work and family in this area in medieval and early modern society. However, social and family relations in the handicraft mode of life only imperfectly fit this model. First, the tension between the workshop economy of production regulated by the guilds and the household economy of consumption and cohabitation has been completely overlooked (Quataert 1985b: 1133–4). Brunner was not concerned with its impact on the organization of family labour in the home or, more specifically, with the demarcation of work spheres by gender. Therefore the concept of *das ganze Haus* in no way matches the family-based household economy introduced by English feminist economic historians such as Alice Clark and reformulated by Tilly and Scott in their concept of the pre-industrial artisan family economy. Second, it has to be emphasized that accommodation of the artisan labour force in the master's household was only partial, as it varied from complete integration in the case of apprentices and unmarried journeymen to complete separation in the case of married journeymen. Even in the middle ages, the variability of both the degree of integration and the length of stay makes the picture considerably more complex than the model of *das ganze Haus* would have us believe (Quataert 1985b; Mitterauer 1984; Reininghaus 1983).

Furthermore, the degree of integration of the artisan labour force in the master's household varied considerably both in time and space. In Central European towns many, possibly most, journeymen continued to live unmarried in their master's house (in what the Germans call *hausrechtliche Abhängigkeit* or *Einbindung*) well into the nineteenth century (Kocka 1990: 144–51; Ehmer 1991: 159ff). Only then did a formal wage relationship emerge. It would be wrong to assume, however, that these unmarried, live-in journeymen were fully integrated into the household, because they formed a highly mobile part of the artisan labour force (Kocka 1990: 187–8). In trades which operated with many wage labourers, such as the building trades, married journeymen formed only the core of the labour force. Michael Sonenscher (1989: 197) found few traces of kin-based workforces in eighteenth-century France. Instead, the workforce of the great majority of the urban trades consisted overwhelmingly of young, single men. He gave no information of their place of residence. In England it seems to have been more usual for married journeymen to live in their own households and to go out to work elsewhere, at least after the sixteenth century. In the nineteenth century it was only in certain specific trades such as bakers and butchers that journeymen and apprentices lived with their masters. As a consequence, the age of marriage and family formation in English and Central European towns differed considerably (Ehmer 1991).

There is no proof whatsoever that the pre-industrial artisan family (man, wife and children) had originally formed a unit of production, still less that this unit dissolved under the impact of industrialization and proletarianization. On the contrary, it can be shown that in many cases the capitalist transformation of artisan production in the nineteenth century forced masters' or journeymen's families to work together in a family work unit. The introduction of the putting-out system in urban industries in the nineteenth century tended to destroy the traditional separation of workshop and household. This happened for example in the tailoring business. In large European cities, such as London, Paris, Vienna, Berlin and Amsterdam, journeymen-tailors had always carried out their trade in their masters' shops. The basic unit of production was not the family but a team of skilled male workers. Even if the wives of skilled tailors were employed in the garment trades, the location of their work and the nature of their tasks would be different from that of the men. In the 1830s and 1840s (in Amsterdam some fifty years later) the ready-made garment industry expanded enormously at the cost of custom tailoring.[41] Tailors began to cut labour costs by reducing the number of their shop workers and turning to home workers instead. These home workers mostly worked with family members in a family unit of labour. For skilled tailors, proletarianization meant a move from the master's workshop to their own household. From then on income depended on his marshalling of family labour. Similar developments can also be found in the shoe industry (Ehmer 1991: 214–28; Schmiechen 1982).

The development of labour relations in the silk industry in Lyon, Krefeld and Vienna in the nineteenth century provides another illuminating example of this process of 'familization' of urban production. Unlike tailoring, silk weaving had been dominated by the putting-out system before the nineteenth century. Manufacturers gave out silk to formally-independent master weavers with their own work-force of journeymen weavers, often living in the master's home. In the nineteenth century, family labour increasingly replaced the labour of journeymen. By setting up a family workshop, it became possible for journeymen to leave the household of the master and to profit from the expanding putting-out industry. Small masters thereby lost the traditional method of controlling dependent labour. As silk weaving required auxiliary workers, family labour was increasingly used. Family labour, especially women's labour, provided masters with a ready solution to the emerging labour shortage in their changing household economy. The household shop came to consist essentially of the wife working alongside her husband and some of their children. As in tailoring, these family work units in the silk industry were created, not by artisan tradition but by its exact opposite: the destruction of this tradition by the establishment of the capitalist manufacturing system.[42]

10 Conclusion: family economy, family strategies and labour markets in pre-industrial Europe

The concept of family economy, introduced in the 1970s in the debates on women's labour by Louise Tilly and Joan Scott and on the proto-industry by Hans Medick, had a very specific meaning derived from the theories of Chayanov on the economic behaviour of the Russian peasantry. The family economy was conceived essentially as a unit of production or a unit of co-operative labour, and was considered typical of the way pre-industrial or proto-industrial labour in Europe was organized. It was supposed that the majority of parents and children worked together in a unitary household, based in or immediately around their own home. If anything, the foregoing review of the historiography on the subject of labour in the pre-industrial family after the pioneering and path-breaking work of Medick and of Tilly and Scott has shown that these central suppositions can no longer be sustained. First, the pre-industrial family, be it rural or urban, did not necessarily constitute a unit of production or labour. It is therefore misleading to generalize about the family work unit or 'household mode of production' as a general denominator of pre-industrial labour organization. Even in proto-industrial production the labour of the family proved to be highly diversified. Second, there was no universal phased evolution from one form of labour organization (family labour) to another (wage labour), nor from one form of family labour organization (family economy) to another (family wage economy). Consequently, theories that try to relate other aspects of family behaviour, such as marriage and fertility, to this supposed evolution of family labour organization must also fail.

The failure of the concept of pre-industrial or proto-industrial family economy becomes evident in three problems. The first is gender segregation in medieval, early modern and modern labour. Contrary to widespread feminist opinion, based on the work of the first generation of English feminist economic historians and in essence, though in a somewhat different form, adopted by Tilly and Scott, there has never been a 'golden age' of women's work in family economy. In the middle ages as well as in early modern or modern industrial times, women have generally been clustered in low skilled, low-status and low-paying occupations. In spite of the integration of part of the artisan work-force in the household of the masters, labour in the household and in the workshop remained separate spheres.

The second problem is that, as far as rural society is concerned, the effects of the social differentiation of the peasantry in much of western and central Europe since the sixteenth century have been ignored or, at least, undervalued. The crucial question is the organization and allocation of family labour time in different strata of the peasantry. The concept of family economy clearly underestimates the extent of wage labour and labour markets in early modern or pre-industrial European society, and therefore seems inadequate for describing the many forms and combinations of labour in the family. The same holds, in a somewhat different fashion, for urban production. Many day labourers and journeymen were married and did not live or work in their masters' households.

The third, closely related, problem is that in most regions, proto-industry was based not on co-operative labour by all members of the family but on individual labour of some of them. Activities of rural lower-class families were often highly diversified. They included different kinds of wage work, industrial production and the cultivation of tiny plots of land. Also, the gender division of labour in proto-industry proved to be important, for instance between female spinning and male weaving.

Notions such as 'economy of make-shifts' (Hufton), 'adaptive family economy' (Wall) or, a more formal neo-classical economic expression, 'utility-maximizing behaviour' that is aimed at an optimal allocation of the labour time of the family, are more adequate descriptions of the behaviour of the pre-industrial family than the static concept of family economy. This is not to say that the outcome of this adaptive or utility-maximizing behaviour was achieved by measuring earning differentials or opportunity costs alone. The poor family's various labour tasks had to be attuned to seasonal variations in labour demand in specific economic and ecological settings. In the process of adaptation to the alternation of opportunities and constraints, people appeared to allocate and co-ordinate their labour within the family in many more varied ways than was originally assumed in the concept of family economy. In this context I have drawn attention to the ideas of Mitterauer and Löfgren about the influence of historical 'ecotypes' on the organization of the 'family labour cycle'. What seems important is that this approach challenges conceptions of a phased and essentially uniform and unilinear development of family labour organization and labour relations. To a large extent the ecological setting determined the heterogeneous outcome of what on a macro-level appears to be a uniform process of proletarianization. In pre-industrial society there was no uniform working class. The forms of wage labour varied enormously: day labourers, crofters, cottagers, proto-industrial workers, migrant labourers, peasant-workers, and so on. These different types of proletarianization, or semi-proletarianization, also influenced family organization and the allocation of family labour in different ways. Only in the nineteenth century did a permanent and more or less uniform industrial proletariat emerge.

Notes

1 This chapter is reprinted, with kind permission of the publisher, in a slightly modified form from *Family strategies and changing labour relations*, Economic and Social History in the Netherlands Volume 6, Amsterdam: NEHA (1994): 19–60.

2 To which, it seems, historians of family structure, including those of the 'Cambridge Group' are increasingly turning their attention, as becomes apparent from their journal *Continuity and Change.*

3 The tendency has been very strong in German-speaking countries. German work in this field in the 1970s is reviewed by Lee (1981). Some important German works include Kriedte, Medick and Schlumbohm (1981); Rosenbaum (1982); Sieder (1987). Of special and continuing interest is the work of Michael Mitterauer and his 'Vienna school' in family history. Some of their latest and most important works include: Ehmer and Mitterauer (1986); Mitterauer (1990 and 1992a); Ehmer (1991). Examples of a combination of family history with labour history by English-speaking authors are: Tilly and Scott (1975 and 1977); Levine (1984 and 1987); Seccombe (1992).

4 Good, if critical, introductions to the subject are: Clarkson (1985) and Hudson (1992). The concept is completely rejected by Coleman (1983), and by Houston and Snell (1984). These and other critics were answered by Kriedte, Medick and Schlumbohm (1983 and 1993). This is also an almost complete review of the literature since their 1977 *Industrialisierung vor der Industrialisierung*, but see also Lewis 1994. Special issues on proto-industry by the *Journal of Family History* volume 17, number 2 (1992) and *Continuity and Change* volume 8, number 2 (1993) give evidence of continuing interest and debate. See also Prak and Schlumbohm in this volume.

5 Medick (1976); Tilly and Scott (1975 and 1977). Anderson (1980: 92–3) valued Medick's study as 'seminal in every way'; Tilly and Scott's as 'a seminal work pioneering the modern use of the concept of family economy'.

6 Tilly and Scott (1977, introduction to the 1987 edition: 6).

7 According to Tilly (1987, quotation on p. 124). The phrase 'cooperative conflicts' is from Sen (1990).

8 Cf. Chayanov (1966). The debt to Chayanov is clear from the many references in Medick (1976: 298ff), Tilly and Scott (1975: 44, 46, 50). The importance of Chayanov can also be seen in earlier formulations in Tilly (1974).

9 Cf. Foster-Carter (1978); Wolpe (1980); Meillassoux (1979). Kriedte, Medick and Schlumbohm were clearly very much influenced by the articulation debate. It has

also been the basic principle of J. L. van Zanden's (1993a) analysis of Dutch merchant capitalism.

10 The most convincing criticisms on this subject can be found in several papers by Mark Harrison, partly written against the influential 'Chayanovist' T. Shanin (1972): Harrison (1974/5, 1976/7a, 1976/7b, 1979/80). Harrison and others placed Chayanov in a strong ideological tradition in Russian peasant studies by labelling him a 'neo-populist' as opposed to the Marxists, of whom the young Lenin was the most prominent: cf. among others Littlejohn (1977); Ennew, Hirst and Tribe (1976/7); Patnaik (1978/9).

11 The theoretical and practical implications of this supposed absence of a labour market in the Chayanovian peasant economy are excellently reviewed in Harrison 1974/5. The issue is raised in an historical context also by Mendels (1978), and Smith (1984); see also Gatrell (1982).

12 The incompatibility is particularly stressed by Schmitt (1988), but see also Mendels (1978), and Pfister (1991, 1992a and 1992b). Schmitt nevertheless presents Chayanov as a precursor of modern neo-classical economics of family labour time allocation, developed by Becker (1965), which, however, contains only a small paragraph on the division of labour within families (on p. 512); the implications for the allocation of labour within the family are explored in Becker (1981). Becker's neo-classical approach has been criticized – correctly, in my opinion – for ignoring gendered and generational inequalities in the process of labour allocation: see for instance Sen (1983).

13 There are many studies on contemporary Third-World agrarian labour relations that implicitly or explicitly corroborate this criticism of the Chayanovian approach; see for example van Schendel (1981); Breman (1985).

14 Cf. Blum (1978: 109–15, 171–7). The work of Charles Tilly (1981 and 1984) is also important in this context. However, as a sociologist he is too much inclined to interpret different and reversible processes of social differentiation as a general European and uniform evolution of proletarianization. See also Lis and Soly (1979), and Soly (1987).

15 Pfister (1991: 71, 88, 94, and 1992b: 223). Robert Lee, in a review of Kriedte, Medick and Schlumbohm, *Industrialisierung vor der Industrialisierung* in *Social History* 4 (1979) 375–9, was one of the first to raise doubts about Medick's adoption of Chayanov's self-exploitation model, partly because it 'tended to ignore such important factors as the mediating impact of migrant labour on the social relations between individual households, and the problem of the sexual division of labour within the individual family'. Admittedly, Schlumbohm in his contribution to *Industrialisierung vor der Industrialisierung* already raised doubts about Medick's idea of a 'differential profit', earned by the putting-out merchant because of the 'self-exploitation' of the proto-industrial family (Kriedte, Medick and Schlumbohm 1977: 60, 112–14 and 209 n. 36).

16 There is an illuminating illustration of this diversification in Schlumbohm (1982). See also from a different angle Cohen (1989/90).

17 Löfgren (1974, 1976, 1978, and 1980). See also the references to Löfgren's ideas in Anderson (1980: 75–6), and Lis (1984: 383), who explicitly invokes Löfgren's research to reject the idea of the prevalence of a 'household mode of production'.

18 In this context it may be relevant to note that the conception of the Historical School of capitalism as a way of industrial organization differs considerably from the Marxist view of capitalism as a social formation.

19 Clark (1919) is the best known. Interesting accounts of the intellectual origins of this first wave of feminist economic history are provided by Thirsk (1985), and Berg (1992).

20 The popularity of this scheme was reinforced by some of the 'classics' of feminist sociology in the 1970s such as Zaretski (1976), Oakley (1976) and Rowbotham (1973). For an early criticism see Kloek (1981: 32–47).

21 One of the best accounts in British history based on this perspective is Hill (1989). Barbara Hanawalt also proves very receptive to Tilly and Scott's 'pre-industrial' family economy: see her introduction in Hanawalt (1986b).

22 Wall (1986a: 265). Laslett (1983: 556), concludes: 'The Chayanov model will not fit the English case, and it would seem to me to be difficult to use as a way of discriminating area from area in Europe'.

23 Cf. the expert review essay by Bennet (1988). A similar critique has been formulated in a Marxist fashion by Chris Middleton (1979, 1983 and 1985).

24 Hilton (1975). See also Gatrell (1982). There is a scathing review of Macfarlane's *Origins* by Hilton: 'Individualism and the English Peasantry', *New Left Review* 120 (1980): 109–11. Other critics mainly focused on Macfarlane's treatment of property rights: S. D. White and R. T. Vann, 'The Invention of English Individualism: Alan Macfarlane and the Modernization of Pre-Modern England', *Social History* 8 (1983): 345–63; L. R. Poos and Ll. Bonfield, 'Law and Individualism in Medieval England', *ibid.* 11 (1986): 285–301. Hanawalt (1986a) essentially follows Hilton in her definition of the peasantry as a social group, as is also clear from her review 'Reflections on Land, Kinship and Life-Cycle', *Peasant Studies* 15 (1988): 137–48.

25 The phrase originates in research dating back to the beginning of this century: Johnson (1909); see also Habakkuk (1969). The literature on the sixteenth century is summarized in Spufford (1974: chapter 2), 'The problem: the disappearance of the small landowner'. The classical study on the sixteenth century is Tawney (1912). Interest in the problem has been revived by the Brenner debate.

26 A summary is provided by Clay (1984: 92–101). See also Spufford 1974; Thirsk (1984a); Everitt (1967).

27 Cooper in Aston and Philpin (1985: 138–91, quote on p. 143). Brenner's answer, that in France there were large numbers of mini-peasant producers alongside the great farms 'who needed to hire themselves out as wage labourers in order to make ends meet' seems completely beside the point: Brenner (1985b: 312, and 1985a: 62 n. 111).

28 Cooper in Aston and Philpin (1985: 167–8). French authors such as Goubert (1965) point at the increasing proletarianization of the peasantry in northern France in the second half of the seventeenth century.

29 Cf. de Vries (1974); van Zanden (1985). However, the actual extent of wage labour and its relation with self-employed family labour in agriculture in different parts of the Netherlands is by no means clearly established. Theoretically it may be plausible to claim that agricultural commercialization in the coastal provinces went hand in hand with rural proletarianization in the sixteenth and seventeenth centuries (cf. van Zanden 1988), but to my knowledge there have been no empirical studies that prove its extent or describe its appearances.

30 Cf. on the eastern province of Drente: Bieleman (1987), the review by J. L. van Zanden, 'De landbouw op de zandgronden van oost-Nederland', *Tijdschrift voor Geschiedenis* 101 (1988): 190–205, and the response by J. Bieleman, 'Boeren en rekenmeesters: een repliek', *ibid.*: 206–21. For a wholeheartedly Chayanovian account of the peasant economy in the southern province of North-Brabant: van den Brink (1991). This account ignores the social differentiation in this area, which must have been very similar to the adjacent Belgian Campine area as analyzed in depth by Vanhaute (1992); for the importance of day labourers see also Trienekens (1993). An interpretation of the development of cottage industries in Brabant in the nineteenth century with the help of the concept of the proto-industrial family economy in Klep (1987).

31 Mooser (1984). Mooser's concept of 'rural class society' is conceived as an alternative to the concept of 'peasant society' without completely rejecting it. See also Dipper (1986). For an interesting critique of the mainstream German historiography of rural society, see Farr (1986).

32 Löfgren (1974); Tenfelde (1979); Devine (1984); Mitterauer (1985); van den Brink (1989).

33 Cf. Löfgren (1976); Mitterauer (1992b); also Gaunt (1977a and b).

34 Löfgren (1976). On the marginality of Holland's rural communities in the sixteenth century: de Vries (1974), and Knotter (1986).

35 Mitterauer (1992a: 58–148) ('Geschlechtsspezifischische Arbeitsteilung und Geschlechter-
    rollen in ländlichen Gesellschaften Mitteleuropas'). As a symbol of universal gender
    specific work roles, the use of the scythe as a male preserve as opposed to the sickle as a
    female preserve, is a much favoured topic (*ibid.*: 94–101); Wiegelmann (1975); Roberts
    (1979).
36 On the influence of the diffusion of new technology: Wiegelmann (1975); on the impact
    of intensification: Sabean (1977).
37 Lucassen refers to literature on France, Spain, Italy, Germany, Great Britain and Ireland.
38 There is a useful introduction to the historiography of revisionism and counter-
    revisionism in this debate in Turner (1984); see also Turner (1989). Some of the best
    counter-revisionist research on the subject in recent years includes Neeson (1989); Snell
    (1985); Allen (1992).
39 The importance of the contribution of women is particularly stressed by Humphries
    (1990); see also Malcolmson (1988).
40 Howell (1986a and b). Howell's evidence appears to be very thin, as was suggested for the
    Dutch city of Leiden by Kloek (1987).
41 On Paris: Johnson (1979); Scott (1984). On London: Schmiechen (1982); also Thompson
    and Yeo (1984); on Berlin: Quataert (1985b); on Amsterdam: Knotter (1991: 147–63).
42 On Vienna: Ehmer (1984); see also Ehmer (1980); on Lyons: Sheridan (1984 and 1979);
    on Krefeld: Kriedte (1991).

9 Mobilization of labour in early modern Europe

Jan Lucassen

Towards the end of the three centuries that we today call the early modern period, Adam Smith awarded labour a key role in his influential economic theory. His *Inquiry into the Nature and Causes of the Wealth of Nations* circulated widely in English and in many translations all over Europe immediately after its publication in 1776. Smith (1986: bk. 1, chapter 5: 133) proclaimed: 'What is bought with money or with goods is purchased by labour, as much as what we acquire by the toil of our own body.' Smith was also well aware of the historical significance of the mobilization of labour (*ibid.*):

> Every man is rich or poor according to the degree in which he can afford to enjoy the necessaries, conveniences, and amusements of human life. But after the division of labour has once thoroughly taken place, it is but a very small part of these with which a man's own labour can supply him. The far greater part of them he must derive from the labour of other people, and he must be rich or poor according to the quantity of that labour which he can command, or which he can afford to purchase.

According to Smith (1986: bk. 1, chapter 3: 124–5; bk. 1, chapter 5: 133–4), economic development was originally concentrated in the Mediterranean, in Bengal and in China, where agriculture led to an accumulation of capital, the development of industry and widespread use of money. However, for a sound economy more was required: a 'tolerable security' should be guaranteed to the owners of capital and to the industrious. This condition was not so easily fulfilled, as was demonstrated by serfdom and feudalism, by the slump in international trade in medieval Europe and, Smith (1986: bk. 2, chapter 1: 380) suggested, in contemporary 'Turkey, in Hindostan, and, I believe, in most other governments of Asia.'

As Smith apparently saw it, the history of successful economic development had been interrupted virtually everywhere by such long periods of insecurity. Fresh starts had been made in the Byzantine Empire, the world of Islam under the Abbasids and in Moorish Spain, and later in Christian Europe with the Italian cities, whose example was then followed by other urbanized parts of Europe, such as Switzerland, the Low Countries and finally Great Britain.[1]

This Smithian understanding of economic development on the basis of improved labour productivity in agriculture, urbanization and urban industries is to a great extent compatible with the classic Marxian proletarianization scheme. However, Karl Marx was more Eurocentric than his Scottish[2] predecessor. For him, modern economic developments began only in fourteenth-century northern Italy. According to Marx (1971, volume 1: 743–50) it was not so much the development of productivity, division of labour or urbanization that were crucial but rather the proletarianization of the serfs (in Italy) and of the small but independent farmers (in fifteenth-century England), developments aggravated by the mass spoliation of ecclesiastical landed property during the Reformation followed by the enclosures. Expropriation and subsequent exploitation, often by state-sanctioned force, stands at the heart of Marx's analysis of early modern economic developments. This becomes clear in his treatment of the Dutch Republic as the 'model capitalist nation of the seventeenth century'. Not only were 'by 1648 the people of Holland more over-worked, poorer, and more brutally oppressed than those of all the rest of Europe put together', but the Dutch also managed to enslave and massacre the Indonesians (Marx 1971, volume 1: 779–86, quote on p. 782; also Lourens and Lucassen 1992; van der Linden 1997a).

In modern analyses of labour markets, proletarianization has become a key concept. In his seminal 1984 article, Charles Tilly provided a thumb-nail sketch of the quantitative outlines of the transition from independent farming to wage labour, mainly in industry. According to his estimates, the percentage of western Europeans depending on wages, grew from twenty-five in 1500 to over fifty in 1750, and seventy by the middle of the nineteenth century. It has not changed substantially after that point. Tilly's analysis of these trends offers an alternative to Smith's equating of urbanization and proletarianization. Tilly places proto-industry, a rural development, squarely in the middle of his argument.

Recent studies of labour markets and labour mobilization in early modern Europe now allow us to go one step further and propose a more complex but ultimately richer analysis of this vital process. To the approaches offered by Smith and Tilly respectively, four major amendments suggest themselves.

First, if we take Europe as a whole, the existence of unfree labour in its many forms has been seriously underestimated: slavery in southern and south-eastern Europe, serfdom in eastern Europe, and in many countries (in western Europe too) convict and other systems of forced labour far exceeding purely penal requirements (Brass and van der Linden 1997).

Second, most labour market theories underestimate the role of the state as an employer, dominating not merely a still underdeveloped sector of public servants, but also huge armies and navies, including those deployed for colonial use (Tilly 1990; Lucassen and Zürcher 1998).

Third, although industry has now been defined much more broadly to include proto-industry and more recently also 'worker-peasantries' and 'partially proletarian peripheral labour' (see contributions by Knotter and Schlumbohm in this volume), one important sector of industry still tends to be overlooked in discussions about proletarianization: the urban independent artisans, as a rule organized in craft guilds. Adam Smith (1986: bk. 1, chapter 8: 168) himself wrongly believed that their numbers were insignificant: 'in every part of Europe, twenty workmen serve under a master for one that is independent'. This misrepresentation has had a long life, but should be revised in the light of modern studies on guilds and the petite bourgeoisie.[3]

And finally, proletarianization was mainly conceived as vertical or social mobility,[4] while its geographical (or horizontal) form was narrowly understood to consist of two patterns. Either impoverished farmers and peasants were shown to migrate over short distances from the countryside into urban dwellings, or they were pictured as long-distance migrants, destined for life as settlers in overseas colonies, particularly in North America. Both these processes were thought to be heavily concentrated in the nineteenth century. But modern migration history has added a new dimension to the picture, by demonstrating that early modern European populations were far more mobile than was once assumed, and showing how substantial numbers covered middle-range distances. Part of this was again unfree migration (cf. the first point above), but many people simply packed up because they hoped for a better life, not unlike migrants in the nineteenth and twentieth centuries (Moch 1992; Lucassen and Lucassen 1997).

1 Five modes of labour mobilization

An attempt to merge all these new insights with the traditional approaches implies that we have to analyse labour mobilization of free and unfree labourers, of migrating and less mobile people, of people who exchanged unfree labour or – under different degrees of external pressure – a more or less independent or even self-sufficient existence for life as dependent wage labourers in agriculture, industry, commerce, or in the service of the state.

Given this range of possibilities, the process of proletarianization displayed many varieties in Europe between *c.* 1500 and 1800. Schematically however, five trajectories can be discerned by combining the poles of free vs. unfree mobilization, and of short-distance vs. long-distance (here foreshortened as national vs. international) mobilization, as they occur in continental vs. maritime states (see figure 9.1).[5]

The two dominant continental trajectories of mobilization, one with mainly free labour in western Europe (1) and one with mainly unfree labour in eastern Europe

	Free	Unfree
National	Continental (1) Maritime (3)	Continental (2)
International	Maritime (4)	Maritime (5)

Figure 9.1 Trajectories of labour mobilization

(2), are characterized by a generally slow evolution. In contrast, maritime and commercial expansion was based as a rule on a more intensive and faster process of labour mobilization, for manning ships and for trade-related activities, for military recruitment and for colonization. In these cases, the relation between supply and demand in the different maritime nations can be shown to have been very different, and therefore within this category three more modes may be discerned: national maritime mobilization (3), international free mobilization (4), and international unfree mobilization (5).

In discussing these five modes or trajectories it should be emphasized that we shall use the Weberian 'ideal type' approach. This means that although (groups of) countries are singled out to exemplify a dominant mode, it should be borne in mind that at the same time other trajectories may have been at work, albeit less predominant.

Trajectory 1: Gradual local mobilization of free labour in continental western Europe

In continental western Europe, in particular in France, in the western half of Germany and in Scandinavia, urbanization was increasing slowly; at times the process was even reversed (de Vries 1984a: 166, 257–8). Consequently, the shift from independent, mostly small-scale farming (alongside larger-scale farming, partially based on serf labour) to artisan production and cottage industry was gradual. Among craftsmen, part of the career of all and the whole career of some, consisted of wage-dependency as a journeyman. Even in proto-industry, the share of labour dependent exclusively on wages varied considerably.

In this trajectory, geographical mobility was restricted mainly to short distances, except for the tramping years of limited categories of journeymen. This pattern had its origins in the middle ages. It was only gradually changed by the Industrial Revolution, which from the second quarter of the nineteenth century accelerated the process of proletarianization and international migration in these areas (Rosenthal 1999: 18–20). These parts of Europe did not send many emigrants overseas in the seventeenth and eighteenth centuries.[6] In France this situation contrasted with the preceding ages,[7] in Germany and Scandinavia with those to come, when the agricultural, artisan and in particular the proto-industrial basis of the economy became more dynamic.

Significantly, the countries in areas of gradual labour mobilization had to resort to early forms of conscription for their military recruitment, a system fully developed around 1800 by France and subsequently by Prussia. Telling earlier examples are the Swedish army during the Thirty Years War and at the end of that century the navy, the French *conscription navale* under Louis XIV,[8] and the Prussian army during the Seven Years War. Characteristic of all these recruitment systems was that potential and actual draftees could generally continue their normal occupations as independent producers in years of peace. This was in contrast with military employment systems, to be discussed below, which depended either on unfree labour or on dependent wage labour, i.e. mercenaries.

Trajectory 2: National mobilization of unfree labour in continental eastern Europe

East of the Elbe, the second trajectory consisted of a gradual but continuous shift from independent farming to increasing degrees of serfdom. This trajectory is best known as the 'second serfdom'. It was accompanied by a very low degree of urbanization. The erosion of peasant freedom in Russia took place in three phases, marked by legislation in 1497 and 1649, introducing first the restriction and finally the prohibition of movement by the peasants (Kolchin 1987). Alongside the enserfment of the peasantry, the expanding state reverted to similar systems of labour mobilization. In Russia, from the time of Peter the Great military recruitment was also based on unfree labour. He re-organized the army and navy, introducing life-long service to be provided by villagers, i.e. serfs. This system was reduced to a 25-year term in 1793, but at the prevailing life-expectancy this made little difference to the recruits (Kolchin 1987: 42, 204, 367–8; Hirschbiel 1978).

The refeudalization of eastern Europe in the early modern period was not a smooth process and on the southern and south-eastern borders of the Russian Empire defections were a constant problem (Kolchin 1987: 278–85). Nevertheless, David Eltis' question about the differences in acceptability of unfree labour in western Europe and America could also be applied to eastern Europe. On several occasions Eltis has raised this question about the 'impossibility' of unfree labour in northwestern Europe and of its 'inevitability' elsewhere – especially in the Americas – and recently concluded that:[9]

> Cultural values were, however, just as important as economic and demographic factors in shaping the direction and composition of migration to the English (and by implication, non-English) Americas. Specifically these values ensured the growth of the slave trade from Africa when English population levels declined after 1660. Attitudes to consumption and work within Europe and shifting European perceptions of insider and outsider are just as important as developments in ocean-going technology and the skills of merchants in explaining the nature of transatlantic migration – particularly in the switch from the mainly European to the mainly African stream that the English initiated.

Only in the nineteenth century, first in Prussia and later in Russia, was serfdom abolished and replaced by a free labour market, and even then only partially.

Trajectory 3: National mobilization of free labour in maritime western Europe (Spain, Southern Netherlands, England)

Rapid and impressive commercial and maritime expansion, based on mobilization of free labour from the hinterlands of the ports, and as a rule within national borders, is exemplified by Spain from the sixteenth and by England from the seventeenth century, and to a certain extent the Southern Netherlands. The Spanish expansion into Central and South America involved the recruitment of sailors for a fleet served by 30,000 men in the early seventeenth century and 40,000 in the century and a half to follow. Moreover, between 1493 and 1600 on average 1,300 colonists left the Iberian peninsula annually.[10] Although Spain also had to recruit mercenaries abroad, especially for its great international wars (such as the Dutch Revolt), the great majority of these men and women came from Spain itself. The Crown could even afford to be so fastidious as to introduce a declaration of *limpieza de sangre* for those aspiring to sail for America, thus barring descendants of Jewish or Muslim origin (Jacobs 1995: 111–20). On top of this, the Spanish government expelled all Jewish and Morisco inhabitants between the end of the fifteenth and the beginning of the seventeenth centuries.[11]

Likewise, the Southern Netherlands managed to sustain their impressive commercial expansion without significant labour recruitment outside their territories (Morsa 1996). England's urbanization required the displacement of large numbers of people. Nonetheless, recruitment was almost exclusively from within the British Isles. This pattern was at most temporarily upset by the wave of immigrants from Flanders and Brabant during the early phase of the Dutch Revolt. By and large the new inhabitants of fast-growing London, as well as those of other English towns, came from other areas in Britain.[12]

Britain's international expansion originally demanded mainly colonists for the extremely unhealthy Caribbean, which claimed many lives, but from the Civil War onwards increasing numbers of sailors (from 16,000 at the end of the sixteenth century to 55,000 a century later, and 95,000 during the Napoleonic wars) and soldiers were needed. Surprisingly, these huge numbers could be found within the British Isles. In times of emergency the 'press' might have to be applied, but mostly recruits offered themselves voluntarily. Besides, these same Isles abounded to such a degree in men that they practised a large-scale convict system until far into the nineteenth century. Under this system men were first shipped against their will to North America, and after the United States became independent, to Australia. The greatest intensity of emigration, however, was over by the eighteenth century.[13] This was the result of an increasing domestic demand for labour, as a consequence of the Industrial Revolution.

However important the Spanish and English cases may be – and we have only to look at the world-wide expansion of their languages – not all maritime nations could afford this trajectory of free labour mobilization within national boundaries. Some were simply too small (trajectory 4), while others had to come to terms with fierce international competition (trajectory 5).

Trajectory 4: International mobilization of free labour in maritime western Europe (Venice and the Dutch Republic)

The earliest examples of the emergence of a truly international free labour market are found in the Italian commercial centres, especially Genoa and Venice. Ultimately the more successful of the two, the Venetian Republic, recruited its sailors, soldiers and craftsmen from a wide area outside its relatively small territory. Its catchment area was not just northern Italy but also the Dalmatian coast and the Levant. Greeks and Albanians in particular were important for the Venetian labour market. However, as we shall see shortly with trajectory 5, at certain times, and increasingly from the middle of the sixteenth century onwards, Venice was also forced to resort to unfree labour.[14]

The only example in the early modern era of massive recruitment of foreign labour on a completely free basis, therefore, is the Dutch Republic. Seasonal migrants, migrant labourers (such as sailors, soldiers and servants), and permanent migrants were indispensable for the Dutch Golden Age. Elsewhere, this author presented estimates suggesting that half the male labour market of the western core parts of the Republic depended on foreigners.[15] To put it differently: whereas nowadays 7 per cent of the Dutch population is born abroad, this was more than 10 in the early seventeenth century (Lucassen and Penninx 1998).

The combination of religious tolerance and economic prosperity attracted approximately half a million settlers to the United Provinces, which for most of their existence had only two million inhabitants. They took up occupations mainly in the shops and workshops of the towns and cities in the maritime provinces. Guilds in this part of the country were rather open to immigrants, in contrast to the inland provinces and even more so to adjacent countries (Lourens and Lucassen 1999 and 2000).

In addition to these permanent settlers an even greater number of labour migrants were employed as soldiers in the Dutch army, and about as many again in the navy, the merchant fleet and in colonial campaigns, mainly in the East Indies. Whereas these were male occupations, hundreds of thousands of foreign females worked as servants in Dutch homes. In the second part of the seventeenth century a pattern of migrant labour, mostly seasonal, from the east and south to the coastal parts of the country, also emerged, encompassing as many as 30,000 seasonal workers annually in the eighteenth century.

Migrants to the Netherlands were drawn there by the prospect of labour opportunities, either in the country itself or in its colonial empire overseas. The narrow coastal strip where most of the economic activity in the country was concentrated covered a mere 15,000 square kilometres, an area much smaller than Greater London, even before the Second World War. The domestic demographic basis for this explosion of activities was too narrow. For the Dutch expansion migrants were indispensable.

Geographically, one may discern several partially overlapping concentric circles around the Republic, more or less reflecting the various economic roles of migrants. One circle has a diameter of 200 to 300 kilometres representing the area within which migrant labour was recruited. A larger one, about 500 kilometres in diameter, marks the extent of the area from which the better-paid labour migrants were drawn as well as most permanent settlers. Lower-paid labour migrants (such as soldiers from Scotland and Switzerland and sailors for the navy and the Dutch East India Company, the VOC) and particular groups of refugees (such as part of the Jewish and Huguenot immigrants) were drawn from even further afield.[16]

Trajectory 5: International mobilization of free and unfree labour in maritime western Europe (southern Europe)

The comparison between the Venetian and the Dutch Republics has already pointed to the vulnerability of labour markets dependent on foreign immigration The successful expansion of the Ottoman Empire in the Balkans cut off the Venetian Republic from its main traditional recruitment area, the Adriatic coast and its hinterlands. The fierce competition between the two naval powers in the eastern Mediterranean caused a partial introduction of unfree labour on the Venetian galleys from 1545, and the Ottoman galleys were manned in the same way. As a consequence, in the famous battle of Lepanto (1571) crews identical in origin and labour circumstances fought one another on behalf of the Muslim and Christian adversaries.[17]

However, unfree labour was also widely used in Venice proper and all over the Ottoman Empire (Erdem 1996: chapters 1 and 2; Lucassen and Zürcher 1998). In the Turkish case the Janissaries obviously catch the eye as an example of unfree soldiers. Under this system, from the late fourteenth century onwards boys from Christian peasant families were enslaved and enrolled (Lucassen and Zürcher 1998: 409).

Venice's problems were far from unique. Portugal, another sparsely populated maritime power – with roughly as few inhabitants as the Dutch Republic and the Venetian Republic – faced fierce competition in international labour markets. Spain, with its impressive labour demands (the Spanish navy comprised ten to twenty times more sailors than that of its western neighbour), as well as the Barbary states severely restricted Portugal's possibilities. No wonder that the Portuguese emulated the system of slavery, for they knew it very well from the Mediterranean sugar cane plantations, where it was practised by the Genoese and Venetians (Phillips 1991; Verlinden 1977).

On the mainland too the Portuguese had recourse to unfree labour. Although the importance of African slave labour in Portugal itself is still under debate, there are telling parallels between the abolition process in Portugal and the Ottoman Empire, which underlines our suggestion that they are part of one and the same trajectory.[18]

This fifth trajectory also draws our attention to the blurred line between the European and the non-European labour markets of the maritime empires. In the Portuguese case, and to a lesser degree this is also true for Italy and the Ottoman Empire, it is very hard indeed to distinguish between slave labour in the metropolis and slavery in the overseas possessions; the system therefore proved to be persistent in both cases for much longer than in the northern slave-trading societies.

There are, however, good reasons to emphasize these borderlines in the case of those other countries engaged in the slave trade and exploiting slaves overseas. First, certainly in relative and perhaps even in absolute numbers, the Portuguese were the most important nation involved in the trans-Atlantic slave transportations. Their share (in combination with Brazil) was 35 per cent. Next came England and France, both far more populous countries than Portugal. The three nations together accounted for 90 per cent of the total traffic. The Dutch were responsible for another 5 per cent (Postma 1990: 296–302).[19] Second, slavery was not (or only under very special conditions) allowed in countries such as the Dutch Republic and England. Third, at least in the Dutch, English and French cases, slavery was not equally important in all colonies. To take just the Dutch example: in the Caribbean it was essential, without any doubt, especially in the Guyanas. In the East-Indies, however, it was far less significant. The VOC directly employed unfree labour in the production of cloves, nutmeg and mace. The importance of this monopoly may be estimated in two ways: its products accounted for one-quarter of VOC sales in Amsterdam, and its organization engaged between one-third of its overseas free personnel at the beginning of the VOC monopoly, but only a tenth at its end.[20]

2 Merchant capitalism and labour mobilization

It is perhaps too early to understand the background to the different patterns in the proletarianization process. Their economic causes are manifold and complex, and these developments do not belong exclusively to the economic domain. As has been suggested for the Low Countries, explanations taking into account the inter-dependence of politics, religion, culture and economics should be preferred over purely economic ones (Davids and Lucassen 1995). Nevertheless, three problems should be addressed briefly here: the unities first of time and second of space that have been used, and consequently the question whether the occurrence of so many different trajectories is characteristic of the period and geographical region studied here.

This chapter set out to describe patterns of development between roughly 1500 and 1800. Now that we have reached some conclusions as to what happened in those centuries, it is important to establish to what extent these trajectories were specific to the early modern period. In other words: are they a continuation of preceding patterns and did they survive into the industrial era? Clearly, proletarianization did not begin in 1500 but probably several centuries earlier, when the European towns started growing, when the differentiation of the labour market between various types of agriculture and crafts gained strength, and when the circulation of money became important in everyday life. Nonetheless, there is a clear-cut contrast between the middle ages and the early modern period. The large-scale employment of unfree labour initially, and subsequently the slow reversal of this pattern in the late middle ages, suggest a much more uniform pattern than the diverging trajectories described here for the early modern period. A similar argument seems to apply to the nineteenth and twentieth centuries, when convergence in the development of industrial capitalism, characterized by free labour mobilization, seems to be the trend through-out most of Europe.

Whatever corrections need to be made to the estimates provided by Tilly in 1984, they are unlikely to explain away the growth spurt of proletarian labour that he revealed for western Europe during the early modern period. Only in eastern and south-eastern Europe was proletarianization mainly a nineteenth-century phenom-enon. It will also prove difficult to challenge Tilly's conclusion that by the middle of the nineteenth century proletarianization had reached an all-time high. Nevertheless, behind a virtually immobile rate, changes certainly did take place during the last century and a half. In the twentieth century for example, more women may have become wage-dependent, as against fewer children and elderly people.

As to the spatial dimension, proletarianization certainly was not an exclusively European phenomenon before the Age of Imperialism. Adam Smith, with his sharp eye for developments in the Near East and in other parts of South and East Asia, urges us to reconsider proletarianization as typically European. Unfortunately, this awareness seems to have been long lost in European history. Although proletarianization is certainly not one of his main concerns, a reappraisal of sorts of the role of non-European developments is present in Braudel's picture notion of a Mediterranean unity, encompassing both the African and Asian coastal regions. These starting points certainly need a vigorous follow-up (see for example Goody 1996: 221–5; Prakash 1995; Perlin 1994: 81–7).

If we can indeed regard the diverging trajectories of labour mobilization as characteristic of the early modern period in Europe (and possibly – but that would require a separate discussion – also for parts of Asia), does this give a specific unity to the era? A unity which deserves the application of an epithet like 'merchant capitalism', for example? This brings us to the difficult problem of the definitions of capitalism and its periodization. Even if we cannot claim to solve this problem, the foregoing discussion of labour-market developments warrants several remarks.

Scholars who have attempted to give the early modern period a name of its own disagree in at least two respects. Some claim that the concept of capitalism is an essential tool in understanding the developments discussed here. Others reject the concept completely. In his analysis of the Dutch economy, Jan Luiten van Zanden (1993a) favours the use of the concept capitalism, whereas Jan de Vries and Ad van der Woude (1997a: 690–3) in their book on the same subject voice strong objections.[21] Among those who embrace the concept of capitalism, just some and then only recently, are of the opinion that merchant or commercial capitalism should be contrasted with industrial capitalism, and is therefore a useful specification of this 'early modern' period.[22]

Adam Smith called the society that emerged in western Europe after the demise of feudalism simply 'civilised society', sometimes with the addition 'advanced'.[23] Marx and Engels used for the same period expressions such as 'capitalist mode of production', 'world market' and 'world history', but not yet 'capitalism' (Hilger 1982: 442–3; cf. Schumpeter 1954: 391, 552 n. 15, 899 n. 17). Only Werner Sombart in the beginning of the twentieth century coined the word 'capitalism' for an historical period, at the same time as Max Weber used the concept in the title of his most famous book. Sombart also introduced the distinction between early capitalism (in German *Hochkapitalismus*) from the middle of the thirteenth to the middle of the nineteenth century, and full and late capitalism thereafter.[24] The replacement of early capitalism by commercial capitalism is even more recent: since the 1970s historians such as Kriedte (1983) and later van Zanden (1993a: chapter 1) have promoted its use (see also Duplessis 1997; Schlumbohm 1996).

Already when Sombart was launching the concept of capitalism in 1902, objections were raised. Gustav Schmoller may have been the first: 'From the newspapers it will not disappear. But whether it should have the important place in science claimed by Sombart, I'm not so sure'; many were to follow (Hilger 1982: 444; Goody 1996: 216–17). In recent historical research Douglass North and Robert Paul

Thomas (1973: 102 and *passim*) may have been the most influential. They have recently been followed by de Vries and van der Woude (1997a).

This long tradition of criticism notwithstanding, van Zanden in 1993 published the scheme for an economic theory of 'merchant capitalism'. In his book (1993a), he used as his point of departure, and indeed the linchpin of his analysis, what he considered to be the distinctive character of patterns of early modern labour mobilization, as compared to those of the industrial era.[25] In van Zanden's words (van Zanden *et al.* 1997: 189–190):

> Merchant capitalism is viewed as an open system: it arises and develops as a capitalistic 'island' in a world that is dominated by precapitalist modes of production. [. . .] The reproduction of labor power occurs largely outside of the sphere of merchant capitalism, namely, in the precapitalist modes of production. [. . .] [I]n merchant capitalism a dualistic system often evolved, in which the reproduction of labor power and the production of the surplus were separated from each other.

If this description of merchant capitalism is applied to the typology provided in this essay, it suggests a distinctive relationship between one of the five trajectories distinguished here, the fourth one, and all of the others, as well as with the non-European world. The maritime trajectory of free-labour mobilization by the Dutch Republic was dependent on mobilizing labour in and from the other regions under discussion, van Zanden claims. This is not necessarily inconsistent with what has been said before, although van Zanden seems to emphasize the unilateral links between one system and all the others more than has been done in the previous pages here.

Opinions diverge, however, on the nature of the inter-regional relations and in particular on the conditions under which this free-labour mobilization took place.[26] Obviously, from a very broad national perspective the recruitment of adult, fit, and often trained labour may be cheaper by way of immigration than by natural growth. In the latter case – which according to van Zanden applies to the industrial era (van Zanden *et al.* 1997: 263–6) – the burden of feeding the proletariat in the years of childhood, before it becomes productive, rest on the shoulders of the national economy. From that same perspective it may also be cheaper to be able to send seasonal workers away during the lean winter season, to help lift the financial burden on the poor-relief institutions.

On the other hand, seen from the perspective of the individual firm or employer, the engagement of immigrants does not seem to have been cheaper during the early modern period. In Holland there is no proof that wages earned by migrant workers – temporary or permanent – were lower for the same jobs than those earned by the indigenous population. Wage differentials have not been found in the urban artisan sector, dominated by the guilds, nor in the free, non-organized sector outside the corporate system, whether urban or rural.[27] Is it possible that immigrants replaced Dutch workers in jobs which, as a consequence of their social 'degradation', lagged below in the occupational ranking and consequently in remuneration? Although there is no direct evidence available to demonstrate or falsify this possibility, we can say that such a development is unlikely to have taken place. Significantly, wages for unskilled labourers in the coastal provinces of the Dutch Republic were higher than those in adjacent countries, except England, at the end of the eighteenth century (de Vries and van der Woude 1997a: 620). The very low wages for seamen, who, as we saw earlier, were in Holland to a great extent of foreign origin, were roughly equal in England and the Netherlands. Moreover, they showed the same tendency to rise in the eighteenth century, compared to those for unskilled labour (data in Davids 1997: 68; Earle 1997: 83; Palmer and Williams 1997: 102–4). Apparently the presence of many foreign immigrants on the lower reaches of the wage ladder did not influence the wage rate negatively, nor did it create obvious comparative cost advantages for Dutch entrepreneurs internationally.[28]

The patterns of development in labour mobilization sketched in this chapter do not allow us to arrive at a final verdict on the pros and cons of the use of such potentially competing concepts as 'capitalism' and 'modern economic growth', or 'merchant capitalism' and 'industrial capitalism'. What can and has been argued here, however, is that there was no monolithic and straightforward process of proletarianization between 1500 and 1800. To the extent the proletarianization did occur (and there is no denying that it did), this was the outcome of a remarkably diverse set of responses to regionally variable circumstances of labour demand, recruitment potential, and competititon for labour. To pinpoint one of numerous trajectories as superior, or otherwise more influential, than the others, is to miss a crucial point about the early modern era. Such dominant influence was possible only under an entirely new set of circumstances, as was created by the Industrial Revolution.

Notes

1 Smith (1986: bk. 3 chapter 2: 494; chapter 3: 503). Smith leaves out Germany and his judgement of the Hansa is much more negative than his opinion of the once powerful Northern Italian and Flemish towns (1986: bk. 3 chapter 4: 519–20). Karl Marx, in the footsteps of Friedrich List, follows the same line of thought (Lourens and Lucassen 1992: 432–3).

2 Schumpeter (1954: 390 n. 11) calls Marx an English economist.

3 Recent works on guilds include: Lis and Soly (1997a); Epstein (1998); Guenzi, Massa and Caselli (1998); Schulz (1999). On artisans, see: Crossick and Haupt (1984, 1995); Crossick (1997); also Tomlins (1999) and the responses to that article. A more pessimistic assessment of the number of independent artisans is Lis and Soly (1997b).

4 Of course, other forms of upward and downward vertical mobility than proletarianization also occurred in the early modern period, e.g. impoverishment of the nobility or the ennoblement of merchants. These remain outside the scope of this discussion.

5 Here I build on my earlier attempts to systematize the history of European labour markets, especially Lucassen (1995; see also Lucassen 1994, 1996 and 1997) and I refrain from repeating detailed references already given in these publications.

6 For Germany: Fertig (1994 and 1997); the emigration to Eastern Europe and to the Dutch Republic – both much more important in magnitude than the insignificant emigrations to North America – do not affect this conclusion; for France: Moogk (1994).

7 See the French colonization efforts in the Mediterranean and subsequent ones on Madeira and of the French migrations to Spain, from the middle ages to the early

seventeenth century: Phillips (1994), Moch (1992, pp. 28–9 and 83–8), Martínez Sopena (1996).

8 France fits least well in this typology of military recruitment, because of its unfree labour on the galleys (Zysberg 1987) in the seventeenth century and its (mainly Swiss) mercenary troops.

9 Eltis (1997: 107); cf. van der Linden (1997b: 521–3).

10 These revised figures (46 per cent of the traditional estimates) are in Jacobs (1995); compare also Altman (1997).

11 See also the many examples of de-urbanization in de Vries (1984a: 277–8).

12 Rappaport (1989: 55–6, 80) for the sixteenth century; in the fifteenth century aliens were more important in London: Bolton (1998: 8); for the seventeenth and eighteenth centuries: Lucassen (1995: 378–83) and Lucassen (1996: 172–3, 177–8, 181–2).

13 See the contributions on Ireland, Scotland and England in Canny (1994) and in van Royen, Bruijn and Lucassen (1997).

14 Lucassen (1995: 376–7), mainly based on Lane (1966). For the Albanians, see Alain Ducellier's work, for example Ducellier 1996.

15 Lucassen (1994, 1996 and 1997). In the Dutch edition of de Vries and Van der Woude (1997a, on pp. 96 and 98), the authors present alternative calculations. Their point of departure, however, is different, because they include on the one hand all immigrants, both male and female, in Holland, but on the other take into account only those from outside the Republic, so excluding those from the land provinces migrating to the sea provinces. Nevertheless, their assessment is consistent with mine.

16 The foregoing mainly follows Lucassen (1994: 180–4).

17 Lucassen (1995); cf. also Erdem (1996: 30 and 194 n. 52). On (free) Greek sailors in the eighteenth-century Ottoman Empire, see Todorov (1983: 198–200, 274–6 and 331). On Albanians, Ducellier (1996).

18 Robert Rowland (Lisbon) informs me that the high numbers, given in J. R. Tinhorao, *Os Negros em Portugal: uma Presenca Silenciosa*, Lisbon: Caminho, 1988, pp. 370–4 are still under discussion. He also provided me with the following chronology of the demise of slavery in Portugal: a 1761 decree forbade entry of black slaves from America, Asia or Africa (intended to prevent drainage of slaves from Brazil and explicitly excluding black slaves already in Portugal); in 1767 extended to mulatto slaves; in 1773 freedom for children of slaves born from them in Portugal and for slaves with great-grand-children in Portugal, whereas the rest remained slaves for life. For the process in the Ottoman Empire see Erdem (1996), and for Italy Verlinden (1977: 1020–46).

19 Because these figures relate to the trans-Atlantic traffic, the Italian and Ottoman activities are not included.

20 Gaastra (1991: 134): the three products represented 28.5 per cent of the total sales of the Chamber Amsterdam in 1668–70 and 23.5 per cent in 1738–40) (*ibid.*: 84–6). Overseas personnel on the Moluccas-Banda, on Ambon and on Ternate in 1625 immediately after the establishment of the monopoly was 37 per cent, in 1687/8 17 per cent, in 1700 12.5 per cent, in 1753 9 per cent and in 1780 13 per cent. For a different emphasis, see van Zanden (1993a: 79–84). For the nineteenth century see Knight (1999).

21 For a discussion, see van Zanden (1997); Davids (1997); de Vries and van der Woude (1997b); also van der Linden (1997a).

22 Apart from the discussion in *Review* (van Zanden *et al.* 1997) which follows in the next few pages, see also an interesting discussion about the American case in *Labor History*: Tomlins (1999a and 1999b); Montgomery (1999); Nelson (1999); and Rock (1999).

23 Cf. Schumpeter (1954: 439), where he summarizes 'Marxist evolutionism' *inter alia* as follows: 'All the cultural manifestations of "civil society" – to use the eighteenth century term – are ultimately functions of its class structure'.

24 Influential in its English version: Sombart (1930: esp. p. 206); see also Schumpeter (1954: 815–20) and Goody (1996: 215–18) on Sombart (and Weber).

25 See van Zanden 1993 (originally published in Dutch in 1991) and the debate in *Review*: van Zanden *et al.* (1997), with contributions by A. Knotter, C. Lis and H. Soly, and I. Wallerstein. In his work van Zanden refers repeatedly to my earlier work on migration history, as do some of the discussants in *Review*.

26 I have to refrain here from a discussion of the relations between European core regions and the non-European world. I do not disagree with van Zanden's interpretation of the function of slavery for European merchants and entrepreneurs. I do think, however, that particularly in Asia slavery is not the only key for understanding labour relations (cf. note 20).

27 Examples for seasonal work are given in Lucassen (1987: 54, 59, 69, 75, 81, 85, 95–7). In the records of Dutch craft guilds no evidence was found of wage differences for native and immigrant journeymen.

28 Gaastra and Bruijn (1993) do not find such advantages for the VOC if compared to competitors abroad. See also Knight (1999).

Part III

Conclusion

10 Economic growth before and after the Industrial Revolution

A modest proposal

Jan de Vries

Once upon a time – but, in truth, not so long ago – the story of economic growth possessed a clear dramatic structure. It began with a seemingly interminable and directionless first chapter, followed by a brief, action-packed, pivotal second chapter, and concluded with a soaring, triumphant finale, a happy ending without end. This structure was a dramatic masterpiece, but the story itself was full of loose ends and puzzles, and this narrative incoherence was not lessened by the peculiar custom of having different groups of story tellers narrate the first and third chapters.

Coherent accounts of historical economic growth are difficult to achieve only in part because of the venerable jurisdictional boundaries that have for so long governed the training of professional historians. Antiquated historical categories continue to guard the high walls separating 'early modern' history from 'late modern' history. But now, after the waves of revisionism to which both the French and Industrial Revolutions have been subjected, it is time to explore seriously ways to reintegrate the histories of the eighteenth and nineteenth centuries.

One might suppose that what historians tear asunder with their conventions of periodization, economists would stitch together with the healing balm of theory. But in practice this has not been the case. Before some point in the eighteenth or nineteenth century economists tend to apply models drawn from the classical tradition and predicated on the existence of pervasive diminishing marginal returns. A hypothesized binding constraint, usually related to the fixed supply of land, governs all such models, whether Malthusian, Smithian, or Ricardian in their details. After that point, neo-classical models are assumed to govern, with their basic assumptions of constant returns to scale and substitutability at all margins. These assumptions have the significant consequence of banishing time and space – history and geography – from modern growth theory. Institutions can be compensated for and scarce resources have their substitutes, while technology, which can be produced at constant costs, is effectively exogenous and available to all.

Just as historians can break open the rusted lock of an historical *Problemstellung* by challenging the ancient joints of periodization, economists can gain new perspectives on the nature of historical economic growth by setting aside the intentionally ahistorical assumptions of their models. Fernand Braudel often noted that mankind is more than waist deep in the routines of everyday life; it is no less true that academics are more than waist deep in disciplinary 'conventional wisdom'. How could we function if this were not true? Still, once in a long while, intellectual currents conspire with 'facts on the ground' to encourage a rethinking of the venerable conventions.

The British Industrial Revolution as a historical concept is today not what it was twenty years ago (O'Brien 1993). Its 'diminution', if that is the right word, leaves many with a sense of loss. But one might take heart in the knowledge that its historiographical pendant, the French Revolution, is – in the words of its leading modern historian – over, *fini* (Furet 1978; Kaplan 1995: 122–43). These twin gatekeepers to the modern world have been subject to new questioning in part because the modern world has not become what was long thought by many to be inherent within it to become.[1]

In economics a multi-stranded literature has emerged in the past decade to question core assumptions about the operation of markets. Bearing labels such as 'new growth theory', 'path dependence', 'co-ordination failure', and 'general equilibrium search', the new concepts have in common a belief in the importance of historical contingency in explaining actual market outcomes, and a belief that such an outcome does not inevitably identify a unique and optimal equilibrium, but more often occupies one of multiple 'stable attractors' that only appear to be such equilibria. The appeal of the new approach resides in its capacity to address questions of local and regional dynamism and non-linear processes that loom so large in the contemporary economy. It gains this appeal at a price – the abandonment of the key neo-classical assumptions that make for mathematical tractability and predictability. If this price is now deemed worth paying – and to many it still is not – it is chiefly because the conventional models now appear to skim the surface of growth processes, taking for granted much of what needs to be explained (David 1993; also Krugman 1991; Diamond 1984; Arthur 1990).

1 Modern economic growth

Let me begin by reviewing the conventional wisdom on the nature of economic growth in the epochs either side of the Industrial Revolution. Because of its great authority, we shall have to start at the end rather than the beginning: with the concept of 'modern economic growth'. Many scholars have participated in the task of defining and measuring modern economic growth, but Simon Kuznets surely presented the fullest, most systematic account of the phenomenon, and most other scholars have been content to follow his lead. To Kuznets, modern economic growth is not simply a statistical artefact of economic activity; rather it is a direct reflection of a single, unified process of economic life that has a recognizable trend. Indeed, Kuznets insisted that each epoch of economic life is based on an epochal innovation, which establishes a characteristic *Weltanschauung*[2] and which manifests a single long-term trend line. To Kuznets, the trend line of the modern epoch is characterized by three essential and interlocking features: rapid growth, relative steadiness (low volatility), and divergence among national economies.[3]

Kuznets not only led in defining modern economic growth as a theoretical concept and, of course, establishing the methods of measuring that growth via the national accounting framework. He also laboured to assemble historical data to establish the temporal boundaries of his epochal phenomenon. We can turn to English leaders in this empirical project for an authoritative statement of the historical character of modern growth. W. A. Cole and Phyllis Deane (1965: 1–2) launched their chapter 'The Growth of National Income' in the *Cambridge Economic History of Europe* with the claim that

> The characteristic which distinguishes the modern period in world history from all past periods is the fact of economic growth. It began in Western Europe and spread first to the overseas countries settled from Europe. . . . The effective beginning of the transformation can be placed in eighteenth-century Europe.

They conceded that earlier periods had not been altogether devoid of interesting economic developments, 'but', they went on:

> The economic advances of pre-industrial societies . . . were different in kind, in magnitude, and in continuity from the economic growth that springs from an industrial revolution. In so far as they were sufficiently far-reaching to affect whole nations, and not merely favoured regions or cities or social groups, their benefits were readily cancelled by the disasters of wars or epidemics and by the brute fact of population pressure.

The actual measurement of growth in the modern epoch has been refined continuously since the pioneering generation of Kuznets, Deane *et al.* Angus Maddison's ongoing enterprise of data collection and interpretation offers an up-to-date statement. In *Dynamic Forces in Capitalist Development* Maddison defines the seventeen decades since 1820 as 'constituting the capitalist epoch', and in this period the advanced capitalist countries (sixteen countries for which he assembled systematic data) have grown 70-fold. This achievement decomposes into a 5-fold growth of population and a 14-fold growth of per capita product. In addition, he notes, this growth was achieved in the face of a halving of annual hours worked and together with a doubling of life expectancy at birth (Maddison 1991: 8; updated in Maddison 1995).

Clearly, nothing approaching this had ever happened before. Indeed, Kuznets offered an iron-clad proof for the claim that the trend line established by the Industrial Revolution could not have existed for any significant period before then. 'Data on per capita product over long periods in premodern times are lacking', Kuznets (1966: 69–70) conceded, but the unique character of modern economic growth could be confirmed

> by projecting the modern rates of growth backward. A rate of 15 per cent per decade . . . means that in a century per capita product rises to over four times its initial level; in two centuries the rise is to 14 times its initial level; in three centuries to 66.2 times. . . . Thus if per capita product had grown 15 per cent per decade for three centuries before the 1960s, per capita product in the 1660s

would have been 1/66 of the present level. But a per capita income at even a twentieth of the present level [*c.* 1960] could not have sustained the population of even the most developed countries, and the assumed rates of growth could not have been maintained, in most countries, for over two centuries.

In short, there had to be a substantial break in the trend line of modern growth, and logically it could not have occurred long before the beginning of the nineteenth century.

The Kuznetsian concept of modern economic growth establishes a sturdy framework for measurement and description. Supplementing it with an explanation of growth, as it were, is the neo-classical growth model associated with the name of Robert Solow. The neo-classical assumptions that gave the Solow model its power are the familiar ones of constant returns to scale and diminishing marginal returns to inputs. One consequence of these assumptions is that the efficiency of capital must decline as it is accumulated in ever larger amounts, which means that the long-term rate of growth of national economies should be inversely related to their initial levels of national income – the convergence property.

A second consequence of this, and of any model with diminishing marginal returns to inputs, is the expectation of deceleration and ultimate cessation of growth. Therefore the unceasing character of modern economic growth depends entirely on a constant stream of technological progress, generated at constant cost and quickly diffused to all parties, so as not to violate the neo-classical assumptions of competitive markets. In short, modern economic growth depends on a special form of a force (technological change) that is exogenous to the model that seeks to explain it.[4]

The concept of modern economic growth is an impressive creation: it is demonstrably unique, it has internal coherence, and it shares with the Christian religion the claim to a universal significance while simultaneously possessing a tangible, historical birth place.[5] For all the neo-classical finery in which it is draped, however, its dependence on a variable whose behaviour it cannot shed light on and whose existence it can only identify as a residual, is a striking feature. It nonetheless gained wide acceptance, in part because of its evident utility, but also because the claims of modern growth to unique status were readily conceded by another concept – one is tempted to say, a co-dependent concept – that emerged to account for economic change in the long centuries preceding the industrial revolution.

2 The neo-Malthusian model

The neo-Malthusian model of the pre-industrial economy was constructed from the only comprehensive quantitative data generally available for this era – population and prices – and fashioned into a model inspired by the teachings of the classical economists in general and Malthus in particular. There is no single figure who gave this model a definitive shape, but a short list of influential scholars, in rough chronological order, must include: François Simiand (1932a and b), Wilhelm Abel (1935: part 2, chapters 2–4), Fernand Braudel (1972; 1982–84), Michael Postan (1972), E. H. Phelps Brown and Sheila Hopkins (1956 and 1981), B. H. Slicher van

Bath (1963: 98–131), Emmanuel Le Roy Ladurie (1966) and the team of E. A. Wrigley and R. S. Schofield (1981). Each of these historians deploys the basic model in somewhat different ways, but the needs of clarity may be served by first presenting the 'essence' of the model.

The dominant economic relationship in pre-industrial economic life is assumed to be that between movements in population (driven by the basic postulate of Malthus (1798: 11) that 'the passion between the sexes is necessary, and will remain nearly in its present state'), and the available supply of land, which is taken to be essentially fixed. While industrial production might take place under conditions of constant returns to scale, agriculture is unavoidably dominant, and it necessarily faces diminishing returns. Food producers are assumed always to work near their techno-logical frontier (leaving no unexploited opportunities) and in conditions approaching autarky (Grantham 1996). These constraints ensure that only technological change can bring about growth, and this is assumed to be, at most, very limited. With supply thus defined, the model posits a set of demand elasticities that vary from close to zero for basic foodstuffs to progressively higher than unity for livestock products, industrial crops and manufactured goods, in that order. Population growth provokes rising prices: most for bread grains; least – indeed, often not at all – for labour. Population decline reverses the pattern. Over the course of a cycle, the movement of relative prices generates major redistributions of income as it constrains demographic behaviour, whether via Malthus's positive or preventive checks. This model is given motion by population change, which is variously assumed to be launched by exogenous forces or to oscillate within a homeostatic system embracing population and the sluggish economic regime invoked above.[6]

It is given motion, but not direction. Le Roy Ladurie (1966: 49–50), for example, introduces his *grand cycle agraire* to analyse the rural society of Languedoc. The cycle begins at a demographic low point (*c.* 1500), where the surviving population forms 'a sturdy, vigorous, well-nourished populace. . . . Purified and rejuvenated by a century of trials and tribulations, . . . ready, for the second time, to launch an assault on the hermes and the wastes'. Thereupon the population multiplied 'like mice in a grange' until, through subdivision of land and pauperization, the social advance of the sixteenth century succumbed to every manner of societal ill.

It has been said that Le Roy Ladurie embarked on his study in search of Marx (to uncover the secrets of capitalist accumulation) and instead found Malthus. He did not hesitate to project this 'respiration of the social organism' onto all of French and European history, in his remarkable lecture '*L'histoire immobile*'. From the eleventh to the eighteenth century French history had been essentially motionless: 'Twelve to thirteen generations of peasants were busy reproducing themselves within limits of finite possibilities whose constraints proved inexorable' (Le Roy Ladurie 1977: 122).

The key feature of the neo-Malthusian model in all its variants is a hypothesized constraint that is irremovable within the terms of the economic system. Any growth had to be temporary. Indeed, the tendency to overshoot sustainable economic levels, or to react to the approach of looming ceilings, or to be destabilized by exogenous shocks, set counter-movements in motion that traced out the slow cycles, or the secular trend, that emerges as the great historical protagonist. For it set limits on peasants and potentates alike (in Braudel's account),[7] or presented society with weak tools which could be worked within narrow margins in order to change hard landings into soft ones – or high pressure regimes into low pressure regimes (in Wrigley and Schofield's model).

Whether presented with the Gallic flair of Le Roy Ladurie, the *gründlichkeit* of Abel, or the empirical commonsensicality of Postan, a common model gained broad acceptance as representing the essential reality of the pre-industrial economy. At once, the model integrated the available data into a coherent picture, defined the epoch's distinctive economic character and potential, and gave it a sturdy periodization.[8]

Many of the scholars active in early modern European economic history over the past generation have focused on developments that go beyond the elemental inter-action of man and land, and of demographic and agricultural regimes, to show how at least portions of Europe expanded their non-agricultural sectors, developed commercial and financial institutions, constructed urban networks and transport facilities, etc. But they have yet to overthrow the model. None of the celebrated developments on the way toward a more complex economic life could overcome the critical constraints enforcing the essential features of the pre-industrial economy captured by the neo-Malthusian model.[9]

Defending the model in the face of this new appreciation of the early modern economy's complexity has required the invocation of Adam Smith, who combined a penetrating understanding of the salutary effects of commercial development via specialization and market extension (for which he is best known), with a conviction that these ultimately could not prevail against the inexorable force of diminishing returns. Tony Wrigley draws out the Smithian argument with acuity and elegance in his *Continuity, Chance and Change*, where he holds up for inspection the example – provided by Smith himself – of the Dutch Republic as the end of the road of Smithian growth. The Netherlands, wrote Smith (1986: bk. 1, chapter ix, 197) in a much-quoted passage, had 'acquired the full complement of riches which the nature of its soils and climate and its situation with respect to other countries, allowed it to acquire'. It could, he went on to conclude, advance no further.

This is my point of entry into the topic of historical growth models. My recent book (1997a) on Dutch economic history, with co-author Ad van der Woude, carries the title *The First Modern Economy*. This heterodox gesture requires some justifi-cation, the theoretical grounds for which I seek to develop in what follows. Some might argue that the 'unique' Dutch economy of the seventeenth century can hardly serve as the basis of far-reaching generalizations (a position I would contest). But no such dismissive claim can easily dispose of the British Industrial Revolution, which is unquestionably a phenomenon at the heart of economic history as a discipline. And the persistence of what I have described as two co-dependent growth concepts is deeply implicated in a conventional appreciation of the Industrial Revolution.

3 The Industrial Revolution

The neo-Malthusian model and the concept of modern economic growth formed suitable bookends to hold upright the sacred scriptures of economic history that revealed the mysteries of the Industrial Revolution. This key concept has the pivotal role of explaining how an economy governed by the dynamic of the secular trend could yield to one driven on to rapid, steady, and unending growth. The great challenge has been to define and explain the key transformations that first can be observed to occur in northern England during the reign of George III, and second can plausibly claim to establish the new growth epoch on a universal scale.[10]

Today, this centrepiece in the grand narrative of economic history is under siege.[11] Revisionist studies have effectively removed the central tenets of brevity and rapid acceleration of aggregate economic growth and even questioned the traditional significance given to mechanical invention.[12] Defenders of the Industrial Revolution have cogent arguments to make, to be sure, and even the revisionists do not deny the momentous structural changes it brought about and its profound social consequences. But their revisions do undermine the narrative structure that unites the two growth models. The neo-Malthusian model, the Industrial Revolution, and the concept of modern economic growth formed an interdependent triad. Revision – one might, as before, say diminution – of the central element does not leave the other two unaffected. For, in John A. Davis's words (1989: 49), 'once the identification between industrialization [mechanized production] and economic growth is loosened . . . the process of economic growth necessarily becomes more open ended, making it difficult, if not impossible to establish any single optimal path [to modern economic growth]'.

The reduction by more than half of measured growth rates in the British economy 1760–1830 does not simply remove most of the acceleration and discontinuity needed to launch the new epoch of modern economic growth. This indeed, may not even constitute an irreparable objection. The revisions also leave a British economy on the eve of the Industrial Revolution that was more industrial in structure and with a significantly higher per capita income than had earlier been supposed. And yet this richer pre-industrial Britain was not the richest of nations; it would take an entire eighteenth century of economic development for it to secure that honour.[13]

At once, this revisionism re-inserts the important achievements of the British industrial revolution in their European context – a major industrial advance occurring within a growing commercial economy – and qualifies their nineteenth-century impact – just one form of specialization in a multi-stranded development process. Revisionism along these lines imposes upon us the requirement to rethink the two growth models that bracket the Industrial Revolution.

To begin with, the unity of the entire period since that event – a key Kuznetsian tenet – now seems less compelling.[14] It is only after 1870 that the average growth rate for Angus Maddison's 'core European countries' shifts from a long-run average of under 1 per cent per annum to a growth path twice as fast. The revised estimates of British growth show an acceleration long before 1870, of course, but even here no trend line consistent with post-1870 British experience can be extended back as far as 1830.

For many years, the notion of a 'second industrial revolution' in the late nineteenth century has rattled about the literature of our discipline without ever achieving a solid historiographical position. As long ago as 1981 Douglass North argued vigorously for a re-periodization when he sought to distinguish a 'second economic revolution' from the 'first industrial revolution'. This 'economic revolution', he associated with the 'new power of science to lift the last great constraint on economic growth – knowledge'. Scientific knowledge, North (1981: 171) argued, established the economic world where 'the underlying assumptions of neo-classical economics [became] realizable: . . . where new knowledge could be produced at constant costs, and substitutions at all margins made possible persistent and sustained growth'.[15]

Similarly, the neo-Malthusian character of the long era preceding the Industrial Revolution also appears in need of revision. Indeed, if my characterizations of the seventeenth- and eighteenth-century Dutch economy are not steeped in grievous error, the Industrial Revolution can fruitfully be viewed as the culmination of a process with deep roots in the preceding two centuries. On other grounds, Wrigley (1988: 12) argued similarly that 'the transformation that gave rise to the Industrial Revolution is better regarded as spread over a period lasting more than two centuries'.

Conceivably, the solution to our problems could be the addition of a third growth model – appropriate from, say, the seventeenth century to *c.* 1870 – to stand between the two existing ones. While this cannot be dismissed out of hand, it is very much a historian's solution, adding periods like Ptolemy added epicycles to the movement of heavenly bodies. What I prefer to argue is that the two models – one cyclical and the other linear – are both inadequate, in the sense of being incomplete. Each relies on forces exogenous to the model for their key characteristics and each derives its considerable power from assumptions that divert our attention from important elements of the dynamics of economic growth in both periods – that is, they are both too narrowly focused.

My aspiration is to make the modern growth model more historical, released from its modernist rigidities, and the neo-Malthusian model more economic, more attentive to the growth potential of the times. I do not seek to deny the large differ-ence in the pace and scope of economic growth in the two epochs, but rather to allow for less-stylized and more-penetrating accounts of how growth could be, and hence can be, achieved, and how economic retardation is directly related to the process of growth itself.

4 Re-thinking economic growth

Re-thinking the character of economic growth on either side of the Industrial Revolution is no small task, but we might begin by considering a few basic issues. First, in what sense is modern growth 'sustained' growth; how linear is it? Second, what really constrained pre-industrial growth; could it only be cyclical?

Modern growth

According to Kuznets, modern growth is the outward manifestation of a unitary process. So long as it lasts, it defines the epoch with a single, long-term trend. How literally are we to take this claim? There is abundant empirical evidence that appears inconsistent with this assertion, describing major temporal shifts and significant national differences that characterize the growth paths of the past century (Maddison 1991: 54–5). The true purpose of the Kuznetsian doctrine seems not so much to describe reality, which it does poorly, as to justify the claims of modern economic growth to exclusivity: a growth pattern deemed to be at variance with it (not fast enough, not steady enough) must be the product of an essentially different economy.

Related to this assertion of the unitary character of modern economic growth is the convergence property of the Solow growth model. To be sure, this was not Kuznets's problem; as we have seen, he believed in divergence. But the intensity of the contemporary debate among economists about convergence signals the high stakes for the model that seeks to 'explain' modern growth.

The current defensive line drawn by the upholders of the neo-classical growth model is 'conditional convergence': the claim that only economies capable of sustained modern growth will tend over time to converge, to grow at rates inversely related to their initial per capita income level. This capacity (Barro 1997: 1–2) required of members of the converger's club depends on a long list of factors – savings propensity, population growth rate, government policy, property rights – which are much easier to assess *ex post* than *ex ante*. This is so because historical growth itself periodically disrupts and re-defines the determinants of conditionality. If technological change were always steady and quickly diffused – effectively a uniform, exogenous influence on the converging world as a whole – this would not occur, but the historical record reveals what the 'new growth theory' seeks to formalize: that at times technological change is closely associated with specific, local processes of growth and accumulation, generating windfall 'Schumpeterian' profits to temporary monopolists, and spilling over via indivisibilities and technical complementarities to generate increasing returns. Moreover, the investment process in such settings provides occasions for learning effects that can accumulate and concentrate technological improvements faster than they can be diffused, resulting in large and irreversible positive externalities (David 1997). The standard competitive assumptions cannot hold in such environments, nor are Pareto conditions met.

Convergence does not describe an economic environment where increasing returns are strong and technological progress is sufficiently radical to be incapable of rapid diffusion. Such environments are not ubiquitous of course, and there are certainly times when convergence is a useful characterization of a competitive, integrating economic world. But these times, in turn, are interrupted by the disruptive impact of technical and organizational achievements that trigger positive feedback processes. The British Industrial Revolution was a good example of such a phenomenon. But it was not the only one. Nor did the others all occur after the Industrial Revolution.

George Grantham (1993b) makes a compelling case for understanding the rapid emergence of the Flemish cloth towns in the eleventh and twelfth centuries as a sequence of endogenous responses to market expansion that fed on each other in a circle of positive feedbacks. Division of labour (the result of private decisions whose implications depend on the complementary decisions of others) and the extent of the market (whose aggregate size depends on the willingness of agents to specialize) interacted to create an economic environment benefiting from increasing returns to scale.

The re-assembly of long-distance trade in the Netherlands in the context of what Braudel termed a 'decentred' international economy at the end of the sixteenth century followed a dynamic with similar features. Here, too, division of labour did not simply follow from market extension, but interacted with it (de Vries and van der Woude 1997a: 668–72, 693–9).

The 'eruptive' and site-specific quality of innovative economic growth, which undermines the linear growth model, is accompanied by forces that lead to deceleration and relative decline in pre- and post-industrial revolution economies alike. Neither the Netherlands nor Britain found long-term growth after their initial transformations to be anything like a smooth or self-sustained process.[16] Both encountered self-limiting forces, but neither was in any sense Malthusian in character. Rather, they represented the long-term implications of sunk costs: of capital and institutional commitments that imposed a degree of path dependence on the economy. Both the Netherlands in the eighteenth century and Britain beginning in the late nineteenth faced transitions between discrete states that had very high adjustment costs and necessarily required much time. Neither of these difficult transitions represented a society hitting a Malthusian ceiling, or attaining Smith's 'full complement of riches' allowed by nature. Rather they are early examples of a ubiquitous feature of modern economic life, operative at the sectoral, regional, and national levels.

These considerations move us away from models of linearity and convergence toward a mixed pattern of discontinuous growth and deceleration – of 'rounds of growth', as the Dutch title of *First Modern Economy* has it.[17] Could it be that some form of the secular trend continues to operate in the modern epoch?

Years ago J. R. Hicks could not resist speculating, in a footnote on the final page of *Value and Capital* (1946), that 'The whole Industrial Revolution of the last two hundred years [i.e., era of modern economic growth] has been nothing but a vast secular boom, largely induced by the unparalleled rise in population'. Orthodox Kuznetsianism frowns on such thought, and Hicks's footnote long circulated as evidence of the great man's eccentricity. This dismissive interpretation was certainly not called into question by the nature of the studies which, over the years, sought to apply long-cycle modelling to the modern economy. Almost all of them were doomsday prophecies, pointing variously to the internal contradictions of capitalism, the impending exhaustion of resources, collapse of the environment, or the over-population of the world (for example Mandel 1980; Tylecote 1991; Meadows 1972). In the past several years, the wave theorists have shifted from writing Jeremiads to offering panegyrics, but they seem no less breathlessly credulous than their predecessors.[18]

All these efforts to press modern times into 'great waves' that bear a strong resemblance to the Braudelian secular trend tend to reflect (and magnify, as in a fun-fair mirror) the basic weaknesses of the secular trend concept as currently developed: its dependence on the notion of one, big, binding constraint.[19]

Pre-industrial growth

Those who are prepared to concede that the pre-industrial past offers episodes of significant economic growth can still object that it was never sustained for long. The doctrine of sustained, indeed self-sustaining, growth serves to distinguish modern growth from what is held to be the essentially cyclical character of growth in earlier times. We have here a distinction of degree, for which there is much evidence, converted into a distinction of kind that serves to rule out of bounds whole categories of historical comparisons (and future speculations), which is sustained mainly as a matter of faith.

A generation ago Deane and Cole presented the doctrine with great confidence. The upward trend in material welfare that had its origins in the eighteenth century and was associated, whenever it appeared, with industrialization differed from all earlier experiences of this kind in that it proved to be irreversible in the long run. It is restated with equal conviction today. Joel Mokyr (1993: 131) brings his recent assessment of the Industrial Revolution literature to a conclusion with the same vocabulary: 'After 1750 the fetters on sustainable economic change were shaken off. . . . What ultimately matters is the irreversibility of the events.'

Deane and Cole (1965: 3) considered the possibility of setbacks of various kinds, but concluded that 'recovery is inevitable because the system carries within itself the seeds of its own resurgence'. While this claim appears to be about the future, it is really about the past. The gospel of sustained, irreversible and unending growth highlights the essence of what distinguishes the pre- and post-Industrial Revolution epochs. Before, economic life faced a binding constraint; after, it did not. Before the Industrial Revolution, classical economics reigned; after, neo-classical.

Perhaps the single most important feature of the neo-Malthusian model that convinces scholars of the essential non-comparability of economic life before and after the industrial revolution is the association of per capita income growth in the pre-industrial society with periods of population decline and economic contraction (for example van der Woude 1973). An economic system that secures improved well-being only for the survivors of plagues, crises and depressions is patently pre-modern. Indeed, Kuznets took the precaution of requiring that modern growth combine growth of per capita product and population growth so as to exclude from consideration income growth that bore a resemblance to growth episodes in the pre-industrial past.[20]

Whether we consult Abel, Slicher van Bath, Phelps Brown and Hopkins, Braudel and Spooner, or nearly any other quantitative study of the purchasing power of labour, we will be confronted with the 'Golden Age of Labour' enjoyed by the generations surviving the Black Death. Silvia Thrupp (quoted in Chambers 1972: 22) objected that 'if the fifteenth century was a golden age, it was a golden age of bacteria', but the time series, which inevitably measures a limited form of day-wage purchasing power rather than real earnings, goes on to trace a cyclical descent which Braudel and Spooner (1967: 429) summarized as follows: 'From the late fifteenth century until well into the eighteenth century, the standard of living in Europe progressively declined'. Indeed, a literal reading of the time series of Phelps Brown and Hopkins shows the building labourer of southern England regaining the purchasing power of his fifteenth-century ancestors only in 1880!

All this, of course, is grist to the Malthusian mill, yet it remains the case that even confirmed adherents to this article of faith recognize that it is not the whole truth. The eras of population growth were unquestionably periods of economic achievement and development. But not of growth?

Braudel dealt with this problem in effect by moving in the opposite direction to Kuznets. Instead of the economy forming a unitary process with a single trend, it consisted in the pre-industrial era of a multi-layered, multi-durational process with contradictory trends. In *Méditerranée* Braudel (1972, volume 2: 892) spoke of the need to 'visualize a series of overlapping histories, developing simultaneously'. In *Civilization and Capitalism* he emphasized the simultaneous flourishing of economy, social order and state during the upswings of the secular trend. This expansiveness was the context in which all manner of economic achievement could take place, except for one: 'During every period [of population growth] until at least the eighteenth century, economic progress was inevitably at the expense of the ever increasing masses, the victims of 'social massacres.'[21]

In Braudel's view, society consisted of co-existing spheres that reacted differently to population growth. The material world was firmly Malthusian, a world of inflexibility, inertia, and slow motion. Still, its physical expansion, however stressful, allowed for the refinement of the more dynamic market economy, which in turn offered new possibilities for capitalism, riding on the broad back of material life and trying to penetrate and control these productive resources. 'Thus we have two universes, two ways of life foreign to each other yet whose wholes explain one another' (Braudel 1977: 6).

To the historian accustomed to a national accounts approach, these assertions suggest an economy of intense inequality subject to gigantic social redistributions of income. During the expansion phases, great achievements rest on the backs of peasants and workers whose share of national income shrinks simultaneously with the decline in their productivity; as their numbers fall their productivity increases and they are also able to retain a greater share of their expanded per capita output. The neo-Malthusian model is one of redistributions rather than of growth, as 'labour's share' expands and contracts radically.

One might appreciate the ability of this model to capture the dynamics of redistribution yet still believe that enduring economic growth could occur across the cycles, so to speak. However, the model has nothing to say about such growth. Braudel's view (1982–84, volume 3: 534–5) was that whatever long-term growth had been achieved in early modern Europe had not sufficed to distinguish it from the rest of the world: 'it is virtually beyond question that Europe was less rich than the worlds it was exploiting, even after the fall of Napoleon when Britain's hour of glory was dawning'.

Braudel's authority notwithstanding, this position is certainly not 'virtually beyond question'.[22] The revised view of British macro-economic performance during the

Industrial Revolution would appear to require that significant pre-industrial economic growth took place in the long run. And much of the research done in the economic history of early modern Europe over the past generation is an investigation of the factors that advanced economic performance across the cycles that have mesmerized so many earlier scholars. Those factors include institutional development, urbanization, demographic control mechanisms, market expansion, agriculture, industrial organization, and technology.[23] The power of diminishing returns is certainly not irrelevant to the working of these factors, but neither is it the iron cage holding all of early modern Europe immobilized in its cold embrace. The secular trend is something more than a repeating cycle.

5 From two models to one

In a polemic directed against revisionists of the Industrial Revolution, David Landes excoriates economists in general and Cliometricians in particular for being 'passionate seekers after the One Cause, the prime mover'. As they found one candidate after another inadequate single-handedly to 'explain' the Industrial Revolution, Landes relates, they began to doubt its importance. He observes that these methodologically sophisticated economists forget that everything is substitutable and hence nothing is indispensable. Historians, he goes on to claim, are more mindful of this economic axiom. 'They do not pursue the will-o'-the-wisp of the single essential factor. Indeed, they rejoice and gain honor by multiple causation . . .' (Landes 1993: 152).

Here Landes fails to acknowledge that the search of the One Cause of the Industrial Revolution arises from the need to explain the lifting of the great constraint that defines the neo-Malthusian model. And this model is certainly one in which historians have invested at least as heavily as economists. The structure of our growth models demands that the Industrial Revolution be discussed in 'essentialist' terms. It cannot, as Wrigley argues in *Continuity, Chance and Change* (1988: 3), be understood as 'a cumulative, progressive, unitary phenomenon'.

François Crouzet sketches just such a gradualist scenario in *Britain Ascendant*. 'One could see the Industrial Revolution', he muses, 'as having emerged quite naturally out of the most advanced of the *ancien régime* economies, which had attained to such a degree of maturity that it effected the transition to a higher degree without any particular force, whether exogenous or endogenous, impelling it.' Crouzet (1990: 24) then quickly adds: 'To invoke an argument of this kind is merely to sidestep the difficulty'. That difficulty, of course, is how to account for the lifting of the constraints of the neo-Malthusian model.

But must we really choose between denying anything needs to be explained and identifying the One Cause that finally allows growth to occur? In their interpretation of economic–demographic interaction that ends *The Population History of England*, Wrigley and Schofield posit a sequence of models in which the negative feedback loops (fed by Malthusian constraints) gradually weaken while the positive feed-back loops (located in the industrial and urban sectors) gradually gain in strength. Referring to the former, they write (1981: 478) that

... [T]he old relationships [negative feedbacks] fell into decay one by one, until by the end of the nineteenth century they remained only as logical possibilities and not as part of observable reality, like the fading grin of the proverbial Cheshire Cat.

This is an image I would like to appropriate in order to critique the neo-Malthusian model more generally. I make three claims.

First, food production in medieval and early modern times was not inevitably inelastic in the face of rising demand. The cornerstone of the neo-Malthusian model has been subjected to a revisionist assault in recent years from medievalists and early modernists alike, with work based on both England and France – plus, less surprisingly, the Low Countries.

According to the new literature, agriculture in most times and places operated well below a technologically-determined ceiling. Correspondingly, the practical problems faced by agriculture were located more in markets and institutions than in technology (Grantham 1995, 1996). Indeed, the British Industrial Revolution has been interpreted not as a triumph over Malthusianism but as a process launched by a sequence of resource reallocations that flowed from a more productive agriculture (Crafts 1985).

Second, the fundamentally greater elasticity of energy from mineral rather than from organic sources, so compellingly argued by Wrigley (1988), was more a theoretical than an actual factor in limiting production in the most advanced pre-industrial economies. While the flow of organic energy sources is necessarily limited, economic use was subject to economizing and substitution. And while the supply of mineral energy sources can rise rapidly, this is always at a price, because the discovery and exploitation of such sources always requires investment, technical change and the mobilization of labour. Thus while agriculture and energy supplies are both physically constrained in theory, in practice supplies are usually governed by the expenses producers were prepared to incur. This depended on the expected returns – that is, on prices.

Third, both agriculture and energy supplies had considerable scope for expansion in the pre-industrial economy, and where demand pressure was brought to bear effectively, the experience of meeting these demands could generate a flow of techno-logical advances, via learning-by-doing, which could advance the economy to a new level and move the theoretical constraint further away.[24] To formulate my position most provocatively: Smithian growth could lead to innovations that generated increasing returns, a Schumpeterian growth that led in turn to new rounds of market expansion. The one type of growth is not superseded by the other; they interact with each other, in the past as in the present, for Smithian commercial development supplied information (knowledge, not in the first instance technical knowledge) that was often the operative constraint to continued economic growth.

The enduring value of Braudel's understanding of long-term change is located in his conviction that the very essence of historical change involves the interaction of different durational processes and different economic regimes. His account of these economic regimes is, in my view, not particularly helpful, but the new, complex approaches to economic change that I have alluded to seem themselves to require a layered, interactive framework. Much of economic life is subject to diminishing marginal returns, in the past as in the present. Constant returns to scale certainly obtains sufficiently for much of it as well, and another class – its size is what is really now at issue – is subject to increasing returns. We possess economic models that rely on each of these, but they are either presented as rival models or are viewed as sequentially applicable, governing the economic life of successive historical epochs.[25]

A more historical approach would see them as simultaneously, at least latently, present and potentially interactive. Their relative weights have certainly changed over time, because the depth and breadth of market information and communication directly affect those weights, but all three dynamic processes – Malthusian, Smithian and Schumpeterian, as William Parker labelled them – existed in both the pre-industrial past and the modern present.[26] A single, common model developed in this spirit – Braudelian in its structure but more rigorously economic in content – might supply a common vocabulary to study economic growth both before and after the Industrial Revolution.

Notes

1 This is a 'Crocean' argument comparable to that used by Cannadine (1984).

2 Kuznets found he could not dispense with this German word, there being no suitably evocative English equivalent. Would his concept have been different had he reached for the French *mentalité*? My discussion of Kuznets' thought is based on his *summum opus* (1966).

3 The third of these features, divergence, seemed necessary to Kuznets (1966: 70–1) since even slight differentials among economies whose growth paths were steep and steady would, in time, inevitably lead to large differences in the coefficients of multiplication. This teaching of Kuznets is now not much discussed, since neo-classical theory has long had a stake in 'convergence theory', the belief that differential rates of capital efficiency in a world of exogenous technological change should lead to growing similarities among national economies, that is, that the rate of growth should be inversely related to the initial level of per capita GDP.

4 A recent defence of the neoclassical growth model is Barro (1997).

5 With apologies to Joel Mokyr, who has often drawn such analogies, referring to Britain as 'the Holy Land of industrialization'.

6 The assumption of exogeneity is explicit in Lee (1973). The interactive model is most fully developed in Wrigley and Schofield (1981).

7 In Braudel's *Méditerranée* population change is the great historical protagonist. He estimated ('stepping beyond the limit of prudence', 1972, Volume 1: 402) a doubling of population in the Mediterranean region in the course of the sixteenth century (from 30 to 60 million), and went on to claim that 'this biological revolution was the major factor in all the other revolutions with which we are concerned, more important than the Turkish conquest, the discovery and colonization of America, or the imperial vocation of Spain' (*ibid.*: 402–3).

It was also more important than the 'price revolution', Braudel argued, because '[t]his increase [of population] lay behind all the triumphs and catastrophes of the century during which man was first a useful worker and then, as the century wore on, a growing burden. . . . Toward 1600 this overload [i.e., overpopulation] halted expansion in new directions and . . . prepared the way for the bitter awakenings of the seventeenth century' (*ibid.* volume 1: 403).

Why did this growth of population so quickly overwhelm Mediterranean society? '[I]n the end this forward movement was brought to a halt by the very inelasticity of agriculture, under the same conditions as in the thirteenth century [i.e., the previous crest of population growth]. . . . The logic of later Malthusian arguments was already visible . . . the inelasticity of agricultural production had reached its ceiling and the result of this impasse was to be the "refeudalization" of the seventeenth century, an agricultural revolution in reverse' (*ibid.*: 427).

Braudel did not depart from this view in *Civilization and Capitalism*. 'This humanity in perpetual motion controls a good share of the destiny of mankind' he wrote in *Afterthoughts on Capitalism and Material Civilization*. '[T]heir ebbs and flows reveal the rules for the long-term trends that continued to operate until the eighteenth century' (1977: 9).

8 Habakkuk said as much as early as 1958 (p. 1484): 'For those who care for the over-mastering pattern, the elements are evidently there for a heroically simplified version of English history before the nineteenth century in which long-term movements in prices, in income distribution, in investment, in real wages, and in migration are dominated by changes in the growth of population.'

9 'It is clearly proper to give first attention to the elements within the system whose relationship promotes negative feedback since by definition they must predominate in a pre-industrial economy. What is meant, indeed, by a pre-industrial economy is a system in which movements of incipient expansion cannot fructify in a sustained exponential growth, but rather tend to provoke changes that will make continued growth more and more difficult to secure.' Wrigley and Schofield (1981: 463, emphasis added).

10 A fine critical review of the literature is provided in Mokyr (1993). Complaints that the Industrial Revolution is a 'misnomer' generally fail to understand the true reason for the term. Like other great revolutions, it refers to a specific historical phenomenon that claims universal significance.

11 Eric Jones (1988: 26) put the matter succinctly: 'Once upon a time it seemed we had a definite event to learn about. Growth began with, growth was, an industrial revolution in late eighteenth-century Britain. Now we know quite securely that the event was really a process, smaller, far less British, infinitely less abrupt, part of a continuum, taking much more time to run.'

12 Crafts and Harley (1992). In Harley (1993) we find the following statements: 'British economic growth accelerated only gradually before the middle of the nineteenth century' (p. 216); 'The famous technical breakthroughs . . . of the "Industrial Revolution" were . . . probably quite a small part of the process of growth' (p. 224). Harley also emphasizes the role of agriculture as a catalyst of structural change – an odd escape route from the Malthusian world. Indeed, in the Crafts–Harley 'Solow-style' assessment of the sources of British growth, only about 20 per cent of GDP growth can be attributed to the residual (deemed to track total factor productivity) in the period 1760–1830. In 1831–60 TFP accounts for 40 per cent of growth – as it had earlier, in the period 1700–60. See Harley (1993: 198).

13 For a comparison of British and Dutch national income estimates for the eighteenth century, see de Vries and van der Woude (1997a: 707). New nineteenth-century Dutch growth estimates were published recently: see Smits, Horlings and van Zanden (2000).

14 Kuznets (1966: 1–8) held that 'the epochal innovation that distinguishes the modern economic epoch is the extended application of science to problems of economic production.' Few economic historians have followed Kuznets in believing that science was the decisive factor in the British Industrial Revolution, but they did believe that a new growth path was established then, so Kuznets' exaggerated views about the great influence of science and the enormous early impact of the steam engine were tolerated as a non-fatal error. But the revised growth estimates now give new credence to the view that the modern epoch (by Kuznets' own standards) cannot have begun until a century later.

15 Support for such a re-dating can also be found in Persson's (1988: 140) studies of long-term growth. His 'controlled conjectures' generated pre-industrial growth rates in Europe (with special emphasis on the middle ages) that traced a slow upward trend from 1100 into the nineteenth century. Technological progress, 'the outcome of an endogenous although intensified growth of knowledge' stood behind this pre-industrial growth record (to which we shall return later), and these growth rates were not definitively exceeded during the Industrial Revolution. The high modern rates of growth could not be achieved until there was 'a radical change in the determinants of technological progress which occurs with the forceful intervention of science in technology in the second half of the nineteenth century.'

16 Wrigley (1988: 16–17). Wrigley refers to 'an intriguing paradox: . . . No sooner had the Industrial Revolution taken place than the relative success began to evaporate, even though absolute progress continued'.

17 *Nederland 1500–1815. De eerste Ronde van Moderne Economische Groei* (The Netherlands, 1500–1815. The First Round of Modern Economic Growth), Amsterdam: Balans, 1995.

18 See for example Snooks (1996), who invokes 'great waves of economic change' to advance his belief that English GDP grew 20-fold between Domesday and the Glorious Revolution. See also Fischer (1996), where long-term societal progress is said to advance in the very periods Snooks regards as least propitious.

19 The secular trend has also made its way into the most recent textbook in general economic history. Cameron (1989), unwilling to honour the events of the Industrial Revolution with its traditional title, sidestepped the term by deploying the concept of 'logistics'. These successive waves of economic advance and retrenchment bear a strong family resemblance to the secular trend. Cameron introduces the logistic to his readers with the observation 'It is virtually certain that each accelerating phase of population growth in Europe was accompanied by economic growth, in the sense that both total and per capita output were increasing. . . . This is most clearly attested for the third logistic (and the incipient fourth), for which statistical evidence is relatively plentiful, but there is also much indirect evidence for similar behavior during the first and second logistics' (1989: 17).

20 Kuznets (1966: 19–20). Easterlin (1996) has as one of his central tasks the defence of the view that population stagnation and decline in developed economies will not undermine the processes of modern economic growth. Chapter 9 has the title 'Secular stagnation resurrected'.

21 Braudel (1972, Volume 2: 895). Similarly (in 1982–84, volume 3: 87), he claims: 'Paradoxically, things were worse for [the masses] when all the indicators were set fair'.

22 Angus Maddison's most recent estimates of world GDP posit a 50 per cent difference between the general level of European and non-European per capita incomes. The difference between Asian income levels and the most advanced European countries was then of the order of two-to-one. By 1820 (shortly after the fall of Napoleon) Maddison's more secure estimates reveal a larger differential: two-to-one between Europe and the non-Western world in general, and three-to-one between major Asian societies and Northwestern Europe (Maddison, World Economic Growth (OECD, 1997, Table B-18).

23 This, at any rate, is my reading of recent scholarship. For a brief survey of the achievements, see de Vries (1994).

24 The argument here is that technological change was 'endogenous' in the sense that it primarily took the form of adaptive innovations, encouraged by the growth of market outlets. Mokyr (1990) makes the distinction between micro-innovations and macro-innovations, the latter being conceptual breakthroughs on which the flow of adaptive improvements and extensions ultimately depend. But even the fundamental advances often depend on a specific economic environment and are not wholly exogenous.

25 Yet it was Alfred Marshall who warned the readers of his *Principles* not to confuse short-term equilibrium (determinate and reversible, governed by diminishing returns as manifested in the familiar shape of supply and demand curves) with economic processes

operating over extended periods of time (indeterminate and irreversible, subject to increasing returns as manifested in falling long-run supply prices).

26 Parker (1984: 191): 'These three expansionary processes are not conceived wholly as stages, and do not follow each other in linear sequence over the historical record. All three are tendencies continuously active.'

Bibliography

Abel, W. (1935; second ed. 1966) *Agrarkrisen und Agrarkonjunktur*, Berlin: Parey.

Abel, W. (1980) *Agricultural Fluctuations in Europe. From the Thirteenth to the Twentieth Centuries*, Eng. trans., London.

Abrams, P. (1978) 'Towns and Economic Growth: Some Theories and Problems', in P. Abrams and E. A. Wrigley (eds.) *Towns in Societies. Essays in Economic History and Historical Sociology*, Cambridge: Cambridge University Press, pp. 9–33.

Aguirre Rojas, C. A. (1992) 'Between Marx and Braudel. Making History, Knowing History', *Review* 15: 175–219.

Allen, Robert C. (1991) 'The two English Agricultural Revolutions, 1450–1850', in B. M. S. Campbell and M. Overton (eds.) *Land, Labour and Livestock: Historical Studies in European Agricultural Productivity*, Manchester: Manchester University Press, pp. 236–54.

Allen, Robert C. (1992) *Enclosure and the Yeoman. The Agricultural Development of the South Midlands 1450–1850*, Oxford: Clarendon Press.

Allmand, C. (1988) *The Hundred Years War. England and France at War c. 1300–c. 1450*, Cambridge: Cambridge University Press.

Altman, I. (1997) 'Moving Around and Moving On: Spanish Emigration in the Sixteenth Century', in J. Lucassen and L. Lucassen (eds.) *Migration, Migration History, History*, Bern: Peter Lang, pp. 253–69.

Ambrosoli, M. (1992) *Scienziati, contadini e proprietari. Botanica e agricoltura nell'Europa occidentale*, Turin: Einaudi.

Ames, E. and Rosenberg, N. (1963) 'Changing Technological Leadership and Industrial Growth', *Economic Journal* 73: 13–31.

Amin, Sh. and Linden, M. van der (eds.) (1996) ' "Peripheral" Labour: Studies in the History of Partial Proletarianization', *International Review of Social History* Supplement 4, Cambridge: Cambridge University Press.

Amman, H. (1953) 'Die Anfang der Leinenindustrie des Bodenseegebietes', *Alemannisches Jahrbuch*.

Amman, H. (1954) 'Deutschland und die Tuchindustrie Nordeuropas im Mittelalter', *Hansische Geschichtsblätter* 72: 1–63.

Anan'ich, B. V. and Lebedev, S. K. (1990) 'Russian Finance during the French Revolution and the Napoleonic Wars', paper presented to Session B1, 'Economic Effects of the French Revolutionary and Napoleonic Wars' of the Tenth International Congress of Economic History, Leuven, 19–24 August 1990.

Anderson, M. (1980) *Approaches to the History of the Western Family 1500–1914*, London: Macmillan.

Anderson, M. (1992) 'New Insights into the History of the Family in Britain', in A. Digby, C. Feinstein and D. Jenkins (eds.) (1992) *New Directions in Economic and Social History* vol. 2, London: Macmillan, pp. 125–35.

Antoni, T. (1982) 'Note sull'arte vetraria a Pisa fra il Tre e il Quattrocento', *Bollettino storico pisano* 51: 295–305.

Arthur, W. A. (1990) 'Positive feedback in economics', *Scientific American* 251: 92–9.

Astill, G. and Langdon, J. (eds.) (1997) *Medieval Farming and Technology. The Impact of Agricultural Change in Northwest Europe*, Leyden: Brill.

Ashton, T. S. (1959) *Economic Fluctuations in England 1700–1800*, Oxford: Clarendon.

Aston, T. H. and Philpin, C. H. E. (eds.) (1985) *The Brenner Debate. Agrarian Class Structure and Economic Development in Pre-Industrial Europe*, Cambridge: Cambridge University Press.

Astorri, A. (1998) *La Mercanzia a Firenze nella prima metà del Trecento. Il potere dei grandi mercanti*, Florence: Olschki.

Aymard, M. (ed.) (1982) *Dutch capitalism and World Capitalism*, Cambridge: Cambridge University Press.

Arrighi, G. (1998) 'Capitalism and the Modern World-System. Rethinking the Nondebates of the 1970s', *Review* 21: 113–29.

Bailey, M. (1988) 'The Rabbit and the Medieval East Anglian Economy', *Agricultural History Review* 36: 1–20.

Bailey, M. (1998) 'Peasant Welfare in England, 1290–1348', *Economic History Review* 51: 223–51.

Bairoch, P. (1976) 'Europe's Gross National Product, 1800–1975', *Journal of European Economic History* 5: 273–340.

Bairoch, P. (1983) 'Energy and Industrial Revolution: New Approaches', *Revue de l'énergie* no. 356.

Bairoch, P. (1985) 'L'énergie et l'industrie manufacturière entre le monde traditionnel et le monde industrialisé: approche quantitative', in P. Bairoch and A. M. Piuz (eds.) *Les passages des économies traditionnelles européennes aux sociétés industrielles*, Genève: Droz.

Baratier, E. (1961) *La démographie provençale du XIIIe au XVIe siècle*, Paris.

Bardini, C. (1998) *Senza carbone nell'età del vapore*, Milan: Bruno Mondadori.

Barro, R. J. (1997) *Determinants of Economic Growth. A Cross-Country Empirical Study*, Cambridge, Mass.: MIT Press.

Becker, G. S. (1965) 'A Theory of Allocation of Time', *Economic Journal* 75: 493–517.

Becker, G. S. (1981) *A Treatise on the Family*, Cambridge, Mass.: Harvard University Press.

Bennet, J. M. (1988) 'History that Stands Still: Women's Work in the European Past', *Feminist Studies* 14: 269–83.

Bentzien, U. (1990) *Bauernarbeit im Feudalismus. Landwirtschaftliche Arbeitsgeräte und Verfahren in Deutschland von der Mitte des ersten Jahrtausends u. Z. bis um 1800*, Vaduz: Topos.

Berg, M. (1987) 'Women's Work, Mechanisation and the Early Phases of Industrialisation in England', in P. Joyce (ed.) (1987) *The Historical Meanings of Work*, Cambridge: Cambridge University Press, pp. 64–98.

Berg, M. (1992) 'The First Women Economic Historians', *Economic History Review* 45: 308–29.

Berg, M. and Hudson, P. (1992) 'Rehabilitating the Industrial Revolution', *Economic History Review* 45: 24–50.

Bergier, J. F. (1963) *Genève et l'économie européenne de la Renaissance*, Paris: S.E.V.P.E.N.

Berkner, L. K. (1972) 'The Stem Family and the Developmental Cycle of the Peasant House-hold: An Eighteenth-Century Austrian Example', *American Historical Review* 77: 398–418.

Berthe, M. (1984) *Famines et épidémies dans les campagnes navarraises à la fin du Moyen Age*, Paris: S.F.I.E.D.

Bieleman, J. (1987) *Boeren op het Drentse zand 1600–1910* AAG-Bijdragen vol. 29, Wageningen: Landbouwuniversiteit.

Biller, P. P. A. (1980) 'Birth Control in the West in the Thirteenth and Early Fourteenth Centuries', *Past and Present* 94: 3–26.

Bisson, T. N. (1986) *The Medieval Crown of Aragon. A Short History*, Oxford: Clarendon.

Blanchard, I. (1985) 'La loi minière anglaise 1150–1850. Une étude de la loi et de son impact sur le développement économique', unpublished paper presented at the Ecole des Hautes Etudes en Sciences Sociales, Paris.

Blanchard, I. (1986) 'The Continental European Cattle Trades, 1400–1600', *Economic History Review* 39: 427–60.

Blanchard, I. (1992) 'Introduction', in I. Blanchard, A. Goodman and J. Newman (eds.) (1992) *Industry and Finance in Early Modern History. Essays Presented to George Hammersley to the Occasion of His 74th Birthday*, Stuttgart: Steiner, pp. 13–26.

Blanchard, I. (1993) The Changing Relationships of European Regions, 14th–18th Centuries: Mining, Trade in Ores and Metals, Edinburgh University: Studies in Economic and Social History. Discussion Paper, No. 93-1.

Blanchard, I. (1996) *The Middle Ages: A Concept Too Many?* Inaugural Lecture, Edinburgh.

Blanchard, I. (1998) ' "The Long Sixteenth Century", 1450–1650', paper presented at the Twelfth International Congress held at Seville, Madrid, 12–18 August 1998.

Blanchard, I. (in press) *The International Economy in the Age of the Discoveries, 1470–1570* vol. 1: *The English Merchants' World*, London: Routledge.

Blanchard, I., Goodman, A. and Newman, J. (eds.) (1992) *Industry and Finance in Early Modern History. Essays Presented to George Hammersley on the Occasion of his 74th birthday* Vierteljahrschrift für Sozial- und Wirtschaftsgeschichte, Beihefte vol. 98, Stuttgart: Franz Steiner Verlag.

Blockmans, W. (1993) 'The Economic Expansion of Holland and Zeeland in the Fourteenth–Sixteenth Centuries', in E. Aerts, B. Henau, P. Janssens and R. Van Uytven (eds.) (1993) *Studia Historica Oeconomica. Liber Amicorum Herman Van der Wee*, Louvain: Leuven University Press, pp. 41–58.

Blomme, J., Buyst, E. and Van der Wee, H. (1994) 'The Belgian Economy in a Long-Term Perspective', in A. Maddison and H. van der Wee (eds.) (1994) *Economic Growth and Structural Change*, Milan: Università Bocconi, pp. 77–96.

Blum, J. (1978) *The End of the Old Order in Rural Europe*, Princeton: Princeton University Press.

Bois, G. (1984) *The Crisis of Feudalism: Economy and Society in Eastern Normandy* (Engl. trans.), Cambridge: Cambridge University Press.

Bolton, J. L. (1998) *The Alien Communities of London in the Fifteenth Century. The Subsidy Rolls of 1440 and 1483–4*, Stamford: Richard III and Yorkist History Trust.

Boserup, E. (1965) *The Conditions of Agricultural Growth*, London: Earthscan.

Boserup, E. (1981) *Population and Technological Change*, Oxford: Blackwell.

Boserup, E. (1983) 'The Impact of Scarcity and Plenty on Development', in R. I. Rotberg and Th. K. Rabb (eds.) (1983) *Hunger and History. The Impact of Changing Food Production and Consumption Patterns on Society*, Cambridge: Cambridge University Press, pp. 185–209.

Boyer, G. R. (1990) *An Economic History of the English Poor Law 1750–1850*, Cambridge: Cambridge University Press.

Boyer-Xambeu, M.-T., Deleplace, G. and Gillard, L. (1986) *Monnaie privée et pouvoir de princes. L'économie des relations monétaires à la Renaissance*, Paris: Editions du CNRS.

Brandt, A. von (1954) 'Waren- und Geldhandel um 1560', *Zeitschrift des Vereins für Lübeckische Geschichte*, 34.

Brass, T. and van der Linden, M. (eds.) (1997) *Free and Unfree Labour. The Debate Continues*, Bern: Peter Lang.

Braudel, F. (1972, French orig. 1949, second ed., 1966) *The Mediterranean and the Mediterranean World in the Age of Philip II*, two vols. New York: Fontana/Collins.

Braudel, F. (1977) *Afterthoughts on Capitalism and Material Civilization*, Baltimore: Johns Hopkins University Press.

Braudel, F. (1982–84, French orig. 1979) *Civilization and Capitalism, 15th–18th Century*, three vols., London: Collins.

Braudel, F. (1985) *Une leçon d'histoire de Fernand Braudel, Châteauvallon/octobre 1985*, Paris: Arthaud-Flammarion.

Braudel, F. and Spooner, F. (1967) 'Prices in Europe from 1450 to 1750', in E. E. Rich and C. H. Wilson (eds.) (1967) *The Cambridge Economic History of Europe* vol. 4, Cambridge: Cambridge University Press, pp. 374–486.

Braun, R. (1960) *Industrialisierung und Volksleben. Veränderungen der Lebensformen unter Einwirkung der verlagsindustriellen Heimarbeit in einem ländlichen Industriegebiet (Zürcher Oberland) vor 1800* Winterthur: Verlag P. G. Keller.

Breman, J. (1985) *Of Peasants, Migrants and Paupers: Rural Labour Circulation and Capitalist Production in West India*, Delhi: Oxford University Press.

Brenner, R. (1976) 'Agrarian Class Structure and Economic Development in Pre-industrial Europe', *Past and Present* 70: 3075 (repr. in T. H. Aston and C. H. E. Philpin (eds.) *The Brenner Debate*, Cambridge: Cambridge University Press).

Brenner, R. (1977) 'The Origins of Capitalist Development: a Critique of Neo-Smithian Marxism', *New Left Review* 104: 25–92.

Brenner, R. (1982) 'The Agrarian Roots of European Capitalism', *Past and Present* 97: 16–113 (repr. in T. H. Aston and C. H. E. Philpin (eds.) *The Brenner Debate*, Cambridge: Cambridge University Press).

Brezis, E. S., 'International Capital Flows During the Eighteenth Century: Did Holland Finance the British Industrial Revolution?', unpublished paper.

Bridbury, A. (1962) *Economic Growth. England in the Later Middle Ages*, London: George Allen and Unwin.

Bridbury, A. (1973) 'The Black Death', *Economic History Review* 26: 557–92.

Bridbury, A. (1982) *Medieval English Clothmaking. An Economic Survey*, London: Heineman.

Brink, G. van den (1989) 'De Structuur van het Huishouden te Woensel, 1716–1803', in G. van den Brink *et al.* (eds.) (1989) *Werk, kerk en bed in Brabant. Demografische ontwikkelingen in oostelijk Noord-Brabant 1700–1920*, 's-Hertogenbosch: BRG, pp. 33–52.

Brink, G. van den (1991) 'De arbeid is alles, de mensch niets. . . . Aard en ontwikkeling van het boerenbedrijf in de Kempen 1800–1900', *Tijdschrift voor Sociale Geschiedenis* 17: 50–72.

Britnell, R. (1993) *The Commercialisation of English Society 1000–1350*, Cambridge: Cambridge University Press.

Brulez, W. (1962) 'Les routes commerciales d'Angleterre en Italie au XVI siècle', *Studi in onore di Amintori Fanfani* vol. 4, Milan: Giuffrè, pp. 120–84.

Brunner, O. (1968, orig. 1950) 'Das ganze Haus und die alteuropäische Ökonomik', in: O. Brunner, *Neue Wege der Verfassungs- und Sozialgeschichte*, Göttingen: Vandenhoeck & Ruprecht, pp. 103–27.

Cameron, R. (1989) *A Concise Economic History of the World*, Oxford: Oxford University Press.

Campbell B. M. S. (ed.) (1991) *Before the Black Death. Studies in the 'Crisis' of the Early Fourteenth Century*, Manchester: Manchester University Press.

Campbell B. M. S. (1995) 'Progressiveness and Backwardness in Thirteenth- and Early Fourteenth-Century English Agriculture: The Verdict of Recent Research', in J. M. Duvosquel and E. Thoen (eds.) (1995) *Peasants and Townsmen in Medieval Europe. Studia in Honorem Adriaan Verhulst*, Ghent, pp. 541–59.

Campbell B. M. S. (1997a) 'Matching Supply to Demand: Crop Production and Disposal by English Demesnes in the Century of the Black Death', *Journal of Economic History* 57: 827–58.

Campbell B. M. S. (1997b) 'Economic Rent and the Intensification of English Agriculture, 1086–1350', in G. Astill and J. Langdon (eds.) (1997) *Medieval Farming and Technology*, Leyden: Brill, pp. 225–49.

Campbell B. M. S. (1998) 'Constraint or Constrained? Changing Perspectives on Medieval English Agriculture', *NEHA-Jaarboek* 61: 15–35.

Campbell B. M. S. and Overton M. (eds.) (1991) *Land, Labour and Livestock: Historical Studies in European Agricultural Productivity*, Manchester: Manchester University Press.

Campbell B. M. S. and Overton M. (1993) 'A New Perspective on Medieval and Early Modern Agriculture: Six Centuries of Norfolk Farming c. 1250–c. 1850', *Past and Present* 141: 38–105.

Cannadine, D. (1984) 'The Past and the Present in the English Industrial Revolution, 1880–1980', *Past and Present* 103: 131–72.

Canny, N. (ed.) (1994) *Europeans on the Move. Studies on European Migration, 1500–1800*, Oxford: Clarendon Press.

Caracciolo, A. (1973) 'La storia economica', in R. Romano and C. Vivanti (eds.) (1973) *Storia d'Italia* vol. iii, Turin: Einaudi.

Caracciolo, A. and Morelli, R. (1996) *La cattura dell'energia. L'economia europea dalla protostoria al mondo moderno*, Roma: La Nuova Italia Scientifica.

Carande, R. (1949) *Carlos V y sus banqueros*, Madrid: Sociedad de Estudios y Publicaciones.

Carrère, Cl. (1976) 'La draperie en Catalogne et en Aragon au XVe siècle', in M. Spallanzani (ed.) (1976) *Produzione commercio*, Florence: Olschki, pp. 475–510.

Carswell, J. (1960) *The South Sea Bubble*, London: Stanford University Press.

Carter, A. (1953a) 'The Dutch and the English Public Debt in 1777', *Economica*, New Series, 20, No. 78.

Carter, A. (1953b) 'Dutch Foreign Investment 1738–1800' *Economica*, New Series, 20, No. 80.

Chambers, J. D. (1952) 'Enclosure and Labour Supply in the Industrial Revolution', *Economic History Review* 5: 319–43.

Chambers, J. D. (1972) *Population, Economy and Society in Pre-industrial England*, Oxford: Oxford University Press.

Chatelain, A. (1970) 'Les usines-internats et les migrations féminines dans la région lyonnaise. Seconde moitié du XIXe siècle et début XXe siècle', *Revue d'histoire économique et sociale* 48, 373–94.

Chayanov, A. V. (1966) *On the Theory of Peasant Economy*, ed. D. Thorner, B. Kerblay and R. E. F. Smith, Homewood (repr. with a foreword by T. Shanin (1986): Manchester: Manchester University Press).

Chevalier, B. (1982) *Les Bonnes Villes de France du XIVe au XVIe Siècle*, Paris: Aubier.

Chiappa Mauri, L. (1997) *Terra e Uomini nella Lombardia Medievale*, Bari.

Chirot, D. and Hall, T. D. (1982) 'World-System Theory', *Annual Review of Sociology* 8: 81–106.

Chittolini, G. (1987) 'La città europea tra Medioevo e Rinascimento', in P. Rossi (ed.) (1987) *Modelli di città. Strutture e funzioni politiche*, Turin: Einaudi, pp. 371–92.

Chorley, G. P. H. (1981) 'The Agricultural Revolution in Northern Europe, 1750–1880: Nitrogen, Legumes, and Crop Productivity', *Economic History Review* 34: 71–93.

Chorley, P. (1997) 'The Evolution of the Woollen 1300–1900', in N. B. Harte (ed.) (1997) *The New Draperies*, Oxford: Oxford University Press, pp. 7–34.

Ciccone, A. and Hall, R. E. (1996) 'Productivity and the Density of Economic Activity', *American Economic Review* 86: 54–70.

Cipolla, C. (1962), *The Economic History of World Population*, Harmondsworth: Penguin.

Cipolla, C. (1963) 'Currency Depreciation in Medieval Europe', *Economic History Review* 15: 413–22.

Cipolla, C. (1964) 'Economic Depression of the Renaissance?', *Economic History Review* 16: 517–27.

Clark, A. (1919, repr. 1968) *Working Life of Women in the Seventeenth Century*, London: Frank Cass.

Clark, G. (1987) 'Productivity Growth Without Technical Change in European Agriculture before 1850', *Journal of Economic History* 47: 419–32.

Clark, G. (1988) 'The Cost of Capital and Medieval Agricultural Technique', *Explorations in Economic History* 25: 265–94.

Clarkson, L. A. (1972) *The Pre-industrial Economy in England 1500–1750*, New York: Schocken Books.

Clarkson, L. A. (1985) *Proto-Industrialization: The First Phase of Industrialization?*, London: Macmillan.

Clay, C. G. A. (1984) *Economic Expansion and Social Change: England 1500–1700* vol. 1: *People, Land and Towns*, Cambridge: Cambridge University Press.

Cohen, M. (1989/90) 'Peasant Differentiation and Proto-Industrialisation in the Ulster Countryside: Tullylish 1690–1825', *Journal of Peasant Studies* 17: 413–32.

Cole, W. A. and Deane, P. (1965) 'The Growth of National Incomes', in H. J. Habakkuk and M. M. Postan (eds.) (1965) *The Cambridge Economic History of Europe* vol. 6, Cambridge: Cambridge University Press, pp. 1–55.

Coleman, D. C. (1983) 'Proto-industrialization: A Concept Too Many', *Economic History Review* 36: 435–48.

Collins, T. (1993) 'Power Availability and Agricultural Productivity in England and Wales 1840–1939', in E. Buyst, G. de Jong, B. van Ark and J. L. van Zanden (eds.) (1993) *Historical Benchmark Comparisons of Output and Productivity 1750–1990*, Louvain: Katholieke Universiteit Research Papers, pp. 78–98.

Comba, R. (1988) 'Vasellame in legno e ceramica di uso domestico nel basso Medioevo', in R. Comba, *Contadini, signori e mercanti nel Piemonte medievale*, Roma: Laterza, pp. 111–24.

Cortonesi, A. (1995) 'Note sull'agricoltura italiana fra XIII e XIV secolo', in *Europa en los umbrales de la crisis: 1250–1350*, pp. 87–128.

Cottereau, A. (1987) 'Justice et injustice ordinaire sur les lieux de travail d'après les audiences prud'homales (1806–1866)', *Le mouvement social* 141: 25–59.

Cotts Watkins, S. and Menken, J. (1985) 'Famines in Historical Perspective', *Population and Development Review* 11: 647–75.

Crafts, N. F. R. (1977) 'Industrial Revolution in Britain and France: Some Thoughts on the Question "Why was England First?"', *Economic History Review* 30: 429–41.

Crafts, N. F. R. (1983) 'British Economic Growth, 1700–1831: a Review of the Evidence', *Economic History Review* 36: 177–99.

Crafts, N. F. R. (1985) *British Economic Growth During the Industrial Revolution*, Oxford: Oxford University Press.

Crafts, N. F. R. and Harley, C. K. (1992) 'Output Growth and the British Industrial Revolution: a restatement of the Crafts–Harley View', *Economic History Review* 45: 703–30.

Crossick, G. (ed.) (1997) *The Artisan and the European Town, 1500–1900*, Aldershot: Scolar Press.

Crossick, G. and Haupt, H.-G. (eds.) (1984) *Shopkeepers and Master Artisans in Nineteenth-Century Europe*, London: Methuen.

Crossick, G. and Haupt, H.-G. (1995) *The Petite Bourgeoisie in Europe 1780–1914. Enterprise, Family and Independence*, London: Routledge.

Crouzet, F. (1990) *Britain Ascendant: Comparative Studies in Franco-Bridish Economic History*, Cambridge: Cambridge University Press.

David, P. (1993) 'Historical Economics in the Long Run: Some Implications of Path-Dependence', in G. D. Snooks (ed.) (1993) *Historical Analysis in Economics*, London: Routledge, pp. 29–40.

David, P. (1997) 'Path Dependence and the Quest for Historical Economics', Oxford: All Souls College, unpublished paper.

Davids, K. (1995) 'Shifts in Technological Leadership in Early Modern Europe', in K. Davids and J. Lucassen (eds.) (1998) *A Miracle Mirrored*, Cambridge: Cambridge University Press, pp. 338–66.

Davids, K. (1997) 'Van moderne groei naar moderne neergang? De economische geschiedenis van Nederland in de vroeg-moderne tijd', *Bijdragen en Mededelingen tot de Geschiedenis der Nederlanden* 112: 57–65.

Davids, K. (1997) 'Maritime Labour in the Netherlands, 1570–1870', in van Royen, Bruijn, Lucassen (eds.) (1997) *Those Emblems from Hell?*, St John's, Newfoundland: International Maritime Economic History Association, pp. 41–71.

Davids, K. and Lucassen, J. (eds.) (1995) *A Miracle Mirrored. The Dutch Republic in European Perspective*, Cambridge: Cambridge University Press.

Davies, K. G. (1952a) 'Joint-stock Investment in the Later Seventeenth Century', *Economic History Review* 4: 283–301.

Davies, K. G. (1952b) 'The Origins of the Commission System in the West India Trade', *Transactions of the Royal Historical Society*, Fifth Series, 2: 89–108.

Davies, K. G. (1957) *The Royal African Company*, London: Longmans.

Davis, J. A. (1989) 'Industrialization in Britain and Europe before 1850. New Perspectives and Old Problems', in P. Mathias and J. A. Davis (eds.) (1989) *The First Industrial Revolutions*, Oxford: Blackwell, pp. 44–68.

Daviso di Charvensod, M. C. (1961) *I pedaggi delle Alpi occidentali nel medio evo*, Turin.

Deane, P. (1969) *The First Industrial Revolution*, Cambridge: Cambridge University Press.

Deane, P. and Cole, W. A. (1962) *British Economic Growth 1688–1959. Trends and Structures*, Cambridge: Cambridge University Press.

de la Roncière, C. M. (1976) *Florence centre économique régional au XIVe siècle*, five vols, Aix-en-Provence: S.O.D.E.B.

de Mas-Latrie, R. (1866) 'Le droit de marque ou de représailles au moyen age', *Bibliothèque de l'École des Chartes*, 27: 529–77.

Del Panta, L. (1980) *Le epidemie nella storia demografica italiana (secoli XIV–XIX)*, Turin: Loescher.

Del Panta, L., Livi Bacci, M., Pinto, G. and Sonnino, E. (1996) *La popolazione italiana dal Medioevo a oggi*, Bari/Rome: Laterza.

Delsalle, P. (1985) *La brouette et la navette: Tisserands, paysans et fabricants dans la région de Roubaix et de Tourcoing 1800–1848*, Westhoek: Editions de Beffrois.

Dersch, W. (1918) 'Hennebergisch–Polnische Beziehungen im 16. Jahrhundert', *Historische Monatsblätter der Provinz Posen* 19.

Derville, A. (1987) 'Dîmes, rendements du blé et "révolution agricole" dans le Nord de la France au moyen âge', *Annales ESC* 42: 1411–32.

Desai, M. (1991) 'The Agrarian Crisis in Medieval England: A Malthusian Tragedy or a Failure of Entitlements?', *Bulletin of Economic Research* 43: 223–58.

Devine, T. M. (ed.) (1984) *Farm Servants and Labour in Lowland Scotland, 1770–1914*, Edinburgh: Donald.

Diamond, P. A. (1984) *A Search-equilibrium Approach to the Micro-foundations of Macro-economics*, Cambridge, Mass.: MIT Press.

Dietz, A. (1910–25) *Frankfurter Handelsgeschichte*, Frankfurt-am-Main: Minjon.

Dillen, J. G. van (1964) 'Oprichting en functie der Amsterdamsche Wisselbank, in de zeventiende eeuw, 1609–1686', in J. G. van Dillen (1964) *Mensen en Achtergronden. Studies uitgegeven ter gelegenheid van de tachtigste verjaardag van de schrijver*, Groningen: Wolters.

Dipper, Chr. (1986) 'Bauern als Gegenstand der Sozialgeschichte', in W. Schieder and V. Sellin (eds.) (1986) *Sozialgeschichte in Deutschland. Entwicklungen und Perspektiven im internationalen Zusammenhang, Band IV, Soziale Gruppen in der Geschichte*, Göttingen: Vandenhoeck & Ruprecht, pp. 9–33.

Dobb, M. (1963, orig. 1946) *Studies in the Development of Capitalism*, New York: International Publishers.

Dubois, H. (1988) 'L'essor médiévale', in J. Dupâquier (ed.) (1988) *Histoire de la population française*, vol. 1: *Des origines à la Renaissance*, Paris: PUF, 207–66.

Ducellier, A. (1996) 'L'insertion professionnelle et civique des immigrés dans les villes d'Italie au moyen âge: l'exemple des Albanais', in D. Menjot and J.-L. Pinol (eds.) (1996) *Les migrants et la ville*, Paris: Editions l'Harmattan, pp. 63–81.

Dufourcq, Ch.-E. and Gautier Dalché, J. (1976) *Histoire économique et sociale de l'Espagne chrétienne au Moyen Age*, Paris: Armand Colin.

Dunlavy, C. A. (1994) *Politics and Industrialization. Early Railroads in the United States and Prussia*, Princeton: Princeton University Press.

DuPlessis, R. S. (1997) *Transitions to Capitalism in Early Modern Europe*, Cambridge: Cambridge University Press.

Dyer, C. (1989) *Standards of Living in the Later Middle Ages. Social Change in England, c. 1200–1520*, Cambridge: Cambridge University Press.

Dyer, C. (1998) 'Did the Peasants Really Starve in Medieval England?', in M. Carlin and J. T. Rosenthal (eds.) (1998) *Food and Eating in Medieval Europe*, London-Rio Grande: Hambledon Press, pp. 53–71.

Dyos, H. J. and Aldcroft, D. H. (1969) *British Transport: an Economic Survey from the Seventeenth to the Twentieth Century*, Leicester: Leicester University Press.

Earle, P. (1997) 'English Sailors, 1570–1795', in P. C. van Royen, J. R. Bruijn and J. Lucassen (eds.) (1997) *'Those Emblems of Hell'? European Sailors and the Maritime Labour Market, 1570–1580*, Research in Maritime History 13, St John's, Newfoundland: International Maritime Economic History Association, pp. 73–92.

Easterlin, R. (1996) *Growth Triumphant. The Twenty-first Century in Historical Perspective*, Ann Arbor: University of Michigan Press.

Ebeling, D. and Mager, W. (eds.) (1997) *Protoindustrie in der Region. Europäische Gewer-belandschaften vom 16. bis zum 19. Jahrhundert*, Bielefeld: Verlag für Regionalgeschichte.

Ehmer, J. (1980) *Familienstruktur und Arbeitsorganisation im frühindustriellen Wien*, Vienna: H. Böhlau's Nachfahren.

Ehmer, J. (1984) 'The Artisan Family in Nineteenth-Century Austria: Embourgeoisement of the Petite Bourgeoisie?', in G. Crossick and H.-G. Haupt (eds.) (1984) *Shopkeepers and Master Artisans in Nineteenth-Century Europe*, London/New York: Methuen, pp. 195–218.

Ehmer, J. (1991) *Heiratsverhalten, Sozialstruktur, ökonomischer Wandel. England und Mitteleuropa in der Formationsperiode des Kapitalismus*, Göttingen: Vandenhoeck & Ruprecht.

Ehmer, J. and Mitterauer, M. (eds.) (1986) *Familienstruktur und Arbeitsorganisation in ländlichen Gesellschaften*, Vienna/Cologne: Böhlau.

Ehrenberg, R. (1922) *Der Zeitalter der Fugger. Geldkapital und Kreditverkehr im 16. Jahrhundert*, Jena: Gustav Fischer Verlag.

Eltis, D. (1997) 'Seventeenth Century Migration and the Slave Trade: The English Case in Comparative Perspective', in J. Lucassen and L. Lucassen (eds.) (1997) *Migration, Migration History, History*, Bern: Peter Lang, pp. 87–109.

Emsbach, K. (1982) *Die soziale Betriebsverfassung der rheinischen Baumwollindustrie im 19. Jahrhundert*, Bonn: Rohrscheid.

Engelen, Th. (1994) 'Family, Production and Reproduction: on the Relationship Between Economic and Demographic Processes', *Economic and Social History in the Netherlands* 6: 61–82.

Ennew, L. J., Hirst, P., and Tribe, K. (1976/7) 'Peasantry as an Economic Category', *Journal of Peasant Studies* 4: 295–322.

Epstein, S. R. (1989) 'The Textile Industry and the Foreign Cloth Trade in Late Medieval Sicily (1300–1500): a "Colonial Relationship"?', *Journal of Medieval History* 15: 141–83.

Epstein, S. R. (1991) 'Cities, Regions and the Late Medieval Crisis: Sicily and Tuscany Compared', *Past and Present* 130: 3–50.

Epstein, S. R. (1992) *An Island for Itself. Economic Development and Social Transformation in Late Medieval Sicily*, Cambridge: Cambridge University Press.

Epstein, S. R. (1993) 'Town and Country: Economy and Institutions in Late Medieval Italy', *Economic History Review* 46: 453–77.

Epstein, S. R. (1998a) 'Craft Guilds, Apprenticeship and Technological Change in Pre-Modern Europe', *Journal of Economic History* 53, 3: 684–713.

Epstein, S. R. (1998b) 'Italy', in T. Scott (ed.) (1998) *The Peasantries of Europe*, London: Longman, pp. 75–110.

Epstein, S. R. (1998c) 'Nuevas aproximaciones a la historia urbana de Italia: el Renacimiento temprano', *Història* 58: 417–38.

Epstein, S. R. (1999) 'Market Structures', in W. Connell and A. Zorzi (eds.) (1999) *Florentine Tuscany: Structures and Practices of Power*, Cambridge: Cambridge University Press.

Epstein, S. R. *et al.* (eds.) (1998) *Guilds, economy and society*, Proceedings of the Twelfth International Economic History Congress, August 1998, Seville: Fundación Fomento de la Historia Económica.

Epstein, S. R. (ed.) (2000) *Town and Country in Europe*, Cambridge: Cambridge University Press.

Erdem, Y. H. (1996) *Slavery in the Ottoman Empire and its Demise, 1800–1909*, New York: Macmillan.

Etemad, B. and Luciani, J. (1991) *World Energy Production 1800–1985*, Genève: Droz.

Europa en los umbrales de la crisis: 1250–1350. XXI Semana de Estudios Medievales, Estella, 18–22 julio 1994, Pamplona: Departamento de Educacion y Cultura.

Everitt, A. (1967) 'Farm Labourers', in J. Thirsk (ed.) (1967) *The Agrarian History of England and Wales* vol. 1: 1500–1640, Cambridge: Cambridge University Press, pp. 396–465.

Farr, I. (1986) 'Tradition and the Peasantry: On the Modern Historiography of Rural Germany', in R. J. Evans and W. R. Lee (eds.) *The German Peasantry. Conflict and Community in Rural Society from the Eighteenth to the Twentieth Centuries*, London: Croom Helm.

Fertig, G. (1994) 'Transatlantic Migration from the German-Speaking Parts of Central Europe, 1600–1800: Proportions, Structures, and Explanations', in N. Canny (ed.) (1994) *Europeans on the Move*, Oxford: Clarendon Press, pp. 192–235.

Fertig, G. (1997) 'Eighteenth-Century Transatlantic Migration and Early German Anti-Migration Ideology', in J. Lucassen and L. Lucassen (eds.) (1997) *Migration, Migration History, History*, Bern: Peter Lang, pp. 271–90.

Fischer, D. Hackett (1996) *The Great Wave. Price Revolutions and the Rhythm of History*, Oxford: Oxford University Press.

Fischer, G. (1929) *Aus Zwei Jahrhundert Leipziger Handelsgeschichte, 1470–1650*, Leipzig.

Fitz, A. J. (1985) *Die Frühindustrialisierung Vorarlbergs und ihre Auswirkungen auf die Familienstruktur*, Dornbirn.

Fogel, R. (1992) 'Second Thoughts on the European Escape from Hunger: Famines, Chronic Malnutrition, and Mortality', in S. R. Osmani (ed.) (1992) *Nutrition and Poverty*, Oxford: Clarendon, pp. 243–86.

Fogel, R. (1994) 'The Relevance of Malthus for the Study of Mortality Today: Long-run Influences on Health, Mortality, Labour Force Participation, and Population Growth', in K. Lindahl-Kiessling and H. Landberg (eds.) (1994) *Population, Economic Development, and the Environment*, Oxford: Oxford University Press, pp. 231–84.

Fontaine, L. (1996) *History of Pedlars in Europe*, Engl. transl., Oxford: Polity.

Fontaine, L. and Schlumbohm, J. (2000) 'Household Strategies for Survival: an Introduction', *International Review of Social History*, vol. 45, supplement, pp. 1–17.

Foster-Carter, A. (1978) 'The Modes of Production Controversy', *New Left Review* 107: 47–77.

Fourquin, G. (1964) *Les campagnes de la région parisienne à la fin du Moyen Âge du milieu du XIIIe siècle au début du XVIe siècle*, Paris: Publications de la faculté des lettres et sciences humaines de Paris.

Fourquin, G. (1979) *Histoire économique de l'Occident médiéval*, Paris: Colin, third ed.

Friel, I. (1995) *The Good Ship. Ships, Shipbuilding and Technology in England 1200–1520*, Baltimore: Johns Hopkins University Press.

Fudge, J. D. (1995) *Cargoes, Embargoes and Emissaries. The Commercial and Political Interaction of England and the German Hanse, 1450–1510*, Toronto: University of Toronto Press.

Furet, F. (1978) *Penser la Révolution française*, Paris: Gallimard.

Gaastra, F. S. (1991) *De geschiedenis van de VOC*, Zutphen: Walburg Pers.

Gaastra, F. S. and Bruijn, J.R. (1993) 'The Dutch East India Company's Shipping, 1602–1795, in a Comparative Perspective', in J. R. Bruijn and F. S. Gaastra (eds.) (1993) *Ships, Sailors and Spices. East India Companies and their Shipping in the 16th, 17th and 18th Centuries*, Amsterdam: NEHA, pp. 177–208.

Galloway, J. (2000) 'Town and Country in England, 1300–1570', in S. R. Epstein (ed.) (2000) *Town and Country in Europe*, Cambridge: Cambridge University Press.

Gascon, R. (1971) *Grand commerce et vie urbaine au XVIe siècle. Lyons et ses marchands*, Paris: SEVPEN.

Gatrell, P. (1982) 'Historians and Peasants. Studies of Medieval English Society in a Russian Context', *Past and Present* 96: 22–50 (repr. in T. H. Aston (ed.) (1982) *Landlords, Peasants and Politics in Medieval England* (Cambridge, 1987) 394–422).

Gaunt, D. (1977a) 'Pre-Industrial Economy and Population Structure. The Elements of Variance in Early Modern Sweden', *Scandinavian Journal of History* 2: 183–210.

Gaunt, D. (1977b) 'Natural Resources, Population, Local Society: The Case of Pre-Industrial Sweden', *Peasant Studies* 6: 137–41.

Genet, J. P. (1995) 'Le développement des monarchies d'Occident est-il une conséquence de la crise?, in *Europa en los umbrales de la crisis: 1250–1350*, pp. 63–86.

Gerding, M. A. W. (1995) *Vier eeuwen turfwinning. De verveningen in Groningen, Friesland, Drenthe en Overijssel tussen 1550 en 1950* AAG-Bijdragen vol. 35, Wageningen: Landbouwuniversiteit.

Gerschenkron, A. (1962) *Economic Backwardness in Historical Perspective*, New Haven: Harvard University Press.

Glick, T. F. (1970) *Irrigation and Society in Medieval Valencia*, Cambridge, Ma.: Harvard University Press.

Goldberg, P. J. P. (1992) *Women, Work, and Life Cycle in a Medieval Economy. Women in York and Yorkshire c. 1300–1520*, Oxford: Clarendon.

Goldthwaite, R. (1993) *Wealth and the Demand for Art in Italy, 1300–1600*, Baltimore: Johns Hopkins University Press.

Goodman, J. and Honeyman, K. (1988) *Gainful Pursuits. The Making of Industrial Europe 1600–1914*, London: Arnold.

Goody, J. (1996) *The East in the West*, Cambridge: Cambridge University Press.

Goubert, P. (1965) 'The French Peasantry of the Seventeenth Century: A Regional Example', in: T. Aston (ed.) (1965) *Crisis in Europe 1560–1660*, London: Routledge.

Grafton, A. (1997) *Commerce with the Classics: Ancient Books and Renaissance Readers*, Ann Arbor: University of Michigan Press.

Grantham, G. W. (1993a) 'Divisions of Labour: Agricultural Productivity and Occupational Specialization in Pre-Industrial France', *Economic History Review* 46: 478–502.

Grantham, G. (1993b) 'Economic Growth Without Causes: A Re-examination of Medieval Economic Growth and Decay', Tucson, Ariz.: unpublished paper, History Association Annual Meetings.

Grantham, G. (1995) 'Time's Arrow and Time's Cycle in the Medieval Economy', Montreal: unpublished paper, McGill University.

Grantham, G. (1996) 'Contra Ricardo: The Macroeconomics of Pre-Industrial Agrarian Economies', Montreal: unpublished paper, McGill University.

Grantham, G. (1997) 'Espaces privilégiés. Productivité agraire et zones d'approvisionnement des villes dans l'Europe préindustrielle', *Annales HSS* 52: 695–725.

Gray, J. (1992/93) 'Rural Industry and Uneven Development: The Significance of Gender in the Irish Linen Industry', *Journal of Peasant Studies* 20: 590–611.

Griffiths, R. T. (1982) 'The Creation of a National Dutch Economy: 1795–1909', *Tijdschrift voor geschiedenis* 95: 513–37.

Gual Camarena, M. (1976) 'Orígenes y expansión de la industria textil lanera catalana en la edad media', in M. Spallanzani (ed.) (1976) *Produzione commercio*, Florence: Olschki, pp. 11–24.

Guenzi, A., Massa, P. and Piola Caselli, F. (eds.) (1998) *Guilds, Markets and Work Regulations in Italy, 16th–19th Centuries*, Aldershot: Ashgate.

Gullickson, G. L. (1982) 'Proto-industrialization, Demographic Behavior and the Sexual Division of Labor in Auffay, France, 1750–1850', *Peasant Studies* 9: 106–18.

Gullickson, G. L. (1983) 'Agriculture and Cottage Industry: Redefining the Causes of Proto-industrialization', *Journal of Economic History* 43: 831–50.

Gullickson, G. L. (1986) *Spinners and Weavers of Auffay. Rural Industry and the Sexual Division of Labor in a French Village, 1750–1850*, Cambridge: Cambridge University Press.

Gullickson, G. L. (1991) 'Love and Power in the Proto-industrial family', in M. Berg (ed.) (1991) *Markets and Manufacture in Early Industrial Europe*, London/New York: Routledge, pp. 205–26.

Gustafsson, B. (1987) 'The Rise and Economic Behaviour of Medieval Craft Guilds. An Economic-theoretical Interpretation', *Scandinavian Economic History Review* 35: 1–40.

Habakkuk, H. J. (1952) 'The Long-term Rate of Interest and the Price of Land in the Seventeenth Century', *Economic History Review* 5: 26–45.

Habakkuk, H. J. (1958) 'The Economic History of Modern Britain', *Journal of Economic History* 18: 1484–501.

Habakkuk, H. J. (1969) 'La disparition du paysan anglais', *Annales ESC* 20: 649–63.

Hajnal, J. (1965) 'European Marriage Patterns in Perspective', in D. V. Glass and D. E. C. Eversley (eds.) (1965) *Population in History*, London: Edward Arnold, pp. 101–43.

Haldon, J. (1993) *The State and the Tributary Mode of Production*, London: Verso.

Hanagan, M. (1986) 'Agriculture and Industry in the Nineteenth-Century Stéphanois: Household Employment Patterns and the Rise of a Permanent Proletariat', in M. Hanagan and C. Stephenson (eds.) (1986) *Proletarians and Protest. The Roots of Class Formation in an Industrializing World*, New York: Greenwood Press, pp. 77–106.

Hanagan, M. (1989) *Nascent Proletarians. Class Formation in Post-Revolutionary France*, Oxford: Blackwell.

Hanawalt, B. (1986a) *The Ties That Bound. Peasant Families in Medieval England*, Oxford: Oxford University Press.

Hanawalt, B. (ed.) (1986b) *Women and Work in Preindustrial Europe*, Bloomington Ind.: Indiana University Press.

Hanham, A. (ed.) (1975) *The Cely Letters 1472–1488*, London: Early English Text Society.

Hanham, A. (1985) *The Celys and Their World. An English Merchant Family of the Fifteenth Century*, Cambridge: Cambridge University Press.

Hareven, T. K. (1991) 'The History of the Family and the Complexity of Social Change', *American Historical Review* 96: 95–124.

Harley, C. K. (1993) 'Reassessing the Industrial Revolution', in J. Mokyr (ed.) (1993) *The British Industrial Revolution*, Boulder, Co.: Westview, pp. 171–226.

Harrison, M. (1974/5) 'Chayanov and the Economics of the Russian Peasantry', *Journal of Peasant Studies* 2: 389–411.

Harrison, M. (1976/7a) 'Resource Allocation and Agrarian Class Formation: The Problem of Social Mobility among Russian Peasant Households, 1880–1930', *Journal of Peasant Studies* 4: 127–61.

Harrison, M. (1976/7b) 'The Peasant Mode of Production in the Work of A. V. Chayanov', *Journal of Peasant Studies* 4: 323–36.

Harrison, M. (1979/80) 'Chayanov and the Marxists', *Journal of Peasant Studies* 7: 86–100.

Harriss, G. L. (1975) *King, Parliament, and Public Finance in Medieval England to 1369*, Oxford: Clarendon.

Hart, M. C. 't (1993) *The Making of a Bourgeois State. War, Politics and Finance During the Dutch Revolt*, Manchester: Manchester University Press.

Harte, N. B. (ed.) (1997) *The New Draperies in the Low Countries and England, 1300–1800*, Oxford: Oxford University Press.

Harvey, B. F. (1991) 'Introduction: the "Crisis" of the Early Fourteenth Century', in B. M. S. Campbell (ed.) (1991) *Before the Black Death*, Manchester: Manchester University Press, pp. 1–24.

Harvey, P. D. A. (1991) *Medieval Maps*, London: British Library.

Hatcher, J. (1993) *The History of the British Coal Industry*, vol. 1: Before 1700, Oxford: Clarendon Press.

Heers, J. (1976) 'La mode et les marchés des draps de laine: Gênes et la montagne à la fin du Moyen Age', in M. Spallanzani (ed.) (1976) *Produzione commercio*, Florence: Olschki, pp. 199–220.

Henning, F.-W. (1974) *Das vorindustrielle Deutschland, 800 bis 1800*, Paderborn: Schöningh.

Henning, F.-W. (1991) *Deutsche Wirtschafts- und Sozialgeschichte im Mittelalter und in der frühen Neuzeit*, Paderborn: Schöningh.

Herlihy, D. (1982) 'Demography', in J. R. Strayer (ed.) (1982) *Dictionary of the Middle Ages*, vol. 4, New York: Scribner, pp. 136–48.

Herlihy, D. (1987) 'Outline of Population Developments in the Middle Ages', in B. Herrmann and R. Sprandel (eds.) (1987) *Determinanten der Bevölkerungsentwicklung im Mittelalter*, Weinheim: VCH, pp. 1–23.

Herlihy, D. (1997) *The Black Death and the Transformation of the West*, Cambridge, MA: Cambridge University Press.

Herrick, B. H. and Kindleberger, Ch. P. (1983) *Economic Development*, New York: McGraw Hill.

Herten, B. van der (forthcoming) De economische evolutie van transport en communicatie in België 1830–1913. Een kwantitatieve en kwalitatieve analyse, Ph.D. thesis, Catholic University Louvain.

Hicks, J. R. (1946) *Value and Capital. An Inquiry into Some Fundamental Principles of Economic Theory*, Oxford: Clarendon.

Hildebrandt R. (1981) 'Interkontinentale Wirtschaftsbeziehungen und ihre Finanzierung in der 1. Hälfte des 17. Jahrhunderts', in H. Kellenbenz (ed.) (1981) *Weltwirtschaftliche und währungspolitische Probleme seit dem Ausgang des Mittelalters* Forschungen zur Sozial- und Wirtschaftsgeschichte vol. 23, Stuttgart/New York: Fischer.

Hildebrandt R. (1992) 'The Effects of Empire: Changes in the European Economy after Charles V', in Blanchard *et al.* (eds.) (1982) *Industry and Finance*, Stuttgart: Steiner, pp. 58–76.

Hilger, M.-E. (1982) 'Kapital, Kapitalist, Kapitalismus', in O. Brunner, W. Conze and R. Koselleck (eds.) (1982) *Geschichtliche Grundbegriffe. Historisches Lexikon zur politisch-sozialen Sprache in Deutschland* vol. 3, Stuttgart: Klett-Cotta, pp. 399–454.

Hill, B. (1989) *Women, Work, and Sexual Politics in Eighteenth-Century England*, Oxford: Blackwell.

Hilton, R. H. (1965) 'Rent and capital formation in feudal society', in *Second International Conference of Economic History, Aix-en-Provence, 1962*, vol. 2, Paris: Mouton, 33–68.

Hilton, R. H. (1975) *The English Peasantry in the Late Middle Ages. The Ford Lectures for 1973 and Related Studies*, Oxford: Clarendon.

Hilton, R. H. (1977) 'Reasons for Inequality among Medieval Peasants', *Journal of Peasant Studies* 5: 271–84.

Hilton, R. H. (1985) 'Medieval Market Towns and Simple Commodity Production', *Past and Present*, 109: 3–23.

Hilton, R. H. (1992) *English and French Towns in Feudal Society. A Comparative Study*, Cambridge: Cambridge University Press.

Hirschbiel, H. H. (1978) 'Conscription in Russia', in J. L. Wieczynski (ed.) *The Modern Encyclopedia of Russian and Soviet History*, vol. viii, Gulf Breeze, Flor.: Academic International Press, pp. 4–9.

Hoffman, Ph. T. (1996) *Growth in a Traditional Society: The French Countryside, 1450–1789*, Princeton: Princeton University Press.

Hoffmann, A. (1972) 'Die Agrarisierung der Industriebauern in Österreich', *Zeitschrift für Agrargeschichte und Agrarsoziologie* 20: 66–81.

Hohenberg, P. M. and Hollen Lees, L. (1985) *The Making of Urban Europe 1000–1950*, Cambridge, Mass.: Harvard University Press.

Holbach, R. (1994) *Frühformen von Verlag und Grossbetrieb in der gewerblichen Production (13.–16. Jahrhundert)*, Stuttgart: Steiner.

Holden, J. M. (1955) *The History of Negotiable Instruments in English Law*, London.

Holmes, D. R. (1989) *Cultural Disenchantments. Worker Peasantries in Northeast Italy*, Princeton N.J.: Princeton University Press.

Holmes, D. R. and Quataert, J. H. (1986) 'An Approach to Modern Labor: Worker Peasantries in Historic Saxony and the Friuli Region over Three Centuries', *Comparative Studies in Society and History* 28: 191–215.

Holton, R. J. (1985) *The Transition from Feudalism to Capitalism*, London: Macmillan.

Holton, R. J. (1986) *Cities, Capitalism and Civilization*, London: Allen and Unwin.

Hopkins, E. A. (1992) 'Nobleman and His Debts: John, Second Earl of Bridgewater, 1622–1686' in J. Blanchard *et al.* (eds.) (1992) *Industry and Finance*, Stuttgart: Steiner, pp. 77–91.

Hoppenbrouwers, P. (1997) 'Agricultural Production and Technology in the Netherlands, *c.* 1000–1500', in G. Astill and J. Langdon (eds.) *Medieval Farming and Technology*, Leyden: Brill, 89–114.

Hoppenbrouwers, P. (2000) 'Town and Country in Holland, 1300–1550', in S. R. Epstein (ed.) (2000) *Town and Country in Europe*, Cambridge: Cambridge University Press.

Hoppenbrouwers, P. and Zanden, J. L. van (eds.) (in press) *Peasants into Farmers? The Transformation of the Rural Economy and Society in the Coastal Areas of the Low Countries During the Later Medieval and Early Modern Periods*.

Hoppit, J. (1986) 'Financial Crises in Eighteenth-Century England', *Economic History Review* 39: 39–58.

Hoppit, J. (1987) *Risk and Failure in English Business 1700–1800*, Cambridge: Cambridge University Press.

Horrell, S. (1996) 'Home Demand and British Industrialization', *Journal of Economic History* 56: 561–604.

Horlings, E. (1995) *The Economic Development of the Dutch Service Sector 1800–1850. Trade and Transport in a Premodern Economy*, Amsterdam: NEHA.

Houston, R. and Snell, K. D. M. (1984) 'Proto-industrialization? Cottage Industry, Social Change, and Industrial Revolution', *Historical Journal* 27: 473–92.

Howell, M. C. (1986a) *Women, Production, and Patriarchy in Late Medieval Cities*, Chicago: University of Chicago Press.

Howell, M. C. (1986b) 'Women, the Family Economy, and the Structures of Market Production in Cities of Northern Europe', in Hanawalt (ed.) (1986b) *Women and Work*, 198–220.

Hudson, P. (1989) 'The Regional Perspective', in P. Hudson (ed.) (1989) *Regions and Industries. A Perspective on the Industrial Revolution in Britain*, Cambridge: Cambridge University Press, pp. 5–38.

Hudson, P. (1992) 'Proto-industrialisation', in A. Digby, Ch. H. Feinstein and D. T. Jenkins (eds.) (1992) *New Directions in Economic and Social History*, vol. 2, London: Macmillan, pp. 11–22.

Hudson, P. and Lee, W. R. (1990) 'Women's Work and the Family Economy in Historical Perspective', in *idem* (eds.) (1990) *Women's Work and the Family Economy in Historical Perspective*, Manchester: Manchester University Press, pp. 2–47.

Hufton, O. H. (1974) *The Poor of Eighteenth-Century France 1750–1789*, Oxford: Clarendon.

Humphries, J. (1990) 'Enclosures, Common Rights, and Women: The Proletarianization of Families in the Late Eighteenth and Early Nineteenth Centuries', *Journal of Economic History* 50: 17–42.

Hymer, S. and Resnick, S. (1969) 'A Model of an Agrarian Economy with Nonagricultural Activities', *American Economic Review*, 59: 493–506.

Iradiel Murugarren, P. (1974) *Evolución de la industria textil castellana en los siglos XIII–XVI*, Salamanca: Salamanca University Press.

Isacson, M. and Magnusson, L. (1987) *Proto-industrialisation in Scandinavia. Craft Skills in the Industrial Revolution*, Leamington Spa: Berg.

Jacobs, A. P. (1995) *Los moviementos migratorios entre Castilla e Hispanoamerica durante el reinado de Felipe III, 1598–1621*, Amsterdam.

Jardine, L. (1996) *Worldly Goods. A New History of the Renaissance*, London: Macmillan.

Jesse, W. (1928) *Der Wendische Münzverein*, Lübeck: Hansischer Gedichtsverein.

Johnson, A. H. (1909, repr. 1963) *The Disappearance of the Small Landowner*, Oxford: Oxford University Press.

Johnson, C. (1979) 'Patterns of Proletarianization: Parisian Tailors and Lodève Woollen Workers', in J. Merriman (ed.) (1979) *Consciousness and Class Experience in Nineteenth Century Europe*, New York: Holmes and Meier, pp. 65–84.

Jonas, R. A. (1991) 'Peasants, Population, and Industry in France', *Journal of Interdisciplinary History* 22: 177–200.

Jones, C. I. (1998) *Introduction to Economic Growth*, New York/London: W. W. Norton.

Jones, E. L. (1988) *Growth Recurring. Economic Change in World History*, Oxford: Blackwell.

Jones, D. W. (1988) *War and Economy in the Age of William III and Marlborough*, Oxford: Blackwell.

Jordan, W. C. (1996) *The Great Famine. Northern Europe in the Early Fourteenth Century*, Princeton: Princeton University Press.

Kander, A. (1996) 'Swedish Forests as Historical Sinks for CO_2', paper presented at the ESTER-Seminar, Montecatini.

Kander, A. (1998) 'Energy Consumption and Forestry in Sweden, 1800–1990', MA thesis, Lund University.

Kaplan, S. L. (1995) *Farewell, Revolution. The Historians' Feud, 1789/1989*, Ithaca, NY: Cornell University Press.

Kaschuba, W. and Lipp, C. (1982) *Dörfliches Überleben. Zur Geschichte materieller und sozialer Reproduktion ländlicher Gesellschaft im 19. und frühen 20. Jahrhundert*, Tübingen.

Kaye, H. J. (1984) *The British Marxist Historians. An Introductory Analysis*, Cambridge: Polity.

Keene, D. and Harding, V. (1987) *Historical Gazetteer of London before the Great Fire*, 1. Cheapside, Cambridge (microfiche).

Kellenbenz, H. (1973) 'Industries rurales en Occident de la fin du Moyen Age au XVIIIe siècle', *Annales E.S.C.* 18: 832–82.

Kellenbenz, H. (ed.) (1975) *Agrarisches Nebengewerbe und Formen der Reagrarisierung im Spätmittelalter und 19./20. Jahrhundert*, Stuttgart: Fischer.

Kellenbenz, H. (1979) 'Die Konkurrenten der Fugger als Bankiers der spanischen Krone', *Zeitschrift für Unternehmensgeschichte* 24.

Kellenbenz, H. (1986) 'Wirtschaft und Gesellschaft Europas 1350–1650', in W. Fischer *et al.* (eds.) (1986) *Handbuch der Europäischen Wirtschafts- und Sozialgeschichte*, vol. 3, Stuttgart: Klett-Cotta, pp. 1–386.

Kerblay, B. (1975) 'Chayanov and the Theory of Peasantry as a Specific Type of Economy', in T. Shanin (ed.) *Peasants and Peasant Societies*, Harmondsworth: Penguin.

210   Bibliography

Kerridge, E. (1967) *The Agricultural Revolution*, London: George Allen and Unwin.

Kerridge, E. (1969) *Agrarian Problems of the Sixteenth Century and After*, London: George Allen and Unwin.

Kindleberger, Ch. P. (1991) 'The Economic Crisis of 1619 to 1623', *Journal of Economic History* 51: 149–75.

King, G. (1696) *Natural and Political Observations and Conclusions upon the State and Condition of England.*

Kjaergaard, Th. (1994) *The Danish Revolution 1500–1800*, Cambridge: Cambridge University Press.

Kleineke, H. (1997) *Towns and Trade in Southern England c. 1400. A Database*, mimeo, London.

Klep, P. M. M. (1987) 'Over de achteruitgang van de Noordbrabantse huisnijverheid, 1810–1920', *Brabants Heem* 39: 79–94.

Kloek, E. (1981) *Gezinshistorici over vrouwen. Een overzicht van het werk van gezinshistorici en de betekenis daarvan voor de vrouwengeschiedenis*, Amsterdam: SUA.

Kloek, E. (1987) 'Vrouwenarbeid aan banden gelegd? De arbeidsdeling naar sekse volgens de keurboeken van de oude draperie van Leiden, *ca.* 1380–1580', *Tijdschrift voor Sociale Geschiedenis* 13: 373–402 (repr. in *ibid.* (1990) *Wie hij zij, man of wijf. Vrouwengeschiedenis in de vroeg-moderne tijd: drie Leidse studies*, Hilversum: Verloren).

Klundert, Th. van de (1997) *Groei en instituties. Over de oorzaken van economische ontwikkeling*, Tilburg: Tilburg University Press.

Knight, G. R. (1999) 'Coolie or Worker? Crossing the Lines in Colonial Java, 1780–1942', *Itinerario* 23: 62–77.

Knotter, A. (1986) 'The Amsterdam Shipping Trade and the Countryside of North-Holland in the 16th and 17th Centuries. The Problem of the Labour Market', in *Storia della Città. Rivista Internazionale di Storia urbana e territoriale* 10: 47–52.

Knotter, A. (1991) *Economische transformatie en stedelijke arbeidsmarkt. Amsterdam in de tweede helft van de negentiende eeuw*, Amsterdam/Zwolle: Waanders.

Kocka, J. (1990) *Weder Stand noch Klasse. Unterschichten um 1800*, Bonn: Dietz.

Kolchin, P. (1987) *Unfree Labor. American Slavery and Russian Serfdom*, Cambridge, Mass.: Harvard University Press.

Komlos, J. (1993) 'The Secular Trend in the Biological Standard of Living in the United Kingdom, 1730–1860', *Economic History Review* 46: 115–44.

Komlos, J. (1996) 'Modern Economic Growth and the Biological Standard of Living', paper presented at the Second Congress of the European Association of Historical Economics, Venice.

Kreutz, B. M. (1973) 'Mediterranean Contributions to the Medieval Mariner's Compass', *Technology and Culture*, 14 (July): pp. 367–83.

Kriedte, P. (1982) 'Die Stadt im Prozess der europäischen Proto-Industrialisierung', *Die alte Stadt* 9: 19–51.

Kriedte, P. (1983) *Peasants, Landlords and Merchant Capitalists. Europe and the World Economy, 1500–1800*, Leamington Spa: Berg.

Kriedte, P. (1991) *Eine Stadt am Seidenen Faden. Haushalt, Hausindustrie und soziale Bewegung in Krefeld in der Mitte des 19. Jahrhunderts*, Göttingen: Vandenhoeck and Ruprecht.

Kriedte, P. (1997) 'Zwischen Ehrerbietung und Aufsässigkeit? Zum Verhältnis der Handweber zu den Verlegern im niederrheinischen Seidengewerbe im 19. Jahrhundert', in A. Lubinski *et al.* (eds.) *Historie und Eigensinn. Festschrift für Jan Peters*, Weimar: Hermann Böhlaus Nachfolger, pp. 215–26.

Kriedte, P., Medick, H. and Schlumbohm, J. (1981) *Industrialization Before Industrialization: Rural Industry in the Genesis of Capitalism*, Cambridge: Cambridge University Press (German original 1977).

Kriedte, P., Medick, H. and Schlumbohm, J. (1981) *Industrialisierung vor der Industrialisierung. Gewerbliche Warenproduktion auf dem Land in der Formationsperiode des Kapitalismus*, Göttingen: Vandenhoeck & Ruprecht.

Kriedte, P., Medick, H. and Schlumbohm, J. (1983) 'Die Proto-Industrialisierung auf dem Prüfstand der historischen Zunft. Antwort auf einige Kritiker', *Geschichte und Gesellschaft* 9: 87–105 (translated as 'Proto-industrialization on Test with the Guild of Historians: Response to Some Critics', *Economy and Society* 15 (1986) 255–72).

Kriedte, P., Medick, H. and Schlumbohm, J. (1993) 'Proto-industrialization Revisited: Demography, Social Structure, and Modern Domestic Industry', *Continuity and Change* 8: 217–252 (orig. 'Sozialgeschichte in der Erweiterung – Proto-Industrialisierung in der Verengung? Demographie, Sozialstruktur, moderne Hausindustrie: eine Zwischenbilanz der Proto-Industrialisierungs-Forschung', *Geschichte und Gesellschaft* 18: 70–87, 231–55).

Kriedte, P., Medick H. and Schlumbohm, J. (1998) 'Eine Forschungslandschaft in Bewegung. Die Proto-Industrialisierung am Ende des 20. Jahrhunderts', *Jahrbuch für Wirtschaftsgeschichte* (special issue on Proto-industrialization), pp. 9–20.

Krugman, P. (1991) *Geography and Trade*, Louvain: Leuven University Press.

Krugman, P. (1996) *The Self-Organizing Economy*, Cambridge, Mass.: Blackwell.

Kussmaul, A. (1981) *Servants in Husbandry in Early Modern England*, Cambridge: Cambridge University Press.

Kussmaul, A. (1990) *A General View of the Rural Economy of England 1538–1840*, Cambridge: Cambridge University Press.

Kuznets, S. (1966) *Modern Economic Growth. Rate, Structure and Spread*, New Haven: Yale University Press.

Labrousse, E. (1933) *Esquisse du mouvement des prix et des revenus en France au XVIIIe siècle*, two vols, Paris: Dalloz.

Ladero Quesada, M. A. and Gonzalez Jimenez, M. (1979) *Diezmo ecclesiastico y producción de cereales en el reino de Sevilla (1408–1503)*, Seville.

Lal, D. (1998) *Unintended Consequences. The Impact of Factor Endowments, Culture, and Politics on Long-run Economic Performance*, Cambridge Mass.: MIT Press.

Landes, D. S. (1969) *The Unbound Prometheus. Technological Change and Industrial Development in Western Europe from 1750 to the Present*, Cambridge: Cambridge University Press.

Landes, D. S. (1993) 'The Fable of the Dead Horse, or, the Industrial Revolution Revisited', in J. Mokyr (ed.) *The British Industrial Revolution*, Boulder, Co.: Westview, pp. 132–70.

Landes, D. S. (1998) *The Wealth and Poverty of Nations: Why Some are So Rich and Some So Poor*, New York: Norton.

Lane, F. C., (1966) *Venice and History*, Baltimore: Johns Hopkins University Press.

Lane, F. C. (1973) *Venice. A Maritime Republic*, Baltimore: Johns Hopkins University Press.

Langdon, J. (1986) *Horses, Oxen and Technological Innovation. The Use of Draught Animals in English Farming from 1066–1500*, Cambridge: Cambridge University Press.

Lapeyre, H. (1953) *Simon Ruiz et les 'assientios' de Philippe II*, Paris: Armand Colin.

Laslett, P. (1983) 'Family and Household as Work Group and Kin Group: Areas of Traditional Europe Compared', in R. Wall, J. Robin and P. Laslett (eds.) (1983) *Family Forms in Historic Europe*, Cambridge: Cambridge University Press, pp. 513–63.

Lavoissier, A. L. (1988) *De la richesse territoriale du Royaume de France*, C. Perrot (ed.) (1988) Paris: Comité des travaux historiques et scientifiques.

Lee, R. D. (1973) 'Population in Pre-industrial England: an Econometric Analysis', *Quarterly Journal of Economics* 87: 581–607.

Lee, W. R. (1981) 'The German Family: A Critical Survey of the Current State of Historical Research', in R. J. Evans and W. R. Lee (eds.) (1981) *The German Family. Essays on the Social History of the Family in Nineteenth- and Twentieth-Century Germany*, London: Croom Helm, pp. 19–50.

Lee, W. R. (1990) 'Women's Work and the Family: Some Demographic Implications of Gender-Specific Work Patterns in Nineteenth-Century Germany', in P. Hudson and W. R. Lee (eds.) (1990), *Women's Work*, Manchester: Manchester University Press, pp. 50–75.

Lehning, J. (1980) *The Peasants of Marlhes: Economic Development and Family Organization in Nineteenth Century France*, Chapel Hill, N.C.: University of North Carolina Press.

Le Mené, M. (1982) *Les campagnes angeivines à la fin du Moyen Age (vers 1350–vers 1530). Étude économique*, Nantes.

Le Roy Ladurie, E. (1966, abridged ed.) *The Peasants of Languedoc*, Champaign-Urbana, Ill. (orig. published as *Les paysans de Languedoc*).

Le Roy Ladurie, E. (1967) *Histoire du climat depuis l'an mil*, Paris: Flammarion.

Le Roy Ladurie, E. (1977) 'Motionless History', *Social Science History* 1 (orig. 'L'histoire immobile', *Annales E.S.C.* 29 (1974): 673–92).

Lesger, C. M. (1994) 'Urban Systems and Economic Development in Holland During the Later Middle Ages and the Early Modern Period', in *Proceedings, XI International Economic History Congress, Milan. Recent Doctoral Research in Economic History*, Milan: Universita Bocconi, pp. 69–79.

Leverotti, F. (1989) 'Dalla famiglia stretta alla famiglia larga. Linee di evoluzione e tendenze della famiglia rurale lucchese (secoli XIV–XV)', *Studi storici*, 30: 171–202.

Levine, D. (ed.) (1984) *Proletarianization and Family History*, Orlando, Fla.: Academic Press.

Levine, D. (1987) *Reproducing Families. The Political Economy of English Population History*, Cambridge: Cambridge University Press.

Lewis, G. (1994) 'Proto-Industrialization in France', *Economic History Review* 47: 150–64.

Lewis, W. A. (1954) 'Economic Development with Unlimited Supplies of Labour', *The Manchester School* 22: 139–91.

Linden, M. van der (1997a) 'Marx and Engels, Dutch Marxism and the "Model Capitalist Nation of the Seventeenth Century"', *Science and Society* 61: 161–92.

Linden, M. van der (1997b) 'The Origins, Spread and Normalization of Free Wage Labour', in T. Brass and M. van der Linden (eds.) (1997) *Free and Unfree Labour*, Bern: Peter Lang, pp. 501–23.

Lis, C. (1984) 'Gezinsvorming en vrouwenarbeid tijdens een versnellingsfase in de ontwikkeling van het kapitalisme, 1750–1850', *Tijdschrift voor Sociale Geschiedenis* 10: 380–405.

Lis, C. and Soly, H. (1979) *Poverty and Capitalism in Pre-Industrial Europe*, Brighton: Harvester Press.

Lis, C. and Soly, H. (eds.) (1994) *Werken volgens de regels. Ambachten in Brabant en Vlaanderen, 1500–1800*, Brussels: VUB Press.

Lis, C. and Soly, H. (eds.) (1997a) *Werelden van verschil. Ambachtsgilden in de Lage Landen*, Brussels: VUB Press.

Lis, C. and Soly, H. (1997b) 'Different Paths of Development. Capitalism in the Northern and Southern Netherlands During the Late Middle Ages and the Early Modern Period', *Review* 20: 211–42.

Littlejohn, G. (1977) 'Chayanov and the Theory of Peasant Economy', in B. Hindess (ed.) (1977) *Sociological Theories of the Economy*, London: Macmillan.

Liu, T. P. (1994) *The Weaver's Knot: The Contradiction of Class Struggle and Family Solidarity in Western France, 1750–1914*, Ithaca, N.Y.: Cornell University Press

Livi Bacci, M. (1990) *Population and Nutrition. An Essay on European Demographic History*, Engl. transl. of second Italian ed., Cambridge: Cambridge University Press.

Löfgren, O. (1974) 'Family and Household among Scandinavian Peasants', *Ethnologia Scandinavica. A Journal of Nordic Ethnology* 2: 17–52.

Löfgren, O. (1975) 'Arbeitsteilung und Geschlechterrollen in Schweden', *Ethnologia Scandinavica* 3: 47–72.

Löfgren, O. (1976) 'Peasant Ecotypes. Problems in the Comparative Study of Ecological Adaptation', *Ethnologia Scandinavica* 4: 100–15.

Löfgren, O. (1978) 'The Potato People. Household Economy and Family Patterns among the Rural Proletariat in Nineteenth-Century Sweden', in S. Akerman *et al.* (eds.) (1978) *Chance and Change. Social and Economic Studies in Historical Demography in the Baltic Area*, Odense: Odense University Press, pp. 95–106.

Löfgren, O. (1980) 'Historical Perspectives on Scandinavian Peasantries', *Annual Review of Anthropology* 9: 187–215.

Lopez, R. S. (1953) 'The Origin of the Merino Sheep', *The Joshua Starr Memorial Volume: Studies in History and Philology*, New York, pp. 161–8.

Lopez, R. S. and Miskimin, H. (1962) 'The Economic Depression of the Renaissance', *Economic History Review* 14: 408–26

Lourens, P. and Lucassen, J. (1992) 'Marx als Historiker der niederländischen Republik', in M. van der Linden (ed.) (1992) *Die Rezeption der Marxschen Theorie in den Niederlanden*, Schriften aus dem Karl-Marx-Haus vol. 45, Trier: Karl-Marx-Haus, pp. 430–54.

Lourens, P. and Lucassen, J. (1999) 'Gilden und Wanderung', in K. Schulz (ed.) (1999) *Handwerk in Europa*, Schriften des Historischen Kollegs, Kolloquien 41, Munich: Oldenbourg, pp. 65–79.

Lourens, P. and Lucassen, J. (2000) 'Zunftlandschaften in den Niederlanden und im benachbarten Deutschland', in W. Reininghaus (ed.) (2000) *Zunftlandschaften in Deutschland und den Niederlanden im Vergleich*, Schriften des Historischen Kommissions für Westfalen, Münster: Aschendorf, pp. 11–43.

Lucassen, J. (1987) *Migrant Labour in Europe. The Drift to the North Sea*, London: Croom Helm.

Lucassen, J. (1991) Dutch Long Distance Migration: A Concise History 1600–1900, IISH Research Papers, no. 3, Amsterdam: International Institute of Social History.

Lucassen, J. (1994) 'The Netherlands, the Dutch, and Long-Distance Migration in the Late Sixteenth to Early Nineteenth Centuries', in N. Canny (ed.) (1994) *Europeans on the Move*, Oxford: Clarendon Press, pp. 153–91.

Lucassen, J. (1995) 'Labour and Early Modern Economic Development', in K. Davids and J. Lucassen (eds.) (1995) *A Miracle Mirrored*, Cambridge: Cambridge University Press, pp. 367–409.

Lucassen, J. (1996) 'The North Sea: a Crossroad for Migrants?', in J. Roding and L. Heerma van Voss (eds.) (1996) *The North Sea and Culture (1550–1800)*, Hilversum: Verloren, pp. 168–84.

Lucassen, J. (1997) 'The International Maritime Labour Market (Sixteenth–Nineteenth Centuries)', in P. C. van Royen, J. R. Bruijn and J. Lucassen (eds.) (1997) *'Those Emblems of Hell'?*, Research in Maritime History, 13, St John's, Newfoundland: International Maritime Economic History Association, pp. 11–23.

Lucassen, J. and Lucassen, L. (eds.) (1997) *Migration, Migration History, History*, Bern: Peter Lang.

Lucassen, J. and Penninx, R. (1997) *Newcomers. Immigrants and their Descendants in the Netherlands 1550–1995*, Amsterdam: Het Spinhuis.

Lucassen, J. and Zürcher, E. J. (1998) 'Conscription as Military Labour: The Historical Context', in *International Review of Social History* 43: 405–19.

Lütge, F. (1967) 'Der Handel Nürnbergs nach Osten im 15. und 16. Jahrhunderts' *Beiträge zur Wirtschaftsgeschichte Nürnbergs* vol. 1: Stadtrat zu Nürnberg.

Lyons, J. S. (1989) 'Family Response to Economic Decline: Handloom Weavers in Early Nineteenth-Century Lancashire', *Research in Economic History* 12: 45–91.

Macfarlane, A. (1978a) *The Origins of English Individualism. The Family, Property and Social Transition*, Oxford: Blackwell.

Macfarlane, A. (1978b) 'The Peasantry in England before the Industrial Revolution. A Mythical Model?', in D. Green, C. Hasselgrove and M. Spriggs (eds.) (1978) *Social Organization and Settlement*, Oxford: Oxford University Press, pp. 325–41.

Macfarlane, A. (1984) 'The Myth of the Peasantry: Family and Economy in a Northern Parish', in R. M. Smith (ed.) (1984) *Land, Kinship and Life-Cycle*, Cambridge: Cambridge University Press, pp. 333–49.

MacKay, A. (1977) *Spain in the Middle Ages. From Frontier to Empire, 1000–1500*, Houndmills and London: Macmillan.

Macleod, C. (1986) 'The 1690s Patents Boom: Invention or Stock Jobbing?', *Economic History Review* 39: 549–71.

Maddicott, J. R. (1975) *The English Peasantry and the Demands of the Crown, 1294–1341*, Oxford: Past and Present Society.

Maddison, A. (1991) *Dynamic Forces in Capitalist Development*, Oxford: Oxford University Press.

Maddison, A. (1995) *Monitoring the World Economy, 1820–1992*, Paris: OECD Development Centre Studies.

Maddison, A. and van der Wee, H. (eds.) (1994) *Economic Growth and Structural Change. Comparative Approaches Over the Long Run on the Basis of Reconstructed National Accounts*, Eleventh International Economic History Congress Milan 1994, Session B 13, Milan: Universitá Bocconi.

Mainoni, P. (1994) *Economia e politica nella Lombardia medievale. Da Bergamo a Milano fra XIII e XV secolo*, Cavallermaggiore.

Makkai, L. (1981) 'Productivité et exploitation des sources d'énergie (XIIe–VIIe siècle)', in S. Mariotti (ed.) (1981) *Produttività e tecnologie nei secoli XII–XVIII*, Firenze: Le Monnier, pp. 165–81.

Malanima, P. (1994) 'Italian Economic Performance, 1600–1800', in A. Maddison and H. Van der Wee (eds.) (1994) *Economic Growth and Structural Change*, Milan: Universitá Bocconi, pp. 59–70.

Malanima, P. (1996a) *Energia e crescita nell'Europa pre-industriale*, Rome: La Nuova Italia Scientifica.

Malanima, P. (1996b) 'Energy Sources and Energy Consumption in Pre-industrial Europe', paper presented at the Second Congress of the European Association of Historical Economics, Venice.

Malanima, P. (1998) *Economia pre-industriale. Mille anni: dal IX al XVIII secolo*, Milan: Bruno Mondadori.

Malcolmson, R. W. (1988) 'Ways of Getting a Living in Eighteenth-Century England', in R. E. Pahl (ed.) (1988) *On Work. Historical, Comparative and Theoretical Approaches*, Oxford: Blackwell, pp. 48–60.

Malden, H. E. (ed.) (1900) *The Cely Letters*, London: Camden Society, Third Series, vol. I.

Malthus, T. R. (1798) *First Essay on Population*, facsimile reprint (1966) with notes by James Bonar, London: Macmillan.

Mandel, E. (1980) *Long Waves of Capitalist Development: The Marxist Interpretation*, Cambridge: Cambridge University Press.

Martin, J. M. (1984) 'Village Traders and the Emergence of a Proletariat in South Warwickshire, 1750–1851', *Agricultural History Review* 32: 179–88.

Martínez Sopena, P. (1996) 'Les "francos" dans les villes du chemin de Saint-Jacques au moyen âge', in D. Menjot and J.-L. Pinol (eds.) (1996) *Les immigrants et la ville*, Paris: Editions l'Harmattan, pp. 9–25.

Marx, K. (1964) *Pre-capitalist Economic Formations* (introduction by Eric Hobsbawm) London: Lawrence and Wishart.

Marx, K. (1971) *Das Kapital*, three vols, Berlin: Dietz.

Mate, M. (1982) 'The Impact of War on the Economy of Canterbury Cathedral Priory, 1294–1340', *Speculum* 57: 761–78.

Mate, M. (1991) 'The Agrarian Economy of South-east England before the Black Death: Depressed or Buoyant?', in B. M. S. Campbell (ed.) *Before the Black Death*, Manchester: Manchester University Press, pp. 79–109.

McCloskey, D. N. (1991) 'The Prudent Peasant: New Findings on Open Fields', *Journal of Economic History* 51: 343–55.

McCloskey, D. N. and Nash, J. (1984) 'Corn at Interest: the Extent and Cost of Grain Storage in Medieval England', *American Economic Review* 74: 174–87.

Meadows, D. L. (1972) *The Limits to Growth. A Report to the Club of Rome Project on the Predicament of Mankind*, London: Earth Island.

Medick, H. (1976) 'The Proto-Industrial Family Economy: The Structural Function of Household and Family during the Transition from Peasant Society to Industrial Capitalism', *Social History* 1: 291–315.

Medick, H. (1996) *Weber und Überleben in Laichingen 1650–1900: Lokalgeschichte als allgemeine Geschichte*, Göttingen: Gandenboeck & Ruprecht.

Meiksins Wood, E. (1996) 'Capitalism, Merchants and Bourgeois Revolution. Reflections on the Brenner Debate and its Sequel', *International Review of Social History* 41: 209–32.

Meillassoux, C. (1979) *Femmes, Greniers et Capitaux*, Paris: Maspero.

Mendels, F. (1978) 'La composition du ménage paysan en France au XIXe siècle: une analyse économique du mode de production domestique', *Annales ESC* 33: 780–802.

Melis, F. (1964) 'Werner Sombart e i problemi della navigazione nel Medio Evo', in G. Barbieri *et al. L'opera di Werner Sombart nel centenario della nascita*, Milan: Giuffrè, pp. 85–149.

Melis, F. (1984) *I vini italiani nel Medioevo*, ed. A. Affortunati Parrini, Florence: Le Monnier.

Mendels, F. (1972) 'Proto-industrialization: the First Phase of the Industrialization Process', *Journal of Economic History* 32: 241–61.

Mendels, F. (1981a) 'Les temps de l'industrie et les temps de l'agriculture. Logique d'une analyse régionale de la proto-industrialisation', *Revue du Nord* 63: 21–33.

Mendels, F. (1981b) *Industrialization and Population Pressure in Eighteenth-century Flanders*, New York: Arno Press (orig. PhD Dissertation, University of Wisconsin, 1970).

Mendels F. (1984a) 'Niveau des salaires et âge au mariage en Flandre 17–18e siècles', *Annales ESC* 39: 939–56.

Mendels, F. (1984b) 'Des industries rurales à la protoindustrialisation. Historique d'un changement de perspective', *Annales ESC* 39: 977–1000.

Menjot, D. and Pinol, J.-L. (eds) (1996) *Les immigrants et la ville. Insertion, intégration, discrimination (XII–XXe siècles)*, Paris: Editions l'Harmattan.

Middleton, C. (1979) 'The Sexual Division of Labour in Feudal England', *New Left Review* 113/114.

Middleton, C. (1983) 'Patriarchical Exploitation and the Rise of English Capitalism', in E. Gamarnikow, P. Morgan and J. Purvis (eds.) *Gender, Class and Work*, Aldershot: Gower, pp. 11–27.

Middleton, C. (1985) 'Women's Labour and the Transition to Pre-Industrial Capitalism', in L. Charles and L. Duffin (eds.) *Women and Work in Pre-Industrial England*, London: Croom-Helm, pp. 181–206.

Miller, E. (1975) 'War, Taxation and the English Economy in the Late Thirteenth and Early Fourteenth Centuries', in J. M. Winter (ed.) (1975) *War and Economic Development. Essays in Memory of David Joslin*, Cambridge: Cambridge University Press, 11–31.

Miller, E. and Hatcher, J. (1995) *Medieval England. Towns, Commerce and Crafts 1086–1348*, London/New York: Longman.

Mitchell, B. R. (1975) *European Historical Statistics*, New York: Columbia University Press.

Mitchell, B. R. and Deane, P. (1962) *Abstract of British Historical Statistics*, Cambridge: Cambridge University Press.

Mitterauer, M. (1979) 'Zum familienbetrieblichen Struktur im zünftischen Handwerk', in H. Knittler (ed.) *Wirtschafts- und sozialhistorische Beiträge. Festschrift für Alfred Hoffmann zum 75. Geburtstag*, Munich: Oldenbourg, pp. 190–219, (repr. in M. Mitterauer (1979) *Grundtypen alteuropäischer Sozialformen. Haus und Gemeinde in vorindustriellen Gesellschaften*, Stuttgart: Fromann-Holzboog, 98–122).

Mitterauer, M. (1981) 'Lebensformen und Lebensverhältnisse ländlicher Unterschichten', in H. Mattis (ed.) (1981) *Von der Glückseligkeit des Staates. Staat, Wirtschaft und Gesellschaft in Österreich im Zeitalter des aufgeklärten Absolutismus*, Berlin: Dunckler and Humblot, pp. 315–38 (repr. in *ibid.* (1992a) *Familie und Arbeitsteilung*, Cologne/Vienna: Böhlau, pp. 33–57).

Mitterauer, M. (1984) 'Familie und Arbeitsorganisation in städtische Gesellschaften des späten Mittelalters und der frühen Neuzeit', in A. Haverkamp (ed.) (1984) *Haus und Familie in der spätmittelalterlichen Stadt*, Cologne/Vienna: Böhlau, pp. 1–36 (repr. in Mitterauer (1992a) *Familie und Arbeitsteilung*, pp. 256–300).

Mitterauer, M. (1985) 'Gesindedienst und Jugendphase im europäischen Vergleich', *Geschichte und Gesellschaft* 10: 177–204 (transl.: 'Servants and Youth', *Continuity and Change* 5 (1990) 11–38).

Mitterauer, M. (1986) 'Formen ländlicher Familienwirtschaft. Historische Ökotypen und familiale Arbeitsorganisation im österreichen Raum', in J. Ehmer and M. Mitterauer (eds.) (1986) *Familie und Arbeitsorganisation*, Vienna/Cologne: Böhlau, pp. 185–324.

Mitterauer, M. (1990) *Historisch-anthropologische Familienforschung. Fragestellungen und Zugangsweisen*, Vienna/Cologne: Böhlau.

Mitterauer, M. (1992a) *Familie und Arbeitsteilung. Historisch-vergleichende Studien*, Vienna/Cologne: Böhlau.

Mitterauer, M. (1992b) 'Peasant and Non-Peasant Family Forms in Relation to the Physical Environment and the Local Economy', *Journal of Family History* 17: 139–59 (orig. 'Ländliche Familienformen in ihrer Abhängigkeit von natürlicher Umwelt und lokaler Ökonomie', in M. Mitterauer (1990) *Historisch-anthropologische Familienforschung*, Vienna/Cologne: Böhlau, pp. 131–45).

Moch, L. Page (1992) *Moving Europeans. Migration in Western Europe since 1650*, Bloomington, Ind.: Indiana University Press.

Mokyr, J. (1976) *Industrialization in the Low Countries 1795–1850*, New Haven: Yale University Press.

Mokyr, J. (1985a) 'Demand vs. Supply in the Industrial Revolution', in J. Mokyr (ed.) *The Economics of the Industrial Revolution*, London: Allen and Unwin, pp. 97–118.

Mokyr, J. (1985b) 'The Industrial Revolution and the New Economic History', in J. Mokyr (ed.) (1985) *The Economics of the Industrial Revolution*, London: Allen and Unwin, pp. 1–52.

Mokyr, J. (1987) 'Has the Industrial Revolution been Crowded Out? Some Reflections on Crafts and Williamson', *Explorations in Economic History* 24: 293–319.

Mokyr, J. (1988) 'Is there Still Life in the Pessimist Case? Consumption During the Industrial Revolution, 1790–1850', *Journal of Economic History* 48: 69–92.

Mokyr, J. (1990) *The Lever of Riches. Technological Creativity and Economic Progress*, Oxford/New York: Oxford University Press.

Mokyr, J. (1991) 'Was there a British Industrial Revolution?', in J. Mokyr (ed.) (1991) *The Vital One: Essays in Honour of Jonathan R. T. Hughes*, Research in Economic History Supplement 6, Greenwich/London, pp. 253–86.

Mokyr, J. (1993) 'Editor's Introduction', in *ibid.* (ed.) (1993) *The British Industrial Revolution: An Economic Perspective*, Boulder, Co.: Westview, pp. 1–131.

Montgomery, D. (1999) 'Christopher Tomlins: Why Wait for Industrialism? Morris, Industrialism, and Materialism', *Labor History* 40: 35–9.

Mooers, C. (1991) *The Making of Bourgeois Europe*, London: Verso Books.

Moogk, P. (1994) 'Manon's Fellow Exiles: Emigration from France to North America before 1763', in N. Canny (ed.) (1994) *Europeans on the Move*, Oxford: Clarendon Press, pp. 236–60.

Mooser, J. (1984) *Ländliche Klassengesellschaft 1770–1848. Bauern und Unterschichten, Landwirtschaft und Gewerbe im östlichen Westfalen*, Göttingen: Vandenhoeck & Ruprecht.

Morineau, M. (1977) 'France', in C. Wilson and G. Parker (eds.) (1977) *Introduction to the Sources*, London: Weidenfeld and Nicolson, pp. 155–89.

Morsa, D. (1996) 'Les immigrants dans les villes des principautés belges (XVIIe–XVIIIe siècles)', in D. Menjot and J.-L. Pinol (eds.) *Les immigrants et la ville*, Paris: Editions l'Harmattan, pp. 171–92.

Mulhall, M. G. (1898) *A Dictionary of Statistics*, London: G. Routledge and Sons.

Munro, J. H. (1991) 'Industrial Transformations in the North-west European Textile Trades, c. 1290–c. 1340: Economic Progress or Economic Crisis?', in B. M. S. Campbell (ed.) *Before the Black Death*, Manchester: Manchester University Press, pp. 110–48.

Munro, J. H. (1997) 'The Origin of the English "New Draperies": The Resurrection of an Old Flemish Industry, 1270–1570', in N. B. Harte (ed.) *The New Draperies*, Oxford: Oxford University Press, 35–128.

Myllyntaus, T. (1996) 'Society on Wooden Legs. The Environmental Effects of Forest Exploitation in 19th-century Finland', paper presented at the First European Social Science History Conference, Noordwijkerhout.

Neeson, J. M. (1989) 'Parliamentary Enclosure and the Disappearance of the English Peasantry, Revisited', in G. Grantham and C. S. Leonard (eds.) (1989) *Agrarian Organization in the Century of Industrialization: Europe, Russia, and North America* Research in Economic History suppl. 5, Greenwich/London, pp. 89–120.

Nelson, D. (1999) 'Labor and Modern Industry: Better than Ever', *Labor History* 40: 39–42.

Neumann, M. (1865) *Geschichte des Wuchers in Deutschland*, Halle: Waisenhaus.

Newman, J. (1983) 'Anglo-Dutch Commercial Co-operation and the Russia Trade in the Eighteenth Century', in *The Interactions of Amsterdam and Antwerp with the Baltic Region 1400–1800. Papers Presented at the Third International Conference of the Association Internationale d'Histoire des Mers Nordiques de l'Europe, Utrecht, August 30th–September 3rd 1982*, Leiden: Nijhoff, pp. 95–104.

Newman, J. (1992) ' "A Very Delicate Experiment": British Mercantile Strategies for Financing Trade in Russia, 1680–1780', in I. Blanchard *et al.* (eds.) (1982) *Industry and Finance*, Stuttgart: Steiner, pp. 115–41.

Nijman, D. G. (1991) 'Louis de Geer (1587–1652), vader van de Zweedse industrie?', *Tijdschrift voor geschiedenis* 104: 213–32.

North, D. C. (1981) *Structure and Change in Economic History*, New York: Norton.

North, D. C. and Thomas, R. P. (1973) *The Rise of the Western World*, Cambridge: Cambridge University Press.

Nussbaum, F. L. (1968, orig. 1935), *A History of the Economic Institutions of Modern Europe*, New York: A. M. Kelley.

Oakley, A. (1976) *Housewife*, Harmondsworth: Penguin.

O'Brien, P. K. (1982) 'European Economic Development: the Contribution of the Periphery', *Economic History Review* 35: 1–18.

O'Brien, P. K. (1993) 'Introduction: Modern Conceptions of the Industrial Revolution', in *id.* and R. Quinault (eds.) (1996) *The Industrial Revolution and British Society*, Cambridge: Cambridge University Press, pp. 1–30.

O'Brien, P. K. (1996) 'Path Dependency, or Why Britain Became an Industrialized and Urbanized Economy Long Before France', *Economic History Review* 49: 213–49.

Ogilvie, S. and Cerman, M. (eds.) (1996) *European Proto-industrialization*, Cambridge: Cambridge University Press.

Olson, M. (1965), *The Logic of Collective Action. Public Goods and the Theory of Groups*, Cambridge, Mass.: Harvard University Press.

Olson, M. (1982) *The Rise and Decline of Nations. Economic Growth, Stagflation, and Social Rigidities*, New Haven/London: Yale University Press.

Opitz, C. (1994) 'Neue Wege in der Sozialgeschichte? Ein kritischer Blick auf Otto Brunners Konzept des ganzen Hauses', *Geschichte und Gesellschaft* 19: 88–98.

Ormrod, M. (1995) 'The West European Monarchies in the Later Middle Ages', in R. Bonney (ed.) *Economic Systems and State Finance*, Oxford: Oxford University Press, 123–60.

Overton, M. (1996) *Agricultural Revolution in England. The Transformation of the Agrarian Economy*, Cambridge: Cambridge University Press.

Overton, L. M. and Campbell, B. M. S. (1991) 'Productivity Change in European Agricultural Development', in B. M. S. Campbell and M. Overton (eds.) (1991) *Land, Labour and Livestock*, Manchester: Manchester University Press, pp. 1–50.

Overton, M. and Campbell, B. M. S. (1997) 'Production et productivité dans l'agriculture anglaise, 1086–1871', *Histoire et Mesure* 11: 255–97.

Palmer, S. and Williams, D. M. (1997) 'English Sailors, 1570–1795', in P. C. van Royen, J. R. Bruijn and J. Lucassen (eds. (1997) *'Those Emblems of Hell'?*, St John's, Newfoundland: International Maritime Economic History Association, pp. 93–118.

Parker, W. N. (1984) *Europe, America and the Wider World*, Cambridge: Cambridge University Press.

Patnaik, U. (1978/9) 'Neo-Populism and Marxism: The Chayanovian View of the Agrarian Question and its Fundamental Fallacy', *Journal of Peasant Studies* 6: 375–420.

Penn, S. A. C. and Dyer, C. (1990) 'Wages and Earnings in Late Medieval England: Evidence from the Enforcement of the Labour Laws', *Economic History Review* 43: 356–76.

Perlin, F. (1994) *Unbroken Landscape. Commodity, Category, Sign and Identity: Their Production as Myth and Knowledge from 1500*, Aldershot: Variorum.

Persson, K. G. (1988) *Pre-Industrial Economic Growth. Social Organization and Technological Growth in Europe*, Oxford: Blackwell.

Persson, K. G. (1991) 'Labour productivity in medieval agriculture: Tuscany and the "Low Countries"', in B. M. S. Campbell and M. Overton (eds.) (1991) *Land, Labour and Livestock*, Manchester: Manchester University Press, 124–43.

Pfister, U. (1989) 'Work Roles and Family Structure in Proto-industrial Zürich', *Journal of Interdisciplinary History* 20: 83–105.

Pfister, U. (1991) 'Die protoindustrielle Hauswirtschaft im Kanton Zürich des 17. und 18. Jahrhunderts', in: D. Petzina (ed.) (1991) *Zur Geschichte der Ökonomik der Privathaushalte*, Berlin: Duncker and Humblot, pp. 71–108.

Pfister, U. (1992a) *Die Zürcher fabriques. Protoindustrielles Wachstum vom 16. zum 18. Jahrhundert*, Zürich: Chronos.

Pfister, U. (1992b) 'The Proto-industrial Household Economy: Toward a Formal Analysis', *Journal of Family History* 17: 201–32.

Pfister, U. (1996) 'Proto-industrialization in Switzerland', in S. Ogilvie and M. Cerman (eds.) (1996) *European Proto-industrialization*, Cambridge: Cambridge University Press, pp. 137–54.

Pfister, U. (1998) 'Proto-industrielles Wachstum: ein theoretisches Modell', *Jahrbuch für Wirtschaftsgeschichte*: 21–48.

Phelps Brown, E. H. and Hopkins, S. (1956) 'Seven Centuries of the Prices of Consumables, Compared with Builders' Wage-rates', in *Economica* 23: 296–314.

Phelps Brown, E. H. and Hopkins, S. (1981) *A Perspective on Wages*, London.

Phillips, S. (1994) 'The Medieval Background', in N. Canny (ed.) (1994) *Europeans on the Move*, Oxford: Clarendon, pp. 9–25.

Phillips, W. D., Jr. (1991) 'The Old World Background of Slavery in the Americas', in B. L. Solow (ed.) (1991) *Slavery and the Rise of the Atlantic System*, Cambridge: Cambridge University Press, pp. 43–61.

Pike, R. (1966) *Enterprise and Adventure: The Genoese at Seville and the Opening of the New World*, Ithaca: Cornell University Press.

Pinchbeck, I. (1969, orig. 1930) *Women Workers and the Industrial Revolution 1750–1850*, London: Cass.

Pinna, M. (1984) *La storia del clima. Variazioni climatiche e rapporto clima–uomo in età postglaciale*, Rome: Società Geografica Italiana.

Pinto, G. (1995) 'Popolazione e comportamenti demografici in Italia (1250–1348)', in *Europa en los umbrales de la crisis*, pp. 37–62.

Ploss, E. E. (1973) *Ein Buch von alten Farben. Technologie der Textilfarben im Mittelalter mit einem Ausblick auf die festen Farben*, third ed., Munich: Moos.

Poehlmann, E. (1993) Economic Growth in Late Medieval England: A Challenge to the Orthodoxy of Decline, M.Sc. Dissertation, London School of Economics.

Pohl, H. (1971) 'Köln und Antwerpen um 1500', *Köln, das Reich und Europa* Mitteilungen aus dem Stadtarchive von Köln 60, Cologne: Neubner, pp. 469–552.

Pollard, S. (1988) *Peaceful Conquest: the Industrialization of Europe, 1760–1970*, Oxford: Oxford University Press

Pollard, S. (1994) 'Regional and Inter-regional Economic Development in Europe in the Eighteenth and Nineteenth Centuries', in *Proceedings of the Eleventh International Economic History Congress (Milan, September 1994)*, vol. A: *Debates and Controversies in Economic History*, Milan: Università Bocconi, pp. 57–92.

Poni, C. (1990) 'Per la storia del distretto industriale serico di Bologna (secoli XVI–XIX)', *Quaderni storici* 25: 93–167.

Poos, L. (1991) *A Rural Society After the Black Death. Essex 1350–1525*, Cambridge: Cambridge University Press.

Postan, M. M. (1928) 'Credit in Medieval Trade', *Economic History Review* 1 (repr. in E. M. Carus-Wilson (ed.) (1955) *Essays in Economic History* vol. 1, London: Arnold, pp. 61–87).

Postan, M. M. (1967) 'Investment in Medieval Agriculture', *Journal of Economic History* 27, 4: 576–87.

Postan, M. M. (1972) *The Medieval Economy and Society*, Berkeley: University of California Press.

Postan, M. M. (1973) *Essays on Medieval Agriculture and General Problems of the Medieval Economy*, Cambridge: Cambridge University Press.

Postan, M. M. and Titow, J. Z. (with statistical notes by J. Longden) (1958–9) 'Heriots and Prices on Winchester Manors', *Economic History Review* 11: 392–417.

Postma, J. M. (1990) *The Dutch in the Atlantic Slave Trade 1600–1815*, Cambridge: Cambridge University Press.

Pounds, N. J. G. (1985) *An Historical Geography of Europe 1800–1914*, Cambridge: Cambridge University Press.

Pounds, N. J. G. and Parker, W. N. (1957) *Coal and Steel in Western Europe. The Influence of Resources and Techniques on Production*, London: Faber and Faber.

Power, E. (1933) 'The Wool Trade in the Fifteenth Century', in E. Power and M. M. Postan (eds.) (1933) *Studies in English Trade in the Fifteenth Century*, London: Routledge.

Prak, M. (1994) 'Regions in Early Modern Europe', in *Proceedings of the Eleventh International Economic History Congress (Milan, September 1994)*, vol. A: *Debates and Controversies in Economic History*, Milan: Università Bocconi, pp. 19–55.

Prakash, O. (1995) *Asia and the Pre-modern World Economy*, IIAS Lecture Series 4, Leiden: International Institute for Asian Studies.

Prestwich, M. (1972) *War, Politics and Finance under Edward I*, London: Faber and Faber.

Price, J. M. (1980) *Capital and Credit in British Overseas Trade: the View from the Chesapeake, 1700–1776*, Cambridge, Mass.: Harvard University Press.

Price, R. (1975) *The Economic Modernisation of France*, New York: Wiley.

Price, R. (1983) *The Modernization of Rural France: Communications, Networks and Agricultural Market Structures in Nineteenth-century France*, London: Hutchinson.

Quataert, J. H. (1984) 'Social Insurance and the Family Work of Oberlausitz Home Weavers in the Late Nineteenth Century', in J. C. Fout (ed.) (1989) *German Women in the Nineteenth Century. A Social History*, New York: Holmes and Meier, pp. 270–94.

Quataert, J. H. (1985a) 'Combining Agrarian and Industrial Livelihood: Rural Households in the Saxon Oberlausitz in the Nineteenth Century', *Journal of Family History* 10: 145–62.

Quataert, J. H. (1985b) 'The Shaping of Women's Work in Manufacturing: Guilds, Households and the State in Central Europe', *American Historical Review* 90: 1122–48.

Quataert, J. H. (1988) 'A new view of industrialization: "protoindustry" or the role of small-scale, labor-intensive manufacture in the capitalist environment', *International Labour and Working-class History* 33: 3–22.

Ragin, Ch. and Chirot, D. (1984) 'The World System of Immanuel Wallerstein: Sociology and History as Politics', in Theda Skocpol (ed.) (1984) *Vision and Method in Historical Sociology*, Cambridge: Cambridge University Press, pp. 276–312.

Rappaport, S. (1989) *Worlds Within Worlds: Structures of Life in Sixteenth-century London*, Cambridge: Cambridge University Press.

Ravallion, M. (1987) *Markets and Famines*, Oxford: Clarendon.

Razi, Z. (1980) *Life, Marriage and Death in a Medieval Parish: Economy, Society and Demography in Halesowen, 1270–1400*, Cambridge: Cambridge University Press.

Reed, M. (1984) 'The Peasantry of Nineteenth-Century England: a Neglected Class?', *History Workshop Journal* 18: 53–76.

Reed, M. (1986/87) 'Nineteenth-Century Rural England: A Case for "Peasant Studies"?', *Journal of Peasant Studies* 14: 78–99.

Reher, D. S. (1990) *Town and Country in Pre-industrial Spain*, Cambridge: Cambridge University Press.

Reinicke, C. (1989) *Agrarkonjunktur und technisch-organisatorische Innovationen auf dem Agrarsektor im Spiegel niederrheinischer Pachtverträge 1200–1600*, Cologne/Vienna: Böhlau.

Reininghaus, W. (1981) *Die Entstehung der Gesellengilden im Spätmittelalter*, Wiesbaden: Steiner.

Reininghaus, W. (1983) 'Das "ganze Haus" und die Gesellengilden: Über die Beziehungen zwischen Meistern und Gesellen im Spätmittelalter', in R. S. Elkar (ed.) *Deutsches Handwerk im Spätmittelalter und frühen Neuzeit*, Göttingen: Schwartz, pp. 55–70.

Reynolds, T. S. (1983) *Stronger than a Hundred Men. A History of the Vertical Water Wheel*, Baltimore/London: Johns Hopkins University Press.

Riddle, J. M. (1991) 'Oral Contraceptives and Early-term Abortifacients During Classical Antiquity and the Middle Ages', *Past and Present* 132: 3–32.

Riden, Ph. (1977) 'The Output of the British Iron Industry Before 1870', *Economic History Review* 30: 442–59.

Riley, J. C. and McCusker, J. J. (1983) 'Money Supply, Economic Growth, and the Quantity Theory of Money: France 1650–1788', *Explorations in Economic History* 20: 274–93.

Roberts, M. (1979) 'Sickles and Scythes: Women's Work and Men's Work at Harvest Time', *History Workshop Journal* 7: 3–28.

Rock, H. B. (1999) 'Artisans and Paradigms', *Labor History* 40: 42–5.

Rösener, W. (1994) *The Peasantry of Europe*, Oxford: Blackwell.

Romano, R. (1962) 'Per una valutazione della flotta mercantile europea alla fine del secolo XVIII' in *Studi in Onore di Amintore Fanfani* vol. V, Milan: Giuffrè.

Rose, S. O. (1988) 'Proto-Industry, Women's Work and the Household Economy in the Transition to Industrial Capitalism', *Journal of Family History* 13: 181–93.

Rosenbaum, H. (1982) *Formen der Familie. Untersuchungen zum Zusammenhang von Familienverhältnissen, Sozialstruktur und sozialen Wandel in der deutschen Gesellschaft des 19. Jahrhunderts*, Frankfurt am Main: Suhrkamp.

Rosenthal, J.-L. (1993) 'Credit Markets and Economic Change in South-eastern France 1630–1788', *Explorations in Economic History* 30: 129–57.

Rosenthal, P.-A. (1999) *Les sentiers invisibles. Espace, familles et migrations dans la France du 19e siècle*, Paris: Éditions de l'École des Hautes Études en Sciences Sociales.

Rostow, W. W. (1961) *The Stages of Economic Growth. A Non-communist Manifesto*, Cambridge: Cambridge University Press.

Roy, T. (1998) 'Indian Handlooms in the 20th Century', *Jahrbuch für Wirtschaftsgeschichte*, 129–52.

Royen, P. C. van, Bruijn, J. R. and Lucassen, J. (eds.) (1997) *'Those Emblems of Hell'? European Sailors and the Maritime Labour Market, 1570–1870*, Research in Maritime History 13, St John's, Newfoundland: International Maritime Economic History Association.

Rowbotham, S. (1973) *Hidden from History*, London: Pluto Press.

Rudolph, R. L. (1992) 'The European Family and Economy: Central Themes and Issues', *Journal of Family History* 17: 119–38.

Ruiz-Martin, F. (1965) *Lettres marchandes échangées entre Florence et Medina del Campo*, Paris: SEVPEN.

Ryan, M. P. (1982) 'The Explosion of Family History', *Reviews in American History* 10: 181–95.

Sabean, D. (1977) 'Intensivierung der Arbeit und Alltagserfahrung auf dem Lande', *Sozial-wissenschaftliche Informationen für Unterricht und Studium* 6: 148–52 (transl. 'Small Peasant Agriculture in Germany at the Beginning of the Nineteenth Century: Changing Work Patterns', *Peasant Studies* 7 (1978) 218–24).

Sabean, D. W. (1990) *Property, Production and Family in Neckarhausen, 1700–1870*, Cambridge: Cambridge University Press.

Sakellariou, E. (1996) The Kingdom of Naples under Aragonese and Spanish Rule. Population Growth, and Economic and Social Evolution in the Late Fifteenth and Early Sixteenth Centuries, Ph.D. thesis, University of Cambridge.

Sanchez León, P. (2000) 'Town and Country in Castile, 1400–1650', in S. R. Epstein (ed.) (2000) *Town and Country in Europe*, Cambridge: Cambridge University Press.

Schendel, W. van (1981) *Peasant Mobility: The Odds of Life in Rural Bangladesh*, Assen: Van Gorcum.

Scheuermann, L. (1929) *Die Fugger als Montanindustrielle in Tirol und Kärnten. Ein Beiträg zur Wirtschaftsgeschichte des 16. und 17. Jahrhunderts* Studien zur Fuggergeschichte vol. 8, Munich/Leipzig: Duncker and Humblot.

Schlumbohm, J. (1982) 'Agrarische Besitzklassen und gewerbliche Produktionsverhältnisse: Grossbauern, Kleinbesitzer und Landlose als Leinenproduzenten im Umland von Osnabrück und Bielefeld während des frühen 19. Jahrhunderts', in *Mentalitäten und Lebensverhältnisse. Beispiele aus der Sozialgeschichte der Neuzeit. Festschrift für Rudolph Vierhaus*, Göttingen: Vandenhoeck & Ruprecht, pp. 315–34.

Schlumbohm, J. (1983) 'Seasonal Fluctuations and Social Division of Labour: Rural Linen Production in the Osnabrück and Bielefeld Regions and the Urban Woollen Industry in the Niederlausitz, *c.* 1770–*c.* 1850', in M. Berg *et al.* (eds.) *Manufacture in Town and Country Before the Factory*, Cambridge: Cambridge University Press, pp. 92–123.

Schlumbohm, J. (1985) 'Proprietà fondiaria e produzione di tele nelle campgagne di Osnabrück e Bielefeld all'inizio del XIX secolo', *Quaderni storici* 59: 373–401.

Schlumbohm, J. (1994) *Lebensläufe, Familien, Höfe: Die Bauern und Heuerleute des Osnabrückischen Kirchspiels Belm in proto-industrieller Zeit, 1650–1860*, Göttingen: Vandenhoeck & Ruprecht.

Schlumbohm, J. (1995) 'Quelques problèmes de micro-histoire d'une société locale: Construction de liens sociaux dans la paroisse de Belm (17e–19e siècles)', *Annales HSS* 50: 775–802.

Schlumbohm, J. (1996) ' "Proto-industrialization" as a Research Strategy and a Historical Period – a Balance-sheet', in S. Ogilvie and M. Cerman (eds.) (1996) *European Proto-industrialization*, Cambridge: Cambridge University Press, pp. 12–22.

Schlumbohm, J. (ed.) (1998) *Mikrogeschichte–Makrogeschichte: komplementär oder inkommensurabel?*, Göttingen: Wallstein.

Schmiechen, J. A. (1982) *Sweated Industries and Sweated Labour. The London Clothing Trades, 1860–1914*, Urbana Ill./New York: University of Illinois Press.

Schmitt, G. (1988) 'Ein bedeutender Agrarökonom ist wieder zu entdecken: Alexander Tschajanow. Zu seinem hundersten Geburtstag 1988', *Zeitschrift für Agrargeschichte und Agrarsoziologie* 36: 185–216.

Schofield, R. (1983) 'The Impact of Scarcity and Plenty on Population Change in England, 1541–1871', in R. I. Rotberg and Th. K. Rabb (eds.) (1983) *Hunger and History. The Impact of Changing Food Production and Consumption Patterns on Society*, Cambridge: Cambridge University Press, pp. 67–93.

Scholliers, E. (1983) 'Werktijden en arbeidsomstandigheden in de pre-industriële periode' in E. Scholliers and P. Scholliers (eds.) (1983) *Werktijd en werktijdverkorting*, Brussel: VUB Press, pp. 11–18.

Schöttler, P. (1985) 'Die rheinischen Fabrikengerichte im Gormärz und in der Revolution von 1848/49', *Zeitschrift für Neuere Rechtsgeschichte* 7: 160–80.

Schüttenhelm, J. (1984) 'Zur Münzprägung und Silberversorgung süddeutscher Münzstätten im frühen 16. Jahrhundert', in W. Kroker and E. Westermann (eds.) (1984) *Montanwirtschaft Mitteleuropas vom 12. bis 17. Jahrhundert. Stand, Wege und Aufgaben der Forschung*, Der Anschnitt, Beiheft 2, Bochum: Vereinigung der Freunde von Kunst und Kultur im Bergbau.

Schulz, K. (ed.) (1999) *Handwerk in Europa. Vom Spätmittelalter bis zur frühen Neuzeit* Schriften des Historischen Kollegs, Kolloquien 41, Munich: Oldenbourg.

Schumpeter, J. A. (1954) *History of Economic Analysis*, London: George Allen and Unwin.

Scott, J. W. (1984) 'Men and Women in the Parisian Garment Trades: Discussions of Family and Work in the 1830s and 1840s', in: P. Thane, G. Crossick and R. Floud (eds.) (1984) *The Power of the Past. Essays for Eric Hobsbawm*, Cambridge: Cambridge University Press, pp. 67–93 (revised edition 'Work Identities for Men and Women. The Politics of Work and Family in the Parisian Garment Trades in 1848', in *ibid.* (1988) *Gender and the Politics of History*, New York: Columbia University Press, pp. 93–112).

Scott, T. (ed.) (1998) *The Peasantries of Europe: from the Fourteenth to the Eighteenth Centuries*, London: Longman.

Scott, T. and Scribner, B. (1996) 'Urban Networks', in B. Scribner (ed.) (1996) *Germany. A New Social and Economic History* vol. I. 1450–1630, London/New York: pp. 113–43.

Scott, W. R. (1910–12) *The Constitution and Finance of English, Scottish and Irish Joint-stock Companies to 1720*, three vols, Cambridge: Cambridge University Press.

Seccombe, W. (1992) *A Millenium of Family Change. Feudalism to Capitalism in Northwestern Europe*, London/New York: Verso.

Sen, A. (1981) *Poverty and Famines. An Essay on Entitlement and Deprivation*, Oxford: Clarendon.

Sen, A. (1983) 'Economics and the Family', *Asian Development Review* 1: 14–26.

Sen, A. (1990) 'Gender and Cooperative Conflicts', in I. Tinker (ed.) (1990) *Persistent Inequalities: Women and World Development*, New York: Oxford University Press, pp. 123–49.

Sereni, E. (1981) 'Note di storia dell'alimentazione nel Mezzogiorno: I Napoletani da "mangiafoglia" a "mangiamaccheroni"', in *ibid.* (1981) *Terra nuova e buoi rossi e altri saggi per una storia dell'agricoltura europea*, Turin, pp. 292–371.

Shanin, T. (1972) *The Awkward Class. Political Sociology of Peasantry in a Developing Society, Russia 1910–1925*, Oxford: Clarendon.

Sheridan, G. J. (1979) 'Household and Craft in an Industrializing Economy. The Case of the Silk Weavers of Lyons', in J. Merriman (ed.) (1979) *Consciousness and Class Experience in Nineteenth Century Europe*, New York: Holmes and Meier, pp. 107–28.

Sheridan, G. J. (1984) 'Family and Enterprise in the Silk Shops of Lyon: The Place of Labor in the Domestic Weaving Economy, 1840–1870', in G. Saxonhouse and G. Wright (eds.) (1984) *Technique, Spirit and Form in the Making of the Modern Economies: Essays in Honor of William N. Parker*, Research in Economic History Suppl. 3, Greenwich/London: JAI Press, pp. 33–60.

Sieder, R. (1987) *Sozialgeschichte der Familie*, Frankfurt/Main: Suhrkamp.

Silva, J.-G. de (1969) *Banque et crédit en Italie au XVIIe siècle*, two vols, Paris: Publication de la faculté des lettres et sciences humaines de Paris-Nanterre.

Simiand, F. (1932a) *Les fluctuations économiques à longue période et la crise mondiale*, Paris: Félix Alcan.

Simiand, F. (1932b) *Recherches anciennes et nouvelles sur le mouvement général des prix du XVIe au XIXe siècle*, Paris: Domat Montchrestien.

Simon, J. L. (1977) *The Economics of Population Growth*, Princeton: Princeton University Press.

Simsch, A. (1970) *Die Handelsbeziehungen zwischen Nürnberg und Posen im europäischen Wirtschaftsverkehr des 15. und 16. Jahrhunderts*, Wiesbaden: Otto Harrassowitz.

Sivéry, G. (1976) 'Les profits de l'éleveur et du cultivateur dans le Hainaut à la fin du Moyen Âge', *Annales ESC* 31: 604–30.

Skocpol, Th. (1977) 'Wallerstein's World Capitalist System: a Theoretical and Historical Critique', *American Journal of Sociology* 82: 1075–90.

Slicher van Bath, B. H. (1957) *Een samenleving onder spanning. Geschiedenis van het platteland in Overijssel*, Assen: Van Gorcum.

Slicher van Bath, B. H. (1963) *The Agrarian History of Western Europe, 500–1850*, London: Arnold.

Smelser, N. J. (1959) *Social Change in the Industrial Revolution: An Application of Theory to the Lancashire Cotton Industry 1770–1840*, London: Routledge & Kegan Paul.

Smil, V. (1994) *Energy in World History*, San Francisco/Oxford: Westview Press.

Smith, A. (1986, orig. 1776) *The Wealth of Nations* (introduction by Andrew Skinner) Harmondsworth: Penguin.

Smith, R. M. (1984) 'Some Issues Concerning Families and their Property in Rural England 1250–1800', in R. M. Smith (ed.) (1984) *Land, Kinship and Life-Cycle*, Cambridge: Cambridge University Press, pp. 1–86.

Smith, R. M. (1991) 'Demographic Developments in Rural England, 1300–48: a Survey', in B. M. S. Campbell (ed.) (1991) *Before the Black Death*, Manchester: Manchester University Press, pp. 25–78.

Smits, J. P. (1995) Economic Growth and Structural Change in the Dutch Service Sector 1850–1913, Ph.D. thesis, Free University at Amsterdam.

Smits, J. P., Horlings, E. and Zanden, J. L. van (2000) *Dutch GNP and its Components, 1800–1913*, Groningen Growth and Development Centre Monograph Series, vol. 5, Groningen.

Snell, K. D. M. (1985) *Annals of the Labouring Poor. Social Change and Agrarian England 1660–1900*, Cambridge: Cambridge University Press.

Snooks, G. D. (1990) 'Economic Growth During the Last Millennium: A Quantitative Perspective for the British Industrial Revolution' *Working Paper in Economic History*, no. 140, Australian National University.

Snooks, G. D. (1992) 'Great Waves of Economic Change: Very Long Run Growth in Britain, 1086–1990', Flims: paper presented at the 22nd IARIW Conference.

Snooks, G. D. (1993) *Economics Without Time. A Science Blind to the Forces of Historical Change*, London: Macmillan.

Snooks, G. D. (1996) *The Dynamic Society: Exploring the Sources of Global Change*, London: Routledge.

Soly, H. (1987) 'Proletarisering in West-Europa, 1450–1850', in F. van Besouw *et al.* (eds.) (1987) *Balans en Perspectief. Visies op de geschiedwetenschap in Nederland*, Groningen: Wolters-Noordhoff/Forsten, pp. 101–18.

Sombart, W. (1930) 'Capitalism', in E. R. A. Seligman (ed.) (1930) *Encyclopaedia of the Social Sciences* vol. 2, New York: Macmillan, pp. 195–208.

Sonenscher, M. (1989) *Work and Wages. Natural Law, Politics and the Eighteenth-Century French Trades*, Cambridge: Cambridge University Press.

Spallanzani M. (ed.) (1976) *Produzione commercio e consumo dei panni di lana (nei secoli XII–XVIII)* Florence: Olschki.

Sprandel, R. (1969) 'La production du fer au Moyen Age', *Annales ESC* 24: 305–21.

Sprandel, R. (1971) 'Gewerbe und Handel', in H. Aubin and W. Zorn (eds.) (1971) *Handbuch der deutschen Wirtschafts- und Sozialgeschichte* vol. 1, Stuttgart: Union Verlag, pp. 335–57.

Spufford, M. (1974) *Contrasting Communities. English Villagers in the Sixteenth and Seventeenth Centuries*, Cambridge: Cambridge University Press.

Stabel, P. (1997) *Dwarf among Giants. The Flemish Urban Network in the Late Middle Ages*, Leuven/Apeldoorn: Garant.

Sussman, N. (1998) 'The Late Medieval Bullion Famine Reconsidered', *Journal of Economic History* 58: 126–54.

Sweezy, P. *et al.* (1978, orig. 1976) *The Transition from Feudalism to Capitalism* (introduction by Rodney Hilton), London: Verso.

Sylla, R. and Toniolo, G. (eds.) (1991) *Patterns of European Industrialization: The Nineteenth Century*, London/New York: Routledge.

Szostak, R. (1991) 'Institutional Inheritance and Early American Industrialization', in J. Mokyr (ed.) (1991) *The Vital One: Essays in Honour of Jonathan R. T. Hughes* Research in Economic History Supplement 6, Greenwich/London, pp. 287–308.

Tanner, A. (1982) *Spulen, Weben, Sticken. Die Industrialisierung in Appenzell-Ausserrhoden*, Zürich.

Tanner, A. (1986) 'Arbeit, Haushalt und Familie in Appenzell-Ausserrhoden. Veränderungen in einem ländlichen Industriegebiet im 18. und 19. Jahrhundert', in J. Ehmer and M. Mitterauer (eds.) (1986) *Familienstruktur und Arbeitsorganisation*, Vienna/Cologne: Böhlau, pp. 459–94.

Tawney, R. H. (1912) *The Agrarian Problem in the Sixteenth Century*, London: Longmans, Green.

Tenfelde, K. (1979) 'Landliches Gesinde in Preussen. Gesinderecht und Gesindestatistik', *Archiv für Sozialgeschichte* 19: 189–229.

Terrier, D. (1996) *Les deux âges de la proto-industrie: les tisserands du Cambrésis et du Saint-Quentinois, 1730–1880*, Paris: Editions de l'EHESS.

Thirsk, J. (1984a) 'Seventeenth-Century Agriculture and Social Change', in J. Thirsk, *The Rural Economy of England. Collected Essays*, London: Hambledon Press (orig. in J. Thirsk (ed.) (1970) *Land, Church and People. Essays Presented to Professor H. P. R. Finberg, Agricultural History Review* 18, Supplement).

Thirsk, J. (1984b) 'Industries in the Countryside', in J. Thirsk, *The Rural Economy of England*, pp. 217–33 (orig. in: F. J. Fisher (ed.), *Essays in the Economic and Social History of Tudor and Stuart England in Honour of R. H. Tawney*, 1961).

Thirsk, J. (1985) 'Foreword', in M. Prior (ed.) *Women in English Society 1500–1800*, London: Methuen, pp. 1–21.

Thirsk, J. (1987) *England's Agricultural Regions and Agrarian History, 1500–1750*, Basingstoke/London.

Thirsk, J. and Cooper, P. (1972) *Seventeenth-Century Economic Documents*, Oxford: Oxford University Press.

Thoen, E. (1990) 'Technique agricole, cultures nouvelles et économie rurale en Flandre au bas Moyen Age', in *Plantes et cultures nouvelles en Europe occidentale, au Moyen Age et à l'époque moderne*, Valence-sur-Boise: Auch, pp. 51–67.

Thoen, E. (1997) 'The Birth of "the Flemish Husbandry": Agricultural Technology in Medieval Flanders', in G. Astill and J. Langdon (eds.) *Medieval Farming and Technology. The Impact of Agricultural Change in Northwest Europe*, Leiden: Brill, pp. 69–88.

Thompson, E. P. (1991) *Customs in Common*, London: the Merlin Press.

Thompson, E. P and Yeo, E. (eds.) (1984) *The Unknown Mayhew. Selections from the Morning Chronicle 1849–1850*, Harmondsworth: Penguin.

Thomson, J. K. J. (1983) 'Variations in Industrial Structure in Pre-Industrial Languedoc', in M. Berg, P. Hudson and M. Sonenscher (eds.) (1983) *Manufacture in Town and Country Before the Factory*, Cambridge: Cambridge University Press, pp. 61–91.

Tilly, C. (1981) 'Proletarianization: Theory and Research', in *id.* (1981) *As Sociology Meets History*, New York/London: Academic Press, pp. 179–89.

Tilly, C. (1984) 'Demographic Origins of the European Proletariat', in D. Levine (ed.) (1984) *Proletarianization and Family History*, Orlando, Fla.: Academic Press, pp. 1–85.

Tilly, C. (1990) *Coercion, Capital and European states AD 990–1990*, Oxford: Blackwell.

Tilly, L. A. (1974) 'Comments on the Yans-MacLaughlin and Davidoff Papers', *Journal of Social History* 7: 452–9.

Tilly, L. A. (1987) 'Beyond Family Strategies, What?', *Historical Methods* 20: 113–25.

Tilly, L. A. and Scott, J. W. (1975) 'Women's Work and the Family in Nineteenth-Century Europe', *Comparative Studies in Society and History* 17: 36–64.

Tilly, L. A. (1977, repr. 1987) *Women, Work, and Family*, New York: Holt, Rinehart and Winston.

Timbal, P.-Cl. (1958) 'Les lettres de marque dans le droit de la France médiévale', in *L'Étranger* Recueils de la Société Jean Bodin vol. X, pt. 2, Brussels, pp. 108–38.

Tits-Dieuaide, M.-J. (1975) *La formation des prix céréaliers en Brabant et en Flandre au XVe siècle*, Brussels: Editions de l'Université de Bruxelles.

Tits-Dieuaide, M.-J. (1987) 'L'évolution des prix du blé dans quelques villes d'Europe occidentale du XVe siècle au XVIIIe siècle', *Annales ESC* 42: 529–48.

Todorov, N. (1983) *The Balkan City 1400–1900*, Seattle: University of Washington Press.

Tomlins, Ch. (1999a) 'Why Wait for Industrialism? Work, Legal Culture, and the Example of Early America – An Historiographical Argument', *Labor History* 40: 5–34.

Tomlins, Ch. (1999b) 'Not Just Another Brick in the Wall: A Response to Rock, Nelson, and Montgomery', *Labor History* 40: 45–52.

Topolski, J. and Wyczanski, A. (1982) 'Les fluctuations de la production agricole en Pologne XVIe–XVIIIe siècles', in J. Goy and E. Le Roy Ladurie (eds.) (1982) *Prestations paysannes, dîmes, rente foncière et mouvement de la production agricole à l'époque préindustrielle* vol. 1, Paris: Editions de l'EHESS.

Toutain, J.-C. (1961) 'Le produit de l'agriculture française de 1700 à 1958, I: Estimation du produit au XVIIIe siècle', *Cahiers de science appliquée*, no. 115.

Travers, A. P. (1976) The Practice of Usury in Mid-Sixteenth Century England, Ph.D. thesis, University of Edinburgh.

Trienekens, G. (1993) 'Integrale geschiedenis in wording. Aarle-Rixtel en Wanroij in de negentiende en het begin van de twintigste eeuw', in *ibid.* and J. van Oudheusden (eds.) (1993) *'Een pront wijf, een mager paard en een zoon op het seminarie'. Aanzetten tot een integrale geschiedenis van oostelijk Noord-Brabant*, 's-Hertogenbosch: BRG, pp. 211–313.

Turner, M. E. (1984) *Enclosures in Britain 1750–1830*, London: Macmillan.

Turner, M. E. (1989) 'Benefits But at Costs: The Debates about Parliamentary Enclosure', in G. Grantham and C. S. Leonard (eds.) (1989) *Agrarian Organization in the Century of Industrialization: Europe, Russia, and North America* Research in Economic History Suppl. 5, Greenwich/London, pp. 49–67.

Tylecote, A. (1991) *The Long Wave in the World Economy*, London: Routledge.

Unger, R. W. (1980) *The Ship in the Medieval Economy 600–1600*, London: Croom Helm.

Unger, R. W. (1983) 'Integration of Baltic and Low Countries Grain Markets, 1400–1800', in J. M. van Winter (ed.) (1983) *The Interactions of Amsterdam and Antwerp with the Baltic Region, 1400–1800*, Leiden: Nijhoff, pp. 1–10.

Unger, R. W. (1984) 'Energy Sources for the Dutch Golden Age: Peat, Wind and Coal', *Research in Economic History* 9: 221–53.

Vandenbroeke, Ch. (1984) 'Le cas flamand: Evolution sociale et comportements démographiques aux 17e–19e siècles', *Annales ESC* 39: 915–38.

Vanhaute, E. (1992) *Heiboeren. Bevolking, arbeid en inkomen in de 19de-eeuwse Kempen*, Brussel: VUB Press.

Vazquez de Prada, V. (1988) 'La conyuntura de la mineria y la metalurgia europeas (siglo xiii–xvii)', *Revista de Historia Economica*, 6: 257–76.

Verhulst, A. (1985) 'L'intensification et la commercialisation de l'agriculture dans les Pays-Bas méridionaux au XIIIe siècle', in J.-L. Delattre (ed.) *La Belgique rurale du Moyen Âge à nos jours. Mélanges offerts à Jean-Jacques Hoebanx*, Brussels: Editions de l'Université de Bruxelles, pp. 89–100.

Verhulst, A. (1990) 'The "Agricultural Revolution" of the Middle Ages Reconsidered', in B. S. Bachrach and D. Nicholas (eds.) (1990) *Law, Custom and the Social Fabric in Medieval Europe. Essays in Honor of Bryce Lyon*, Kalamazoo: Western Michigan University, pp. 17–28.

Verlinden, Ch. (1977) *L'esclavage dans l'Europe médiévale*, Gent: Rijksuniversiteit te Gent.

Viazzo, P. P. (1989) *Upland Communities. Environment, Population and Social Structure in the Alps Since the Sixteenth Century*, Cambridge: Cambridge University Press.

Ville, S. P. (1990) *Transport and the Development of the European Economy, 1750–1918*, Basingstoke: Macmillan.

Vlachovic, J. (1964) *Slovenska med v 16. a 17. storoci*, Bratislava: Vydavatelstvo Slovenskej akadémie vied.

Vogel, W. (1915) 'Zur Grosse der Europäischen Handelsflotten im 15., 16. und 17. Jahrhundert', *Festschrift Dietrich Schäfer*, Jena, pp. 268–333.

Voort, R. van der (1994) *Overheidsbeleid en overheidsfinanciën in Nederland, 1850–1913*, Amsterdam: NEHA.

Vries, J. de (1974) *The Dutch Rural Economy in the Golden Age, 1500–1700*, New Haven: Yale University Press.

Vries, J. de (1976) *The Economy of Europe in an Age of Crisis, 1600–1750*, Cambridge: Cambridge University Press.

Vries, J. de (1981), *Barges and Capitalism. Passenger Transportation in the Dutch Economy, 1632–1839*, Utrecht: HES.

Vries, J. de (1984a) *European Urbanization 1500–1800*, London: Methuen.

Vries, J. de (1984b) 'The Decline and Rise of the Dutch Economy 1675–1900', in G. Saxonhouse and G. Wright (eds.) (1984) *Forms and Methods in Economic History: Essays in Honor of William N. Parker*, Greenwich, pp. 149–89.

Vries, J. de (1992) 'The Labour Market', *Economic and Social History in the Netherlands* 4: 55–78.

Vries, J. de (1994) 'The Industrial Revolution and the Industrious Revolution', *Journal of Economic History* 54: 249–70.

Vries, J. de (1999) 'Great Expectations. Early Modern History and the Social Sciences', *Review* 22: 121–49.

Vries, J. de and van der Woude, A. (1997a) *The First Modern Economy. Success, Failure and Perseverance of the Dutch Economy, 1500–1815*, Cambridge: Cambridge University Press.

Vries, J. de (1997b) 'Nederland de eerste moderne volkshuishouding. Een zinsbegoocheling of wenkend perspectief?', *Bijdragen en Mededelingen tot de Geschiedenis der Nederlanden* 112: 66–77.

Waal, A. de (1990) 'A Re-assessment of Entitlement Theory in the Light of the Recent Famines in Africa', *Development and Change*, 21: 469–90.

Wall, R. (1986a) 'Work, Welfare and the Family: An Illustration of the Adaptive Family Economy', in L. Bonfield, R. M. Smith and K. Wrightson (eds.) (1986) *The World We Have Gained. Histories of Population and Social Structure. Essays Presented to Peter Laslett on his Seventieth Birthday*, Oxford: Blackwell, pp. 261–94.

Wall, R. (1986b) 'Arbeit, Fürsorge und Familie. Eine vergleichende Betrachtung von Handwerkern, Bauern und Arbeitern in Devon und Westflandern', in J. Ehmer and M. Mitterauer (eds.) (1986), *Familienstruktur und Arbeitsorganisation*, Vienna/Cologne: Böhlau, 495–521.

Wallerstein, I. (1974) *The Modern World-System* vol. 1: *Capitalist Agriculture and the Origins of the European World-Economy in the Sixteenth Century*, New York: Academic Press.

Wallerstein, I. (1979) *The Capitalist World-Economy. Essays by Immanuel Wallerstein*, Cambridge: Cambridge University Press.

Wallerstein, I. (1980) *The Modern World-System* vol. 2: *Mercantilism and the Consolidation of the European World-Economy, 1600–1750*, New York: Academic Press.

Wallerstein, I. (1989) *The Modern World-System* vol. 3: *The Second Era of Great Expansion of the Capitalist World-Economy, 1730–1840s*, San Diego: Academic Press.

Wallerstein, I. (1991) *Unthinking Social Science. The Limits of Nineteenth-Century Paradigms*, Cambridge: Polity.

Wallerstein, I. (1997) 'Merchant, Dutch, or Historical Capitalism?', *Review* 20: 243–54.

Wallerstein, I. and Smith, J. (eds.) (1992) *Creating and Transforming Households. The Constraints of the World-Economy*, Cambridge/Paris: Cambridge University Press.

Walter, J. and Schofield, R. (1989) 'Famine, Disease and Crisis Mortality in Early Modern Society', in J. Walter and R. Schofield (eds.) (1989) *Famine, Disease and the Social Order in Early Modern Society*, Cambridge: Cambridge University Press, pp. 1–74.

Ward, J. R. (1974) *The Finance of Canal Building in Eighteenth-Century England*, Oxford: Oxford University Press.

Watson, A. M. (1983) *Agricultural Innovation in the Early Islamic World. The Diffusion of Crops and Farming Techniques, 700–1100*, Cambridge: Cambridge University Press.

Watts, D. G. (1967) 'A Model for the Early Fourteenth Century', *Economic History Review* 20: 543–7.

Wee, H. Van der (1963) *The Growth of the Antwerp Market and the European Community (Fourteenth–Sixteenth Centuries)*, 3 vols, The Hague: Nijhoff.

Wee, H. Van der and Blanchard, I. (1992) 'The Habsburgs and the Antwerp Money Market: the Exchange Crises of 1521 and 1522–3' in I. Blanchard *et al.* (eds.) (1992) *Industry and Finance*, Stuttgart: Steiner, pp. 22–57.

Wee, H. Van der and Peeters, T. (1970) 'Un modèle dynamique de croissance interséculaire du commerce mondial (XIe–XVIIe siècles)', *Annales ESC* 25: 100–26.

Weir, D. R. (1995) 'Family Income, Mortality, and Fertility on the Eve of the Demographic Transition: A Case Study of Rosny-sur-Bois', *Journal of Economic History* 55: 1–26.

Westermann, E. (1971a) *Eislebner Garkupfer und seine Bedeutung für den europäischen Kupfermarkt, 1460–1560*, Cologne/Vienna.

Westermann, E. (1971b) 'Das "Leipziger Monopolprojekt", als Symptom der mittel-europäischen Wirtschaftskrise um 1527/8', *Vierteljahrschrift für Sozial- und Wirtschaftsgeschichte* 58: 1–23.

Westermann, E. (1972) 'Die Bedeutung des Thüringer Saigerhandels für den mittel-europäischen Handel an der Wende vom 15. und 16. Jahrhundert', *Jahrbuch für Geschichte Mittel- und Ostdeutschlands* 21.

Wiegelmann, G. (1975) 'Bäuerliche Arbeitsteilung in Mittel- und Nordeuropa: Konstanz oder Wandel?', *Ethnologia Scandinavica. A Journal for Nordic Ethnology* 3: 5–22.

Wielandt, F. (1971) 'Münzen, Gewichte und Masse bis 1800', in H. Aubin and W. Zorn (eds.) (1971) *Handbuch der deutschen Wirtschafts- und Sozialgeschichte* vol. 1, Stuttgart: Union Verlag, pp. 658–78.

Wiesner, M. E. (1986) *Working Women in Renaissance Germany*, New Brunswick, NJ: Rutgers University Press.

Wilkinson, R. G. (1973) *Poverty and Progress. An Ecological Model of Economic Development*, London: Methuen.

Wilson, C. (1941) *Anglo-Dutch Commerce and Finance in the Eighteenth Century*, Cambridge: Cambridge University Press.

Wilson, C. (1977) 'The British Isles', in C. Wilson and G. Parker (eds.) (1977) *Introduction to the Sources*, London: Weidenfeld and Nicolson, pp. 115–54.

Wilson C. and Parker, G. (eds.) (1977) *An Introduction to the Sources of European Economic History 1500–1800*, London: Weidenfeld and Nicolson.

Wolff, Ph. (1976) 'Esquisse d'une histoire de la draperie en Languedoc du XIIe au début du XVIIe siècle', in M. Spallanzani (ed.) *Produzione commercio e consumo dei panni di lana*, Florence: Olschki, pp. 435–62.

Wolpe, H. (ed.) (1980) *The Articulation of Modes of Production. Essays from Economy and Society*, London: Routledge and Kegan Paul.

Woude, A. M. van der (1973) 'Het gebruik van begrippen ontleend aan de sociale wetenschappen bij het analyseren van economische en sociale verschijnselen in het verleden', *A.A.G. Bijdragen* 18: 3–22.

Woude, A. M. van der, Hayami, A. and Vries, J. de (eds.) (1990) *Urbanization in History. A Process of Dynamic Interactions*, Oxford: Clarendon.

Wrigley, E. A. (1978) 'A Simple Model of London's Importance in Changing English Society and Economy 1650–1750', in P. Abrams and E. A. Wrigley (eds.) (1978) *Towns in Societies*, Cambridge: Cambridge University Press, pp. 215–43.

Wrigley, E. A. (1987) 'Urban Growth and Agricultural Change: England and the Continent in the Early Modern Period', in *id.* (1987) *People, Cities and Wealth*, Oxford: Blackwell, pp. 157–193.

Wrigley, E. A. (1988) *Continuity, Chance and Change. The Character of the Industrial Revolution in England*, Cambridge: Cambridge University Press.

Wrigley, E. A. and Schofield, R. S. (1981) *The Population History of England, 1541–1871. A Reconstruction*, London: Arnold.

Young, A. (1993) 'Invention and Bounded Learning by Doing', *Journal of Political Economy* 101: 443–72.

Yun, B. (1994a) 'Economic Cycles and Structural Changes', in T. Brady, H. A. Oberman and J. Tracy (eds.) (1994) *Handbook of European History, 1400–1600. Late Middle Ages, Renaissance and Reformation*, vol. 1, Leyden: Brill, pp. 377–411.

Yun, B. (1994b) 'Proposals to Quantify Long Term Performance in the Kingdom of Castile, 1550–1800', unpublished paper presented at the Session 'Economic Growth and Structural Change', Eleventh International Economic History Congress, Milan.

Yntema, R. J. (1992) 'The Brewing industry in Holland, 1300–1800: a study in industrial development', unpublished PhD thesis, University of Chicago.

Zanden, J. L. van (1985) *De economische ontwikkeling van de Nederlandse landbouw in de negentiende eeuw, 1800–1914,* AAG-Bijdragen vol. 25, Wageningen/Utrecht: Landbouwhogeschool.

Zanden, J. L. van (1987) 'De economie van Holland in de periode 1650–1805: groei of achteruitgang?', *Bijdragen en mededelingen betreffende de geschiedenis der Nederlanden* 102: 562–609.

Zanden, J. L. van (1988) 'De prijs van de vooruitgang? Economische modernisering en sociale polarisatie op het Nederlandse platteland na 1500', *Economisch- en Sociaal-Historisch Jaarboek* 51: 80–92.

Zanden, J. L. van (1989) 'Dutch Economic History of the Period 1500–1940: a Review of the Present State of Affairs', *Economic and Social History in the Netherlands* 1: 9–30.

Zanden, J. L. van (1992) 'Economic Growth in the Golden Age', *Economic and Social History in the Netherlands* 4: 5–26.

Zanden, J. L. van (1993a) *The Rise and Decline of Holland's Economy. Merchant Capitalism and the Labour Market,* Manchester: Manchester University Press.

Zanden, J. L. van (1993b) 'The Dutch Economy in the Very Long Run', in E. Szirmai *et al.* (eds.) (1993) *Explaining Economic Growth,* Amsterdam: North-Holland, pp. 267–84.

Zanden, J. L. van (1997) 'De laatste ronde van pre-moderne economische groei', *Bijdragen en Mededelingen betreffende de geschiedenis der Nederlanden* 112: 49–56.

Zanden, J. L. van (1998) 'The Regional Pattern of Agricultural Development, 1500–1800', *NEHA-Jaarboek voor de economische, bedrijfs- en techniekgeschiedenis* 61: 66–85.

Zanden, J. L. van (1999) 'Wages and the Standard of Living in Europe, 1500–1800', *European Review of Economic History* 3: 175–98.

Zanden, J. L. van *et al.* (1997) 'Merchant Capitalism', *Review* 20: 189–270.

Zaretski, E. (1976) *Capitalism, the Family, and Personal Life,* London: Pluto Press.

Zeeuw, J. W. de (1978) 'Peat and the Dutch Golden Age. The Historical Meaning of Energy Attainability', *AAG-Bijdragen* 21: 3–31.

Zulaica Palacios, F. (1994) *Fluctuaciones económicas en un período de crisis. Aragón en la baja Edad Media.* Saragossa: Institucion 'Fernando el Catolico'.

Zupko, R. E. (1977) *British Weights and Measures. A History from Antiquity to the Seventeenth Century,* Madison/London: University of Wisconsin Press.

Zysberg, A. (1987) *Les galériens. Vies et destins de 60 000 forcats sur les galères de France 1680–1748,* Paris: Seuil.

Index